New Terrains in Southeast Asian History

This series of publications on Africa, Latin America, Southeast Asia, and Global and Comparative Studies is designed to present significant research, translation, and opinion to area specialists and to a wide community of persons interested in world affairs. The editor seeks manuscripts of quality on any subject and can usually make a decision regarding publication within three months of receipt of the original work. Production methods generally permit a work to appear within one year of acceptance. The editor works closely with authors to produce a high-quality book. The series appears in a paperback format and is distributed worldwide. For more information, contact the executive editor at Ohio University Press, Scott Quadrangle, University Terrace, Athens, Ohio 45701.

Executive editor: Gillian Berchowitz
AREA CONSULTANTS
Africa: Diane M. Ciekawy
Latin America: Thomas Walker
Southeast Asia: William H. Frederick

The Ohio University Research in International Studies series is published for the Center for International Studies by Ohio University Press. The views expressed in individual volumes are those of the authors and should not be considered to represent the policies or beliefs of the Center for International Studies, Ohio University Press, or Ohio University.

Singapore University Press Pte Ltd is the publishing arm of the National University of Singapore (NUS). Organized as a private limited company, the Press is 100% owned by the University, and operates on a not-for-profit basis. A Board of Directors appointed by the University oversees the operation of the Press, and a Publishing Committee drawn from the ranks of the academic staff at the National University of Singapore approves all books. Publishing activities of the Press are handled by Peter Schoppert, Managing Director, and Paul Kratoska, Publishing Director.

The goal of the Press is to serve the needs of scholars, students and the English-speaking public in Singapore, Southeast Asia and the Asia-focused global community, by publishing books for academic, professional and trade markets. The current emphasis of the Press' commissioning and acquisition efforts is on Asia-related social sciences and humanities, as well as business subjects of relevance to the region.

Contact information for the Press is as follows: Singapore University Press Pte Ltd, Yusof Ishak House, National University of Singapore, 31 Lower Kent Ridge Road, Singapore 119078 (email: supbooks@nus.edu.sg).

New Terrains in Southeast Asian History

EDITED BY

Abu Talib Ahmad and Tan Liok Ee

OHIO UNIVERSITY
RESEARCH IN INTERNATIONAL STUDIES
SOUTHEAST ASIA SERIES NO. 107
OHIO UNIVERSITY PRESS
ATHENS

SINGAPORE UNIVERSITY PRESS
NATIONAL UNIVERSITY OF SINGAPORE

© 2003 by the Center for International Studies
Ohio University
Printed in the United States of America
All rights reserved

First published in 2003 by Singapore University Press Pte Ltd.
Yusof Ishak House,
31 Lower Kent Ridge Rd,
National University of Singapore
Singapore 11 9078
SUP ISBN 9971-69-269-4
11 10 09 08 07 06 05 04 03   5 4 3 2 1

The books in the Ohio University Research in International Studies Series
are printed on acid-free paper ⊖

Library of Congress Cataloging-in-Publication Data
New terrains in Southeast Asian history / edited by Abu Talib Ahmad and
Tan Liok Ee.
    p.   cm. —(Ohio University research in international studies.
Southeast Asia series ; no. 107)
Includes bibliographical references and index.
ISBN 0-89680-228-0 (pbk. : alk. paper)
    1. Asia, Southeastern—Historiography. I. Abu Talib Ahmad.
    II. Tan, Liok Ee. III. Research in international studies.
Southeast Asia series ; no. 107.

DS524.4 .N48 2003
959'.007'2059—dc21

                                            2002029328

Contents

Preface

The articles in this book are drawn from twenty-nine papers presented at the Conference on Southeast Asian Historiography since 1945, Penang, 30 July to 1 August 1999. Generous financial assistance from the Japan Foundation Asia Center and the Southeast Asian Studies Regional Exchange Program (SEASREP) enabled us to bring twenty-one participants from various parts of Southeast Asia to make the conference a meaningful regional discourse. We thank both organizations and in particular Takao Hirota of the Kuala Lumpur Japan Cultural Center (Japan Foundation) and Yumiko Himemoto of SEASREP for their assistance. Moral and financial support from the Center for Advanced Studies, National University of Singapore, helped to see this publication to fruition. We are also grateful to all members of the history section, School of Humanities, Universiti Sains Malaysia, for pitching in to make the organization of the conference a truly cooperative effort and to our former colleagues Cheah Boon Kheng and Paul Kratoska for their suggestions and support. We thank all participants at the conference, who together made what everyone fondly remembered afterward as the Penang Conference such a stimulating, memorable, and enjoyable experience. Last but not least, we would like to express our gratitude to Ohio University Press, especially for the support of Gillian Berchowitz and the dedication of the editor, Nancy Basmajian, and her extremely able team.

Introduction

ABU TALIB AHMAD AND TAN LIOK EE

IN HIS KEYNOTE ADDRESS to the Conference on Southeast Asian Historiography since 1945, Thongchai Winichakul challenged scholars of Southeast Asian history to explore new terrains in the past by relocating themselves, or shifting their angles of visions, to new sites. He suggested in particular that the concepts of interstices and margins offer rich possibilities for opening up epistemological spaces where hitherto displaced or suppressed histories might be hidden. Both *interstices* and *margins,* he pointed out, should not be taken in a purely literal sense to mean physical or geographical locations but should be understood metaphorically and analytically, as locations of alternative temporal and conceptual anchorages from which to make fresh explorations into the past. The feeling that it was time for Southeast Asian history writing "to move on," as Thongchai put it, beyond the clichéd themes and jaded narratives of national history, in search of different templates and alternative trajectories, was echoed in many of the other twenty-eight papers presented at the conference.

Historians of Southeast Asia have met several times in the past, to compare notes, share ideas, and reflect on the state of their field. The most established and influential scholars in the field were invited to present papers at such conferences. Hence the publications originating from them have become important milestones, marking the trails opened by earlier generations of scholars. The first of such collections, containing papers from a conference held at the School of African and Oriental Studies in London in the mid-1950s, was published in 1961.[1] The volume, *Historians of Southeast Asia,* was edited by D. G. E. Hall, whose own voluminous and pathbreaking work on Southeast Asian history was published in 1955.[2] The colonial era was coming to an end and it was in this context that Hall made his famous call for the rewriting of the region's history in its own right, not as an appendage to the history of China or India, nor of the Portuguese, Dutch, English, or any other exogenous powers that may have towered over the region through the ages. Southeast Asian history, said Hall, "cannot be safely viewed from any other perspective until seen from its own."[3]

In 1979 a second collection, *Perceptions of the Past in Southeast Asia,* originated from a conference at the Australian National University, which had become an important center for Asian and Southeast Asian studies.[4] The writers in this later volume were clearly influenced by a decade of debates about Euro-centric and Asia-centric perspectives in history writing, in particular the seminal arguments of John Smail and Harry Benda.[5] The authors of *Perceptions* self-consciously questioned the framework of "modern" and "scientific" historical methods from which they peered into historical texts, especially when these texts reflected different views of the past that had to be understood within the "mental architecture" of people writing in different times and different parts of Southeast Asia. Three years later a third volume, *Moral Order and the Question of Change,* appeared in the United States, where interest in Southeast Asian studies had grown during the Vietnam War years. Articles in this book remained focused on the thinking, beliefs, and perceptions of Southeast Asians, which were identified and interpreted through close studies of various texts.[6] Whether scholars thought in terms of unearthing "stratigraphic" layers to arrive at the "deep structures" of Southeast Asian history, or seeking "autonomous" histories, or delineating indigenous "cultural matrices," the preoccupation since the 1970s, especially among scholars in the West, has been to find the "authentic" local agencies, structures, or forces that moved historical processes within the region.[7]

In these earlier conferences and publications no more than a handful of Southeast Asians participated or contributed papers. Similarly, other volumes on Southeast Asian history published in the last few decades,[8] including *The Cambridge History of Southeast Asia* (1992),[9] have been written mainly by European, American, or Australian scholars, with nominal participation from Southeast Asians. The region is not short of its own scholars, whether they are trained locally or abroad, but, because most of their work is written and published in their own languages and in local journals, they are less well known outside their own countries. A 1995 survey of Thai historical work after 1973, published in an English-language regional journal, revealed how much of the interesting new work produced by Thai scholars is inaccessible to those who cannot read Thai.[10] Where similar surveys of work produced in other Southeast Asian countries are not available, scholarship in various Southeast Asian languages remains largely unknown to a wider audience, including other Southeast Asians.

Southeast Asian scholars researching and writing about their own pasts have rarely come together to compare theoretical assumptions and methodological strategies or to share their preoccupations, predilections, and anxieties. It seemed, therefore, a good idea to bring a group of Southeast Asian scholars together to talk about their ongoing work and that of colleagues in their respective countries. By siting a conference within Southeast Asia itself, with the majority of the papers presented by Southeast Asians, we hoped to capture the dominant currents and emerging countercurrents in Southeast Asian history writing within the region itself. The theme, Southeast Asian Historiography since 1945, identified work produced in the second half of the twentieth century as the special focus, while the timing of the conference, just before the dawning of a new millennium, seemed a particularly appropriate juncture "to step back and reconsider the underlying concepts, assumed theories, and reigning paradigms within which we are refining our craft."[11] Perhaps, as a collection of Southeast Asian voices, we could together identify new milestones and map new trails in Southeast Asian history writing.

However, there is no implication that the work of Southeast Asian scholars is somehow more authoritative or authentic. Whether we think of local researchers as native or indigenous, any claim that they somehow have an innate edge over or are naturally privy to knowledge not accessible to foreigners, is indefensible. The dangers of making too much of this distinction are raised by Thongchai Winichakul in this volume. He suggests a new term—*home* scholar—to avoid the uneasy undertones inherent in the terms *native* and *indigenous,* but freely acknowledges that even this term makes an essentially subjective, even emotive, claim. In any case, all claims, whether based on birth, race, length of stay, or any other criterion, are ultimately subject to dispute. Granted the home scholar may enjoy some advantages, such as linguistic ease or greater sensitivity to the processes and moments of cultural encounters, but these are counterbalanced by other problems, such as the danger of "native blindness."[12] The home perspective is ultimately just one more perspective, "as peculiar as the view from afar," having no privileged access to the truth and equally open to debate. The work of Southeast Asians on Southeast Asian history should be subject to the same critical standards as that of other scholars.

The discussions that took place over our three-day conference in Penang were a marvelous cacophony, revealing that an eclectic heterogeneity of theoretical and methodological strategies were being employed, or thought about, by scholars working in different parts of the region. This volume documents a rare moment of intellectual exchange about Southeast Asian history in which the voices of Southeast Asians are foregrounded. It captures the richness and diversity of historical discourse among Southeast Asian scholars at the end of the twentieth century, the extent to which old paradigms and approaches are being questioned, and the confidence with which history writing is being taken into new terrains. This diversity is due not only to differences in the training and theoretical predilections of individual scholars but also, and perhaps more to the point, to the different politics of writing history in various parts of the region.

The contributions to this volume reflect the wide range of issues and markedly different styles of history writing represented at the conference. A closer reading, however, reveals that there are recurrent themes, related problems, and shared concerns. The three sections of the book demarcate three main themes that emerged at the conference, but there are other interconnections and overlaps, which readers will discern from their own readings of the papers. This introduction attempts to provide a wider overview of the conference by recapturing the main strands of discussions at the conference and relating them to some of the papers that we were unfortunately unable to obtain for publication.

The conference opened with historiographical surveys of work produced since 1945 in seven Southeast Asian countries.[13] All concurred that the dominant motif has been the story of anticolonial struggles laying the foundations for the formation of the nation-state after the departure of a colonial power. The trope of a glorious precolonial past providing the origins of the modern nation-state is another central feature of most attempts to reconstruct, and legitimate, the history of the nation as the "national past." Many conference participants took a highly critical stance toward national histories constructed as "unilinear emplotments along singular trajectories"; reducing the nation's past into one story presented for public consumption as the "grand narrative," the "national odyssey," or the "national pageant."[14]

The political and ideological agendas of such histories, especially if explicit or heavy-handed and even when implicit or subtle, are easily revealed when their texts are subject to a little critical scrutiny. School textbooks, perhaps, are most heavily permeated by the political and didactic functions of history. There was a long, but interesting, discussion into how history textbooks, at the university as well as school level, tend to be "ideological, repetitive and mantra-like," containing little beyond the "officially sanctioned versions of the national narrative."[15] Textbooks are an important genre of history writing that affects entire generations of young Southeast Asians. There was much concern that "mantra-like" textbooks accompanied by uninspired teaching are killing any seeds of interest in the study of the past that might still be left in a generation already uninterested in the histories of their families and societies. It seems that history not only has to be rescued from the nation, but also from bad teachers and boring textbooks!

Conference participants compared notes on who determines the content and structure of history syllabuses and textbooks in their respective countries, a topic that led, inevitably, to discussions on the role, and vested interest, of the state in the project of creating a unitary view of the national past. Many different avenues and overt or covert strategies of restriction can be used to enforce compliance with acceptable structures or themes, eliminate controversy, discourage too many dissonant voices, and impose a uniform shape to national history. In addition, governments can control access to primary sources, refuse entry for foreign scholars, or censor publications. Even without such actions, a generally repressive atmosphere can result in conformity or self-censorship on the part of writers, who may fear loss of employment or promotional prospects, if not deprivation of personal security and freedom. In some Southeast Asian countries, such as Brunei, Indonesia, and Vietnam, the state has played a relatively greater role. But differences in state control among the Southeast Asian countries were, it was agreed, a matter of degrees of subtlety, with none being totally exempt.

History writing cannot be separated from politics. This is one dimension more likely to impinge on the work of "home" scholars, who live within the immediacy of ongoing political changes in their own countries in particular and the region in general, and within the direct range of the state's power. All the country surveys reflected how much trends in local history writing relate to political currents in the countries concerned. Singapore's national narrative may be unique among Southeast Asian countries in being centered on economic development rather than the political struggle to form a post-colonial nation-state. But, by fusing the national narrative with the trajectory of rational progression into modernity, the celebratory tale of Singapore's progress from the empty marshland Stamford Raffles took over to the international financial hub of the twenty-first century, and its graduation from the Third World into the First, is not so far different from other national histories. It, too, legitimates the national project as defined by the ruling party, the PAP, leaving virtually no room for alternative pathways from the past to the present.

All claims to authenticity in historiography, or attempts to privilege one voice and force a closure on alternative voices or interpretations of the past, are problematic. Thus, for example, Singapore's attempts to identify national heroes in recent years opened a Pandora's box of questions on which the lid had been shut, particularly when a recalcitrant hero refused to fit into the image outlined for him, jarring against the official version of the story. A critical deconstructive analysis of the choice, timing, and scripting of a few heroes, and one heroine, revealed problematic silences as well as interesting hidden subtexts.[16] Memoirs written by historical actors, whether winners or losers in the struggle for political power, can also be a way of imprinting one account of the past as the authentic version, denying possible interlocutors entry into contestations over the past. And even the claims of some scholars to be authentic spokespersons of subaltern groups, whose voices were previously submerged by elitist histories but are now recovered by the scholars' ingenuous interrogation of sources, can and should be challenged.

In a different context, a historian confronted with conflicting versions in traditional Thai and Malay texts, purportedly of the same events, may well suggest that it is rather like a dialogue between two pasts, both with their respective hidden agenda. It is the job of the historian to engage in an intertextual study to decipher and interpret the subtext of the dialogue.[17] Some conference participants were, however, uncomfortable with this sidestepping of the issue of authenticity and we launched into a debate on the whole question of facticity in historical discourse, of shifting lines between myth and reality, and changing standards of what is acceptable as rational, or possible, or true. Whatever the verdict, if there can be one, on these difficult issues, the historian is undeniably and inevitably locked into an unending series of dialogues, between two or more sets of sources and the "facts" they claim to re-present, and between readers located in different points in time and historical sources speaking from the past.

The past can mutate in tandem with the changing present and new voices, or new interpretations in the dialogue of claims and counter-claims about what really happened in the past, can pop up. Well-worn themes may have dominated history writing in most Southeast Asian countries for decades but there have also been periods of heightened activity and interest in revisionist interpretations when political up-heavals displace entrenched authoritarian regimes, and the grounds are thrown open, even if only temporarily, for contestations over his-torical meanings and truths. Moments of historiographical excite-ment and change in Thai and Filipino historiography, already well known to many at the conference, were cited as comparisons to coun-tries such as Myanmar, Brunei, and even Malaysia where there have been few or no major revisionist movements in historical writing. All participants were keenly aware that many countries in Southeast Asia were, at the time of the conference in mid-1999, still experiencing convulsions arising from the social and political ruptures that fol-lowed the 1997 economic crisis. Whether these fissures will allow for the emergence of alternative histories does not depend just on the out-comes of the struggles for political power and control over the nation's future. It will depend no less on where scholars choose to locate them-selves in contestations over the past.

On this issue there were two contradictory views. One group saw historians as very much products of their specific times and societies, their perspectives of the past shaped and bounded by elements be-yond their control, revisionist moments in historiography therefore more the products of history than historians. Disagreeing with this view, a second group argued that historians decide what to look for in the past, though they cannot and should not predetermine what they will find. Notwithstanding the powerful role of the state, histo-rians are ultimately the ones who write people or events into or out of history; what they exclude becomes lost from history and what they choose to write about becomes part of history.

This responsibility of the historian, it was felt, weighs more heavily on local scholars. As nationals, they have been more involved, or implicated, in the writing of national and nationalistic histories than scholars abroad, who as foreigners could be more distanced from the national projects of building an integrated nation and consolidating a national identity.[18] In many countries in Southeast Asia, rewriting history to claim back the authenticity, and in some cases glory, of a precolonial past was part of the anticolonial and nationalist struggle. By centering history on the nation, local scholars found a location from which to write back at colonialist and Orientalist histories. But are the forces of anticolonialism and nationalism receding as nations, maturing beyond the immediate postindependence formation stage, face a new era of globalization? Or should we ask perhaps whether the nation has dominated history for too long? Is it now time for history to be rescued from the nation and released from the confines of a decades-old template? Should historians depart from such homogeneity, generate more debates and controversies, look for the history of differences, listen to more voices from the past, and seek alterities and contrary plots to challenge the hegemony of the unilinear emplotment of the national past?

In the critique of national histories, other questions and criticisms were also raised. Who defines what the nation is and how is this present linked to what it was in the past? One problem certainly is that country histories in which the names of Southeast Asian nations, as they are known today, are applied anachronistically backward in time to establish continuity with the precolonial past and disguise the many changes that have taken place over the centuries, in state systems and over different mappings of territories.[19] Further, there is a great diversity of ethnic groups, languages, cultures, religions, and long histories of in- and out-migration of peoples, in most Southeast Asian societies. Can the histories of such diverse peoples, indigenous and immigrant, be brought under the rubric of a single narrative? Is the history of the nation a composite history of all its people(s)? Is a national history the sum of all the nation's parts? Who or what gets located at the center of the nation's history, and why?

Such questions, and the answers to them, are saturated with political considerations from the present impinging themselves on our perceptions and understanding of the past. How the lines between indigenous and foreign, majority and minority, are drawn can and have changed over time. The privileging of particular themes or sources or languages in history writing, as much as different positionings by local and foreign scholars, has resulted in some groups being centered and others marginalized. The question of how Myanmar's national history has incorporated minority indigenous peoples, such as the Shans and Karens, was raised as one example. The Indians in Malaysia, visible only on the periphery of Malaysian national history, or appearing mainly in plantation or labor histories or studies specific to the Indian community, is another case in point.[20] In the case of the indigenous communities of Sarawak, a multiplicity of languages, separation across geographical distances, and oral rather than written historical traditions make any attempt to construct a single political narrative that can incorporate all the communities highly problematic.[21]

When the nation is consistently placed at the center of historical research, the result often is an inward-looking perspective that displaces or diminishes the attention given to broader issues or stories that cross national boundaries. One example is the history of the Cold War, a hot and bloody event for many Southeast Asian societies, which has been much researched by scholars in the West, but from an "external" perspective. It is time for Southeast Asian scholars to look at the many layers of this entire episode from the *inside,* not in a parochial nationalistic sense, but from a perspective that can take in the local and regional dimensions, relating them to the international strategic factors in the conflicts. Most important perhaps is the utilization of local sources and local knowledge to understand how the international conflicts that were part of the Cold War impinged on the politics and lives of peoples living in the region.[22]

Another consequence of national narratives, usually structured as the story of the formation of the nation-state, is that politics is foregrounded at the expense of cultural, economic, and social structures that may be perceived only from a wider regional or even global perspective. Caught within the national narrative mode, many Southeast Asian scholars work within contemporary national boundaries even when they are not writing national histories. They engage in few comparative studies and even fewer that sweep broadly across the entire region, unlike scholars in the West. There are few works by local scholars comparable in scale to Anthony Reid's Braudelian history of Southeast Asia in the Age of Commerce,[23] or with the scope of Oliver Wolters's regional perspective in identifying the main features of the cultural matrix shared, in his view, by many early Southeast Asian societies,[24] or the breadth of Benedict Anderson's work on nationalism and politics covering several Southeast countries.[25]

Southeast Asian scholars may, indeed, also be admonished for lacking the courage to venture into theoretical discussions that require a broader, comparative, or regional perspective, choosing instead to confine themselves to localized, microcosmic, ethnographic studies. In calling on Southeast Asian scholars to move on to more sophisticated theoretical work, Thongchai Winichakul suggests as a corrective first step that they rethink their conceptions of space and time.[26] The linear emplotments and narrative chronologies of national histories have entrapped researchers, restricting explorations of multiple dimensions of space as well as time. Thinking of space as malleable and open to differing, or even conflicting, conceptualizations can destabilize the hegemonic hold of official or national history's claims over the shape of the past, alerting us against a simplistic unidimensional perspective in studying history.[27] Space can be conceptualized in several ways—in topographic, social, cultural, or even metaphorical terms—as physical landscapes, as sites where new social structures are erected or old ones reassembled, as arenas of social conflict, as contact zones for peoples and cultures, or simply as the terrain of everyday activities. Exploring new spatial metaphors can create the epistemological spaces for local knowledge and subaltern voices to be articulated and also destabilize old concepts of time. In place of linear time, we may think of several temporal trajectories, with different flows and speeds, intersecting gridlike at multiple points.

National or political boundaries are not tight and imporous, peoples and social relations are seldom hemmed in by lines drawn on maps. Transgressions, or trespassing, may be regular, even daily, occurrences. Indeed, movements of people, goods, cultural practices, values, and ways of thinking has been a recurrent theme for centuries in Southeast Asian history. Continuous movements of people make some spaces diasporic. Singapore is one example of a diasporic space in which the "localization of transnational elements" is evident. To enrich this line of thought further, the concept of interstices suggests focal points from which to track different kinds and levels of dynamic movements across space and time, providing the possibility of complex histories of social relations and cultural interchange that traverse or transcend political boundaries. As "locations of culture," interstices can be found wherever encounters, translations, appropriations, and hybridization have occurred or are in process. Seeking new historical narratives at the interstices and on the margins is one way we can find new terrains for research, as well as a higher level of theoretical engagement, to meet the challenge of writing postnational histories.

From another methodological perspective, huge segments of the Southeast Asian past remain in darkness due to scholars' reluctance, or inability, to grapple with the massive amounts of quantitative data that are, in fact, readily available. Patient mining of detailed records and sophisticated strategies of quantitative analysis can yield the kind of illuminating insights, especially into the lives of ordinary people, that we cannot find elsewhere. This is one direction in which more work should be done.[28] While quantitative data provides conventionally acceptable solid ground for historical studies, no historian today can ignore the impact of new theories in other disciplines on the historian's craft. Some may think that historians, who have always engaged with their primary sources as texts requiring skeptical caution and careful analysis, should not find literary theory and the postmodernist emphasis on deconstruction astonishingly new. But the challenge from postmodernist theories, with their insistence that the social world is essentially a constructed reality, goes beyond asking us to treat conventional historical sources with greater care. We will need to rethink our concepts of fact, truth, and objectivity. It is not clear whether we can simply absorb interesting ideas from other disciplines, treating them as new ingredients to be "mixed in an interesting research potion."[29]

Several papers presented at the conference took us away from mulling over such theoretical issues to research on highly specific topics, such as seventeenth-century Phuket, a Chinese kongsi in Johore, migrants in contemporary Vietnam, social bandits in South Sulawesi, the print culture of Tamil Muslims, and the location of Chinese women in Malaysian history.[30] These papers together showed that there is a wealth of histories that can be written that are not more parts of the jigsaw to be forced into the structure of the national narrative. Migratory or marginal groups penetrate national boundaries, bringing uprooted cultural practices and social institutions into new locales. They are examples of interstices around which new webs of social relations are constructed while old structures break apart. The meaning of such histories is to be found not in their location within the larger national narrative but in what they reveal about the dialectics between human agency and the social, political, and cultural structures in which human lives are defined and lived. In the highly personal decisions of individual Vietnamese and their families to move or to stay on when their world was shaken by one seismic change after another, we can see the dynamics between structure and agency in the lives of ordinary people caught in the web of events beyond their control. The lives of Chinese women, situated within translocations of social and cultural practices or migratory movements between China and the Malay Archipelago in a long history of trading and cultural contacts, reveals constantly changing and multiple dimensions in the dynamics between structure and agency.

Histories of migrants, social bandits, and other "marginal" groups may, from one point of view, be considered a counterpoint to "mainstream" history. But this presupposes that the line between center and margin is clear and fixed rather than ambiguous and fluctuating. Migrants can enter, or become part of the political, economic, and cultural, mainstream just as peoples from "the center" may, in certain situations, become migrants. Furthermore, studies of "marginal" groups such as social bandits do not just inform us about the group itself, they also tell us a great deal about the social, economic, and political structures in the society that marginalized them.

In like manner, local histories do illuminate larger themes but they can also suggest alternative delineations of meaningful space or explain the construction of unique local identities, highlighting the saliency of nonnational stories or narratives. Some local histories may require the scholar to pursue sources located literally around the globe, as in the case of seventeenth-century Phuket. Others, for example, the Ngee Heng Kongsi in Johore, draw their meaning mainly from local sources and local knowledge. The wealth that may lie hidden in local records, such as those of state-level religious affairs departments, once discovered can open up to a patient scholar the possibility of entering into the day to day lives of ordinary people and therefore also for writing history from below. And it is the intense interest that local people have in their own history, so clearly illustrated in the history of the Ngee Heng Kongsi, that makes history and knowledge about the past meaningful to those living in the present.

Historians are not the only people interested in the past, and historical writing should not be intended only, or even mainly, for scholarly exchange or aggrandizement. At the conference, Ambeth Ocampo made an impassioned plea for more Southeast Asian academics to bring the fruits of their research out of their ivory towers and share them with a wider public.[31] Historians, like literary writers, produce texts. Without readers, these texts have little meaning. Popular history can also provide an overt or covert challenge to "official history" by taking historical debates to a wider audience. This is one way in which history can be more interesting and meaningful to more people, especially young persons. Citing the experience of the celebration of the centennial of the declaration of Philippine independence on 12 June 1898 as an example, Ocampo suggested that centennials and other commemorations of significant historical events are occasions when scholars and writers can stimulate public debate and join in a wider discourse about the meaning and significance of such events. History most certainly does not belong only to the historians. It also belongs to the people. Writing popular histories is one way in which history can be taken from the ivory tower and returned to the people. Can Southeast Asian historians rise to this as well as all the other challenges that face them in the twenty-first century?

Many calls for new directions of research and writing were made during the Conference on Southeast Asian Historiography since 1945. The title of the conference suggested a backward-looking perspective, appropriately enough for a meeting of historians. Yet many of the papers presented, and the tenor of discussions during the conference, were forward-looking in seeking new epistemological ground, new methodological strategies, new foci, and new audiences. In documenting the intellectual exchange of the conference, we hope this volume will be part of, and contribute further to, the ongoing search for new terrains in the writing of Southeast Asian history.

Notes

1. D. G. E. Hall, ed., *Historians of Southeast Asia* (London: Oxford University Press, 1961).

2. D. G. E. Hall, *A History of Southeast Asia* (1955; reprint, London: Macmillan, 1961).

3. Ibid., vii.

4. Anthony Reid and David Marr, eds., *Perceptions of the Past in Southeast Asia* (Singapore: Heinemann Educational Books, for Asian Studies Association of Australia, 1979).

5. This debate was set off by Hall, *History of Southeast Asia*. John Smail and Harry Benda's seminal pieces were published in the *Journal of Southeast Asian History* (now *Journal of Southeast Asian Studies*) in 1961 and 1962 respectively. Smail's essay "On the Possibility of an Autonomous History of Modern Southeast Asia" is available in *Autonomous Histories, Particular Truths: Essays in Honor of John W. Smail*, ed. Laurie J. Sears, University of Wisconsin Center for Southeast Asian Studies, Monograph 11 (Madison, 1993); Benda's essay "The Structure of South-East Asian History" appears in *Continuity and Change in Southeast Asia: Collected Journal Essays of Harry J. Benda*, Yale University Southeast Asia Studies, no. 18 (New Haven, 1972).

6. David K. Wyatt and Alexander Woodside, eds., *Moral Order and the*

Question of Change: Essays on Southeast Asian Thought, Yale University Southeast Asia Studies, no. 24 (New Haven, 1982).

7. These concepts come from Benda, Smail, and Oliver Wolters. Two useful surveys of changes in Southeast Asian historiography are J. D. Legge, "The Writing of Southeast Asian History" in *The Cambridge History of Southeast Asia,* ed. Nicholas Tarling, 2 vols. (Cambridge: Cambridge University Press, 1992), 1:1–50; and Craig J. Reynolds, "A New Look at Old Southeast Asia," *Journal of Asian Studies* 54, 2 (1995): 419–46.

8. For example, C. D. Cowan and O. W. Wolters, eds., *Southeast Asian History and Historiography: Essays Presented to D. G. E. Hall* (Ithaca: Cornell University Press, 1976); Ruth T. McVey, ed., *Southeast Asian Transitions: Approaches through Social History* (New Haven: Yale University Press, 1978). See also Soejatmoko, Mohammad Ali, G. J. Resinck, and G. McTurnan Kahin, eds., *An Introduction to Indonesian Historiography* (Ithaca: Cornell University Press, 1965).

9. Tarling, *Cambridge History of Southeast Asia.*

10. Thongchai Winichakul, "The Changing Landscape of the Past: New Histories in Thailand since 1973," *Journal of Southeast Asian Studies* 26, 1 (1995): 99–120.

11. Thongchai Winichakul, article in this volume.

12. For an interesting discussion of the problems of a China-centered perspective and the vulnerabilities of an "insider" location in writing the history of China, see Tongji Lin, "The China-Centered Approach: Traits, Tendencies, and Tensions," *Bulletin of Concerned Asian Scholars* 18, 4 (1986): 49–59.

13. Of the seven papers presented at the conference, three are included in this volume: Ni Ni Myint on Myanmar, C. J. W.-L. Wee on Singapore, and Abdul Rahman Haji Ismail and Badriyah Haji Salleh on Malaysia.

14. To borrow the vocabulary used by Milagros Guerrero, "Philippine Historiography: The Teaching of Philippine History since 1946," her survey presented at the conference on Southeast Asian Historiography since 1945, Penang, July 30–August 1, 1990.

15. The discussion on textbooks was sparked after Charnvit Kasetsiri presented "History: 'In and Out' of Textbooks in Thailand," at the conference.

16. See article by Hong Lysa and Huang Jianli in this volume.

17. See article by Kobkua Suwannathat-Pian in this volume.

18. For a discussion on this point, see Soedjatmoko, "The Indonesian Historian and His Time" in *An Introduction to Indonesian Historiography,* 404–15.

19. See article by Paul Kratoska in this volume.

20. This was raised in K. Anbalakan's conference paper, "Doing Justice to Ethnic Minorities in History Writing: The Case of the Indians in Malaysian History."

21. Ooi Keat Gin provided a survey of historical writings about the indigenous communities of Sarawak, at the conference.

22. Richard Mason made this call for a fresh round of revisionist histories of the Cold War from a local perspective in his conference paper entitled "Origins of the Cold War in Southeast Asia: A Survey of Post-Revisionist Interpretations."

23. Anthony Reid, *Southeast Asia in the Age of Commerce, 1450–1680: The Lands below the Winds* (New Haven: Yale University Press, 1988).

24. O. W. Wolters, *History, Culture, and Region in Southeast Asian Perspectives* (Singapore: ISEAS, 1982; rev. ed., Ithaca: Cornell Southeast Asia Program Publications, in association with Institute of Southeast Asian Studies, 1999).

25. See, for example, Anderson's latest collection of essays, *The Spectre of Comparisons: Nationalism, Southeast Asia and the World* (London: Verso, 1998).

26. Winichakul, this volume.

27. These and other ways of conceptualizing space are discussed in Brenda Yeoh's article in this volume.

28. In addition to making these arguments, Radin Fernando's article in this volume also discusses some examples.

29. These issues are discussed in Yong Mun Cheong's article in this volume.

30. Part 3 contains five of these papers (Abu Talib Ahmad, Dhiravat na Pombejra, P. Lim Pui Huen, Andrew Hardy, and Tan Liok Ee).

31. In "Out of the Ivory Tower: Popular History in the Philippines since 1945."

Part One

SEEKING NEW PERSPECTIVES
AND STRATEGIES

Chapter 1

WRITING AT THE INTERSTICES

Southeast Asian Historians and Postnational Histories in Southeast Asia

THONGCHAI WINICHAKUL

A HISTORIAN NORMALLY CARES LESS about theories than a social scientist does. Many historians think it could be detrimental for them to be too rigid about theory and some fear their work would become less charming if they are too explicit about theory. Indeed the ability to weave concepts and theories into skillful storytelling is much more challenging and more illuminating.

There are times, nevertheless, when we need to step back and reconsider the underlying concepts, assumed theories, and reigning paradigms within which we are refining our craft. In recent years, nation and nationalism as concepts and practices have been severely scrutinized. Critics from different methodological orientations and political ideologies have exposed the arbitrariness of the nation as a historical entity and the mechanisms that make it seem natural; they have emphasized its artificiality, pointed to its casualties, and questioned its contribution to the modern world.[1] Nations and nationalisms in Asia are likewise facing criticisms in the context of their colonial and postcolonial experiences.[2] The validity of writing "national history" in Asia is now disputed and the need to "rescue" its "casualties" advocated.[3] The nation as historical Subject, a natural and given assumption glorified by many great thinkers from the eighteenth to the early twentieth century, is now in trouble.

In Southeast Asia, national history is facing similar challenges. Reynaldo Ileto's works not only make the subaltern, who did not truly fight for the nation, the Subject of history, but also offer an alternative, nonlinear plot for a history of the Philippines.[4] Glenn May argues that Bonifacio, one of the most prominent Filipino nationalist leaders of the Katipunan in the 1890s, was possibly a myth rather than a true historical figure.[5] In Thailand too, the official royal/national history has been shaken since the late 1970s, by other kinds of national narratives as well as nonnational ones. Alternative plots of Thai history have been offered.[6] Recently the status of the golden age of Thai history, Sukhothai, was severely undermined when the inscription to which it owes the main story line was said to have been written much later than originally thought. Despite many efforts to rescue the sanctity of the inscription, the cloud over the golden age is unlikely to go away.[7] In Laos and Vietnam there have always been competing national narratives—communist, anticommunist, and others—all laying claim to the nation's past.[8] Keith Taylor's recent article goes radically further, defying a cohesive national or regional frame of Vietnamese history, with its familiar north-south linear narrative.[9] In post-Suharto Indonesia, despite the difficulties in dealing with its traumatic past, it is very likely that hundreds of historiographical flowers will blossom to challenge the national narrative of the state. Regardless of anyone's political preferences, the seismic shifts in its territorial makeup will inevitably result in historiographical shifts as well. Some of these challenges are stimulating alternative narratives of the nation, such as a popular nationalist "history from below" or the nonlinear pluralistic story of a nation, but others are seeking ways to go beyond the national narrative.

Unlike the making of national histories in some countries in Europe, supposedly the origin of the idea of the nation-state, national histories in colonial and postcolonial conditions, such as in Southeast Asia, have taken different trajectories. In most cases, history writing was an elitist craft and knowledge form inherited from, but subsequently practiced in reaction to, colonialism. Their nationalism was not an imperial but an anticolonial or postcolonial one. Even the modern history of a noncolonized country like Siam has been very much anticolonial, or even postcolonial, in character and genesis.[10] National histories in individual countries usually respond dynamically to increasing social plurality, a burgeoning local bourgeoisie, and weakening authoritarian conditions. History is changing, and probably will change even more significantly, in ways that have yet to be seen.

Modern historical knowledge in Southeast Asia, produced in colonial or postcolonial conditions, was part of the modernity project in which there was no religious or intellectual revolution that could break, or secularize, it from traditional perceptions of the past. As a result, the so-called national history is regarded not just as an account of the country's actual past, but as a "true" or "correct" collective ledger, computed in accordance with a scale of spiritual merit and demerit, as well as a repository of the "national spirit and ideology." Therefore, I have no illusions that national histories will go away soon. On the contrary, national histories may be modified or transformed but will survive vigorously everywhere, as long as the nation itself does. The challenges to nations, scholarly or otherwise, will nevertheless pave the way for alternative histories to emerge. The challenges for us, as historians, should be to expose the limitations of the current national histories and to explore other possibilities. It is time to move on.

I would argue that as the spatial configuration of a nation is shaken, and the legitimation of a nation as a spatial identity problematized, with the changing geography comes the possibility of different stories. As the nation-state loses its predominance, so too will a national history. This is as much a serious cause for concern as an opportunity to break the grip of the official ideology and its national narrative. It all depends on how, and in which directions, historians and other historical actors choose to direct it. In this chapter, I do not suggest yet another kind of national narrative, be it a popular one from below or a nationalized local history. A more exciting alternative for historians in Southeast Asia is the concept of writing history "at the interstices." Below I discuss history of the margins and history of the localization of transnational elements as two ways of writing history at the interstices.

My choice is not in any way intended as a prediction that history at the interstices will eventually prevail. On the contrary, it is an expression of my preference, my endorsement so to speak, arising from a sense of excitement that this is an opportunity to propose alternatives, including radical ones, with no romantic aspiration that my preference will emerge as the winner. In this essay I am responding to the call made by O. W. Wolters in 1994 to look at "Southeast Asia as a Southeast Asian field of study."[11]

I will argue that although there is no guarantee that scholars within Southeast Asia can arrive at the "truth" more easily or better than nonnatives, they can approach their study from an angle that could provide a comparative advantage for them to play the most prominent role in theorizing history at the interstices. They should aim high in order to make theoretical contributions to the field of history writing. I am aware of the implications and limitations of the various words used to signify scholars and historians of Southeast Asia. In the present context my preference goes to a new term that is vague enough to allow interpretations and modification but is free of political baggage: *home* scholars, or scholars (historians) of the *home,* by which I mean those who study the country, region, or location that they consider their home, and whose works are read, debated, and become, in a sustained manner, part of the scholarly discourse and cultural politics of their home society.[12] The main purpose of this term is to differentiate such scholars from those who study the home of other people, no matter how much attachment, love, or sympathy they might extend to that place. Regarding a place as a home is more inclusive than exclusive. It does not preclude a long-distance study away from home or exclude the commitment a long-time resident alien may have to a new home, nor does it privilege one kind of rootedness over another. It allows for various subjective claims of, more or less, intimacy and knowledge of the place thought of as home. Of course all such claims, whether based on birth, race, length of stay, or any other criteria, are ultimately subjective and open to dispute.

The Decline of Nation as a
Spatial Identity and Historical Subject

The challenges to national history come from many fronts. Fundamentally, the conditions that fostered the emergence of national history at the beginning—the rising of the national bourgeoisie against the aristocracy, the making of an empire, and anticolonialism—have completely changed. But most important is the fact that consciousness of space and spatial identities, on both the global and local scales, have been fundamentally altered. The nation-state, nationhood, and nationalism can no longer be taken without suspicion and may often even evoke contempt. Although the nation is likely to outlast us, it may not enjoy the same power as *the* dominant spatial identity, which it has held for the past two hundred years. Even the rise of ethnic nationalism in many parts of the world in recent years may raise doubts about the value of nationalism rather than strengthening it.

Mary Louis Pratt has argued in her study on colonial Latin America that colonialism was a form of transculturation. One of its impacts was a new planetary consciousness—that is, a new perception of the world with particular emphasis on how the Europeans understood their positions in relation to others in the world.[13] Colonialism in the eighteenth and nineteenth centuries in Asia produced similar effects. The emergence of the geo-body of a nation, for instance, was a revolution of spatial identity within the new planetary framework of modern geography. Globalization of the late twentieth century onward is likely to introduce another form of planetary consciousness. A small number of national capitals have become world metropolises, in a league of their own, since the colonial period. Currently a small number of closely connected global financial and information hubs, whose affiliations are to corporations as much as to national economies, are forming a layer in a new global landscape. The two-dimensional, politically oriented design of the globe may soon need a major revamp to reflect the new multilayered global entities.

Globalization will have far-reaching effects on spatial identities and thus also on the reformulation of historical subjects in many ways. First, although it is an exaggeration to say that the nation-state is irrelevant, the geopolitical entity is increasingly intersected, disrupted, displaced, and interpolated by the global realms of media (mediascapes), movements of people (ethnoscapes), information (infoscape), and neoliberal capitalism.[14] As the nation-state faces even more challenges in the years to come, it is likely to induce reconfiguration and resistance, provoking alternatives to its present form, while its dominance over the discourse of identity, now subject to challenge, will be reduced.

Second, instead of the homogenization and standardization feared by many, conservatives and radicals alike, globalization is likely to produce and provide opportunities for new kinds of diversity as some existing ones disappear. The maximization of human resources in diverse places will neither destroy nor impede diversity and individuality. On the contrary, the invigoration of local identity and diversity has become an important method for enhancing human resources.[15] Globalization is, in the words of well-known Thai scholar Chai-anan Samudavanija, like a huge net over the world that is full of holes.[16] A new variety of identities (and therefore of historical subjects) some more and some less than a nation, is likely to emerge.

Third and most important, like every other global force in the past, such as Indianization, Sinicization, and European colonialism, the current globalization has its twin, which is the other side of the same moment or process, namely localization. It is unlikely that the world will become faceless or lack particularity. Global forces always assume local forms, as the global must always be made comprehensible or meaningful at the local level. The emerging spatial identities, nonetheless, could either be similar to the old, be totally new, or perhaps be a hybrid. Here the different kinds of agency, and their ingenuity, play a key role. By the late twentieth century, the active agencies of global/localization were no longer the ruling elite. Entrepreneurs, the media, and public intellectuals now undertake this role.

These are among the conditions that could foster new spatial identities. In the reformulation or emergence of spatial identities, new histories are possible. Perhaps, they are inevitable. Why? A spatial identity is always a place—that is, a space loaded with values and meanings for those who identify with it. A spatial identity usually has its story, probably many stories, without which such a place or identity would be meaningless. In fact, a story anticipates a place and a spatial identity. More often than not travelers and surveyors know stories about places even before they get there. After arriving they write about or map the place accordingly. Place and story are thus intertwined. On the one hand, stories can change the ways people think about a place, and therefore redefine it, or give birth to new spatial identities. Stories become resources for the new spatial identity, for formulating the narrative of its birth, development, characteristics, and so on. On the other, as a place changes or a different spatial identity emerges, its story usually changes accordingly. A potentially new spatial identity may inspire, and project, stories that help its emergence.

A national history is the biography of a spatial identity. While the nation is being transformed, or perhaps losing its predominance as the primary historical Subject and the privileged site of history, the raison d'être of a national history in many postcolonial countries, namely anticolonialism, is losing its force as well. No matter how much the regimes in those countries try to call up the specter of neocolonialism as a convenient enemy, especially during the economic crisis, the ghost may not be effective in the long run. The real dynamism that propels changes in the spatial identity of a nation is increasing diversity and complexity within a society. The old national story has served its purpose, to establish a nation-state; it has perhaps run its course. Now other narratives, of nonnational subjects perhaps, begin to emerge and blossom. We are at this transition, when national history is on its way out and narratives of new spatial identities are emerging. I can, however, only talk about postnational history; for the future is in the making, by historians among many others.

History at the Interstices

HISTORY OF THE MARGINS

A national history basically tells a story about how a nation came into being: through the political-economic processes of nation building, or by assuming the "essence" of a nation, such as a core culture, or by identification with a race, a homeland, and so on, that over time evolved until a full-grown nation is realized in the form of the modern nation-state. Most national histories are teleological narratives, stories of preordained destinations.

As the arbitrariness of the world of nations and the limitations of national history come under scrutiny, plenty of alternatives are emerging. Among them are a transnational history of Southeast Asia as a common maritime trading zone;[17] a history of areas that span or cross the borders between different modern nations, especially if they shared a common history before the drawing of modern national boundaries;[18] and subnational histories of regions and locals that once were "autonomous," and not part of the major nations, but were "integrated" with them later. Spatially speaking, these alternatives seek different spatial identities. And, with a different geography, different stories emerge.

A different story of a nonnational spatial identity, however, may or may not be a challenge to the national narrative. As the interest in local history proliferates, it can be a counterhistory, as it often rediscovers a local narrative suppressed or bypassed by the national narrative.[19] It is a challenge to the nation-state if the latter remains vulnerable to local and regional differences. But a local history can be integrated into the national narrative, as regions and locales are drawn into the national administration. In the case of Thailand, the integrity of national sovereignty is no longer under threat from regionalism (with perhaps a few exceptions). Although political centralization is very much in place, the mushrooming of local histories in the past two decades or so and the expressive diversity throughout the country have enhanced the legitimation of the state. The more diverse and more plural society has rendered the Thai state more flexible and more stable. Local histories, instead of being regarded as alternatives, are accommodated and integrated into the national narrative. Indeed they are overtly nationalistic and explicitly subservient to the national narrative and agenda.[20]

I suggest a few more possibilities that could challenge the assumption of the national essence, or disrupt it, thereby changing the ways we think about a national narrative and offering the opportunity for a transition from a national history. This is what I call history at the interstices—the history of the locations and moments between being and not being a nation, becoming and not becoming a nation. Thinking of national history with a spatial perspective, we should explore all the extremities where the domain of national history ends and another history begins, be it the super- or the subnational, especially the ones suppressed by national history. At those interstices, theoretically, it is possible to discern the discursive regime of a national history, its logics, conditions, constitutions, mechanism, reproduction, and so on, in contrast to the adjacent domains of knowledge under different regimes. By doing so, we should understand better how a national history emerges and survives, and probably we will discover other histories that were displaced or suppressed by it.

From a spatial perspective, again, an entity can be comprehensible as a domain of certain meaning within a certain, but not necessarily fixed, boundary. In other words, instead of starting from the center—the supposedly intrinsic essence, the given definition of a subject of study, be it democracy, ethnicity, or a nation—we can approach a subject by looking at how it is defined, its "out-line," the limits of its meaning, or the boundary of such an entity within which a certain meaning claims its authority and beyond which it would become something else. The margin is where the inclusion and exclusion, integration and suppression of certain meanings take place.

A history of the margins of a nation is, therefore, a history of the locations—geographically, temporally, culturally—where it stops being a nation, or being this or that nation. The obvious examples are geographic, such as the autonomous history of those units that never became separate independent nations but had resisted integration or still struggle for autonomy. The cases of the Karen, Mon, Kachin, Aceh, and Irian Jaya, come to mind right away. Similar cases may be found along the borders of most nations. As the modern kind of boundary—margin and sovereignty—were established, such areas have been overlooked as separate entities with their own histories that defy the national ones. A history of each area is usually slipped into a celebratory narrative of the success of national integration.[21] In most cases, as Clive Christie has shown, it is possible to write a counter-history about how each had been different and separate from the core of a nation, thus a history of reluctance to integrate, of resistance or separatism.[22] They are the locations where the national history could have taken a different course. Indeed, in some areas the age-old, prenational polity persists together with the practice of multiple sub-missions and ambiguous sovereignty.[23]

A history of the margins of a nation can be written for a nongeo-graphic subject as well. We may think of a history of a nation's people from the margins, how ethnic and religious minorities are positioned with the construction of citizenship, of discrimination, exclusion, and suppression of various kinds of minorities.[24] Nationhood is always identified by a number of authentic essences, be it the "genuine" culture, "superior" race, royal power, or ancestry linked to a norma-tive history. These are the "centers" without which a nation would lose its character. National history constitutes the domain of histori-cal knowledge whose boundaries mark the distinction between what is considered legitimate, credible history and what is not. The writ-ing of national history involves silencing, suppressing, or excluding certain pasts from becoming part of the national narrative; these are pushed out to the margins of the national.

A history from the different margins of the alleged center would certainly expose the limits of a nation as an entity. These histories of the margins of a nation offer a decentered view of a nation. It is very likely that they will undermine the unifying theme, the essence, the teleology, or the spirit of a nation's history. Besides, because they expose the different edges of the nation, they will remain fragmented and are unlikely to coalesce into a new national history.

HISTORY OF LOCALIZATION

Let us return to globalization. Its pervasiveness is exaggerated and misleading. The limits of globalization are wherever it encounters local conditions. To use a linguistic metaphor, at those points of encounter, globalization cannot avoid translation, which involves the appropriation and interpretation of the globalizing language in order to be intelligible in local contexts.[25] Thus, instead of eliminating or suspending local culture, a localization process will take place. This applies also to cultural products, knowledge, and probably science and technology as well. In fact the current globalization process is not the first global force in the history of transculturation. Historians of Southeast Asia have been familiar with Indianization, an earlier "globalizing" influence. So too was modernity via colonialism in the eighteenth to twentieth centuries. Some earlier historians thought that Southeast Asia was colonized by an imperial power from India. Later, many believed that the region was not colonized but culturally Indianized, as if the preexisting local cultures were insignificant and played no role in the transculturation process. Eventually we have learned to recognize the role of "local genius," those local agencies that were active in selectively adopting and adapting the Indic elements to fit local settings. Historians realized that though the Indic influence in local cultures was widespread, they never made Southeast Asia become Indian.[26] Nor did colonial hegemony or Westernization make us Euro-American. Neither will the current globalization. In short, there is no globalization without localization; the former cannot take place without the latter.

To put this in a spatial perspective, the limits of globalization are reached at those sites where the global and the local collide, and where they produce effects, whether as synthesis, modification, displacement, replacement, or in some other form. Globalization is truly globalized—penetrating into every corner of the globe—only when it allows local variation to take place. The locations where encounters occur have been celebrated by Homi Bhaba as the "in-between" or the "beyond," which are the sites and moments of cultural production and transformation that are actively engaged with transnational influences. Usually these sites are on the margins of the domain of mainstream culture, but they can send waves of changes to the entire cultural realm.[27] In Bhaba's words, they are the "locations of culture." I would like to call them the interstices.

In the following encounters and moments of localization, cultural production took place through translation and appropriation, involving hybridization from both channels of resources. Three significant studies in Philippine history illustrate this point; namely, Ileto's *Pasyon and Revolution,* on the local appropriation of Catholicism as reflected in popular movements between 1840 and 1910; Vicente Rafael's *Contracting Colonialism,* on the conversion to, and translation of, Christianity under early Spanish rule that reformulated the social order in the Philippines; and more recently, Filomeno Aguilar's *Clash of Spirits,* on how local people employed indigenous belief in magic to tame and accommodate capitalism, as well as market and global forces.[28] In his study of an influential historical text by a Thai Marxist, Craig Reynolds has insightfully demonstrated how Marxist historical materialism was appropriated by a Thai radical intelligentsia of the 1950s to produce a subversive, antiroyalist narrative of oppressive and exploitative Thai feudalism, even though there was no equivalent to feudalism in Thai history. This radical discourse turned the concept that was closest to feudalism, namely *sakdina,* from an exalted, honorable connotation into a derogatory one. In another study, Reynolds shows how an ancient Chinese historical romance, *Sanguo yanyi,* became highly popular in modern Southeast Asia, especially Thailand, as a guide for business and political maneuvers. Through being translated into Thai in the late eighteenth century, a Chinese text became a classical Thai literary work that was quite different from the Chinese original, becoming in that process the purveyor of a Sinitic transnationalism.[29]

Such interstices offer exciting subjects of studies that can counter both the globalist, who has an appetite only for studies of worldwide forces, and the nationalist, who can only see the course of national history as determined domestically by indigenous people. Whenever and wherever there is a transnational situation, outside-inside is a false dichotomy and global-local are inseparable parts of the same process.

The issue here resonates what Anna Tsing has argued for in her works. What I call interstices she calls margins.[30] In the following selections she explains the terms *margins* and *local:*

> Margins [are] conceptual sites from which to explore the imaginative quality and the specificity of local/global cultural formation. Margins here are not geographical, descriptive locations. . . . Instead, I use the term to indicate an analytic placement that makes evident both the constraining, oppressive quality of cultural exclusion, and the creative potential of rearticulating, enlivening, and rearranging the very social categories that peripherize a group's existence.

> Local [is] a site in which widespread institutions and cultural configurations take on particular forms, rather than a site of autochthonous cultural formation.[31]

Interest in the localization process, however, has been overshadowed by preoccupation with national history as well as by global studies. Interest in the all-encompassing phenomena of globalization reflects the desire for universal knowledge and for a grand narrative, or theory, that can explain the worldwide process. But the truth is that localization, which is the other side of the same phenomena, is equally global and all-encompassing because globalization is always realized in local forms. The world is full of localization and hybridity.

The terms by which we understand the same phenomenon from opposite approaches can be misleading. In speaking of the global, one alludes to a gigantic phenomenon that is unified and homogeneous and will let nothing escape it. The local, on the other hand, seems to be the many fragmented, individual processes happening in specific conditions, as if they are not everywhere in rendezvous with the global forces and as if the global and local are a separable pair. Conceptually speaking, such a global-centric bias could, and should, be turned around. Not only does this bias make us blind to the other side of the same phenomenon, but the intellectual propensity in favor of universal theory often relegates the particularity of the local, and its derivatives, into nothing more than empirical and ethnographic data, or the proof of theory, or perhaps the exceptions to theory. Most studies of global phenomena usually assume the primary importance of the origins or archetypes from which the process of appropriation and duplication of local variations takes off. Hence the possibility of scientific and universal global studies beyond particular cases, while local and area studies are relegated to the marginal realm of derivative experiences and reactive particularities, with no intellectual significance beyond individual cases. This leads to the attempt at a grand narrative and theoretical formulations about globalization but never of localization. Scholars who tend to study their "home" countries without claims for a universal application, then, usually become appendices or extensions of the more universal theoretical discourse in the academy.[32] In other words, theoretical orientation becomes a comparative advantage of the global-oriented scholarship while the orientation toward particularity becomes a disadvantage, if not a liability, for area specialists and scholars of the home. The comparative advantage or privilege also goes to scholarship that takes Europe as the model for a universal history, from which many theories are derived.[33] Scholars of the home in non-Western countries, therefore, become disadvantaged people in the intellectual strata, for they are too local and too descriptive.

Take studies of nationalism as an example. All the major theoretical propositions of nationalism mentioned at the beginning of this chapter take Western Europe and North America as the origin of, and prototype for, nationalism from which derivative nationalisms "spread" to other places throughout the world.[34] Without denying what happened in history, we may shift our perspectives and the language by which the process is understood. How so? It is undeniable that the so-called derivative experiences consist by far of the majority of cultures and nationalisms throughout the world. They are the reality most people live with. That is to say the nationalisms that were formulated in the colonial and postcolonial contexts are the fully developed ones. They are the norm of the world. The nationalisms of Europe were the ones that came too early, not the fully developed ones. They should be taken as such, no more and no less. Instead of taking the experiences of Western Europe as the authentic or genuine prototype, we should take them as a genealogical ancestor of nationalisms in other parts of the world. One of the consequences of this shifting perspective is that nationalism should normatively be taken as a transcultural, transnational, and hybrid product. The "original" or "authentic" ones in Western Europe should be considered marginal, not central, to world experiences, and can be fully understood only when they encounter different experiences from around the world.

In this view, the process of transculturation and localization must be considered primary and given full credit. A history or genealogy of anything is by no means a simple story of its duplication from its "stem cells." Rather, it involves other conditions and factors at the locations and moments of its development. Instead of looking at the origins and how this spread, attention should be shifted to the moments and locations of "translation," in which new influences and existing ones come into contact, conflict, and struggle, and exchange their meanings and values. The process of resolution—of exchange, conflict, and tension—is simultaneously the process of hybridization. If we suspend for a moment the sense of narrowness and particularity attached to the term *localization,* we would realize how global localization in fact is, and how significant it is, ethnographically as well as theoretically. Localization definitely can and should be theorized as well.

It has been too long that generalizations about Europe or America are taken as theory while studies from other parts of the world are considered descriptive or ethnographic. This is probably the time to go beyond such a false hierarchy and division of labor. Perhaps the study of interstices, or margins, or the edges of the global-local realms, is the way of the future for country and regional studies, like Southeast Asia, to become more theoretical without sacrificing their empirical and ethnographic strength.[35] Anthony Reid tries to salvage area studies by arguing that Southeast Asia is on par with Europe as an experience in the global process.[36] History at the interstices may take one step further—and that is to claim that localization and the margins should be the prime sites of studies that can be theorized—and contribute to both ethnographic and theoretical literature at the same time.

Historians of the Home and Postnational Histories

This brings us to another related question we have heard more frequently in recent years about Southeast Asian studies by Southeast Asians, or the scholars of the home: Is postnational history another excuse for Western scholars to dominate fields such as the history of Southeast Asia? Or is it, on the contrary, the opportunity for historians from Southeast Asia to play a special role in the field?

The calls for a history of Southeast Asia by Southeast Asian scholars who study their homes are getting louder in recent years. There are several factors in favor of the work of the home scholar. First, critiques of Orientalism, especially colonial scholarship and its legacies, and of the U.S.-dominated area studies, point to one thing in common. Both take the form of knowledge of the Other, through the gaze of the powerful West, serving particular political economies of scholarship in the West, but with profound effects on the self-knowledge of the studied areas and people. The call for the scholars of the home is a result of an anticolonial and anti-imperialist conscience that hopes to correct the situation.

Second, the years of the Asian economic miracle have strengthened not only the economies of many countries in Southeast Asia but also boosted the pride and confidence of scholars in the region. While the subsequent crisis hit Asian economies very hard, scholarly confidence was hardly hit. Blame for the economic collapse was placed equally, if not more, on foreigners. Confidence in scholarship of the home has found institutional support in growing regional networks and collaborations, such as SEASREP (the Southeast Asian Studies Regional Exchange Program), as well as with ASEAN becoming stronger as a spatial entity. These conditions, if sustained, could help invigorate regional Southeast Asian scholarship in the long run.

But apart from this circumstantial (i.e., political and economic) support for Southeast Asian scholarship of Southeast Asia, is there a valid intellectual reason for such a turn in favor of home scholarship? What are the virtues or peculiar potential of Southeast Asian scholars who study their homes? Is there a privilege in being historians of the home?

It is assumed that the call for "native" historians to come to the fore is politically correct. Very often it is implied that an account is more accurate and authoritative if it is written by an "insider."[37] A stronger call, such as the one by Wolters, cites intellectual reasons for Southeast Asian history to be written by Southeast Asians, arguing that there is a peculiar historical consciousness in the region such that its people would write history in their own way.[38] Sometimes a history by the home historian is, ipso facto, taken to be an antidote to Orientalism, as implied by Ileto in his critiques of Western historians of Philippine history.[39] On the other hand, Western concepts are pinpointed as the agents of contamination to what would otherwise be "genuine indigenous knowledge." In the Thai case, the mantra is that Western ideas do not fit Thai society and Thai intellectuals, policymakers, perhaps educated people in general, have followed the West too much for too long. I believe a similar sentiment can be found in every other country in the region.

A discussion of knowledge production as having two sides, Western or Southeast Asian, could become a trap, for it is hard to avoid sounding either like a nationalist or an Orientalist. While the critique of Orientalism is well known, I would like here to discuss two underlying assumptions that usually lend authority to the home scholars: first, faith in the higher value of being a "native" scholar, and second the allegedly pristine nature of "indigenous" knowledge.

To start with, who is a native? An assumption that a native scholar has an innate edge, is a politically correct authority, or enjoys a natural privilege in studying his or her own culture and history, in contrast to a foreigner, is nonsense. Let us assume that we are talking about formally trained historians, rather than ordinary people in the street. Kirin Narayan has questioned how native a native still is in today's world of multiple identities and complex relations.[40] As a Sino-Thai, am I supposed to know Thai history and culture better or worse than Thai-Thai historians? Since I have been living outside the country for many years, can I still be considered a native? What if I continue living abroad another twenty years? Is the native essence reduced over time? We simply cannot measure the level or the quality of being native by any rational means.

Suppose that we can measure the native quality by some means, how can we assume that natives know more, or better, or that the knowledge they have is more truthful? A home scholar may have some advantages in his or her intimacy with the local language. But this is neither intrinsic nor given. Nor is it a guaranteed quality, right, or privilege. On the contrary, the belief in such an intrinsic quality is a delusion that could lead to "native blindness." Being a home scholar, in my view, simply means an attachment to, and familiarity with, a particular place. A native perspective is, strictly speaking, the view from a particular point and background, no more no less, with no imputation of authority or privilege or special access to knowledge. It is as peculiar as the view of an outsider, from afar or from a comparative perspective. Any of them can be more, or less, or equally, truthful.

With regard to *indigenous* scholarship, there is an argument that both Southeast Asian studies and knowledge of individual countries are dominated by Western scholarship, and indigenous knowledge has suffered from such domination. This view asserts, implicitly or explicitly, that a "truly indigenous" scholarship would have been better, or more desirable. The issue here is whether scholarship within Southeast Asia is really stymied by Western scholarship. As colonial and American creations, area studies undoubtedly responded to the changing political economy of Western academia. But I would argue that academia and knowledge production in every Southeast Asian country similarly responds primarily to the political and economic conditions of each country. Social sciences and humanities everywhere in the world are disciplines that tend to be more inward oriented than the natural sciences. Their aims, designs, agenda, ideologies, and development respond more to domestic conditions. They are less open to, thus care less about, and hence are less dominated by, international academics than we might think. The trends, fashions, even the field of debates, inside and outside a country, are often not the same.

Undoubtedly, scholarship in the West does have a strong influence over the entire field. However, the influence of area studies in Europe and America over academia in Southeast Asian countries, like every other aspect of transnational culture, is localized in its encounter with local conditions. Instead of suffering from Western domination, I think the situation may well be the reverse—that is, the home scholars may enjoy some special privileges in the production of knowledge of their own country, especially in history and cultural studies. Their homegrown knowledge creates a particular market or audience that has not faced serious critical challenges. The more inwardly oriented their academia and scholarship are, the less critical inquiry and fewer rigorous challenges. To borrow an economic metaphor, protectionism of the internal market for local scholarhip is strong. This is the reason for striking differences in scholarly development and agenda among various countries in the region, and from area studies in Europe and America. For example, in Thailand, whose academia has never been dictated to by a colonial power, colonial knowledge was imported and adapted to serve domestic interests since the late nineteenth century.[41] In my view, the situation has been the opposite to what is generally believed, which is that Thai studies in Thailand have been under the strong influence of the homegrown intellectual traditions, including Buddhism, royalism, and Thai parochialism. Western scholarship on Thailand has suffered from following Thai scholars, most of whom are elite intellectuals, too much and for too long.[42] Therefore, not only is it hard to justify "indigenous" scholarship nowadays, it is also debatable whether it has suffered more from Western scholarship or the other way round.

Some major factors that have stymied scholarship in many countries are local. As we know, scholars operate under politically repressive conditions as well as under self-censorship and self-limitation, either by ideologies such as nationalism or by the desire to serve the collective good, whether that be defined as national security, national confidence, respect to ancestors, or in yet other ways. Apart from such political considerations, there are more profound factors that may be hard to crack indeed. I would like to discuss only a major one, namely the religious tradition of intellectual inquiry. Modern scholarship in most countries in the region was founded upon strong religious traditions that did not undergo any religious or intellectual revolution on their paths to modernity. One of the legacies of the religious approach to knowledge is to accept the Truth as already discovered and well established. The quest for new knowledge is merely the search for current meanings and manifestations of the known Truth. The advance of knowledge is incremental, not through paradigm shifts or breaks with past beliefs. Hence, the emphasis on rote learning and de-emphasis on criticism and originality, as this would confront or supersede existing knowledge. Knowledge production within this intellectual tradition is quite different from, say, how it is understood within the Enlightenment, let alone postmodernism.

If being native does not lend any authority to a scholar of the home, and if indigenous knowledge, assuming there is such a thing, is not necessarily better or worse, what advantages, if any, may a home scholar of Southeast Asia have? Does writing history at the interstices offer any opportunity to amplify such advantages?

Writing at the Interstices

The answer is that there may be some comparative advantages, but none is given, innate, or comes naturally for the home scholars. For years, many Southeast Asianists from within the region have expressed concern over "the old problem of the superiority of indigenous scholars."[43] Kernial Sandhu spells this out clearly: "If Southeast Asians cannot come up with new insights and 'cutting edges' for the study of Southeast Asia, that is those which would advance our understanding of the region and also scholarship in general, we are in serious trouble."[44] As long as the scholars of the home are condemned to empirical and ethnographic studies to test theories, or to add to the grand narrative of universal history, the situation is not likely to change. I would argue that the concept of history at the interstices can, hopefully, contribute to change.

History at the interstices traverses along the margins of national identity and national history, looking for the "in-between" locations of encounters. It would inevitably expose the edges and limits of the national domain and record the changing configurations of national identity along its borders. At the interstices, differences, hybrids, and mixtures come into play. A historian of the interstices should have the sensitivity for nuances of cultural differences and their changes. The most important loci and traces of cultural differences, clashes, hybrids, and shifts are in *language,* in the broad sense, which includes discourses and other forms of cultural communications. In general, the more a subject or methodology requires language sensitivity, the more comparative advantage the *home* scholar would have. An economist, for example, is less required to know the local language than is a literary historian.

History of the margins, or at the interstices of transnational and transcultural processes, is where scholars who are immersed in particular local conditions and cultures, or languages, would have a decisive advantage. This is by no means an ability that is innate or exclusive to "native" scholars. Some foreigners can acquire the same, or even better, language sensitivity. Wolters, for instance, is indisputably one of them. His language sensitivity undoubtedly made him a preeminent historian of localization. Nevertheless, the home scholars generally have better opportunities to hone their sensitivities to detect the process, moments, and locations of cultural encounters and localization that take place along the interstices of the cultures that they are more familiar with.

Despite their comparative advantage in ethnographic and language sensitivity, the home scholars may nevertheless produce an endless number of ethnographic studies, as they have been doing so far. On the other hand, as I have proposed throughout this chapter, they could be confident and ambitious enough to make theoretical contributions as well. Writing history at the interstices is an opportunity to turn the alleged weakness or disadvantages, namely expertise in local matters with particular language and cultural sensitivity, into advantages for theorization. Not only should scholars of the home reclaim the significance of localization in the global and theoretical discourse, but they should, by doing so, also be able to break up the false division of academic labor.

I do not claim that this is the only future for historians or other scholars within Southeast Asia. Nor is this proposition made in the spirit of rivalry with Western scholarship. But writing history at the interstices of cultures, from the limits, the edges, the margins that are no longer marginal, clearly offers home scholars in Southeast Asia the enormous potential to contribute to Southeast Asian studies, to the knowledge of individual countries ethnographically, and above all to theoretical discourse far beyond one country or the region.

Notes

1. See Ernest Gellner, *Nations and Nationalism* (Ithaca: Cornell University Press, 1983); Benedict Anderson, *Imagined Communities* (London: Verso, 1983); Anthony Smith, *The Ethnic Origins of Nations* (Oxford: Blackwell, 1986); and an earlier work by Elie Kadourie, *Nationalism* (London: Hutchinson, 1960). For a coverage of recent debates on nationalism, see Gopal Balakrishnan, ed., *Mapping the Nation* (London: Verso, 1996). A critical review of theorists and theories of nationalism with specific reference to Southeast Asia is David Henley, "Ethnographic Integration and Exclusion in Anti-Colonial Nationalism: Indonesia and Indochina," *Comparative Studies in Society and History* 37, 2 (April 1995): 286–324. For Africa, where nationhood and nationalism are problematic factors in political develop-

ment, see Basil Davidson, *The Black Man's Burden: Africa and the Curse of the Nation-State* (New York: Times Books, Random House, 1992); Mahmood Mamdani, *Citizen and Subject: Contemporary Africa and the Legacy of Late Colonialism* (Princeton: Princeton University Press, 1996).

2. See Partha Chatterjee, *The Nation and Its Fragments: Colonial and Post-colonial Histories* (Princeton: Princeton University Press, 1993); Thongchai Winichakul, *Siam Mapped: A History of the Geo-Body of a Nation* (Honolulu: University of Hawaii Press, 1994); Stein Tønnesson and Hans Antlöv, eds., *Asian Forms of the Nation* (London: Curzon, for the Nordic Institute of Asian Studies, 1996); Henley, "Ethnographic Integration."

3. Prasenjit Duara, *Rescuing History from the Nation* (Chicago: University of Chicago Press, 1995).

4. Reynaldo Ileto, *Pasyon and Revolution: Popular Movements in the Philippines, 1840–1910* (Manila: Ateneo de Manila University Press, 1979), and "Outlines of a Non-Linear Emplotment of Philippine History," in *Reflections on Development in Southeast Asia,* ed. Lim Teck Ghee (Singapore: ISEAS, 1988), 130–59.

5. Glenn May, *Inventing a Hero: The Posthumous Re-Creation of Andres Bonifacio* (Madison: Center for Southeast Asian Studies, University of Wisconsin, 1996).

6. See Thongchai Winichakul, "The Changing Landscape of the Past: New Histories in Thailand since 1973," *Journal of Southeast Asian Studies* 26, 1 (March 1995): 99–120.

7. See the debate in James Chamberlain, ed., *The Ramkhamhaeng Controversy* (Bangkok: Siam Society, 1991). The book, however, could not record the impact of the controversy on the national ideology, such as how many regal gatherings took place to try to alleviate the uneasy qualms.

8. For Laos, see Mayoury Ngaosyvathn and Pheuiphanh Ngaosyvathn, *Paths to Conflagration: Fifty Years of Diplomacy and Warfare in Laos, Thailand, and Vietnam, 1778–1828* (Ithaca: Cornell Southeast Asia Program, 1998). For Vietnam, see Hue-tam Ho Tai, "Representing the Past in Vietnamese Museums," *Curator: The Museum Journal* 4, 3 (September 1998): 187–99, and *The Country of Memory: Remaking the Past in Late Socialist Vietnam* (Berkeley: University of California Press, 2001).

9. Keith Taylor, "Surface Orientations in Vietnam: Beyond Histories of Nation and Region," *Journal of Asian Studies* 57, 4 (November 1998): 949–78.

10. I have argued elsewhere that the genesis of modern Thai history was the Franco-Siamese crisis in 1893 in which the Siamese lost in the contest for the left bank of the Mekong (*Siam Mapped,* ch. 8). The Thai past was reconstructed and shaped by this anticolonial agony.

11. O. W. Wolters, "Southeast Asia as a Southeast Asian Field of Study," *Indonesia* 58 (October 1994): 1–17.

12. My thanks to Christoph Giebel and Hong Lysa for their comments on the term *home* and to Hong Lysa's succinct definition that I have taken almost verbatim. In the original version of this paper, I used the term *indigenous,* which implies rootedness either by birth, residence, race, and is probably used more inclusively. Indeterminate boundaries and implicit discrimination abound in this term's meaning and usage. How much longer will I remain indigenous if I live outside the region? How long would it take for a resident of the region, born elsewhere, to become indigenous? To use this term in the Malaysian context, where the conference was held, and where the term is highly politicized and charged with various emotive meanings, would illustrate its most striking failure for what I intend here. The terms *local* and *native* likewise imply the peripheral and ethnographic particulars as opposed to the center and the universal, located elsewhere. As I will argue against such a division of power and intellectual claims, these two words are self-defeating for this article. Nevertheless I will still use them, even as flawed concepts, when necessary, in contrast to the global in the discussion on globalization.

13. Mary Louis Pratt, *Imperial Eyes: Travel Writing and Transculturation* (London: Routledge, 1992).

14. The ideas and terms here are modified from Arjun Appadurai, *Modernity at Large: Cultural Dimensions of Globalization* (Minneapolis: University of Minnesota Press, 1996).

15. My understanding of the relationship between the invention of local identities and late capitalism owes much to Tim Oaks (Geography, University of Colorado, Boulder), who studies regional identities in China.

16. Chai-anan Samudavanija, "Holes in the Net: Local Culture, Self-Government, and Globalization," keynote address at the International Alumni Convocation, University of Wisconsin, Madison, May 6, 1999. A similar concern was expressed before colonialism swept the world and *industrialization* became *mass production.* As the present world attests, humans in various cultures become alike in some ways but cultural diversity and differences among human societies become even more complex in many other ways. The landscape of difference and diversity has been changed rather than eradicated.

17. Anthony Reid, *Southeast Asia in the Age of Commerce, 1450–1680,* 2 vols. (New Haven: Yale University Press, 1988 and 1993). There is increasing interest in area studies focusing on the oceans or seas and on the economic and social history of the trans–Indian Ocean communities, especially between India and Southeast Asia.

18. There have been several research projects in recent years on border areas that share cultural and economic systems, such as between southern Yunnan, China, Burma, northern Laos and Thailand; the Riau Archipelago and Sumatra; the western coast of Malaysia and northern Sumatra; and the Sulu region and Sabah.

19. The Chinese subnational histories that are "rescued" by Prasenjit Duara in *Rescuing the Nation from History* are those that have been undermined, displaced, or suppressed by the national history. For a local history that has its own life outside the national narrative, see Lorraine Gesick, *In the Land of Lady White Blood* (Ithaca: Cornell Southeast Asia Program, 1996). The histories of potential separatist regions throughout Southeast Asia are certainly against the grain of national histories. See Clive J. Christie, *A Modern History of Southeast Asia: Decolonization, Nationalism, and Separatism* (New York: Tauris Academic Studies, 1996).

20. Thongchai Winichakul, "Changing Landscape," 110–18. A controversy in 1995 over the authenticity of a national heroine in Nakhon Ratchasima, a major city in the northeast, is illustrative. A young historian argued that the heroine may not be a true historical person, tracing instead the process by which a proud local cult was elevated to a national one for political reasons in the 1930s, and revealing how national history was changed to accommodate it. Local people reacted angrily, threatening the historian and calling for the revocation of her degree and the punishment of her advisors. For them, a national heroine cannot be merely based a local cult; and the glory of the city is in being part of the glorified national narrative, not a local one.

21. An example from the Thai case is Tej Bunnag, *The Provincial Administration of Siam, 1892–1915: The Ministry of the Interior under Prince Damrong Rajanubhab* (Kuala Lumpur: Oxford University Press, 1977). The final paragraph of the book is especially revealing.

22. Christie, *History of Southeast Asia*.

23. See Janet Sturgeon, "Practices on the Periphery: Marginality, Border Powers, and Land Use in China and Thailand," Ph.D. diss., Yale School of Forestry and Environmental Studies, 2000.

24. On the making of minorities, see James Scott, "Hill and Valley in Southeast Asia, or . . . Why Civilizations Can't Climb Hills," paper for the Beyond Borders 2001 workshop, Centre d'Études et de Recherches Internationales & Social Science Research Council, Paris, 1–4 June 2000. Patricia Pelley, "Barbarians and Younger Brothers: The Remaking of Race in Post Colonial Vietnam," *Journal of Southeast Asian Studies* 29, 2 (September 1998): 374–91; Jean Michaud, "The Montagnards and the State in Northern Vietnam from 1802 to 1975," *Ethnohistory* 47, 2 (2000): 333–68; Thongchai

Winichakul, "The Others Within: Travel and Ethno-Spatial Differentiation of Siamese Subjects, 1885–1910," in *Civility and Savagery: Social Identity in Tai States,* ed. Andrew Turton (London: Curzon Press, 2000), 38–62; Hjörleifur Jónsson, "Rhetorics and Relations: Tai States, Forests, and Upland Groups" in *State Power and Culture in Thailand,* ed. E. P. Durrenberger (New Haven: Yale University Southeast Asia Studies, no. 44, 1996).

25. Thongchai Winichakul, "The Future of Asian Studies," *Asian Studies Newsletter,* June 1997, 11–12 (discussion at the presidential forum of the annual meeting of the Association for Asian Studies in Chicago in 1997).

26. It is impossible and unnecessary to review the huge debate among historians of Southeast Asia on Indianization versus localization. The state of knowledge is unarguably captured in O. W. Wolters, *History, Culture, and Region, in Southeast Asian Perspectives* (Singapore: ISEAS, 1982; rev. ed., Ithaca: Cornell Southeast Asia Program Publications, in association with Institute of Southeast Asian Studies, 1999). The term *local genius* is Wolters's.

27. Homi Bhabha, *The Location of Culture* (London: Routledge, 1994), 4–9.

28. Ileto, *Pasyon and Revolution;* Vicente Rafael, *Contracting Colonialism: Translation and Christian Conversion in Tagalog Society under Early Spanish Rule* (Durham: Duke University Press, 1992); Filomeno Aguilar Jr., *Clash of Spirits: The History of Power and Sugar Planting Hegemony on a Visayan Island* (Honolulu: University of Hawaii Press, 1998).

29. Craig J. Reynolds, "Tycoons and Warlords: Modern Thai Social Formations and Chinese Historical Romance," in *Sojourners and Settlers: Histories of Southeast Asia and the Chinese,* ed. Anthony Reid (St. Leonards, NSW, Australia: Allen and Unwin, 1996), 115–47.

30. Anna Lowenhaupt Tsing, *In the Realm of the Diamond Queen* (Princeton: Princeton University Press, 1993); see esp. her theoretical argument about the margins on pp. 14–17.

31. The quotations are from Anna Lowenhaupt Tsing, "From the Margins," *Cultural Anthropology* 9, 3 (1994): 279, 282.

32. In Anna Tsing's words, the Third World detail is description, as opposed to theory. See *Diamond Queen,* 31.

33. The best known critique of this is Dipesh Chakrabarty, *Provincializing Europe* (Princeton: Princeton University Press, 2000).

34. The word *spread* is part of the subtitle of Anderson's *Imagined Communities.* An even more conspicuous preference for the prototypes is Liah Greenfield, *Nationalism: Five Roads to Modernity* (Cambridge, Mass: Harvard University Press, 1995), in which the five models come from England, France, Russia, Germany, and North America.

35. O. W. Wolters discusses a similar idea in "'Regional Studies' in the 1990s," in *History, Culture, and Region* (rev. ed., 1999), 206–25.

36. Anthony Reid, "Recent Trends and Future Directions in Southeast Asian Studies (Outside Southeast Asia)," in *Toward the Promotion of Southeast Asian Studies in Southeast Asia*, ed. Taufik Abdullah and Yekti Maunati (Jakarta: Indonesian Institute of Sciences, 1994), 273.

37. I have myself been welcomed many times by foreigners and Thais alike as if I were an embodiment or a site of indigenous Thai knowledge in American academia. This is an ambivalent recognition, since it is simultaneously an acknowledgment of my non-Western scholarship and an implication that my foremost credential is not my scholarship but my being Thai, and an unfortunate perception, since I would be among the last scholars from Thailand prepared to claim to be, intellectually, a genuine Thai.

38. Wolters, "Southeast Asian Field of Study."

39. Reynaldo Ileto, *Knowing America's Colony: A Hundred Years from the Philippine War,* Philippine Studies Occasional Papers Series, no. 13 (Honolulu: Centre for Philippine Studies, University of Hawaii, 1999). Although Ileto strictly attacks only Western scholarship on the Philippines, and does not explicitly say that a native account is better or more accurate, his dichotomous argument, separating Western and Filipino scholarship, leaves not much room to imply otherwise.

40. Kirin Narayan, "How Native is a 'Native' Anthropologist?" *American Anthropologist* 95, 3 (September 1993): 671–86.

41. See David Streckfuss, "The Mixed Colonial Legacy in Siam: Origins of Thai Racialist Thought, 1890–1910," in *Autonomous Histories, Particular Truths: Essays in Honor of John R. W. Smail,* ed. Laurie Sears (Madison, Wis.: Center for Southeast Asian Studies, 1993), 123–53.

42. In the field of history, for example, royal/nationalist history has been the paradigm for Western historians of Thailand from Quaritch Wales to David Wyatt.

43. A. B. Shamsul, "A Comment on Recent Trends and the Future Direction of Southeast Asian Studies," in *Toward the Promotion of Southeast Asian Studies in Southeast Asia,* ed. Taufik Abdullah and Yekti Mautani (Jakarta: Indonesian Institute of Sciences, 1994), 296.

44. Kernial Sandhu, "Southeast Asian Studies: Some Unresolved Problems," in *A Colloquium on Southeast Asian Studies,* ed. Tunku Shamsul et al. (Singapore: ISEAS, 1981), 17, quoted in Shamsul, "Recent Trends," 277.

Chapter 2

CHANGING CONCEPTIONS OF SPACE IN HISTORY WRITING

A Selective Mapping of Writings on Singapore

BRENDA S. A. YEOH

THE SIGNIFICANCE AND POWER OF the concept of space, and its relevance to the historical imagination, have been enduring concerns in historical geography since long before spatial metaphors and cartographies became all the rage in current social theorizing, as found in cultural studies, critical theory, and the humanities in general. Indeed, traditional historical geographers such as Clifford Darby and Gordon East have long subscribed to the view that any history that is totally preoccupied with political relations and incidents, without any attention to the geographic conditions that shape societies, is sterile and unrealistic. The following comments provide a sampling of views that emphasize the importance of the geographic dimension in writing history:

> Historie without geographie like a dead carkasse hath neither life nor motion at all.[1]

> Without a geographical basis, the people, the makers of history, seem to be walking on air, as in those Chinese pictures where the ground is wanting. The soil must not be looked on only as the scene

of action. Its influence appears in a hundred ways, such as food, climate, etc. As the nest, so is the bird. As the country, so are the men.[2]

Human thought and action have their springs, not in a spatial vacuum, but in some definite geographical milieu, which defines in varying degrees the character and orbit of human effort.[3]

At the same time, Marxist historical geographers such as David Harvey have argued that the "geographical imagination" or "spatial consciousness," that which helps one to "recognize the role of space and place in his or her own biography, to relate the spaces one sees around one, and to recognize how transactions between individuals and between organizations are affected by the space that separates them," is a necessary complement to the "sociological imagination," that which enables one to "understand the larger historical scene in terms of its meaning for the inner life and the external career of a variety of individuals."[4]

More recently, the postmodernist tide, awash over several related disciplines, has led to a strengthening of geographers' claims for a centering of spatial concerns, and hence a renaissance of sorts for human geography in academic discourse within the social sciences and humanities. Edward Soja, for example, argues that modern social theory has been overly preoccupied with historicism, with its emphasis on individual and collective biographies, at the expense of spatiality.[5] The power of a "space-blinkered" historical imagination, which has created a "critical silence" where space is concerned, is increasingly challenged, however, by the postmodern move toward dismantling disciplinary privileges and the attention to a consideration of space and time, in tandem, as signposted in the works of Michel Foucault, Henri Lefebvre, and John Berger. Soja reminds us of Berger's view that "prophesying now involves a geographical rather than historical projection; it is space not time that hides consequences from us." He also claims Foucault as a "post-modern geographer" and applauds his "provocative spatialization of power."[6] Chris Philo has argued further that Foucault's critique of a "total history," that "posits a 'central core' to the social world" and often draws on spatialized vocabularies, can be read as a critique of historians' and social scientists' "insensitivity to the geography of the social world that manifests itself in stressing the homogeneity of events, phenomena, and their hypothesized determinations within *spatial* 'great units' (continents and perhaps countries) and in thereby ignoring the reality of smaller-scale aerial differences and distributions."[7] In contrast, Foucault, according to Philo, negotiates "the snares of totalisation" by taking seriously "space, place and geography as sources of fragmentation."[8]

This chapter presents a selective mapping of the different ways in which space has been conceptualized in the writing of Singapore history, drawing from my own experience in trying to mine local historical writings to hone the craft of historical geography. I examine the different ways in which space has been rendered and incorporated into historical analysis in selected texts that narrate Singapore's history.[9] There are, of course, many theoretical and practical difficulties in simultaneously conceptualizing spatial difference, temporal change, and human action in one written account and most works will give emphasis to one aspect at the expense of others.[10] Nevertheless, part of the argument is that the questions raised by a historical geographer, in transgressing into the territory of the historian, can open up important debates on the ways disciplinary boundaries are conventionally drawn around central concepts such as space and time.

"Standard" Histories: Space as Backdrop

Up to now, it can still be said that C. M. Turnbull's *A History of Singapore, 1819–1975*[11] remains the "one and only general history" of Singapore as a separate entity, as opposed to being part of Malayan history.[12] This is a deft account of the political, economic, and social events that shaped Singapore's colonial and immediate postindependence history. Turnbull gives due weight to the role of key individuals and the "clash of personalities and ideologies," to uncover "a ferment of mixing and change, which produced a unique society" beneath the "apparently placid surface of Singapore life." She gives brief cross-sectional period pictures of the social and physical landscape at particular historical junctures, such as the polyglot nature of its people centered around an entrepôt trade economy at the "high noon of empire, 1867–1914" (chapter 3) and the transformation of "slums, squatter shanties and dilapidated *kampungs*" into "modern, high-rise flats, hotels and offices" as a result of "ambitious schemes of urban renewal" in the first decade of independence, from 1965 to 1975 (Chapter 9). Most of the attention however is not focused on re-constructing the changing geographies of the past but on developing and sustaining the historical narrative, in a combination of descriptive and explanatory sketches connecting events, centered mainly on political themes, with the goal of unraveling the "many paradoxes and vicissitudes in Singapore's history."[13]

Turnbull's "general history" treats spatial difference and land-scape changes largely as backdrop, with little to add to the unfolding narrative. Several other more specific works could also be classified in this category. Ernest Chew and Edwin Lee's collection of essays, for example, approaches the history of Singapore thematically, de-voting a chapter at a time to topics relating to economic development and social and political issues.[14] The landscape is given emphasis only by way of a self-contained chapter on housing.[15] The incorporation of spatial questions in historical narrative in the form of a separate chapter on changing landscapes is a common strategy in various other edited collections.[16] Spatial relations, as such, are given very little ana-lytical weight in most general histories. Any interest in the spatial imagination appears satisfied by recourse to a background sketch of the visible landscape as a backdrop to political action, social and eco-nomic changes, and other expressions of human agency.

"Histories from Below": Everyday Spaces of the Marginalized

More recently, the question of space has been the subject of more so-phisticated treatment in historical texts. This stems largely from the development of revisionist histories that champion the everyday worlds of common people as opposed to "the visible terrain of society and dominant individuals and groups."[17] Of late, approaches to colonialism that focus exclusively on, or privilege the impress of, European colonizer, culture, or capital in shaping the shared worlds of colonizer and colonized groups, have come under more critical scrutiny than before. Two particular streams of scholarship are beginning to converge, and possibly crosscut.

The first draws on the ongoing debate on the "indigenization" of academic discourse in the social sciences, a movement that gained momentum in the early 1970s when Third World indigenous scholars, joined by a number of Western counterparts, raised their voices against the implantation of a social science discourse that perpetuated the captivity of mind beyond the colonial era. The plea was for an articulation of grassroots consciousness and a rejection of "borrowed" consciousness, the development of alternative perspectives that could provide an insider's view of reality, and a valorization of historical contexts and cultural specificities in analyzing human societies. In this project, the most difficult task is to move beyond "iconoclastic talk about the 'domination' of alien models and theories" to the construction of alternative conceptual frameworks and metatheories that reflect indigenous worldviews and experiences.[18]

It has been acknowledged, for example, that "to have an academic discourse beyond 'orientalism' and 'occidentalism' is rather a tall order as long as we cannot break away from, and become totally independent of, colonial knowledge."[19] As Bernard Cohn has argued, the colonial project not only invaded and conquered territorial space but also involved the systematic colonization of indigenous epistemological space, such as indigenous thought systems, reconstituting and replacing these by using a wide corpus of colonial knowledge, policies, and frameworks.[20] With decolonization, ex-colonies have regained (sometimes partial) political territory, but seldom the epistemological space. The objective of reclaiming such epistemological spaces has provided the impetus for subaltern studies, a school of political and literary criticism, which considers how the voice of colonial subjects can be represented and heard without distortion.

Calls for resistance to, and alternative readings of, European texts as a means to demystify colonialist power have also been issued. For example, Zawiah Yahya has argued that the most effective way of deconstructing Western discourse is to use "its very own tools of critical theory, . . . not only to dismantle colonialism's signifying system but also to articulate the silences of the native by liberating the suppressed in discourse."[21] Among historians and geographers, there have also been several rereadings of the history of European expansion on the world stage, such as Eric Wolf's attempt to "abrogate the boundaries between Western and non-Western history" and reinstate the "active histories of 'primitives,' peasantries, laborers, immigrants, and besieged minorities" and Jim Blaut's proposal of a nondiffusionist model of the world that seeks to decenter Europe as the maker of world history and geography.[22] In the debates about geographic historiography, there are tentative signs of a repositioning from an engagement with *geography and empire* or *geography and imperialism,* with the accent on the colonizing power, to a consideration of the multiple historical geographies of the colonized world. The recent debate about recasting what passes as the Western geographic tradition as an "irredeemably hybrid product" that "relied upon and appropriated many elements of other local ('indigenous') geographical knowledges" is one such example.[23]

The second impulse relates to the developing critique of mainstream theories of colonial societies and cities that privilege the forms and faces of dominance as the leitmotif of the colonial enterprise. As Anthony King, whose own work has had a major impact on "the study of colonial domination and dispossession," observes in an insightful epilogue to Nezar AlSayyad's *Forms of Dominance,* "the focus on European colonialism, by occupying the historical space of those urban places and people of which it speaks, has marginalized and silenced two other sets of voices: the voices of resistance and the voices of, for want of a better term, 'the vernacular.'"[24] The metanarrative of postcolonial and, ipso facto, colonial discourse, has failed to break with, in fact has extended the reach of, the enterprise and discourse of dominance and dispossession that "should have been dead for half a century."[25] Ironically, it is the critical but exclusive engagement with "the colonizers model of the world" that produces a narration of history from the point of view of those who "claim history as their own," further marginalizing "the people to whom history has been denied."[26]

Work in postcolonial studies and cultural geography that trace their genealogy to Edward Said's notion of the Orient as a hegemonic and homogeneous discursive construction of the West, divorced from lived material practice, has had the effect of writing out the colonized.[27] The continual emphasis on the policies and discourses of the colonial power in "the constant framing and creation of natives as the 'other' in order to facilitate subordination" leaves little epistemological and empirical space for the insertion of conflict and collision, negotiation and dialogue, between colonizer and colonized.[28] In other words, a critical perspective that dissects but still centers the colonial vision inevitably reproduces its dominance, its gaze, and its effects without drawing the colonized body out from the shadow lands to which it has been relegated. In accounts that ignore the agencies, struggles, and practices of the colonized, not only is a false impression of the relative "costs" and "benefits" of the advances of colonialism created, the colonial attitude of homogenizing the colonized as an inferior Other is further reproduced. Non-Western cultures and peoples remain in "an interpretive position as the perpetual inferior."[29]

In the context of Singapore until the late 1980s, the traditional emphasis on colonial history has meant a preoccupation with "British action, reaction and inaction to local happenings." As a result, "[i]n writing about political changes historians' . . . preoccupation with the images of the overlife has resulted in them neglecting critical aspects of Malaysia's (and Singapore's) past by overlooking the roles of ordinary individuals and groups."[30] Since then, the lacuna in terms of work on the "invisible" spaces of the underside has been gradually filled by a number of significant pieces that attempt to "integrate the history of experience of the (common people) into the larger history of Singapore" and to "scan" their everyday universe "at point blank range."[31] These works have tried to destabilize the commonly held interpretation of Singapore as the product of the imposition of the dominant logic of the colonial political and cultural economy onto non-Western time and territory.[32] They have instead valorized everyday practices in the colonial city and taken seriously the hard work of rescuing the common people in colonized territories from the "enormous condescension of posterity" in the fashion of grassroots historians such as E. P. Thompson and George Rudé who worked to restore everyday lives and actions to the "very stuff of history."[33]

It is often the case that simply not enough is known about colonized groups, given the asymmetries in the historical records, for anyone approaching the colonial period to hope to mount a revisionist stance. Historians of the underside have in response mounted concerted efforts to imaginatively mine the official archives and refilter colonial discourse through "other" lenses and, at the same time, widen the net to include hitherto ignored source materials produced by the everyday workings in the life worlds of the colonized. Methodologies to uncover the perspectives of the ordinary people have included existentialist means of encountering people and situations in an intersubjective manner through oral histories, reminiscences, eyewitness accounts, and interviews, as well as phenomenological approaches that look beyond the written record and at people's representations of their life worlds by using, for example, pictorial, visual, and artifactural evidence.

In these "histories from below," writers take pains to take us away from the grandeur of colonial edifices, which often typify accounts of the colonial city, into the hidden spaces of the common people. The following abstract from James Warren is characteristic of such accounts:

> Let us penetrate into the recesses of Chinatown enclosed by its bleak privacy in the 1920s and pay special attention to the housing conditions of the rickshaw pullers. Rickshaw lodging-houses had one or more large rooms; the average number was two or three, the highest being six to nine rooms in a building. The men slept in wooden beds fixed on the wall in tiers, on canvas or straw cots in the centre of the room, and on the floor in the passageway. The lodging-houses were characterised by intensive use of shared bed 'space' which was rented out in some instances for 8- or 12-hour periods. In the biggest compound houses where there

were 130 or more occupants, if a coolie wanted to move about the room he had to literally walk over the bodies of fellow pullers.[34]

Given the attention to everyday, microscale spaces, these narratives are potentially more sensitive to the roles and activities of women, who have hitherto been almost entirely hidden from history, by dint of the fact that political history pays little heed to the private sphere, to which many women are traditionally confined. However, unlike in many nineteenth- and early-twentieth-century cities in the West, where the cult of domesticity confined women to the private spaces of the home and suburbs, immigrant women in colonial Singapore straddled home and workplace, actively contributing to the paid-work economy, both in a formal and informal sense. Some writers have already started giving attention to women who undertook paid work, as laborers, servants, hawkers, and prostitutes.[35] Little, however, has yet been written about women's domestic spaces—the arena of familial ties, intergenerational relations, unpaid housework and home-based paid work, childcare, and religious and recreational activities based in the home. Not only is the topic of women's activity spaces in Singapore history a neglected field of inquiry, there is also little acknowledgment that public and private spheres need to be treated as interpenetrative and interdependent spheres equally crucial to the sustenance of the city.

In treating the ordinary person as an active agent, possessing consciousness, creativity, and emotions, and bringing these qualities to bear on the making of the colonial city, historians such as Warren insist on creating a Singapore with "a powerful sense of . . . character" through interweaving the "attitudes (of ordinary people), the emotional reach and intensity of single events" into the historical narrative.[36] In his work on the rickshaw coolies, Warren argues,

> We can, for instance, evoke an atmosphere of a city that was quietly devastating—the pullers' fear of being assaulted or hit or run over by a motor car in the pitch dark, of an elderly man's craving and not having money to purchase *chandu* (opium), of dying in an empty cubicle or back lane as a "vagrant" or "unknown Chinese"; the chilling incongruities of wealthy tourists dancing in the Raffles at the height

of the Depression while the pullers hovered outside in the grip of misfortune, the rotten stench of sewage, the horrors of tenements, and the mortuaries piled with bodies of cholera victims. . . . This approach and evidence provides the framework for a new kind of history of Singapore.[37]

From this perspective, space and place as conceived in the historical narrative are invested with meanings that are inseparable from the consciousness of those who inhabited them. This is how Warren explains the rickshaw coolie's acute sense of place:

> Space—geographical, sociological, cultural—in Singapore was linked to what rickshaw coolies saw and did during the course of their work cycle every day. . . . The rickshaw puller's perception of the city was built up over the months and years in a kind of shorthand, "a notation of space," replete with minute details on morphology and change in the urban landscape and its relations to their work situation. . . . Some spots on the landscape were closely associated with power and fortune in their minds. . . . Rickshaw pullers also knew other places around the city, though, that were unfavorable; dangerous sites that could affect them adversely. . . . They knew which streets were permissible to work on year in and year out, which markets and stands were forbidden and dangerous, and where the brutal peon or *samseng* might be waiting to swoop down and confiscate their license or intimidate them to pay a bribe.[38]

In attempting to reclaim ordinary people's historical trajectories through their own experiences, it also becomes necessary to reconstruct their spatial mappings through their own eyes. In these reconstructions space is no longer a location or a backdrop but an experience or a relationship that cannot be conceived outside the thoughts, feelings, and everyday struggles that make up the consciousness of its inhabitants.

Contested Histories: The Politics of Space

In my earlier work, I have argued for the importance of going beyond a recovery of the historical geography of the common people to accommodate what might be termed a politics of space in analyses of the colonized world.[39] This is not so much a call for a complete turn-around in perspective from one that valorizes the dominant logic of the colonial enterprise to that which explores the everyday worlds of the colonized peoples. It is a move to examine the intersections between the two in fleshed-out accounts of the processes of conflict, collusion, and negotiation that animated spatial politics. This is an alternative project that draws on notions of the *contact zone,* a multiplicity of re-sistances, and the dynamics of spatial politics as conceptual tools. In other words, there is a need to reconceptualize the colonized world as a contact zone in terms of contest and complicity, conflict and collu-sion, and to tackle the unwritten history of resistance.

The term *contact zone* has been used by M. L. Pratt as an alterna-tive to *colonial frontier,* a term grounded within a European expan-sionist perspective, as "an attempt to invoke the spatial and temporal copresence of subjects previously separated by geographic and histori-cal disjunctures, and whose trajectories now intersect." A *contact* per-spective "emphasizes how subjects are constituted in and by their relations to each other . . . not in terms of separateness or apartheid, but in terms of copresence, interaction, interlocking understandings and practices, often within radically asymmetrical relations of power." In fleshing out the dynamics of the "contact zone," Pratt at-tempts to identify the "parodic, transculturating gestures" on the part of colonized subjects as they undertake to represent themselves in ways that engage with and ultimately reshape colonial discourse.[40]

Drawing on different conceptual tools but with crosscutting aims, I tried in my own work to reconceptualize power relations in the colonial city of Singapore, suggesting that the colonial city can be ana-lyzed as a terrain of conflict and negotiation where the specific tech-niques of disciplinary power and the multiple resistances "formed right at the point where relations of power are exercised"[41] are played out. I point out that the agency of the colonized is not only highly dif-ferentiated but often effective because, whether tacitly or discur-sively, it drew on coherent ideologies, institutional structures, and schemes of legitimation that were independent of and largely impenetrable to the colonial authorities. At the same time, however, it is also circumscribed and modified by the disciplinary techniques of colonial power.[42] It is by treating the colonial enterprise and the colonized world as "different but overlapping and curiously interdependent territories"[43] that one can seek to "faithfully mirror the complex weave of competition, struggle and cooperation within the shifting physical and social landscapes."[44]

Such a project requires a reconsideration of colonial power relations in general and the notion of *resistance* in particular. As S. Pile and M. Keith note, "issues of 'resistance' have only recently become foregrounded in geographers' discussion of power relationships, political identities and spaces, and radical politics."[45] Part of this interest in *resistance* draws from and folds into recent approaches in cultural studies that "invoke a 'tropology of resistance and hybridity' in their analyses of subaltern actors traversing landscapes of culture, power, and social contestation."[46] Geographers' specific contributions to the debate have been primarily in terms of demonstrating the value of a spatial understanding of *resistance,* and in grounding geographic metaphors of space, place, and positionality in situated practices and local contexts. Rather than attempting to trace the complex contours of geographers' recent engagements with the notion of *resistance,* I will briefly summarize two broad strands of the debate that would be useful in informing a contextualized reading of the politics of space in the colonized world.

First, beyond dissecting the strategies and technologies of domination, the domain of resistance and politics must be expanded beyond "heroic acts by heroic people or heroic organizations,"[47] without detracting from the power and poetics of such acts or suggesting that they are scissored out of the fabric of everyday contexts, and reconfigured to include resistant postures, ploys, and strategies woven into "the practice of everyday life."[48] James Scott's work, in particular, was highly influential in valorizing "everyday forms of resistance" as "weapons of the weak."[49] It also attracted the attention of critics like Abu-Lughod, who cautioned against the "tendency to romanticize resistance, to read all forms of resistance as signs of the ineffectiveness of systems of power and the resilience and creativity of the human spirit in its refusal to be dominated."[50]

While we need to guard against trivializing resistance by discerning it in situations everywhere, removing it from its macropolitical status allows us to appreciate the fluid, unstable nature of power relations. This creates the conceptual and creative space to rewrite the colonized world on its own terms rather than accept the dualistic model mirrored in colonizers' accounts of either a passive, quiescent, and ignorant people ripe for reform or salvation under benign colonial rule, or a hotbed of violence, riots, insurrections, and revolts boiling over the moment colonial surveillance and control were relaxed. As A. Vidler points out, albeit in a different context, it is often "[b]etween submission to the intolerable and outraged revolt against it" that ordinary people "somehow define[d] a human existence within the walls and along the passage of their streets."[51]

Second, as P. Routledge writes,

> Resistances may be interpreted as fluid processes whose emergence and dissolution cannot be fixed as points in time [or space]. . . . [They are] rhizomatic multiplicities of interactions, relations, and acts of becoming. . . . Any resistance synthesizes a multiplicity of elements and relations without effacing their heterogeneity or hindering their potential for future rearrangement. As rhizomatic practices, resistances take diverse forms, they move in different dimensions, they create unexpected networks, connections, and possibilities. They may invent new trajectories and forms of existence, articulate alternative futures and possibilities, create autonomous zones as a strategy against particular dominating power relations.[52]

Strategies of resistance may thus be "assembled out of the materials and practices of everyday life," tracing visible lineaments in physical space.[53] They may also "engage the colonized spaces of people's inner worlds" and effect the production of "inner spaces" or "alternative spatialities from those defined th[r]ough oppression and exploitation."[54] Thinking of resistance as "rhizomatic practices"—a metaphor that appropriately insists on a certain grounding of such practices and, at the same time, conceives of resistance as sprouting both above and below ground—points to the contingent nature of power. This allows us to transcend the dichotomy between treating resistant spaces as purely autonomous, "uncolonized" spaces exterior to or dislocated from the spatial parameters of domination, or as purely "underside" spaces of social life confined to, and reacting against, authorized spaces of domination in a strategic fashion where "each offensive from one side serves as leverage for a counter-offensive from the other."[55] Treating resistance as rhizomatic emphasizes its creative and elusive nature, as a subjectivity that is polyphonic, plural, working in many discursive registers, many spaces, many times.[56] In the colonized world, it is important not only to recognize that there were a panoply of resistances inhabiting different spaces but also to underscore the way they connect, collide, diverge, transmute, sometimes in unexpected ways, and often moving in and out of spaces of domination.

Drawing on these ideas, I have tried in my own work to argue that while colonialism does "produce its own space,"[57] it does not do so without the processes of conflict and compromise between those who control space and those who live in it, both of whom must be seen as "participants in the same historical trajectory." Close examination of the "contact zone, the social spaces where disparate cultures meet, clash, and grapple with each other, often in highly asymmetrical relations of domination and subordination,"[58] opens up the possibility of constructing historico-geographic accounts of the colonized world that move away from depicting it as a passive, flattened-out world, stamped upon by more powerful others, and fashioned solely in the image of colonialism.

These intersecting contact points, between the different facets of the colonial world and the multiple constituents of the colonized world, were played out in a variety of ways and occupied different spaces, threaded into the fabric of everyday life and occasionally culminating in flashpoints of crisis proportions. A Chinese coolie immigrant who arrived in colonial Singapore in the early twentieth century was likely to encounter colonial and municipal authority as wielded by its minions in many guises, from the sanitary inspector who ordered the pulling down of his cubicle in a coolie lodging house, the municipal peon who served a disinfection notice on the chief tenant of his house, the registrar of vehicles who issued his license to pull a jinrikisha, the police officer who arrested him for obstruction of public places, to the municipal apothecary who inspected his corpse for signs of infectious disease and the burial grounds inspector who ensured his burial in a municipally sanctioned plot.

The view from the other side of the looking glass is an equally complex one. The colonial authorities had to contend with the continuous, clandestine strategies of evasion and noncompliance of myriad individuals, the voice of influential Chinese leaders in advocating alternative discourses, and the networks in Chinese society, hidden from the colonial gaze, that occasionally drew the masses together in violent backlashes. While the agency of the individual coolie, the leader, and the masses, was seldom concerted and never seamless, it drew sustenance from a clan-centered cultural economy governed by its own ideologies about life, work, health, and death. This was visibly inscribed in the landscape in the form of clan-owned temples, medical halls, sick-receiving houses, burial grounds, schools, lodging houses, shops, and business networks.[59]

As David Arnold has argued, it is only through an awareness of the dialectical nature of the encounters between the colonized people and the colonial state that it is possible to avoid assumptions of mass "passivity" and "fatalism."[60] Historical geographies of the colonized world need to come to grips with these dialectical encounters, not only by dissecting the norms and forms of colonial dominance but also through a variegated account of the strategies and spaces of resistance. The colonized drew on multiple strategies to resist exclusionary definitions, to fend off the intrusive mechanisms of bureaucratic power, and to advance their own claims. English-educated leaders of the Chinese community, for example, were able to defend the sacrosanctity of Chinese burial grounds through representations on various government committees, petitions, memorials, and letters to the press. By drawing on alternative discourses on environmental management as embodied in Chinese geomancy, they sought to challenge Western urban-planning ideas and sanitary science. As colonial authorities could not effectively govern without incorporating a segment of the colonized body into the ruling power structure, the views of those who acted as social brokers commanded sufficient weight for them to be incorporated into decision-making bodies in the colonial government. Policies were occasionally held back to accommodate expressed views, although where policy changes were made, there was seldom any real acknowledgment of the legitimacy of alternative Asian discourses.

While debates provoked by the introduction of legislation, for example of the Burials Bill at the end of the nineteenth century, represented the better-publicized, better-ventilated aspects of conflicts over space, it was but one of multiple contact zones in which the politics over burial space were played out. The debates in discursive space afforded by legislative channels and the media were matched on the ground by the small but pervasive, clandestine acts of illegal burial and exhumation among the Chinese laboring classes, who were equally concerned with protecting their rights to burial even if they were unable to afford the finer points of *feng shui* insisted upon by their wealthier compatriots. Indeed, it was often at the level of daily practices and within the spaces of everyday life that the effects of power were renegotiated or countered.

This is clearly demonstrated, for example, in the catalogue of colonized people's strategies to evade surveillance measures to detect and arrest infectious disease in the city. In Foucault's terms, just as disciplinary institutions employ a panoply of meticulous, minute techniques embodying the "micro-physics" of power, the subjects of discipline are themselves capable of "small acts of cunning endowed with a great power of diffusion."[61] While the strategies used by the Asian people were mainly self-help measures incapable of, nor directed at, upsetting the larger symbolic order of dominance and dependence prescribed for the colonized world, they were also not bereft of effects. They were often widespread enough to thwart the execution of particular policies and to inflect colonial control in everyday life. Nor were these strategies purely idiosyncratic, obstructionist, or irrational, as the colonial authorities often depicted them to be.

Instead, the lack of "cooperation" on the part of the people in implementing disease control in the city, for example, stemmed partly from the fact that they subscribed to different notions of disease and contagion, and what constituted appropriate measures of healing based on their own systems of medical care.

It is in this context that colonial campaigns to sanitize the city were often perceived to be political, cultural, and moral impositions to be "passively resisted" (a phrase used by the authorities themselves to describe the people's reactions) whenever and wherever possible. Furthermore, while the spatial practices of resistance might take visible form through counterstrategies within colonized spaces reacting against the machinery of domination, they often drew on the resources of other, uncolonized, inner spaces outside the prevailing power relations. In other words, the colonized world had its own spatialities of power that were not necessarily circumscribed nor apprehended by the geographies of colonialism, underlining the point made by Pile that "geographies of resistance do not necessarily mirror geographies of domination, as an upside-down or back-to-front or face-down map of the world."[62]

While revolutionary uprisings did not loom very large throughout the history of colonial Singapore, the "verandah riots" of February 1888 demonstrated how everyday rhythms might be disrupted by the culmination of tensions located at different sites in the colonized body and over a span of time. Ostensibly started by a localized confrontation between a group of shopkeepers and municipal inspectors clearing the verandahs of obstructions in one part of town, the involvement of other traders, hawkers, rickshaw coolies, gangland elements, clan groups, and the police, galvanized the outbreak into full-scale rioting, a crisis event that also drew on the fissures within the municipal body itself as well as the rivalry between the two English dailies. An act of resistance, as Routledge has pointed out, synthesizes, albeit temporarily, "a multiplicity of elements and relations."[63]

Not only were acts of resistances in the colonized world fluid processes that run the gamut of different forms, they were also interconnected in unexpected ways as "rhizomatic practices." Just as large-scale, violent clashes might grow out of an accumulation of small run-ins on a daily basis, flashpoints might also subside into everyday forays. The termination of the verandah riots did not signify a satisfactory conclusion to the question of how "public space" should be defined and used; instead, the verandahs were reabsorbed into the daily arena as sites subject constantly to municipal reform on the one hand and recolonization by shopkeepers, traders, and hawkers on the other. The contingent nature of resistance should also be noted, its emergence and dissolution being inextricably linked to the specific context. The withdrawal of customary privileges to use public spaces for communal celebrations during the Chinese Hungry Ghosts Festival season did not provoke a visible response from the Chinese community immediately but clearly surfaced several months later in the ferment building up to the verandah riots.

For some time now the postcolonial critique has argued that colonialism was neither monolithic nor unchanging. In the same way that narratives of colonialism have been subject to closer scrutiny and refinement, accounts of the colonized world must also avoid homogenizing and essentializing the colonized as a category. Neither colonialism nor the colonized were unitary entities immune to the influence of the other. Neither dominance nor resistance forms a closed, complete circuit in itself. As Routledge points out, "practices of resistance cannot be separated from practices of domination, they are always entangled in some configuration. As such they are hybrid practices, one always bears at least a trace of the other, that contaminates or subverts it."[64] Conceptions of space in history will be enriched by taking fuller account of the interweaving of the discourses and practices of domination with those of resistance as these take shape, not through abstract theories, but in the social materiality of colonized spaces.

Diasporic Space

A perspective on space that has not been given enough consideration in Singapore history is to treat Singapore as the product of overlapping diasporas. Recent theoretical treatments of international migration within the context of global capitalist change inspired by poststructuralist ideas about movement and mobility, dislocation and displacement, have drawn on the notion of diaspora as a central concept in rethinking "the notion that there is an immutable link between cultures, people, or identities and specific places."[65] *Diaspora* is used, often in metaphorical rather than material terms, to trace new conceptual maps for understanding deterritorialization, the growth of complex transnational and multiple forms of identification and transborder cultural production in the current phase of globalization.[66] Yet it is certainly not a new phenomenon for Singapore, the quintessential product of nineteenth- and twentieth-century diasporas, a polyglot migrant world constituted by streams of immigrants from China, India, the Malay Archipelago, and other far-flung places and dominated by a small European imperial diaspora. As T. N. Harper says,

> Singapore is a child of diaspora. Its history embodies many of the tensions of blood and belonging that the concept evokes. Singapore testifies to the difficulties of creating a modern nation-state on a model inherited from Europe in a region where history mocks the nation-state's claims to cultural and linguistic exclusiveness. The post-colonial experience of Singapore has been dominated by the attempts of the state—an artifact of British rule—to surmount these constraints and to create a national community bounded by a common culture and a sense of place, and bonded by individual allegiance.[67]

One implication of treating space as diasporic would be to open up a discursive terrain for situating "the contradictions between the notion of discrete territory of the nation [or British colony, in the case of colonial Singapore] and the transgressive fact of migration."[68] It provides a conception of space, which is not bounded and impermeable, but stretched across expanses and in perpetual motion. At the same time, this perspective attempts to make sense of human lives as journeys. In N. Rapport's words,

> The universal way in which human beings conceive of their lives [is] in terms of a moving-between—between identities, relations, people, things, groups, societies, cultures, environments. . . . It is in

and through the continuity of movement that human beings continue to make themselves at home. . . . They recount their lives to themselves and others as movement: they continually see themselves in stories, and continually tell the stories of their lives.[69]

Singapore of the nineteenth and early twentieth centuries in this sense is a place of sojourn, a temporary stopping point for a number of diasporic journeys, journeys that are not unidirectional but often circular or ridden with disruptions and detours.

Diaspora also conjures up a particular kind of imaginative geography, drawing on notions of common interest between heterogeneous groups and grounding them in space and, at the same time, articulating a specific "homeland" to which links can be drawn. This is the underlying assumption in works such as *The Chinese Diaspora* where *diaspora* connotes the binding of diverse peoples as a single body to a homeland.[70] While Wang Gungwu has recently expressed considerable disquiet with the application of the term *diaspora* to the Chinese,[71] this particular framework does allow the geographer to give attention not simply to the processes within a particular bounded territory, but also to conjure up the migrant's spatial imaginaries of what it means to be "home" and "away." More so than other spatial frameworks discussed earlier, this provides a useful way of understanding not only Singapore's collective history but also the individual narratives of the migrants who constituted the lived world of Singapore's past.

Different Spaces

While philosophical debates on the nature of space is a fraught terrain, it is useful to remember David Harvey's point that the question, What is space? is possibly better replaced by the question, "how is it that different human practices create and make use of distinctive conceptualizations of space?"[72] In narrating and reflecting on Singapore's history, different authors have drawn on a number of different notions of space to serve varying purposes. As discussed in this chapter, these include space as a passive backdrop, space as undersides or margins of resistance, space as contested terrain, and space as diasporic interconnectedness. These different ways of inserting a consideration of space into the writing of history has produced more variegated accounts, allowing for history to be written not simply as a monolithic enterprise but refracted through the prism of geographic imaginations to reveal its multiple hues. As historian Theodore Zeldin argues, to find new points of contact in addressing our research questions, we need to look through "two lenses simultaneously, both through a microscope, choosing details that illuminate life in those aspects that touch people most closely, and through a telescope, surveying large problems from a great distance."[73] A sense of space, and the different perspectives that varying scales can offer, is an important touchstone for the writing of history. As the production of knowledge is focused more and more at the interstices between disciplines in the new millennium, it is hoped that the dialogue between the historical and the spatial will bear even more fruit.

Notes

1. Peter Heylyn, *Microcosmus,* a 1621 text, as quoted in H. C. Darby, "On the Relations of Geography and History," *Transactions of the Institute of British Geographers* 19 (1953): 1.

2. Jules Michelet, *Histoire de France,* Preface to 1869 edition, as quoted in Darby, "Relations of Geography and History," 2.

3. G. East, *An Historical Geography of Europe* (London: Methuen, 1966), vii.

4. D. Harvey, *Social Justice and the City* (London: Edward Arnold, 1973), 23–24.

5. E. Soja, *Postmodern Geographies: The Reassertion of Space in Critical Social Theory* (London: Verso, 1989).

6. Ibid., 22, 21.

7. C. Philo, "Foucault's Geography," *Environment and Planning; D, Society and Space* 10 (1992): 142; emphasis in original.

8. Ibid., 144.

9. I make no claims to a comprehensive survey. I will not, for instance, be dealing with works that attempt to locate Singapore's place in pre-

modern Southeast Asia (e.g., P. Wheatley, *The Golden Khersonese: Studies in the Historical Geography of the Malay Peninsula before A.D. 1500*) or as a strategic interest in the rivalry between European trade empires between the sixteenth and eighteenth centuries. E. Lee's "Historiography of Singapore" in *Singapore Studies: Critical Surveys of the Humanities and Social Sciences,* ed. B. Kapur (Singapore: Singapore University Press, 1985), 1–31, provides a brief review of the literature. The focus here is on historical writings on modern Singapore as a place in itself. According to C. M. Turnbull, "interest in the history of Singapore as a separate entity is a comparatively new phenomenon" Turnbull, *A History of Singapore, 1819–1975,* 1st ed. (Singapore: Oxford University Press, 1977). Turnbull's story, until recently, was treated as part of Malayan history. I will also be concerned chiefly with the colonial era in Singapore's history.

10. A. Rogers, "Key Themes and Debates," in *The Student's Companion to Geography,* ed. A. Rogers, H. Viles, and A. Goudie (Oxford: Blackwell, 1992), 233–52.

11. The second edition (Singapore: Oxford University Press, 1989) extended the narrative to 1988.

12. See E. Lee, "Historiography of Singapore," in *Singapore Studies: Critical Surveys of the Humanities and Social Sciences,* ed. B. Kapur (Singapore: Singapore University Press, 1985), pp. 1–31.

13. Turnbull, *History of Singapore 1819–1975,* xiv.

14. E. C. T. Chew and E. Lee, eds., *A History of Singapore* (Singapore: Oxford University of Singapore, 1991).

15. S. E. Teo and V. R. Savage, "Singapore Landscape: A Historical Overview of Housing Image," in Chew and Lee, *History of Singapore,* 312–38.

16. For example V. R. Savage, "Landscape Change: From *Kampung* to Global City," in *The Physical Environment of Singapore: Adjustments to a Changing Landscape,* ed. A. Gupta and J. Pitts (Singapore: Singapore University Press, 1992), 5–31; V. R. Savage and B. S. A. Yeoh, "Urban Development and Industrialization in Singapore: An Historical Overview of Problems and Policy Responses," in *Malaysia and Singapore: Experiences in Industrialization and Urban Development,* ed. B. H. Lee, B. H. Oorjitham, and S. Oorjitham (Kuala Lumpur: University of Malaya, 1993), 22–56; V. R. Savage, "Singapore as a Global City: Change and Challenge for the Twenty-first Century," in *Singapore: Towards a Developed Status,* ed. L. Low (Singapore: Oxford University Press, 1999), 140–69; G. L. Ooi and Y. C. Kog, "Further Urbanization: Impact and Implications for Singapore," in Low, *Singapore,* 170–93.

17. See, for example, P. Rimmer, L. Manderson, and C. Barlow, "The Underside of Malaysian History," in *The Underside of Malaysian History:*

Pullers, Prostitutes, Plantation Workers, ed. P. Rimmer and L. M. Allen (Singapore: Singapore University Press, 1990), 3–22.

18. See Y. Atal, "The Call for Indigenization," *International Social Science Journal* 33, 1 (1981): 189–97.

19. A. B. Shamsul, "Arguments and Discourses in Malaysian Studies: In Search of Alternatives," paper presented at the International Workshop on Alternative Discourses in the Social Sciences and Humanities: Beyond Orientalism and Occidentalism, National University of Singapore, 30 May–1 June 1998.

20. B. Cohn, *Colonialism and Its Forms of Knowledge: The British in India* (Princeton: Princeton University Press, 1996), 4–5.

21. As quoted in S. F. Alatas, "The Theme of 'Relevance' in Third World Human Sciences," *Singapore Journal of Tropical Geography* 16, 2 (1995): 131.

22. E. R. Wolf, *Europe and the People without History* (Berkeley: University of California Press, 1982), x; J. M. Blaut, *The Coloniser's View of the World: Geographical Diffusion and Eurocentric History* (New York: Guilford Press, 1993).

23. See J. D. Sidaway, "The (Re)Making of the Western 'Geographical Tradition': Some Missing Links," *Area* 29, 1 (1997): 72–80.

24. A. D. King, "Rethinking Colonialism: An Epilogue," in *Forms of Dominance: On the Architecture and Urbanism of the Colonial Enterprise,* ed. N. AlSayyad (Aldershot: Avebury, 1992), 343.

25. Ibid.

26. Wolf, *Europe and the People,* 23.

27. See R. J. C. Young, "Foucault on Race and Colonialism," *New Formations* 25 (Summer 1995): 57–65.

28. N. AlSayyad, "Urbanism and the Dominance Equation," in N. AlSayyad, *Forms of Dominance,* 8.

29. S. Tanaka, *Japan's Orient: Rendering Pasts into History* (Berkeley: University of California Press, 1993), ix.

30. Rimmer, Manderson, and Barlow, "Underside of Malaysian History," 8.

31. J. F. Warren, *Rickshaw Coolie: A People's History of Singapore, 1880–1940* (Singapore: Oxford University Press, 1986), 316, 324.

32. Lai Ah Eng, *Peasants, Proletarians, and Prostitutes: A Preliminary Investigation into the Work of Chinese Women in Colonial Malaya* (Singapore: Institute of Southeast Asian Studies, 1986); Warren, *Rickshaw Coolie;* K. L. B. Yeo, "Hawkers and the State in Colonial Singapore: Mid-Nineteenth Century to 1939" (M.A. thesis, Monash University, 1989); Rimmer and Allen, *Underside of Malaysian History;* J. F. Warren, *Ah Ku and Karayuki-san: Pros-*

titution in Singapore, 1870–1940 (Singapore: Oxford University Press, 1993); L. Manderson, *Sickness and the State: Health and Illness in Colonial Malaya, 1870–1940* (Cambridge: Cambridge University Press, 1998).

33. E. P. Thompson, *The Making of the English Working Class* (Harmondsworth: Penguin, 1968), 13.

34. Warren, *Rickshaw Coolie,* 202.

35. For example, Lai, *Peasants, Proletarians, and Prostitutes;* K. Gaw, *Superior Servants: The Legendary Cantonese Amahs of the Far East* (Singapore: Oxford University Press, 1988); Yeo, "Hawkers and the State"; Warren, *Ah Ku and Karayuki-san.*

36. Warren, *Rickshaw Coolie,* 324–25.

37. Ibid., 324.

38. Ibid., 188–92.

39. B. S. A. Yeoh, *Contesting Space: Power Relations and the Urban Built Environment in Colonial Singapore* (Kuala Lumpur: Oxford University Press, 1996).

40. M. L. Pratt, *Imperial Eyes: Travel Writing and Transculturation* (London: Routledge, 1992), 7, 192.

41. M. Foucault, "Power and strategies" in *Michel Foucault: Power/Knowledge, Selected Interviews and Other Writings, 1972–1977,* ed. Colin Gordon (Brighton: Harvester Press, 1980), 142.

42. Yeoh, *Contesting Space,* passim.

43. E. W. Said, "Foreword to Subaltern Studies," in *Selected Subaltern Studies,* ed. R. Guha and G. C. Spivak (New York: Oxford University Press, 1988), viii.

44. D. Harvey, "On the History and Present Condition of Geography: An Historical Materialist Manifesto," *Professional Geographer* 36 (1984): 7.

45. S. Pile and M. Keith, preface to *Geographies of Resistance,* ed. Pile and Keith (London: Routledge, 1997), xi.

46. D. S. Moore, "Remapping Resistance: Ground for Struggle and the Politics of Place," in Pile and Keith, *Geographies of Resistance,* 87.

47. N. Thrift, "The Still Point: Resistance, Expressive Embodiment, and Dance," in Pile and Keith, *Geographies of Resistance,* 125.

48. M. de Certeau, *The Practice of Everyday Life* (Berkeley: University of California Press, 1984).

49. J. C. Scott, *Weapons of the Weak: Everyday Forms of Peasant Resistance* (New Haven: Yale University Press, 1985).

50. J. L. Abu-Lughod, "The Romance of Resistance: Tracing Transformations of Power through Bedouin Women," *American Ethnologist* 17, 1 (1990): 42.

51. A. Vidler, "The Scenes of the Street: Transformation in Ideal and

Reality, 1750–1871" in *On Streets*, ed. S. Anderson (Cambridge, Mass.: MIT Press, 1978), 28.

52. P. Routledge, "A Spatiality of Resistances: Theory and Practice in Nepal's Revolution of 1990," in Pile and Keith, *Geographies of Resistance*, 69.

53. Ibid.

54. S. Pile, introduction ("Opposition, Political Identities and Spaces of Resistance") to Pile and Keith, *Geographies of Resistance*, 3, 17.

55. M. Foucault, "The Politics of Health in the Eighteenth Century," in Gordon, *Michel Foucault*, 163–64.

56. Thrift, "Still Point," 135.

57. H. Lefebvre, *The Production of Space*, trans. D. Nicholson-Smith (Oxford: Basil Blackwell, 1991).

58. Pratt, *Imperial Eyes*, 4.

59. These points and the following examples are more fully fleshed out in Yeoh, *Contesting Space*.

60. D. Arnold, "Touching the Body: Perspectives on the Indian Plague, 1896–1900," in Guha and Spivak, *Selected Subaltern Studies*, 56.

61. M. Foucault, *Discipline and Punish: The Birth of the Prison*, trans. A. Sheridan (London: Penguin Books, 1979), 139.

62. Pile, introduction, 14.

63. Routledge, "Spatiality of Resistance," 69.

64. Ibid., 70.

65. S. Lavie and T. Swedenburg, introduction to *Displacement, Diaspora and Geographies of Identity*, ed. Lavie and Swedenburg (Durham: Duke University Press, 1996), 1.

66. N. G. Schiller, L. Basch, and C. S. Blanc, "Transnationalism: A New Analytic Framework for Understanding Migration," in *Towards a Transnational Perspective on Migration: Race, Class, Ethnicity, and Nationalism Reconsidered*, ed. N. G. Schiller, L. Basch, and Szanton Blanc (New York: New York Academy of Sciences, 1992).

67. T. N. Harper, "Globalism and the Pursuit of Authenticity: The Making of a Diasporic Public Sphere in Singapore," *Sojourn* 12, 2 (1997): 261.

68. P. van der Veer, introduction ("The Diasporic Imagination") to *Nation and Migration: The Politics of Space in the South Asian Diaspora*, ed. P. van der Veer (Philadelphia: University of Pennsylvania Press, 1995), 2.

69. N. Rapport, "Coming Home to a Dream: A Study of the Immigrant Discourse of 'Anglo-Saxons' in Israel," in *Migrants of Identity: Perceptions of Home in a World of Movement*, ed. N. Rapport and A. Dawson (New York: Berg, 1998), 77.

70. Wang Ling-chi and Wang Gungwu, eds., *The Chinese Diaspora: Selected Essays*, 2 vols. (Singapore: Times Academic Press, 1998).

71. Wang is of the view that both China and hostile governments may extract political capital out of the term *diaspora*. From China's perspective, the term may be used to designate a single body of overseas Chinese and used to bring about nationalist and racist binding of all Chinese at home and abroad. In other countries, the term may become a major source of suspicion that Chinese minorities could never feel loyalty toward their own nations. See Wang Gungwu, "A Single Chinese Diaspora? Some Historical Reflections," inaugural lecture for the Center for the Study of the Chinese Southern Diaspora (CSCSD), Australian National University, Canberra, 1999.

72. Harvey, *Social Justice and the City*, 13–14.

73. T. Zeldin, *An Intimate History of Humanity* (New Delhi: Penguin, 1999), 15.

Chapter 3

QUANTIFYING THE ECONOMIC AND SOCIAL HISTORY OF SOUTHEAST ASIA

A Quest for New Evidence and Methods

M. R. FERNANDO

THE ECONOMIC AND SOCIAL HISTORY of Southeast Asia has emerged as a major field of study in the last three decades. There is a substantial literature covering various aspects of the economic and social history of the region over a long span of time, particularly after 1800, although we still have to do a great deal more work before writing a detailed history of the region as a whole. This is indeed a formidable task given the complexity of historical experiences of people in different parts of the region, not to mention the difficulties involved in sifting through a large amount of material in several European languages.[1] Nevertheless, we have a fairly clear view of the broad contours of the socioeconomic transformation that swept across the region after 1820, and historians are now widening the frontiers of scholarship by looking at the early modern period (ca. 1400–1820), which received relatively less attention well into the mid-1980s.

Nearly all work in the fields of economic and social history done since the early 1960s has been written from the point of view of indigenous people or from a local perspective, a conceptual principle that emerged in the course of one of the great debates in writing Southeast Asian history after decolonization. The main characteristics of this guiding principle are well known: focus on the periphery instead of the colonial metropolis and the effects of colonial policies on indigenous populations in the periphery—or rather, how the latter reacted to colonial policies—in order to bring local people to the foreground of history. The best examples of this genre of writings are small in scale and encompass a small area of a country and a relatively short period of time. The assessment of the degree of change in economy and society is, furthermore, based on a careful examination of descriptive evidence spiced occasionally with some statistical evidence. Consequently the conclusions are very difficult to posit beyond a small area and a relatively short period of time. Historians' reluctance to acknowledge, let alone use, the large body of statistical evidence available on many aspects of economic and social change, and covering a long period of time, has had a debilitating effect on the writing of economic and social history of Southeast Asia.

This is precisely what the "cliometric" historians set about to overcome after 1970, claiming that a quantitative approach will not only enable historians to discern the long-term trends of socioeconomic change but will also provide a more scientific basis in comparison with the conventional methods of the study of history.[2] The majority of cliometric historians are reluctant to advocate a rigorous quantitative approach that advocates the possibility of reducing the rich gamut of human experience to pure mathematical formulae. And yet a careful and extensive use of quantitative evidence covering a long span of time seems to provide greater insight into the process of socioeconomic change by examining the statistical evidence on different aspects of human behavior in order to discern the long-term trends and its dynamics.

Much of the progress made in writing Southeast Asian history from below in recent years has been achieved by focusing on commonplace events such as banditry, prostitution, criminality, and riots. Historians have also been using new and unusual source materials to find reflections of people in a wide range of activities.[3] This genre of writings in socioeconomic history still makes use of the conventional methods; methods that have worked very well in some areas of economic and social history such as famines, peasant uprisings, political conflicts involving the colonial state and ordinary people as shown by the highly fashionable writings of the subaltern school, not to mention numerous studies on peasant uprisings in Southeast Asia. Events such as famines and revolts, however, do not involve people en masse. The patterns of behavior of people in production and consumption of food, indebtedness, mobilization, and reproduction, are very difficult if not impossible to discern on the basis of small samples and fragmentary descriptive accounts. We are often forced to qualify our conclusions with vague expressions of measurement.

Most of us working on Southeast Asia are reluctant to make use of the kind of quantitative information that lends itself admirably well to the study of mass phenomenon in economic and social history as the main source of information for the study of common people. We all make use of raw statistics in a casual manner to prove a point, but not on a large enough scale to discern the long-term developments or complex character of the phenomena concerned. If properly used in combination with descriptive information and a modicum of caution by applying rigorous methods, the quantitative approach will broaden our understanding of social and economic history.

In recent years, a few historians have made an effort to project the long-term historical development of Southeast Asia. While recognizing the differences between geographic areas, they postulate a general pattern of behavior since the beginning of the fifteenth century for both Europe and Asia.[4] Quantitative evidence is an indispensable category of evidence for such a broad framework, one that could bring about a radical change in current practices in the study of socioeconomic history.

Current Practice

There has never been any controversy about using quantitative information in studying the economic and social history of Southeast Asia, before or after World War II. Historians have made use of quantitative data, after a fashion, to elucidate population growth, the rise or fall in state revenue and commerce, and the growth of indigenous agriculture.[5] But before World War II, there was no effort to examine the long-term trends of any phenomenon on the basis of quantitative information. The range of issues explored in light of quantitative information was also confined to the issues pertinent to the colonial economic order.

Writing the economic and social history of common people became popular after World War II as a new generation of historians began to ask new questions against the background of rapid socioeconomic changes sweeping across the region. The initial efforts in writing the economic and social history of people at large are impressive and exciting and show the fine results we can achieve by making use of the vast repository of descriptive information available on the mundane economic life of people.[6] The success of this approach inspired the next generation of historians to plumb the depths of colonial archives, leading to a wave of new historical writings within the broad parameters of area studies. The basic idea is simple: to bring common people back to life in the light of historical evidence culled from the colonial sources, we must descend to the local level, far away from the center of gravity of the colonial administration. The resultant change in perspective has been rather impressive, as shown by numerous studies in the 1970s and 1980s.[7]

The first conspicuous characteristic of this genre is a vast amount of descriptive information on the economic and social life of indigenous people caught up in the process of capitalist economic transformation. The second important characteristic is the tendency to measure change over time in light of some quantitative evidence. There is no doubt that this approach has broadened our understanding of the long-term processes of modern economic and social transformation in Southeast Asia after 1830. The basic methodological underpinnings of the current practice of socioeconomic history—that is, writing the history of small local units in order to focus on common people—has unfortunately come to a grinding halt in recent years. Historians are no longer interested in pursuing area studies focused on the economic and social life of indigenous people. We are now

interested in overarching structures, long spans of time and comparative history, all symptomatic of the global change in politics, economy,
and society. Quantitative data and methods provide the most effective
and convenient way to study history in the long run.

There has indeed been some effort to introduce a quantitative approach into the study of the socioeconomic history of Southeast Asia
in the last two decades. There is no doubt that the use of statistics has
given a new dimension to the historians' efforts to delineate change
and continuity in the socioeconomic transformation that swept across
the region from the early decades of the nineteenth century onwards.
But statistics are being used circumspectly and often with an apologia
for the unreliability of such evidence, which is notoriously difficult to
reconcile with the descriptive evidence. This is partly due to the fact
that in some cases the statistics are indeed far from reliable and consistent, and partly because most historians are wary of making use of
sophisticated quantitative methods to make sense of the statistics at
their disposal.

Occasionally, a historian has gone beyond the customary limits of
his craft and examined statistical evidence on its own terms—that is,
using sophisticated quantitative methods to discern the demographic
patterns for a sample population or an episode of crisis mortality with
a degree of success.[8] There is no doubt that a quantitative approach
directed toward discerning the long-term trends in economic growth
and change in Southeast Asia can be illuminating. For instance, despite local variations, we can clearly see a common pattern of economic growth and development across Southeast Asia since 1870, on
the basis of the statistics of production and trade in agricultural commodities.[9] A similar picture will probably emerge from a study of demography and growth of the labor force and service industries, for
which we have ample statistical evidence. A judicious blend of statistical and descriptive evidence has yielded a fascinating picture of the
dynamics of agricultural growth in Indonesia since the 1880s.[10]

It is true that a large corpus of reliable statistics on many variables
of economic and social life for most parts of Southeast Asia becomes
available only after 1850, a state of affairs that has prompted some eco-

nomic historians to ignore the economic history before 1850 altogether. However, while we may not have large compilations of statistics covering a long span of time and many aspects of life, we can still make use of whatever data is available to delineate the long-term trends in demography and economic transformation in Southeast Asia since 1400. A great deal of quantifiable information is indeed available for studies in demography and economic growth for most parts of Southeast Asia after 1400, but all such evidence, and much else besides, is buried in both indigenous and European archives awaiting scholarly attention.[11]

A quantitative approach—the use of quantitative evidence and rigorous analytical tools to bring out the significance of quantitative evidence in the context of the matter being discussed—appears to broaden the scope of historical studies on the economy and society of Southeast Asia and add a new dimension to historical discourse based on descriptive evidence. There are misconceptions, for instance, about the very nature of demographic transformation and its dynamics. These misconceptions are largely due to the reluctance of historians to delve deeply into the archival and published sources to cull relevant statistics and analyze them properly before trying to explain what is considered to be a population explosion since the mid-nineteenth century.[12] The "explosion" becomes less surprising viewed in the context of long-term population growth since 1400 and also in light of the best figures available in contemporary sources, instead of some dubious and sporadic figures usually produced in discussion. At the most basic level, then, a quantitative approach corrects some serious problems inherent in a discursive discourse based on descriptive evidence adorned with some statistical evidence, which does not yield a sharp picture of the trends of change and its dynamics.

There is no shortage of quantitative information for most parts of Southeast Asia after 1800, for a great deal of quantitative information on economic and social matters was collected, sifted through, and published, in most parts of Southeast Asia under colonial rule. The corpus of data is rich for Indonesia, Burma, Thailand, and British Malaya; and remaining parts of the region too have fairly large collections of data covering many aspects of economic and social history.[13] The scope and range of data for some parts of the region, particularly Malaysia, Thailand, Burma, and Vietnam, are yet to be ascertained as a result of the paucity of scholarly works on the social and economic history of those countries in which quantitative information is used to any appreciable extent.

The published annual reports of the colonial administrations of Burma, the Malay Peninsula, and the Dutch East Indies are perhaps exemplary of the statistical data at the disposal of students of history. These reports provide complete runs of statistics for demography, migration, land use, agricultural production, trade, criminality, health, education, and so forth from the early 1820s to the early 1940s, and are supplemented, with an unavoidable gap during the Japanese interregnum, after 1950, when the range and quality of data improve considerably. Some recent studies mentioned above give us an inkling of the richness of this corpus of quantitative information in exploring the material life of the indigenous population of Southeast Asia before and after World War II.

It is not easy to collate and regroup the vast amounts of quantitative information produced by the colonial bureaucracy to suit the interests and needs of historical research. To begin with, a great deal of effort is needed to gather all published reports in places where the original hard copies are not available. This is relatively easy compared with sifting through the reports and identifying the tables that contain relevant information, and it is harder still to impose some discipline on the recalcitrant data grouped, subdivided, aggregated, and dispersed in numerous tables so we can begin to see some general patterns in the phenomenon being observed. Therefore it is highly desirable to have data from these colonial reports reorganized and made available in forms more congenial for quantitative analysis. This task has been achieved with admirable results in the case of Indonesia, as will be shown below. For the rest of Southeast Asia, however, we have no comparable compilations of statistics culled from the colonial reports.

For the period prior to 1820, one has to search in the dusty corners of local and European archives for quantitative (and other) information, which is fortunately abundant, particularly in the archives of international trading companies of the Dutch and English, which had close links with Asia. The riches of historical evidence in the large repositories of the Dutch and English East India companies are still largely unknown, simply because those archives are organized in such way that one layer of documents is concealed behind another, and the quantitative data is often hidden in the lower layers interspersed between long descriptive records. For instance, one of the most fascinating categories of records containing a wealth of quantitative evidence on the domestic economy of insular Southeast Asia is the shipping list for major ports such as Batavia, Melaka, Ambon, and Makassar among others, between 1620 and 1795.

There is an equally fascinating document that provides insight into the daily life of the Dutch garrisons that policed sea-lanes across the region. The list of necessities for garrisons, compiled annually, is a long document that provides details of the wide range of goods needed for their operation. Church records are perhaps more important, as they record vital events of a cross-section of the urban communities in major cities such as Batavia, Melaka, Singapore, Makassar, and Manila. These records are unfortunately not preserved in their entirety, but where we have a reasonably complete run of the records, as in the case of Melaka, we can piece together a fascinating account of the life of the Christian community in the city concerned.[14] The most complete sets of parish records for any part of Southeast Asia before 1820 are to be found in the Philippines and, despite the problems involved in using the rich ores of evidence they contain, these records enable historians to achieve fine results in demographic history comparable to the justly renowned studies in the demographic history of England based on similar records.[15] There are even more fascinating records that can illuminate many aspects of social history with a quantitative dimension buried in the vast repositories of the Dutch East India Company archives.[16] It is quite clear that there is no shortage of quantitative information on many aspects of economic and social history of Southeast Asia since 1400, and the use of quantitative information opens up new avenues of

study into hitherto unexplored areas of the material life of indigenous people.

There is perhaps little dissent about the use of statistics among historians, but using rigorous quantitative methods to analyze that body
of data, and garnish the scholarly discourse with cliometric vocabulary, may well result in a call for arms. The rigorous quantitative
methods sound strange and the familiarization required may take
quite some time, even before evaluating the result of the analysis itself, and the latter seems to occupy so little space compared with the
agonizingly long and complex discussion of the methods of analysis.
The degree to which one can employ rigorous quantitative methods
in analyzing the data has to be decided on the merits of the data depending on their scope and reliability, for it is highly misleading and
inappropriate to subject a set of sporadic and unreliable figures to a
sophisticated analysis. Nevertheless, it is possible to identify several
basic procedures that would bring out the essence of the data in order
to say something new and pertinent on a given issue.

Identifying a trend in a phenomenon is perhaps the most important procedure at our disposal. This can be achieved with ease using
any one of the standard programs for statistical analysis, which also
allow us to perform numerous other procedures such as calculating
the mean and standard deviation of a trend, to identify its components
and correlate different variables, to formulate a hypothesis of or an explanation for a given phenomenon. There is a host of other simple but
effective statistical procedures a student of history can adopt in historical studies of quantitative information, a task made considerably easier, less time consuming, and highly rewarding with the advent of
powerful microcomputers.

The Case of the Economic and Social History of Nineteenth-Century Java

There are several problems in studying social and economic history at
local levels within the parameters of area studies. Social and eco-

nomic change does not stop at district, provincial, or national boundaries, which are arbitrary limits imposed by political fiat. While local differences are genuine and a part of reality, we should not overlook the similarities across local boundaries that become important in drawing broad conclusions covering a large area and a long span of time. The sum total of local examples of a given phenomenon, furthermore, does not necessarily produce a broad picture of the process of social and economic change. This is obvious when we examine the case of Java in the nineteenth century, a subject that has been studied at length during the past three decades.[17] These major works, as well as numerous small contributions, are conceived within the framework of autonomous history writing focused on small areas. The end result of this approach and methodology is that we have a detailed picture of the ways in which the indigenous population in some areas reacted to being incorporated into the modern capitalist economic system under colonial rule. Instead of misleading general views of the ubiquitous impact of colonial policies, we receive a more complex picture of gradual adaptation both on the part of peasants and the colonial administration.

The revision is striking in the case of economic and social changes in rural Java in the middle decades of the nineteenth century. The received wisdom had it that Javanese peasants were impoverished as a result of the forced cultivation of commercial crops that swept through the island. This view in its original form was a result of looking at the situation in Java from a political stance, liberal versus conservative, in light of the fragmentary information couched in emotionally charged language.[18] The received view had a face-lift in the early 1960s, when it was refined in terms of cultural anthropology.[19] The received view is based on several strands of argument premised on the assumption that Javanese peasants hated forced cultivation of commercial crops, did not benefit from it, and experienced great hardship arising from the exploitation of their land and labor. The result was, according to Geertz, a society wherein the burgeoning population was forced to eke out a meager living in a stultifying subsistence agricultural economy.

This perception has undergone a radical change since the early 1970s as historians began to probe into the colonial archives and plumb records at the local levels of administration. It became obvious from the records that there was a degree of flexibility and adaptation of colonial policy at local levels, as the local administration began to implement the basic idea of growing commercial crops with peasant land and labor on a large scale. It was necessary to obtain the cooperation of the peasant communities for this purpose and gradually a modus operandi came into existence that allowed the peasant communities a fair degree of control over how the work was organized and its rewards distributed. This mode of operation, in which local indigenous functionaries down to the village level played a noteworthy role, brought about far-reaching economic and social change in rural Java. The peasant communities, it seems, reacted favorably to the growing of commercial crops once it was absorbed into the agricultural cycle. There was plenty of adjustment in work patterns, including allocation of land and labor, by peasant communities. Despite numerous local nuances and differences, we observe a great deal in common between areas across Java with regard to economic and social change. There was population growth while agricultural production increased and nonagricultural economic activity proliferated, heralding a noticeable change in the standard of living of the Javanese rural population. Socially, a process of differentiation of peasantry was a conspicuous phenomenon; we see a peasantry gradually differentiated in terms of access to land and other sources of income and social standing arising from the improved economic standing.

There is, however, some reluctance among historians to acknowledge that a broad pattern of change swept through the island. The historians concerned look at social and economic change from the vantage point of their bailiwicks and project a picture of the unique conditions in respective areas. They are consequently oblivious to the fact that a given phenomenon could occur elsewhere in Java. This is a result of focusing on a small area and the difficulties involved in sifting through an enormous amount of information covering all parts of the island. When a brave scholar shoulders the task, his ability to project a broad generalization for all Java is hampered by the methodological constraints. For instance, in his recent masterly account of economic and social change in Java under the cultivation system, Robert Elson piles up numerous local instances as if their sheer bulk will produce a broad generalization.[20] The problem is all too clear. On the one hand, we must produce enough evidence from the contemporary sources to lend credibility to our analysis, because most readers do not have access to the sources. On the other, piling up pieces of information covering different areas of Java does not necessarily yield a broad generalization; that requires a sense of proportion and measurement.

This is obvious when we compare two different accounts of the growth of nonagricultural economic activity in Java, one from the conventional stance and the other from a cliometric point of view that combines both the quantitative and descriptive information.[21] It is very difficult to elicit a sense of measurement from the descriptive evidence of social and economic change, not only because the subjective element in reports made colonial officials themselves skeptical about what they described but also because the sheer bulk of information describing the situation in different areas makes forming an overall view rather difficult. Measuring change in the spread of nonagricultural economic activity over time is even more difficult on the basis of descriptive evidence. These difficulties disappear if we compile a simple table combining two or more sets of data covering several decades.[22] To measure social and economic change, we should use quantitative information that reveals the local, regional, and national trends and the proportion of change over a long period of time.

There is in fact no shortage of quantitative information of all kinds covering a wide range of variables in archival and published official records of the former colonial administration of Indonesia. The most reliable and complete statistics on population, food crop and commercial agriculture, trade, industry, prices, national income, money and banking, as well as transport are now accessible to scholars in an exemplary series of publications.[23] This series is justly hailed as a worthy companion to a series of quantitative information for late Tokugawa and early Meiji Japan.[24] The aforesaid series of statistics on Java has appeared too late to be made full use of in local studies carried out in the 1980s. The scholars engaged in studying Java's economic and social history are somewhat wary to use these statistics to ascertain overall and provincial trends in economic changes in Java. For instance, Elson in his recent study presents statistical evidence piecemeal without any effort to draw the long-term trends or to present the statistics of different variables in relation to each other except on one occasion. He does relate different variables in his elaborate discussion, it has to be said in fairness, with due caution about the quality of statistics. The end result of his elaborate discussion of socioeconomic change, full of details of local circumstances, is that the reader has to draw his or her own broad picture of the situation in Java as a whole. This is hard enough for readers who are familiar with the evidence and problems involved. The readers who are unfamiliar with the subject matter may find it harder to get through the overwhelming amount of details to form a sufficiently clear general picture.

The problem could have been satisfactorily resolved by using quantitative data on a large scale and in a consistent manner. For instance, a simple graph showing the overall and regional trends of population growth can provide a clear point of departure for a detailed discussion of the factors contributing to population growth. In fact, a number of important questions can be raised on the basis of this quantitative description of population. The impact of rapid population growth on land and agricultural production, for instance, continues unfortunately to be ignored by historians, partly because we have not yet formed a sufficiently clear picture of the population growth itself. Before the publication of population statistics, only a few historians had access to the annual population counts while all others resorted to using fragmentary figures of dubious provenance to discuss the patterns of population growth and its causes.[25]

The new light statistical evidence can throw on economic change in rural Java is even more evident when we examine the data on food production, price of rice, and nonagricultural economic activities such as domestic manufacturing and rural trade. These variables are closely involved in the ongoing debate about the standard of living of Javanese peasants. There are differences of opinion among scholars as to the criteria necessary to measure change in the standard of living. We do not have household budget studies and all we can do is to gauge the change in general terms at the household level. Given the fact that we are dealing with a peasant society where access to land is an important criterion, we can begin with the vicissitudes in patterns of landholding.

There is evidence of mounting pressure on peasant communities to enlarge the ranks of peasants with access to land who bore the brunt of the burden of cultivation work, which led to a sudden increase in the number of peasants with access to land in the early 1830s. But this trend did not continue for long and, although the number of landholding peasants rose in the next three decades, it was not exactly proportionate to the population growth.[26] While this phenomenon has been observed in some localities, we are still waiting for a general view of the situation in all of Java. Such a picture is extremely difficult to gain from the snippets of descriptive information, because it does not yield a measurement, and isolated local samples of measurement are no substitute for a proper analysis of Java-wide figures. There are numerous problems of definition involved in such an exercise, but when the quantitative information is carefully examined, it projects a picture of the growing differentiation of peasantry into segments as landholding peasants, including tenants and sharecroppers, and landless agricultural laborers. The proportion of landholding peasants remained more or less constant at 65 percent of all peasant households in Java, which suggests a process of increasing differentiation of the rural population as it grew apace and the economy became diversified.[27]

There are plenty of statistics of areas of cultivated arable land under food crops and production of food crops, particularly rice, from the early 1820s onward. This corpus of data has not been properly analyzed as a series and with attention to the regional patterns, although parts of the time series have been examined and two economic historians have given us a picture of long-term developments in rice production in Java.[28] The food supply in the middle decades of the nineteenth century appears to have increased considerably, thus raising per capita food consumption. This conclusion casts serious doubts on the received wisdom that the people of Java experienced serious food shortages as a result of the expansion in commercial agriculture.[29] It is true that there were highly localized famines in Cirebon and Semarang, but the overall food supply was undoubtedly increasing and, with the improved communication facilities, trade in rice gathered momentum and eliminated local food shortages.[30] This subject has not received enough attention from historians, particularly in the analysis of the mass of quantitative information available, to elicit the regional patterns and combine them with the equally large body of descriptive information to weave a broad picture of the indigenous agricultural economy.

As with the food supply, we have not made use of all the quantitative information on other indicators bearing on the issue of standard of living, such as money income, tax burden, and the consumption of opium and of salt, textiles, meat, and other sundry goods necessary for daily life. Two scholars have made a partial effort to redress the imbalance with varying degrees of success. While Boomgard is overtly bent upon proving his view almost entirely on the basis of snippets of statistics, Elson is mostly engrossed in fragmentary descriptive evidence with a modest effort at measuring living standards within the conventional limits of the historian's craft.[31]

I have dealt with the historiography of nineteenth-century Java at some length because it shows the progress in making use of quantitative information far better than any other area in Southeast Asia. This becomes a more difficult task as we enter the world of the scribes of indigenous rulers, for whom history was a subject worthy of poetry, and clerks in trading companies, for whom counting profits was a matter of routine.

The Case of the Malay Archipelago, 1640–1840

The economic and social history of Southeast Asia during the early modern period (1400–1820) is a new phenomenon full of great potential following Reid's highly imaginative study of the "age of commerce" (1450–1680). This interest in the history of the early modern period is partly a result of the need to rethink the origins of the rapid economic growth of Southeast Asia. It is usually associated with the region's rapid incorporation into the modern world capitalist system in the mid-nineteenth century. This view is challenged by recent studies showing a much earlier origin of economic growth dating from the early 1400s.[32] The revival of long-distance trade between China and Europe after 1400 appears to have stimulated economic activity in the region, an ideal situation, given that it was a meeting place for traders from both areas, in addition to being a major supplier of commodities greatly in demand. The broad contours of economic and social developments in Southeast Asia during the early modern period are now clear and we also have some detailed studies of various aspects of the process in different parts of the region.[33] Nevertheless, even the evocative pictorial evidence that Reid has ingenuously brought forth in a conspicuously Braudelian fashion provides us with only a narrow window to look into the life of people. The use of pictorial evidence has underlined how important it is to find new sources for a breakthrough in the study of history.

The detailed studies of the economic and social history of the early modern period are based on the copious records of the indigenous administrations of Burma, Thailand, and Vietnam and the voluminous records of European trading companies. There are layers in the last category of records and until now most historians have confined themselves to the first and second layers of documentation bequeathed to us by the Dutch and English trading companies. Below these layers are to be found further layers of documents, hitherto ignored or marginally used by historians, partly because they contain information of little value for writing political history. Here we find information on economic and social affairs of people at large as well as the ruling elite, as shown by the records of ship movements, which fascinates historians with an interest in using quantitative methods.

The Dutch East India Company records contain runs of shipping records of major ports such as Jambi, Palembang, Melaka, Ambon, and Makassar, in addition to the records of a few ports in Java. These records provide a detailed account of commercial activities of many thousands of indigenous and European traders. The records are lengthy, full of problems, and at times cover long spans of time, as in the case of Melaka, which provides the longest series (1677–1792). Information contained in the shipping lists delights the heart of quantitatively oriented historians, but it also calls for a prodigious amount of time and labor to compile databases and to scrutinize the data using complex statistical programs. However, the results based on work in progress on Makassar, Java, and Melaka are nothing short of revelatory.[34]

The corpus of data from Melaka harbor, which came under Dutch control in 1641 and remained under Dutch control until 1824, is perhaps the most complete of all the series of shipping records. It arguably provides a reliable index of the level of commercial activity involving the local population over a large area including Burma, Thailand, Cambodia, Vietnam, Sumatra, the Malay Peninsula, and Java. The series on ship movements for Melaka is complete except for one major gap (1744–60), and figures are not available for a few months for some years in the first half of the eighteenth century. The overall picture of ship movements into and out of Melaka in the long run, without any adjustment except a trend line, reflects the vicissitudes of indigenous commerce (see fig. 3.1).

It is clear that Melaka remained a major port of call for local traders despite Dutch efforts to stifle it, for the sake of Batavia, as the center of all commercial activity in Indonesian archipelago. The level of commerce waxed and waned and indeed experienced a nadir in the mid-eighteenth century, but picked up momentum after 1760 to rise to a peak toward the end of the eighteenth century. From this evidence, therefore, we have to conclude that the Dutch were unable to restrict, let alone stifle, indigenous trade within the region despite rigorous application of a pass system regulating indigenous traders.

These figures provide the precise magnitude of local commerce conducted by a throng of Malay, Chinese, and European traders from numerous ports in the region. We can identify every one of

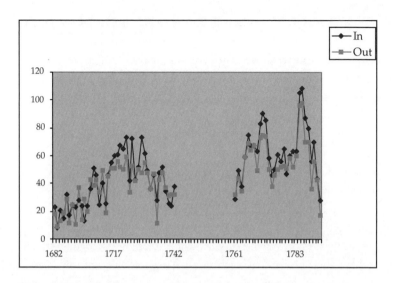

Fig. 3.1. Ship movement into and out of Melaka, 1682–1792

them by name and ethnic background, their place of residence, affiliation with local noblemen and relations with fellow traders, the kind and size of vessels, goods carried on board, and the duration and pattern of travel. This information is enough to write a comprehensive social history of the entire mercantile class operating in the region during the period under review. The mercantile class underwent change over time, as one generation of traders was replaced by another, although the mode of operation remained largely intact. There was a high turnover in traders based in various ports in the archipelago as they moved from one port to another, probably depending on the fortunes they made, the fortunes of the port-polities, and the nature of the cargo. This aspect of mercantile life is easy to capture by quantitative methods, whereas it is likely to elude students working within the confines of traditional boundaries of the craft.

There was a contest for primacy between Malay and Chinese traders in the region, to judge by the continuously changing balance in favor of one group or the other. Malay traders firmly held ground from the late seventeenth to the mid-eighteenth century while Chinese traders gradually rose in number, eventually surpassing the tally of Malay counterparts by 1770. It was a temporary victory, for the Malay traders bounced back in the later years of the eighteenth century.[35] The vicissitudes of Javanese traders, who came to Melaka in large numbers, deserve close attention. Their disappearance in the second half of the eighteenth century is one of the salient features of changing trade patterns in the Malay Archipelago. Tightened Dutch control of main port-polities in Java such as Banten, Cirebon, Semarang, and Surabaya, which affected the mode of operation of indigenous economy, was a major factor contributing to the decline of Javanese traders participating in regional trade. And Java's domestic economy suffered a great deal as a result of the warfare involving rival factions of the royal houses until 1755. When peace returned at long last, Javanese traders had lost their place in regional trade. They seldom ventured beyond Riau, it seems, because commodities from Java came to Melaka via Riau in the second half of the eighteenth century. There is a similar story about European and Eurasian traders settled in local towns. The mercantile community was highly mobile and favored links that cut across ethnic lines when the interests of business or personal reasons necessitated such links. Mapping movements of a particular trader over a period of one or two decades gives a picture of the rising and declining fortunes of a person as well as his base of operation.

Changing fortunes of traders reflect the vicissitudes of port-polities along the trade network encompassing the Malay Archipelago. Information in shipping lists provides a detailed picture of the ways in which a trade network came into existence, connecting important port-polities such as Pegu, Kedah, Siak, Melaka, and Riau. The rise and fall of Riau, not only as a bastion of Malay rule but also as a major center of commerce, is a subject worthy of a major study: our data provides a fascinating account of the dynamics of the mercantile community in Riau. It relied heavily on the political elite at first, but seems to have become more independent in the second half of the eighteenth century. Information of traders' affiliation with noblemen is very important for the social historian and, instead of citing a few examples that do not really convey a measurement of change, a quantitative historian could easily state the vicissitudes in relationships in exact terms covering the entire mercantile community. Similar quests can be undertaken with regard to other centers of commerce, a quest that would yield a fascinating picture of places such as Kedah, which seems to have played an important role as a transit market between the mainland centers of commodity production and major ports in the Malay Archipelago.

The information in the shipping lists that is the hardest to analyze concerns the cargo on board, which has a bearing on the issue of the dynamics of local economies and economic growth. Much of the information on the cargo involves local markets and consumption patterns rather than long-distance trade, which has unfortunately been overemphasized in the literature as a major force of change in local economy. What we find in the shipping lists provides a detailed account of the demand and supply of commodities for local consumption that included a wide range of goods. A close examination of the cargo therefore provides not only a measurement of the state of the local economy but also a feeling for the material life of the local population seldom found in any other source. People were fond of dried fish and fish roe and some groups of people, particularly Europeans, were excessively fond of liquor. Fashions in food as well as dress changed over time and in accordance with times of plenty or scarcity. If we are ever likely to take a peep into the living room of people who lived in this period, it is through the lens of these shipping lists, for no visual representation of the material life has survived to entice students of history to emulate Braudel and Schama.[36]

Information of the cargo on board ships also helps one to gauge the dynamics of local economies. While Reid emphasizes the exogenous factor or long-distance trade as the prime mover, Lieberman focuses on endogenous factors.[37] The data on production of commodities required for the long-distance trade between Europe and Southeast Asia on which Reid has based his argument does not cover the domestic economy.[38] Reid has not taken into account the existence of quantitative information on the domestic economy, partly due to the serious difficulties in retrieving such information from obscure and voluminous sources. On the basis of information on cargo in the Melaka shipping lists, it can be argued that the domestic economy played a major role in changes in material life, although some noteworthy changes occurred in the domestic economy as a result of the expansion in long-distance trade. Economic growth in the Malay Archipelago was thus to a large extent endogenous, a conclusion that goes well with Lieberman's assessment of the situation in mainland Southeast Asia during the early modern period.

The study of the economic and social history of Southeast Asia is still in its infancy, so we would do well to evaluate the best methods to adopt in broadening our understanding of the material culture of people. Historians have been working toward the ideal way of writing autonomous history on the basis of descriptive evidence. This method has undoubtedly broadened our understanding, but its limitations prevent us from exploring new research agendas that would go to the heart of the material culture of indigenous peoples. The quantitative approach will hopefully provide much needed impetus and a point of departure for exploring economic and social history of the region afresh without sacrificing the basic principles of the historian's craft. Furthermore, it widens the scope of inquiry of social and economic history and enables the historian to measure more clearly, if not more precisely, change over time and to explain the dynamics of change lucidly and precisely instead of vaguely. The degree of improvement inherent in adopting a quantitative approach seems to outweigh any possible regrets in stepping over the conventional boundary of the historian's craft to help us overcome some serious methodological constraints in the present mode of study.

Notes

1. Robert Elson's masterly and succinct survey of economic and social change in Southeast Asia after 1800 is by far the most satisfactory effort in this direction. Elson, "International Commerce, the State and Society: Eco-

nomic and Social Change," in *Cambridge History of Southeast Asia,* ed. N. Tarling, 2 vols. (Cambridge: Cambridge University Press, 1992), 2:131–96.

2. For a well-informed and considered discussion of both approaches, see R. W. Fogel and G. R. Elton, *Which Road to the Past?* (New Haven: Yale University Press, 1963).

3. Sartono Kartodirdjo, *The Peasants' Revolt of Banten in 1888* (The Hague: Martinus Nijhoff, 1966); J. Ingleson, "Prostitution in Colonial Java," in *Nineteenth and Twentieth-Century Indonesia,* ed. D. P. Chandler and M. C. Ricklefs (Victoria: Monash University, 1986), 123–40; Cheah Boon Kheng, *The Peasant Robbers of Kedah, 1900–1929* (Singapore: Oxford University Press, 1988); J. Sharpe, "History from Below," in *New Perspectives on Historical Writing,* ed. P. Burke (Oxford: Polity Press, 1991), 24–41.

4. A. Reid, *Southeast Asia in the Age of Commerce, 1450–1680,* vol.1, *The Lands below the Winds* (New Haven: Yale University Press, 1988); vol. 2, *Expansion and Crisis* (New Haven: Yale University Press, 1993); V. Lieberman, "Local Integration and Eurasian Analogies: Structuring Southeast Asian History, c. 1350–c. 1830," *Modern Asian Studies* 27, 3 (1993): 475–572.

5. Among the early efforts to make use of statistics in delineating patterns in economic behavior, the following works are noteworthy: D. H. Burger, *De ontsluiting van Java's binnenland voor het wereldverkeer* (Wageningen: Veenman, 1939); J. S. Furnivall, *Netherlands India* (Cambridge: Cambridge University Press, 1944); C. Robequain, *The Economic Development of French Indochina* (New York: Oxford University Press, 1944).

6. M. Adas, *The Burma Delta* (Wisconsin: University of Wisconsin, 1974); J. C. Ingram, *Economic Change in Thailand, 1850–1970* (Stanford: Stanford University Press, 1950); D. B. Johnston, "Rural Society and the Rice Economy in Thailand, 1880–1930" (Ph.D. diss., Yale University, 1975); J. A. Larkin, *The Pampangans* (Berkeley: University of California Press, 1972); E. Wickberg, *The Chinese in Philippine Life, 1850–1898* (New Haven: Yale University Press, 1965); Guy Gran, "Vietnam and the Capitalist Route to Modernity: Village Cochinchina, 1880–1940" (Ph.D. diss., University of Wisconsin, 1975); E. Sadka, *The Protected Malay States, 1874–1895* (Kuala Lumpur: University of Malaya Press, 1968); Lim Teck Ghee, *Peasants and Their Agricultural Economy in Colonial Malaya, 1874–1941* (Kuala Lumpur: Oxford University Press, 1977); Cheng Siok-Hwa, *The Rice Industry in Burma, 1852–1940* (Kuala Lumpur: University of Malay Press, 1968); Thee Kian Wie, *Plantation Agriculture and Export Growth: An Economic History of East Sumatra, 1863–1942* (Jakarta: LIPI, 1977).

7. W. J. O'Malley, "Indonesia in the Great Depression: A Study of East Sumatra and Jogjakarta in the 1930s" (Ph.D. diss., Cornell University, 1977); R. E. Elson, *Javanese Peasants and the Colonial Sugar Industry*

(Singapore: Oxford University Press, 1984), and *Village Java under the Cultivation System, 1830–1870* (Sydney: Allen and Unwin, 1994); G. R. Knight, *Colonial Production in Provincial Java: The Sugar Industry in Pekalongan-Tegal, 1800–1942* (Amsterdam: VU University Press, 1993); Djoko Suryo, "Social and Economic Life in Rural Semarang under Colonial Rule in the Late Nineteenth Century" (Ph.D. thesis, Monash University, 1982); M. R. Fernando, "Peasants and Plantation Economy" (Ph.D. thesis, Monash University, 1982); P. Boomgaard, *Children of the Colonial State: Population Growth and Economic Development in Java, 1795-1880* (Amsterdam: Free University Press, 1989); N. G. Owen, *Prosperity without Progress* (Berkeley: University of California Press, 1984).

8. Boomgaard's study of Java's population in the middle decades of the nineteenth century is by far the most radical study in which sophisticated methods are used with varying degrees of success. He is unfortunately obsessed with arriving at precise measurements, something impossible to do with the kind of raw data available, and his exposition is so obtuse as to confuse the reader. These problems have probably discouraged other scholars from undertaking any rigorous analysis of population statistics for Indonesia before 1930. P. C. Smith's study of crisis mortality in the Philippines in the mid-1840s is in contrast a model of its kind. Smith, "Crisis Mortality in the Nineteenth-Century Philippines: Data from Parish Records," *Journal of Asian Studies* 38, 1 (1978): 51–76.

9. A. Booth, "The Economic Development of Southeast Asia, 1870–1985," *Australian Economic History Review* 31, 1 (1991): 20–52.

10. Pierre van der Eng, *Agricultural Growth in Indonesia since 1880* (Groningen: Rijksuniversiteit, 1993).

11. V. Lieberman's fascinating study of Burma after 1440 attests to the existence of quantitative evidence on economic affairs in Burma during the early modern period. Lieberman, *Burmese Administrative Cycles: Anarchy and Conquest, c. 1580–1760* (Princeton: Princeton University Press, 1984).

12. The problems involved in the demographic history of Southeast Asia are explained at length in N. G. Owen, "The Paradox of Nineteenth-Century Population Growth in Southeast Asia: Evidence from Java and the Philippines," *Journal of Southeast Asian Studies* 18, 1 (1987): 45–57.

13. The vast corpus of statistical material in print covering all parts of Southeast Asia from the mid-nineteenth century onward is admirably annotated in J. Brewster, ed., *Bibliography of Statistical Sources on Southeast Asia, c. 1750–1990* (Canberra: Australian National University, Research School of Pacific Studies, 1990).

14. The only surviving records of the Dutch reformed church in Melaka are now preserved in the National Archives of Malaysia and microfilm

copies of them are also available in the libraries of the University of Malaya and Singapore National University.

15. The subject matter is discussed at length in E. A. Wrigley et al., eds., *English Population History from Family Reconstruction, 1580–1837,* 2d ed. (Cambridge: Cambridge University Press, 1997), a major work on demographic history of Europe that sets new standards.

16. The records of the civic administration of Melaka town, for instance, provide a wealth of information to write about Europeans and Eurasians in Melaka town in the second half of the eighteenth and early decades of the nineteenth centuries. These papers, now deposited in the British Library, are admirably inventoried in I. Baxter, "Dutch Records from Malacca in the India Office Records," *Journal of Malaysian Branch of Royal Asiatic Society* 56, 2 (1983): 105–33.

17. Elson, *Javanese Peasants,* "Sugar Factory Workers and the Emergence of 'Free Labor' in Nineteenth-Century Java," *Modern Asian Studies* 20, 1 (1986): 139–74, and *Village Java;* G. R. Knight, "From Plantation to Padifield: The Origins of the Nineteenth-Century Transformation of Java's Sugar Industry," *Modern Asian Studies* 14, 2 (1980):177–204, "Peasant Labor and Capitalist Production in Late Colonial Indonesia: The 'Ca'paign' at a North Javanese Sugar Factory," *Journal of Southeast Asian Studies* 19, 2 (1988): 245–65, and "The Peasantry and the Cultivation of Sugar Cane in Nineteenth-Century Java: A Study from Pekalongan Residency, 1830–1870," in *Indonesian Economic History in the Dutch Colonial Era,* ed. A. Booth, W. J. O'Malley, and A. Weideman, Yale University Southeast Asia Studies, no. 35 (New Haven: Yale University Press, 1990), 49–66; Suryo, "Social and Economic Life"; M. R. Fernando, "Growth of Non-Agricultural Economic Activities in Java in the Middle Decades of the Nineteenth Century," *Modern Asian Studies* 30, 1 (1996): 77–119.

18. G. H. van Soest, *Geschiedenis van het kultuurstelsel,* 3 vols. (Rotterdam: H. Nijgh, 1869–1871).

19. C. Geertz, *Agricultural Involution* (Berkeley: University of California Press, 1963).

20. Elson, *Village Java.*

21. Ibid., 255–77; Fernando, "Non-Agricultural Economic Activities."

22. Fernando, "Non-Agricultural Economic Activities," 106–7.

23. P. Creutzberg and P. Boomgaard, eds., *Changing Economy in Indonesia,* 16 vols. (Amsterdam: KIT, 1975–96).

24. K. Ohkawa and P. Shinohara, *Patterns of Japanese Economic Development: A Quantitative Appraisal* (New Haven: Yale University Press, 1979).

25. B. White, "Demand for Labor and Population Growth in Colonial Java," *Human Ecology* 1, 3 (1973): 217–36. The volume on population in

Creutzberg and Boomgaard, *Changing Economy in Indonesia,* appeared in 1991.

26. R. van Niel, *Java under the Cultivation System* (Leiden: KILTV, 1992), 61–86; M. R. Fernando, "Peasants and Plantation Economy" (Ph.D. thesis, Monash University, 1982), 96–107, 157–64; Elson, *Village Java,* 162–70.

27. Fernando, "Non-Agricultural Economic Activities," 104–5.

28. A. Booth, *Agricultural Development in Indonesia* (Sydney: Allen and Unwin, 1988); Eng, *Agricultural Growth.*

29. Soest, *Geschiedenis van het kultuurstelsel,* 3:165–222; G. Gongrijp, *Schets eener economische geschiedenis van Indonesie* (Haarlem: F. Bohn, 1957), 102–4.

30. Fernando, "Peasants and Plantation Economy," 192–235; R. E. Elson, "The Famine in Demak and Grobogan in 1849–1850: Its Causes and Circumstances," *Review of Indonesian and Malaysian Affairs* 19, 1 (1985): 39–85.

31. P. Boomgaard, *Children of the Colonial State,* 96–101; Elson, *Village Java,* 301–17.

32. Reid, *Expansion and Crisis;* Lieberman, "Local Integration."

33. Nguyen Thanh-Nha, *Tableau économique du Vietnam aux dix-septième et dix-huitième siècles* (Paris: Cujas, 1970); V. Lieberman, *Burmese Administrative Cycles: Anarchy and Conquest, c. 1580–1760;* W. Koenig, *The Burmese Polity, 1752–1819: A Study of Kon Baung Politics, Administration, and Social Organization* (Ann Arbor: Center for South and Southeast Asian Studies, University of Michigan, 1990); Charnvit Kasetsiri, *The Rise of Ayuthia* (Kuala Lumpur: Oxford University Press, 1976); A. Reid, ed., *The Last Stand of Asian Autonomies* (London: Macmillan, 1998); L. Nagtegaal, *Riding the Dutch Tiger* (Leiden: KILTV, 1996).

34. H. Sutherland, "Trade in VOC Indonesia: The Case of Makassar," in *Regions and Regional Developments in the Malay-Indonesian World,* ed. Bernhard Dahm, 45–62 (Wiesbaden: Otto Harrassowitz, 1992); Sutherland and D. S. Brée, "Quantitative and Qualitative Approaches to the Study of Indonesian Trade: The Case of Makassar," in *Dari babad dan hikayat sampai sejarah kritis,* ed. T. Ibrahim Alfian, H. J. Soesoemanto, Dharmono Hardjowidjono, and Djoko Suryo (Yogyakarta: Gadjah Mada University Press, 1987), 369–408; Lee Kam Hing, "The Shipping Lists of Dutch Melaka: A Source for the Study of Coastal Trade and Shipping in the Malay Peninsula during the Seventeenth and Eighteenth Centuries," in *Kapal dan harta karam/Ships and Sunken Treasure,* ed. Mohammad Yusoff Hashim et al. (Kuala Lumpur: Persatuan Muzium Malaysia, 1986), 53–76; G. Knaap, *Shallow Waters, Rising Tide* (Leiden: KILTV, 1996); A. Reid and M. R. Fernando, "Shipping on Melaka and Singapore as an Index of Growth, 1760–1840," *South Asia* 19 (special issue, 1996): 59–84.

35. Data supporting this view are given in Reid and Fernando, "Shipping on Melaka and Singapore," 66–67.

36. F. Braudel, *Civilization and Capitalism, Fifteenth–Eighteenth Century*, 3 vols. (London: Collins, 1981–84); S. Schama, *The Embarrassment of Riches* (London: Fontana, 1987).

37. Reid, *Age of Commerce, 1450–1680, The Lands below the Winds*, 1–31; Lieberman, "Local Integration," 488–505.

38. D. Bulbeck, A. Reid, and Lay Cheng Tan, *Southeast Asian Exports since the Fourteenth Century* (Singapore: Institute of Southeast Asian Studies, 1998).

Chapter 4

SOUTHEAST ASIAN HISTORY, LITERARY THEORY, AND CHAOS

YONG MUN CHEONG

MORE THAN TWO DECADES AGO, the borders between history and other disciplines had already begun to blur. Like political science and sociology, history was interested not only in *what* had happened but also in some classification of the types of events that had happened. History seemed to be different from political science or sociology because history was more interested in past events and processes whereas political science and sociology concentrated on present events and processes. But even this distinction between an interest in the past and the present was becoming blurred.

Among the disciplines, history has been the least reluctant to cross boundaries, and borrow shamelessly from other disciplines, to explore the past. Historians of Southeast Asia were inclined to try a range of different methods to get a handle on the history of the societies they were trying to understand. This perhaps is also true of other disciplines but it is a particularly distinctive feature of history for two reasons:

- The past is so nebulous, so unknown, and unknowable, that historians need to adopt the methods of other disciplines in order to exploit all possible means to understand the past.

- There is a certain porosity in the disciplinary boundaries of history that encourages historians to make forays in all directions. After all, the past studied by the historian is not the monopoly of only one person.

Southeast Asian history has accumulated a huge debt in the intellectual exchange with other disciplines. It would appear that the balance is not in history's favor, as historians have borrowed more than they have contributed as far as theory and methodology are concerned. From cultural anthropology, in the footsteps of Geertz's *Agricultural Involution,* historians learned how Dutch policy could be studied in terms of its impact on colonial Java. From political science, historians borrowed J. S. Furnivall's concept of a plural society, and from sociology, historians found the Weberian concept of ideal types useful in reconstructing the trading patterns of the past. Coming closer to the contemporary scene, historians have relied on studies by political economists for a better understanding of the capitalist transformation of Southeast Asia.

The question now is whether historians can ever claim to understand Southeast Asian societies using purely archival and other documentary sources to the exclusion of contributions from other disciplines. Learning from literary analysis, there is already a growing collection of scholarly works that concentrate on the examination of a whole range of different texts. These include such specialized items as Vietnamese poems written in the fourteenth century, inscriptions and oral histories passed down through the ages, as well as nonliterary texts such as pamphlets, posters, and even advertisements. Many outstanding recent historical studies on Southeast Asia bear the trademark influences of literary theory, postmodernism, poststructuralism, critical theory, and the new humanities. In his survey of Southeast Asian history in the *Cambridge History of Southeast Asia,* John Legge has listed some examples, citing in particular authors like Anthony Day, Shelly Errington, Anthony Milner, and James Siegel.[1] In this chapter, the term *literary theory* will denote this genre of work.

Literary theory has raised fundamental questions about historical research. Historians used to be able to assert confidently that they could achieve an understanding of the past based only on documentary sources. But literary theory has raised serious doubts as to whether this is possible. Historians of Southeast Asia and other parts of the world have begun to revisit their primary sources and ask whether it is really possible to reconstruct the past from those sources. According to literary theory, the source materials used by historians are mainly texts, consisting largely of arrangements of words. These arrangements of words, and the words themselves, can possess different meanings in different contexts to different people. Hence, the truth about the past is more elusive than the historian thinks. Texts, of course, extend beyond documentary sources and can include interviews, songs, folktales, and other performance arts. The study of texts thus broadens into what is now termed cultural studies. The challenges from literary theory are complex and arguments about how literary theory impacts upon history are often difficult to understand. Nevertheless, few historians can ignore these challenges.

To illustrate that words are anchored to contexts and cannot be divorced from them, I offer the problem of deciding whether Funan was the first state founded in Southeast Asia.[2] This seemingly innocuous question was usually answered in the affirmative in general textbooks on Southeast Asia because the word *state* was usually understood to connote a degree of trade relations, a wet-rice economy, some technological innovations, an increasing population density, and political centralization. To varying degrees, these were characteristic of Funan. But ask a Chinese ruler in the period before the Christian era and he would add that a state would, by definition, embrace rules of dynastic succession and a defined territorial space.

Words such as *state* are signifiers that are anchored in cultural contexts. Used in different times, by different persons, inside or outside Southeast Asia, *state* carries different connotations and can convey different meanings. In determining whether Funan was the first polity to bear the characteristics of a state, historians faced the danger of working from a vocabulary drawn from external criteria. A literary theory approach provides an opportunity to question afresh previously unchallenged assertions, forcing historians to pause longer before passing judgment. Of course, literary theory cannot provide an answer to the question whether Funan was the first state in Southeast Asia. What it does is to wave red flags of warning against the unquestioning acceptance of past assumptions when ambiguity should be the order of the day.

The use of the word *state* by historians of Southeast Asia is only one example. In the same way, a literary theorist would argue that the languages of ethnicity, community, or nationalism, so commonly employed by historians who do not see them as problematic, are arbitrary tools used to dissect society. They can even be artificial constructions that disguise the fundamentals of a society. Such historical categories had to be reinvented in response to new ideological challenges and social change. Using these categories without questioning their cultural meanings would force the past into a rigid teleological narrative, whereas the past could, in effect, disperse into a variety of historical outcomes at every stage if freed from the confines of the boundaries imposed by such categories.

Help is specially needed to understand the meanings of a whole new set of jargon that has entered the vocabulary of scholarly discussions, history included. At seminars and in publications, participants use phrases like *privileging one group against another, decentering the subject, otherizing one segment of society, deconstruction, closer study of the text,* and of course, the much overworked word *discourse.* What do these terms, which come from the language of literary theory, mean? Often, attempts to understand analyses of Southeast Asia from the standpoint of literary theory have been fruitless. Sometimes, one can only come to conclusions such as the following: the arguments are too difficult to understand; traditional questions, such as what happened and why, seem to have been passed over in favor of others such as, What are the structures of experience?; primary sources are deemed unlikely to provide answers to the questions of traditional history; simple explanations are set aside in favor of more complex ones; and abundance, or the need to produce more knowledge about the past, seems to be out of favor. Instead, the flavor of the month is squeezing all texts for more questions, more complex and abstract interpretations.

Can Primary Sources Reveal the Past?

An attempt to understand the influence of literary theory can begin with the brief but significant debate that appeared in the pages of *Kajian Malaysia* in 1987. Anthony Milner, one of the contributors to the debate, commented that studies of British colonial Malaya were "dated" or "out-of-date" because they were colonial in their preoccupation and perspectives.[3] Such studies were "colonial" in the sense that they portrayed the British as the "principal actors in the period, the initiators of action" when in fact Malay-British relations were much more complex. The history of British colonial Malaya was history written "from above" and "from outside." Whether Malay actors and initiators entered British colonial history depended on whether they made an impact on the civil servants who wrote the reports that were subsequently deposited in the archives. The historian who depends on such primary sources has to beware. The civil servant chronicler viewed the world around him (it was hardly ever "her") through the "prism of his own bureaucratic network." The progenitors of change, if there were thought to be any, would come from within that bureaucratic network and not any outside agency. By extension, these reports tended to influence the kind of questions that inspired the history research enterprise. This conferred tremendous influence upon the civil servant chronicler who could unknowingly dictate the kind of history that was written using those sources.[4] The same argument can be extended to the reports generated by civil servant chroniclers in other colonial territories (e.g., the *Memories van Overgave* or the political reports of the Netherlands East Indies).

Milner's propositions can be understood better if set against intellectual changes enveloping the world. Today more and more historians are being won over to the view that history has much to learn from literature and vice versa. This is a broad and progressive view of interdisciplinary cooperation but from an earlier, perhaps more narrow, scientific and rational worldview, the relationship between history and literature was thought to be the same as that between facts and imagination. It was thought that history is factual, should be built on a foundation of facts, and these facts were to be found not in literature but mainly in the colonial records, which provided modern and rational accounts. Other kinds of primary sources, such as Southeast Asian chronicles, tended to be classified into the category of literature as they were more concerned with the affairs of the other world than this world. They were creative and imaginative.

In fact, this distinction between history and literature is invalid. All records, whether classified as historical or literary, should be subjected to the same standards of analysis. For example, regardless of whether a source is a colonial document or a chronicle, the historian would have to ask, What were the intentions of the author when writing the record or chronicle? Who was the intended audience? Was there other, contradictory evidence to the data in the record? How far removed was the writer from the events he was reporting? What were the vested interests in the production of the report or chronicle?

Milner has recommended that the colonial records can still be used but in addition to reading them in the conventional way, they must also be read against the grain. By this he meant the development of an independent vantage point from which to approach the colonial records. One supposes that this vantage point could be developed from social science concepts and sociological paradigms, an understanding of semiotics, using such common historical categories as nationalism and knowledge of precolonial political and social structures.

Such comments on the British and other colonial records have arisen because of relatively recent doubts about the veracity and reliability of the colonial records that have been stimulated by arguments within literary theory. A thought arises. Can the thousands of meters of colonial records be considered less reliable because they were constructed from a bureaucratic perspective? Sometimes one senses that those who were less confident about the reliability of colonial records may also be those who were less patient about painstakingly leafing through the thousands of reams of colonial archives. To be fair to those who still depend on the colonial records, there has never been wholesale confidence in their reliability. It would be a naive oversimplification to think that historians using archival sources rely on them without checking their reliability. The reliability check can consist of internal consistency as well as compatibility with noncolonial records.

One possible response to the warning about the reliability of colonial records is to ignore it and carry on with business as usual. After all, at the end of the day, when the research is completed, whatever conclusions are drawn about the past can only be considered tentative. They are only accepted as true based on the arguments presented on their behalf. There follows a process of argumentation that is part of seeking the truth about the past, a built-in validation. When new evidence becomes available, the earlier conclusions about the past have to be revised.

A different question to pose would be, What kind of history would be written if a historian were not "shackled" or "imprisoned" by colonial records? Is the concept of a British Malayan history an artificial construct, invented to handle that field intellectually? Still, there was indeed a period of time when a British Malaya existed, and so a British Malayan history was worthy of the name. Other constructs within the same framework would include Federated Malay States and Unfederated Malay States, decentralization, and any other categories that may be used to organize the information found in documents.

Two propositions can be identified from the *Kajian Malaysia* discussions:

- The colonial records not only set the agenda for the historian's research, they dictate the questions.
- The reliability or unreliability of the colonial records cannot be attested to by reference to noncolonial records or a study of the values embedded in the records. Questions about their reliability go to the root of the history enterprise by raising doubts about whether primary sources can be the basis of truth claims that historians make about the past.

History and Literary Theory

What has been the impact of literary theory on Southeast Asian historiography? Although this impact became ubiquitous from the late 1970s onward, its first signs can be traced back to the 1950s, when C. C. Berg, writing about Javanese history, raised some issues concerning the use of a particular text, the fourteenth-century court chronicle the *Negarakertagama,* to understand the history of the Majapahit Empire.[5] Berg was reacting to the practice of prewar Dutch scholarship that relied on chronicles to provide evidence for an actual reality rooted in the past. It was then assumed that such chronicles, if subjected to rigorous internal criticism, could reveal the history of the Majapahit Empire because they contained a modicum of facts. If the mythical elements could be sieved out, the rest could be used. Berg argued that this was the wrong way to use the chronicle. The *Negarakertagama* should be recognized for what it was; it served a magical function by bestowing legitimacy on rulers and transmitting a desired world order. Thus, for example, it was wrong to depend on the *Negarakertagama* for geographic place names to illustrate the extent of the Majapahit Empire. Rather, the *Negarakertagama* merely displayed the geographic knowledge of the author. Berg's work, however, was just an initial stab, as he still worked within the underlying assumption that the past was knowable. Whether historical reality could be uncovered was not an issue. Later historians of Southeast Asia were to raise more fundamental questions about how primary sources, including texts such as chronicles, should be treated.

Following the arguments of literary theory, the primary sources of historians can all be regarded as texts. As texts, they should be studied in terms of their content, their internal consistency, and their relation to other pieces of evidence. But, as texts, Southeast Asian chronicles, literatures, inscriptions, and colonial records should also be treated from the angle of literary theory. And what is that angle? It is none other than the need to deconstruct them to reveal the inner structures that would throw light on how Southeast Asian societies regarded themselves. This can be achieved because the language used in the texts provides the key to understanding the worldview of the writers of these texts. By studying the signs embedded in this language, it is possible to crack the codes in which the meanings are hidden. Using more simple English, one could say that words are not univocal. Each word does not possess only one meaning that is universally known and acknowledged. It is unlikely that a word has no other meaning. Language shapes meaning even as the language is being articulated in speech and writing.[6] Following this mode of thought, there have been studies of Javanese concepts of time, prophecy, and change, Acehnese historical thinking, and political concepts in Malay texts. In the same vein, the methods used to analyze classical chronicles on Southeast Asia should also apply to the Dutch East India Company (VOC) and British colonial records.

An interesting example of how literary theory began to shape the historian's inquiry into the past is Shelly Errington's work on Malay literary texts.[7] He has raised some interesting questions that can be cited as examples of the impact of literary theory on the writing of history. For example, he asked, when translating passages of the Hikayat Hang Tuah into English, what tense should be used? Should the translator use the simple past tense, the present perfect, the future perfect, or the future perfect conditional? For the uninitiated, these ponderings over the different components of English grammar might seem meaningless. However, the questions revealed how a translator, or a historian of Southeast Asia, may impose a temporal relationship between events where there is no evidence that this relationship exists in the text to be translated and annotated.

To take the questions a step further, it is only necessary to open a publication on Southeast Asian history to note how the time element is interwoven into the writings. Phrases like the following are often used: *after that, after some time, after a while, meanwhile*. A historian can only write about *meanwhile* if there is some distance between the historian and the event being described. One might ask whether the *meanwhile* is an artificial intrusion on the part of the historian into the past?

In *The Invention of Politics in Colonial Malaya,* Anthony Milner analyzes Ibrahim Yaacob's *Surveying the Homeland,* (1941), a left-wing analysis of Malay society on the eve of the Japanese invasion.[8] It is also a record of his lecture tour and it is possible to use *Surveying the Homeland* to learn about how the Malays in a particular context were accumulating more knowledge about the past. Yaacob's book explained that the Malays were "jostled" or "pressured" by the invasion of foreign capital, foreign goods, and foreign labor; they were losing land to non-Malays; they were forced out of the markets; along the Pahang River or in Kedah, Malays could not compete with the Chinese. The number of Malays with no work at all increased year by year. These are all substantive bits of knowledge that can be obtained from the text.

However, Milner's analysis of *Surveying the Homeland* went beyond the conventional objective of accumulation of information from a given text. His purpose was not only to discover the anticolonial, anti-imperialist *content* of what Ibrahim Yaacob wrote but also to uncover the anticolonial, anti-imperialist content through dissecting the *form* of writing. And it was at this level that Milner entered a kind of no-man's-land where historians had previously feared to tread, provoking unease or critical comments from other scholars.[9] For example, Milner attempts to deconstruct the meaning of *sedar* (aware), arguing that Ibrahim Yaacob's lecture tour can be regarded as a text designed to make the Malays aware of their emerging nation. It was assumed that the audience listened to the speeches and that by listening the Malays were becoming aware. Milner suggests that the audience was not merely learning awareness from the content of the speeches but also from their style.[10]

Milner notes that *Surveying the Homeland* did not stress religious piety. There were no references to Allah or quotations from the Qur'an. Nor was Allah invoked in the presentation of the text. This was a sharp departure from the common practice of most Malay speakers or writers when introducing their subject. In fact, Ibrahim Yaacob claimed that the book was a gift to the Malay people in the same way that the Malay sultan would make a gift to his subjects when he deigned to take notice. Ibrahim Yaacob thanked all the people who helped him gather the materials for his speeches, including the Tengkus, Rajas, Datuks, Tuans, Inchis, friends and comrades, all in one breath without distinguishing the highly placed from the lowly. This too was a violation of Malay convention. The familiar form, *saya* (I), was used when addressing royalty. The sharp analysis and rational presentation of Ibrahim Yaacob's speeches would also have served as a model for debate and discussion in the growing public sphere. We should note that this mode of analysis includes a study of *silences,* of what Ibrahim Yaacob did not say or do. Historians may balk at having to study the silences as well as the utterances. The latter can be analyzed, but can the former?

These examples demonstrate the range of responses adopted by historians when reacting to the influence of literary theory. These features are not peculiar to Southeast Asian history but, taken together, they can point the way to new research on the region.

First, it would appear that new reading strategies are needed to incorporate literary theory analysis into history. Broadly speaking, the strategies form an intellectual journey with three stages. The first stage starts from within the text. In the second stage, moving outside the text, the focus falls on the circumstances in which the text was generated. In the third stage, the historian returns to the text itself.

During the first stage, the historian would ask the following questions: What was the perceived problem to which the text (e.g., a primary document) was the response? What was the intended purpose when the text was generated? How did the author construct the experience that was described in the text? Was there an especially distinctive mode of explanation? Were there strains or weaknesses in the way the explanations and experiences were constructed? Was the author aware of these strains? How did the author perceive his or her role in the generation of the text? What sort of mask did the author don? Did the author assume the persona of a bureaucrat or a chronicler? A representative of an interest group? Was there a sense of detachment? Was there an identifiable mood or tone adopted in the text? Who was the intended audience for the text? What was the audience expected to do after reading the text? How did the text handle the problem of change (which is such an important concern for historians)? Was change treated positively? Or was stability preferred? Was there a single word, phrase, or section that constituted the critical axis around which the entire text rotated? In the second stage, the questions would shift in focus from the text to the author's background. This would include the community or generation of which the author was a member. How did the explanations of the author differ from those of his or her generation and community? Was the author producing the text within a paradigm of knowledge that was implicit even if it was not explicitly stated? Finally, in the third stage, the historian would ask whether the ideas in the text reflect the contemporary issues of the world in which the text was generated.

Reviewing the three stages, it would not be wrong to suspect that the methods of inquiry developed within literary theory were not really new when compared to the methods already used by the historians before the influence of literary theory was felt. When confronted with a text, historians had never felt confined to the contents of the text, only seeking the causes of events and the facts of an external reality. One of the standard approaches had always been to check the internal consistency of a text, and the constant interaction between the historian and his or her sources (or texts) is a hallmark of history writing.

Furthermore, literary theory, when applied to history, can engage the intellectual faculties of any student, from a freshman to a graduate student. At the conference where this essay originated, there was a lively discussion on how history could be made interesting to attract students to a field that is not well known for being hip or cool. When the conference discussion moved to the subject of history teaching, many conferees were able to chip in. The subject acted like a catalyst for enthusiastic contributions. In comparison, only a select few could speak knowledgeably on more specialized topics such as seventeenth-century Phuket or how to conduct subaltern studies in Southeast Asia. Literary theory, too, can be a catalyst, harnessed to stimulate participation and hence "interest" in a history tutorial. By focusing on the structure of the text and concentrating less on the information that can be squeezed out of the text, all students are placed on the same footing with the professor. There is equality because the professor's mastery of detailed content knowledge has to share the stage with noncontent materials. Each student is empowered to voice his or her own take on the structure of the text, using the reading strategy outlined above. The result for the student is more confidence to participate in a history discussion where the mastery of content knowledge is only part of the exercise. This, it seems, would be superior to employing innovative electronic gadgets to boost a lesson in history.

Lingering Problems Posed by Literary Theory

The incorporation of literary theory into historical research and writing introduced a host of problems. It raised doubts whether the historian can ever get at the past. Can the historian ever recover objective, verifiable events? Would he or she be as confident as before? Yet, the answer must be yes because history, as a form of modern scholarship, is based on evidence and the historian must defend with evidence whether a piece of history writing is a true reflection of the past from a valid reading of a text.[11]

What objections do historians have to the arguments mounted by literary theory? Is literary theory the wave of the future? Not necessarily. For example, it is still not definitively accepted that language is a structure that is internally coherent and shapes the external reality, as argued in literary theory. Equally significant is the suspicion that literary theory is applying standards of readings that are developed in twentieth-century Western civilization to literary products of other cultures and earlier centuries. Exponents of literary theory claim a universal applicability for their views. But what about the relevance of geography, culture, society, political and economic background? Historians are naturally concerned because they have always been reading texts in the light of the backgrounds in which the text was generated.

Another direction that Southeast Asian history could take is the road to chaos. To understand the concept of chaos, it is necessary to attempt an understanding of its opposite: the notion of linearity in history. At first sight, this may seem to be a nonissue. Historians deal with time, often taking it for granted. Time is linear. It cannot be otherwise. The arrow of time flies on and on and history is reconstructed on that assumption.

Many years ago, when Southeast Asia first became a recognizable field of study, the term *linear* was still not discussed in a serious way. In the 1960s H. J. Benda hinted at the linear progress of time but did not elaborate to any extent. In 1979 there appeared a publication on the Southeast Asian conception of time.[12] In the 1990s linear time has regained more attention and might even begin to affect the way historians of Southeast Asia write their history. Two examples of how linearity was treated will suffice.

The first relates to the reaction of Thai historians, after 1973, to royalist national history. Instead of viewing Thai history as a linear path from Sukothai to Bangkok, one Thai historian, Srisak Vallibhotama, proposed a history of interactions between human settlements and the environment that occurred simultaneously in many places.[13]

The second relates to Rey Ileto's criticism of a linear emplotment of Philippines history. In this emplotment, Filipino history was written by *ilustrado* historians, for whom history was a movement from a golden past to a tragic fall (when the country was placed under colonial control), then to an age of revival (nationalism), followed by independence and nation building. In such a linear account, binary classifications tended to prevail. Filipino history progressed linearly from primitive to modern, from religious to secular, from fanatical to rational or programmatic. This ilustrado account was little more than a construction of reality based on the axis of progress and modernity. It was not necessarily a "true" view. Therefore it shared the same status as the constructed reality of the native millennial movements, which had been consigned within linear accounts to the primitive, religious, and fanatical. The only difference was that the ilustrado construction of linear history was regarded as upheld by "current standards of objectivity and truth."[14] According to Ileto, such linear history consigns much data to the margin and an alternative history was needed to rescue such data to allow historians to challenge the "dominant constructs."[15]

It is likely that other historians of Southeast Asia have also used the concepts of linearity in their writings. Linearity could also have been so subconsciously ingrained in the historian's psyche that it has become a dominant paradigm. In contrast, there is a raging controversy in the physical sciences over the concepts of linearity and nonlinearity. The earlier linear world of Newton appears to have been nudged from center stage to make space for the nonlinear world of chaos theory.

Chaos theory has many components that could affect the way history is studied and written. The common meaning of chaos is breakdown or confusion. By definition, chaos is unpredictable behavior. An example of unpredictability relevant for history research is summarized in the phrase "minor actions, major consequences." A particular event or act, though minor, may be the proverbial straw that broke the camel's back, resulting in a catastrophic collapse of the camel. Put simply, one of the central planks of chaos theory is that effects are disproportionate to the cause.[16]

Another component of chaos that is relevant for history is feedback. In human societies, feedback occurs widely, enabling people to respond rapidly to life-threatening events to ensure survival. Chaos theory suggests that there are two kinds of feedback: positive, or change enhancing, and negative, or change minimizing. When the past is examined in terms of both positive and negative feedback, both types can be seen to coexist in a historical situation.

Negative feedback is change minimizing. The classical scientific example to illustrate this concept is the thermostat in an air-conditioning system. This apparatus maintains room temperature at an even level. When the temperature rises, the air-conditioning equipment is adjusted to inject cool air. When the temperature drops, the cooling system is cut off. Thus negative feedback preserves equilibrium. Stability is maintained. What examples of negative feedback can be found in Southeast Asian history? One is reminded of the attempts by the VOC and the Netherlands East Indies government to maintain their contractual relations with Southeast Asian rulers by preserving trade links and excluding other traders. This policy excluded change. The practice was also called monopoly.

Positive feedback, on the other hand, challenges stability or continuity. It feeds on itself by enhancing further change. In Southeast Asian history, an example of positive feedback can be found in the experiences of the Southeast Asian traders in the free-trade environment promoted by the British in the region. Every time a merchant profited from free trade, the news spread and attracted another to experience the same. The result was a further enhancement of this cascading process of free trade, spreading its tentacles to more areas and creating changes even within monopoly areas in the Netherlands East Indies.

In general, chaos theory has a lot to contribute to the historian's understanding of causation and change. According to chaos theory, causation cannot be explained only in terms of billiards, in which cue sticks hit balls that in turn hit other balls, causing them to fly off in certain more or less predictable directions. In chaos theory, this explanation of causation is considered too mechanistic because the same conditions are expected to produce the same results. An example of such mechanistic causation used in Southeast Asian history, and indeed other histories as well, would be the relationship between the level of poverty, or famine, and the occurrence of revolt. This was a powerful explanation that had served us well in exploring past Southeast Asian revolts. However, according to chaos theory, the billiards analogy is less useful in explaining sudden unexpected transformations to new levels of complexity, big changes that eventually fizzle out or, conversely, puny or chance events that balloon into irresistible forces. This last phenomenon is described in chaos theory as "minor actions, major consequences." One is reminded of how Grotius based his legal justification of Dutch colonial architecture in the seventeenth century solely on the capture of the Portuguese ship *Sta. Catarina* in 1603.[17]

Chance as a form of causation is a thorny and philosophical issue in history. Chaos theory has raised this concept to a central feature in explaining causal relations. Borrowing the concept from chaos theory and applying it to Southeast Asian history is not simply a matter of using chance to explain causes that resist being identified. Chaos theory goes one step further. It attempts to stipulate the precise point at which chance enters a chain of events and makes a contribution. Outside of a laboratory, this precise point may be difficult to identify, but the thought of chance playing a role in causation invites further research. The possibility of chance is important in chaos theory, and in Southeast Asian history, because change enhancers and change minimizers are not built into the past, dating from the origins of an event. Enhancers and minimizers can enter the chain of events at any moment. They can constitute the stray factors or "chance" events.

It might be said that Southeast Asian history has always been full of situations of order as well as chaos. For example, much of classical Southeast Asian history was conceived of as cycles moving from order to chaos and then back again. And if chaos celebrates change, then isn't that what history is about? But that is not the meaning of chaos intended by the physical scientists. Rather than conceiving chaos as the opposite of order or stability, chaos is thought of as extremely complex information. Such information is difficult to classify and analyze and is often represented by sharp angular lines on graphs. Here, there is a danger of labeling any historical situation as chaos because it is too complex to be analyzed. That would be abuse rather than expertise.

At the heart of the physical scientists' idea of chaos is the view that chaos does not end in extinction but moves toward increasing complexity. In this sense, chaos theory resonates with the field of literary theory. The study of chaos penetrates into another domain of reality. It reinforces the literary theory argument that the world that is known is only a constructed reality. This constructed reality was understood using the tools of analysis suitable for data existing in an orderly world. If that reality was constructed, then it can also be deconstructed. Repeatedly, in literary theory, the texts are penetrated to reveal the structures beneath. Similarly, in chaos theory the orderly world is penetrated to reveal the complexities existing beyond.

As yet there is no application of chaos theory to seek new questions that would illuminate the past of Southeast Asia. But chaos theory has been applied to restudy Western history, with interesting results.[18] At one time too, there was no application of literary theory to the study of Southeast Asian history but now, literary theory exercises considerable influence over historiography. Who knows what the future will bring for chaos theory when applied to Southeast Asia?

How will Southeast Asian history develop from here? What will be the impact of literary theory and chaos theory upon Southeast Asian history? One possible road to take could be a review of the way Southeast Asian history has been divided into time periods. The categories used thus far—ancient or classical, early modern, modern (including a category for colonialism), contemporary—all represent constructions of the past that can, should, or need to be deconstructed. Indeed, these are time-based linear categories that serve present-centric perspectives. For the purpose of historiography, historians have selected for Southeast Asians when their modern period should be and what aspects of their societies qualify to be sufficiently dominant for the period to be described as modern. In the same way, historians have selected for Southeast Asians what their classical or golden age should be by discovering the past for them. Historians, it appears, have acted like tyrants in this respect. Discussions of this nature have recently been published in the *Journal of Southeast Asian Studies.*[19]

In an essay on historiography, as this one professes to be, attention naturally falls on those materials that have already been published or have seen the light of day in a conference. However, some of the issues about chaos I have just discussed refer to trends in history writing that have not fully matured yet. Definitely these trends have not yet completely transformed the writing of Southeast Asian history. It is therefore appropriate to identify some of the likely directions that this kind of history research on Southeast Asia can take.

To simplify the somewhat diverse trends of critical theory and chaos theory discussed earlier, it can be stated that the study of complexity has entered the domain of historians, including those specializing in Southeast Asia. Literary theory is about complex societies because it is no longer feasible to uncover the "truth" at the face value of documents that describe those societies. Reality is to be found behind or underneath the level of facts in the documents, and there is no certainty that it can be grasped at all. Chaos theory is also about complexity. It is no longer only a world of cause and effect, as described in traditional histories. The past is also filled with chance, and it is the historian's task to explain how chance fits into the scheme of facts.

When literary theory and chaos theory are applied jointly to the study of Southeast Asian history, the challenges are forbidding. References have been made above to various historians who have attempted to apply literary theory to the study of Southeast Asian literature in order to understand societies better. More will follow in their footsteps. How has chaos theory been applied to Southeast Asian history? As far as can be ascertained, chaos theory is still relatively new to Southeast Asian studies. It is also unlikely that all its dimensions will be equally relevant. However, there are a number of ingredients in chaos theory that can nudge historians of Southeast Asia to review their perspectives of the past. To illustrate these ingredients, it would be useful to suggest a direction in which they can be combined to produce new findings.

In chaos theory, time is not conceived as purely linear. Similarly, space is not necessarily predetermined by the nation-state. Chaos theory also places considerable emphasis on feedback mechanisms. These are some of the ingredients that can be mixed in an interesting research potion. For example, the general historiography of Singapore focuses on its growth from a fishing village to a modern port feeding on international trade, giving a linear path of development par excellence for Singapore's history from the past to the present. Instead, it is also valid to focus on the periods when time either remained "stationary" or even reverted to the past, when traders and merchants conducted business using time-honored practices and along time-honored channels. The focus should also not always be placed on Singapore alone. Singapore should be studied in relation to the surrounding region, including parts of Sumatra, the Riau islands, west Borneo, and indeed any other parts of the former Dutch East Indies, for example Bali and Lombok, that maintained links of all kinds, military or even clandestine, with Singapore.

When this broader, more spatial, view is adopted, the research on Southeast Asia shifts from the nation-state, or former British colonies versus former Dutch-controlled areas, to pieces of territories that may bear no name when grouped together. These are the complexities within history that correspond with some of the ingredients of chaos theory. Finally, the powerful impetus to trade provided by the territories listed above cannot be explained only by the attractions of Singapore's location and its laissez-faire policies. There are also the feedback mechanisms, mostly informal, that linked those territories together. Put simply, it was Batavia that imposed negative feedback measures to contain trade but it was Singapore that invited positive feedback measures to attract the trade.

The details resulting from this kind of research cannot be discussed here. Suffice it to say that the same approach can be applied to other territories and regions in Southeast Asia. It will then be possible to sample the kind of research possibilities that literary theory and chaos theory can offer. In this respect, the future of Southeast Asian studies can be very exciting. At the very least, not only can basic questions be raised about how primary sources should be used in history research. It will be equally important to ask whether literary theory and chaos theory, when applied to history, are only passing fads like the cliometrics trend of the 1960s.

Notes

1. J. D. Legge, "The Writing of Southeast Asian History," in *The Cambridge History of Southeast Asia,* ed. Nicholas Tarling, vol. 1, *From Early Times to c. 1800* (Cambridge: Cambridge University Press, 1992), 48.

2. This question was revisited in O. W. Wolters, *History, Culture, and Region in Southeast Asian Perspectives* (Singapore: Institute of Southeast Asian Studies, 1982), 12–15.

3. A. C. Milner, "Colonial Records History: British Malaya," *Kajian Malaysia* 4, 2 (1986): 2–7.

4. Ibid., passim.

5. This discussion on Berg is based on Legge, "Writing of Southeast Asian History," 46–47.

6. N. Katherine Hayles, introduction ("Complex Dynamics in Literature and Science") to *Chaos and Order: Complex Dynamics in Literature and Science,* ed. N. Katherine Hayles (Chicago: University of Chicago Press, 1991), 1–33.

7. Shelly Errington, "Some Comments on Style in the Meanings of the Past," in *Perceptions of the Past in Southeast Asia,* ed. Anthony Reid and David Marr (Singapore: Heinemann Educational Books Asia, 1979), 26–42.

8. Anthony Milner, *The Invention of Politics in Colonial Malaya: Contesting Nationalism and the Emergence of the Public Sphere* (Cambridge: Cambridge University Press, 1994).

9. See review of Milner's book by Cheah Boon Kheng, *New Straits Times,* 5 October 1996, 9; and the brief comment in A. B. Shamsul, "Debating about Identity in Malaysia: A Discourse Analysis," in *Cultural Contestations: Mediating Identities in a Changing Malaysian Society,* ed. Zawawi Ibrahim (London: ASEAN Academic Press, 1998), 42 n 8.

10. Milner, *Invention of Politics,* 258, 262, 266.

11. J. D. Legge, "Clio and Her Neighbors: Reflections on History's Relations with the Surrounding Disciplines," in *Dari babad dan hikayat sampai sejarah kritis: Kumpulan karangan dipersembahkan kepada Prof. Dr. Sartono Kartodirdjo* (From chronicles and tales to critical history: Collection of essays in honor of Professor Dr. Sartono Kartodirdjo)*,* ed. T. Ibrahim Alfian, H. J. Koesoemanto, Dharmono Hardjowidjono, and Djoko Suryo (Yogyakarta Gadjah Mada University Press, 1987), 331–50.

12. Anthony Reid and David Marr, eds., *Perceptions of the Past in Southeast Asia* (Singapore: Heinemann Educational Books, 1979).

13. See Thongchai Winichakul, "The Changing Landscape of the Past: New Histories in Thailand since 1973," *Journal of Southeast Asian Studies* 26, 1 (1995): 109.

14. Reynaldo C. Ileto, "Outlines of a Nonlinear Emplotment of Philippine History," in *The Politics of Culture in the Shadow of Capital,* ed. Lisa Lowe and David Lloyd (Durham: Duke University Press, 1997), 121.

15. Ibid., 99. See also Reynaldo C. Ileto, *Critical Questions on Nationalism: A Historian's View,* Professorial Chair Lecture 3 (Manila: De La Salle University, 1986), 8

16. Michael Aung-Thwin, "The 'Classical' in Southeast Asia: The Present in the Past," *Journal of Southeast Asian Studies* 26, 1 (1995): 90. A

very interesting point is raised: whether the Mongol invasion during the thirteenth century created a crisis in Southeast Asia.

17. Peter Boschberg, "Hugo Grotius, East India Trade, and the King of Johor," *Journal of Southeast Asian Studies* 30, 2 (1999): 225–48.

18. See for example, A. M. Saperstein, "Chaos: A Model for the Outbreak of War," *Nature* 309, 24 (1984): 303–5.

19. Aung-Thwin, "'Classical' in Southeast Asia," 86.

Chapter 5

COUNTRY HISTORIES AND THE WRITING OF SOUTHEAST ASIAN HISTORY

Paul H. Kratoska

Much of the historical writing on Southeast Asia falls within the category of country histories. Since the nation-states in the region only came into being after 1945, such histories generally deal with prior events in the territories that modern countries occupy and the processes that brought them into being. The purpose of this chapter is to discuss some of the strengths and limitations of approaching Southeast Asian history from a country perspective and to suggest how the history of the region might look if written on a different basis. Before turning to these issues, however, it will be useful to consider why country-based histories of Southeast Asia are so pervasive.

The Prevalence of Country-Based History

In part the country approach has dominated the writing of history in Southeast Asia for practical reasons. First, few historians have the linguistic capability to do in-depth research on more than one or two countries. Second, the greater part of the archival record has been assembled by the former colonial powers and the nation-states that succeeded them, and source materials are therefore organized along country lines. Third, universities tend to employ historians on the basis of particular country specialties rather than general knowledge of the region. And finally, books written as country histories suit the needs of publishers looking for titles with readily defined markets.

For professional historians, country studies fulfill yet another objective, in that they concern local rather than foreign institutions and historical figures. The pre-independence writings of J. C. van Leur called for a shift in perspective from the study of Europeans in Asia to a study of Asia itself, and he inspired the postwar generation of historians working on Southeast Asia to make the activities of the indigenous populations of the region their primary focus.[1] A landmark article that appeared in the early 1960s, John R. W. Smail's piece in the newly established *Journal of Southeast Asian History* calling for an "autonomous" history of Southeast Asia, revitalized this effort.[2] Smail's concept of autonomous history similarly departed from the focus on European affairs that had prevailed during the colonial period, although he suggested an approach that was neither Western nor local.

Neither van Leur nor Smail advocated country histories as the solution for the issues they raised. The work of van Leur was written and published in Dutch prior to 1940 but became available to a wider audience in 1955, when a selection of his writings appeared in translation under the title *Indonesian Trade and Society*. The term *Indonesia* appears in titles in that collection ("On the Study of Indonesian History," "On the Eighteenth Century as a Category in Indonesian History") and at numerous points in the text. Writing in the 1930s, van Leur himself did not use the politically charged Indonesia, and in their original form the titles cited above referred to the Indies.[3] The translation was published after Indonesian independence and the change in terminology no doubt seemed both appropriate and desirable, particularly for material that emphasized a local as opposed to a European orientation. However, it shifted the focus from the people living in a loosely defined region to a political entity with clearly defined borders.

Although the goal of writing non-European history inspired the postwar generation of historians, and in the eyes of many students of the region became the only legitimate objective, it was not entirely clear how that goal was to be attained. Did an autonomous, or an indigenous, history require new techniques and if so, what were they? Could both foreigners and local historians, trained at foreign institutions and using the methodology of the historical profession at large, produce such histories?[4] Answers to these questions proved elusive and contentious. John Bastin, writing of van Leur's influence shortly before the appearance of Smail's article, commented that the task of producing "a revolutionary reappraisal of existing historical methods and techniques, and of existing historical concepts and periodization" was "fraught with so many difficulties and hazards that it remains unattempted." He also warned that "a neat deception has been perpetrated by a number of historians who, by concentrating their attention on the evils of Western colonialism in Asia, have come to convince themselves, and their audience, that they have escaped the Europe-centric habit, and succeeded in interpreting Asian history from an Asian viewpoint."[5]

Scholars within the region seized the opportunity offered by independence to write their own national histories and used a wide variety of tools to reassess the colonial state and its opponents. Drawing on theoretical approaches derived from sources as diverse as Max Weber, Karl Marx, Antonio Gramsci, and Michel Foucault, historians of Southeast Asia have examined precolonial state and society, the antecedents of new national states, and hitherto neglected sectors of society such as women, workers, and peasants. But in doing so they have simply followed general trends in historical studies throughout the world. The question of what local history might be, beyond history as drafted by local writers, was left unresolved. However, if the methodology remained to be worked out, an ideal subject matter for an autochthonous, or an autonomous, history seemed to be at hand in the form of the newly independent nation-states of Southeast Asia. Historians portrayed the nation-state as the product of local rather than colonial endeavor, and the success of the nation-state in itself seemed to demonstrate the fallacy of derogatory colonial views concerning the abilities of Southeast Asian peoples. Moreover, studies of the antecedents of the nation-state offered an opportunity to highlight abuses associated with colonial rule, as well as an array of positive achievements by local people that could inspire pride and loyalty among newly enfranchised citizens.

By placing the newly independent states of the region within trajectories of past events, by describing local historical figures whose lives were worthy of study and emulation, and by correcting errors and fallacies in histories written from a colonial perspective, historians became part of a process of nation building. Country histories, written from such a perspective, sometimes coalesced into national or nationalistic histories and occasionally moved into the realm of ideology and hagiography. Most, however, remained empirically grounded and followed established historical methodology in the Western tradition. This work was valuable and important, and the purpose of the present chapter is not to attack the achievements of history written in this mode, but rather to consider some of its weaknesses and to question what seems to be an excessive preoccupation with country-oriented history.

The Past as It Was and How the Present Came to Be

Insofar as an objective of historical writing is to show how the present came to be, country histories are a useful tool for understanding the past. With regard to a second task of history, showing the past as it was, country histories are less successful, for the process of selecting the sequence of events that resulted in the creation of a nation-state often involves disregarding events and circumstances that led in other directions.

The alternatives to country history include studies built around particular topics, or based on units of study other than the territories controlled by modern states. The value of noncountry approaches can be illustrated by examining subjects that have had considerable significance in the second half of the twentieth century but are poorly explained within the country approach. I will touch briefly on five issues: colonialism, political entities that did not form part of the lineage of modern states, minorities, alternatives to the modern nation-state, and economic and social patterns that transcend individual states.

Colonialism

Country histories tend to portray colonialism from a nationalist perspective, as an enemy to be overcome rather than a system to be understood. Attention focuses on foreigners who lived and worked in colonial territories, on extractive mechanisms that directed profits from trade and industry to Europe or America, on the exploitation of local farmers and local or immigrant laborers, and on the struggle to overcome this system. Such an approach omits many crucial features of the period of colonial rule, and, ironically for revisionist history in the spirit of van Leur and Smail, it reflects a continuing preoccupation with the activities of foreigners and a corresponding neglect of local activity. It is rare to find in these accounts a discussion of the administrative arrangements of colonialism, a staple feature in accounts written before independence,[6] even though many colonial institutions still survive. It is equally rare to find a discussion of local elements in the "colonial" system, even though local collaborators were crucial to the success of the colonial endeavor.[7] Finally, there is a neglect of things that happened during the colonial period but had little or nothing to do with colonial rule; studies of religion, of ideas, of agrarian activity and many other topics that are central to the Western historical tradition are largely missing.[8]

At the same time, despite the strong political focus of country histories, some of the central facts of political development are not explored. First, contrary to assertions by political leaders such as Sukarno and Ba Maw, colonial rule was not imposed on "Indonesia" or "Burma," or for that matter on "Malaya" or "The Philippines," for these entities did not yet exist.[9] Colonialism began as a relationship between European powers and certain of the myriad rulers in the region, and was shaped both by Western and local interests. Over time the Western powers developed mutually acknowledged spheres of influence, and they established borders around these territories when trading relations were replaced by formal administrative control, giving rise to the Philippines, the Netherlands Indies, British Malaya, French Indochina, and British Burma. Within these territories, bureaucratic systems of administration gradually displaced local power structures, creating opportunities for the rise of new elites distinguished by their Western educations and their capacity to operate the bureaucratic machinery. However, when histories assume the Philippines, or Indonesia, or Burma existed prior to colonial rule, this process of change is effectively denied.

The most egregious examples of accounts written from a country perspective are school textbooks. Indonesian school texts, for example, project "Indonesia" back into the prehistoric past, and narrate events in "Indonesia" during the "Hindu," "Muslim" and "imperialist" eras that preceded the national uprising and the winning of independence.[10] Recent textbooks on Philippine history show an awareness of the lack of congruence between the modern Philippines and any pre-colonial entity, but they still assume a pre-Spanish territorial unity: one says the Philippines is the name by which "our country" is presently known, and another lists earlier names for "the country." Moreover, perhaps for want of better terms, these books refer to the population prior to Spanish rule as Filipinos, and write of Magellan's expedition to "the Philippines," giving a clear impression that the archipelago constituted a country before the coming of the Spanish.[11]

The country histories that feature in catalogues of academic publishers catering to university audiences are far more sophisticated, but even when authors take pains to avoid unwarranted assumptions about the past, as they generally do, these books by their very format tend to project present political forms into the past. David Wyatt's *Thailand: A Short History* traces "The Beginnings of T'ai History" to the experiences of the T'ai people outside the territory of modern Thailand before the eleventh century and later describes the political developments that followed their movement into the Chao Phraya River basin.[12] The book thus has two elements at its core: the T'ai peoples, and the territory occupied by modern Thailand. An earlier historian dealing with these events, W. A. R. Woods, adopted a similar approach, beginning his *History of Siam* with a chapter on the history of the T'ai people and then considering the situation in "Siam" before the coming of the T'ai people.[13] *A History of Modern Indonesia since c. 1300* by M. C. Ricklefs finds the start of the "Modern Era" around the fourteenth century but declares that the recorded history of "Indonesia" began some thousand years earlier.[14] Ricklefs adopts the name Indonesia without comment to deal with an area that has no other commonly accepted designation; alternatives to the colonial formulation Netherlands [East] Indies include Tropical Holland, Insulinde, and Nusantara.[15] In their *History of Malaysia,* Barbara Watson Andaya and Leonard Andaya use the term Malaysia in discussing a pre-Malaysian past, but note that in doing so they are presenting "the history of *what is now* Malaysia."[16] Whether the caution exercised by these scholars is sufficient to avoid the pitfalls of country history can remain an open question; what is clear is that school textbooks and popular histories ignore such distinctions and identify modern states with the distant past.

Second, despite superficial similarities there are significant differences between colonial entities and the nation-states that succeeded them.[17] Colonial administrators are sometimes criticized for failing to establish national economies or for denying indigenous people political opportunities in their own countries. Such criticisms are misplaced because colonial territories were not incipient nation-states but fragments of empire, and they were governed accordingly. Internally, those in Southeast Asia embraced a variety of different peoples and indigenous institutions and had multiple administrations that reflected these differences. British Burma included an inner core, where the population was primarily Burman, and a group of outlying territories where it was not; the Philippines had special provisions for the Muslim areas in the south, while both French Indochina and British

Malaya had territories that were directly ruled as colonies along with protectorates under indigenous rulers. The Netherlands Indies contained a welter of jurisdictions and administrative arrangements.

These entities began to assume their modern form with the development of centralized bureaucracies between the mid-nineteenth and early twentieth centuries. The Depression accelerated this process, disrupting the international arrangements that underlay colonialism and forcing colonial governments to adopt policies more in line with the needs of self-sufficient nation-states. For example, during the 1930s local sources of food and labor were exploited to a greater degree than before and local officials began to replace foreigners at somewhat higher levels of administration. Nonetheless, colonial states remained loosely integrated collections of territories governed by institutions and policies designed for empires when the Japanese invasion finally destroyed the European colonial system.

British Malaya is a good example of this situation. The name itself is a term of convenience that embraced seven administrative units; one crown colony (the Straits Settlements) and six protectorates (the Federated Malay States and five Malay states outside the federation). It exported a small range of primary products and imported both rice and labor. Because it depended on external sources to supply basic needs and sold its exports in foreign markets, the territory was poorly equipped to stand on its own and, from a colonial point of view, there was no reason for it to do so. Malaya was one small piece of an empire that included both Burma, the world's largest exporter of rice, and India, the source of much of Malaya's workforce. Malaya's economic arrangements conformed to principles of comparative advantage within the British Empire rather than principles of autarky for a single country. During the 1930s, in response to the Depression and to a growing Japanese threat to the region, the government introduced measures to make Malaya more self-sufficient in rice and labor, although much remained undone at the time of the Japanese invasion.[18] Administratively the territory was not unified until after the war.

Because country histories distort colonialism, they also provide an inaccurate picture of nationalism and the transition to independence. In its classic sense, nationalism referred to efforts by groups of people who shared certain cultural characteristics to create a political environment that would allow them to cultivate their cultural identity and buttress it with a political structure. In Southeast Asia nationalism is equated with the fight against colonial rule, undertaken on behalf of multicultural or multiethnic territories and led by radical reformers concerned with modernization. Southeast Asian nationalism mounted strong attacks on the customs and traditions prevalent in the region (including languages, religious practices, "superstitions," and established political authorities) but displayed an ambivalence toward colonialism. The modernizers valued the access to technology and new political philosophies that the colonial state provided even while it depleted economic resources and blocked access to political authority; their quarrel lay with the colonial rulers rather than colonial institutions. Upon gaining independence, these Westernized elites took control of the administrative apparatus of the colonial state, added the forms if not always the substance of democracy, and declared their efforts a victory for nationalism.

The process of making the territories controlled by colonial administrations into unitary states involved the shaping of new "nations" by inducing the people living within their boundaries to adopt "national" languages and cultures, which in many cases were not their own, and to identify with a civic body based on birth and residence rather than shared cultural characteristics. There are many sound reasons for these arrangements, and some groups have seen equally good reasons to oppose them. But histories that portray the gaining of independence as a process whereby preexisting nation-states broke free from colonial control fail to capture the significance of the transition. An understanding of modern Southeast Asia requires an examination not only of the way new states took over existing borders and administrative mechanisms during the transition to independence, but also of the internal transformation of these territories from loosely joined collectivities into unitary states under the dual impetus of nationalist ideology and administrative convenience.

Nonnational Political Entities

Before colonialism the people of Southeastern Asia were governed through a substantial number of small polities, and these were enmeshed in complex networks of hierarchical linkages.[19] Some groupings became extremely large and lasted for considerable periods of time, but they remained loosely controlled alliances within which some subordinate elements enjoyed a considerable degree of autonomy. It is difficult to trace a line of political development from these entities to the modern states of Southeast Asia, for the former were sets of people linked through shifting patron-client connections, while the latter are territorial states with rigid boundaries and fixed rules. Colonialism established borders and introduced Western-style bureaucratic systems and principles of sovereignty that allowed for a much greater degree of central control than was found in traditional society, and these mechanisms were maintained and extended after independence, shaping the modern state.[20]

Country histories portray nationalism as the enemy of colonialism, and the idea that national states have their origins in the colonial state is unpalatable. It is partly for this reason that nationalist histories of Thailand trace its origins to Sukhothai or earlier, of Indonesia to Majapahit or earlier, of Burma to Mandalay and the older capitals found in the Dry Zone. Establishing such lineages lends legitimacy to modern nation-states, but there are few institutional parallels and the attempt to find linkages is rarely rigorous and can involve depicting historical entities as though they were modern states.

A further difficulty arises when an attempt is made to unify the historical experiences of people who were not in the past politically unified. Given that the countries of Southeast Asia became unitary states only with independence, it is not surprising that integrated national histories prove difficult to write. This is particularly true for Indonesia, where a large number of local rulers formally retained their powers until early in the twentieth century, and in practice some continued to do so until independence and even beyond.[21] Similarly, East Malaysia, formerly Sabah and Sarawak, and the states of the Malay Peninsula, only became a single country in 1963, and before that date their histories had little in common apart from the fact that the administration of all three areas fell to the British Colonial Office after 1945. Attempts to produce an integrated history of Malaysia generally founder on this difficulty, and indeed the search for common features seems misdirected, since one important element of the story is the way these diverse territories were integrated after their political union.

Minorities

The drawing of colonial boundaries in Southeast Asia created new sets of minority and majority peoples. Colonial regimes viewed ethnic and religious minorities as weak and vulnerable and in some instances established separate administrative areas and special laws or regulations to protect their interests. With independence, minorities were drawn into a process of nation building that required them to adhere to national identities based in many cases on the cultural characteristics of a politically dominant group. The processes of modernization and development that ensued often denigrated their cultures and traditions as backward and nonprogressive.

The treatment of indigenous minorities after independence has ranged from patronizing to abusive; there are few instances where the traditions and political aspirations of minorities have been respected, or where they have been allowed to pursue their own way of life without interference.[22] Reflecting the political preoccupations of the national elite, country histories pay little attention to minorities and tend to follow modernizing political leaders in portraying them as an impediment to progress, as a burden to be shouldered, or as a threat to national unity.

Nonindigenous minorities, consisting for the most part of members of Chinese, Indian, or Arab trading communities, fare little better. The transnational character of their communities, their ties with their homelands, and the wealth and power they have accumulated, do not fit comfortably into the nation-state model used in country histories. Their role in shaping regional and local economies, and the political and physical attacks they have endured over the years, receive little attention. In some cases even very substantial minorities, such as the Chinese in Malaysia, have largely been omitted from nationalistic country histories. In the story of the modern nation-state, minorities are peripheral or even subversive. However, their experiences are important to an understanding of the Southeast Asian past and help explain many of the conflicts that have troubled the region in the latter part of the twentieth century.

Alternative Anticolonialism

Country histories characterize the modern nation-states of Southeast Asia as a triumph of secular nationalism, parliamentary democracy, and capitalist economics and pay scant attention to other aspects of the anticolonial movement in the region. Many young reformers became interested in the Marxist critique of imperialism and in socialist principles during the 1920s and 1930s, and these ideals featured prominently in the anticolonial struggle. However, most of the independent regimes created in postwar Southeast Asia were hostile to the left, and a number became involved in armed conflict with communist groups. Marxist ideology and leftist organizations are largely omitted from nationalist histories and, if acknowledged as part of the anticolonial struggle, are portrayed in a negative and cursory way.

Another alternative to the secular nationalism adopted from Western Europe might be termed theocratic nationalism. Religion was a central feature of local identity in much of Southeast Asia, and religious leaders played a part in the struggle to end colonial rule and create national identities and independent states. Religious leaders offered theocratic alternatives to secular nationalism, but these initiatives were unsuccessful—often because the European colonial leadership, or the Japanese, found the secular opposition more congenial and gave it preferential treatment. Theocratic nationalism receives little notice in country histories and is portrayed either as a minor part of the process of shaping local identity or sometimes as a movement prone to excesses and fanaticism. Histories of Indonesia, for example, characterize religious organizations such as Muhammadijah and Nahdatul Ulama as apolitical, and therefore outside the line of nationalist development, because they did not adopt explicitly political programs or engage in party politics, although they clearly helped shape national identity and nationalist feeling.

Traditional rulers offered yet another alternative to colonialism. Nationalist activity rarely centered on these figures, despite their considerable potency as possible symbols of national identity, and country histories tend to represent them in a negative light, as leaders who treated their people badly by imposing excessive taxes and making harsh demands or as traitors who assisted the colonial powers. In the Marxist historical tradition, they represent nonprogressive feudal elements. At the very least, these images are ahistorical, criticizing past rulers for disloyalty to ideas and political entities that did not exist during their time. Such attacks also help mask how far modern ideologies and political structures have departed from indigenous models.

Country and Region

Finally, country histories provide an incomplete picture of institutions and events that do not fall within a single country unit. Trade and production, for example, are more often examined from a country than from a regional perspective. However, products such as rubber, rice, coconuts, and tin were produced across Southeast Asia, and it is more useful to define a field for analysis by examining where these items are produced and marketed than to base research on political units.

Similarly, accounts of the Chinese in Southeast Asia are almost always based on particular countries, and there is no major study that examines the Chinese on a regional basis.[23] Although understandable given the immensity of the subject, the situation is nonetheless anomalous in that the significance of the Chinese lay precisely in the linkages or networks that transcended both indigenous and colonial states.

Country studies are an essential part of the historical literature on Southeast Asia. Without them, it would be difficult to gain an accurate understanding of some of the key events and institutions found in the region. However, country histories alone cannot provide a satisfactory picture of Southeast Asia's past, and the purpose of this chapter has been to consider briefly certain topics that illustrate this point. The dominance of the country approach has contributed to a distortion of important aspects of Southeast Asian history, notably colonialism and anticolonial activity, nonnational political entities, minorities, and economic and social history. It has also left Southeast Asia with a large number of political studies, but a shortfall of studies dealing with other topics of importance to the region.[24] For example, there is no history of the Malay people or the T'ai people, or of most other identifiable cultural groups within the region. Similarly, geographic units such as the Java Sea or the Melaka Straits or the Mekong River could provide a natural focus for historical studies, but to date little has been done along these lines. Country studies are valuable, but Southeast Asian history could profitably move in other directions.

Notes

1. See J. C. van Leur, *Indonesian Trade and Society: Essays in Asian Social and Economic History,* trans. *James S. Holmes and A. van Marle* (The Hague: W. Van Hoeve, 1955).

2. Smail's article "On the Possibility of an Autonomous History of Modern Southeast Asia" appeared in the *Journal of Southeast Asian History* 2, 2 (1961): 72–102. It has been reprinted in *Autonomous Histories, Particular Truths: Essays in Honor of John Smail,* ed. Laurie Sears (Madison: Center for Southeast Asian Studies, University of Wisconsin, 1993), 39–70.

3. J. C. van Leur, "Enkele aantekeningen met betrekking tot de

beoefening der Indische geschiedenis" and "Eenige aanteekeningen betreffende de modelijkheid der 18e eeuw als categorie in de Indische geschiedschrijving," in *Indonesian Trade and Society,* 147–56, 268–89.

4. On this issue see the remarks by Thongchai Winichakul in this volume.

5. John Bastin, "The Western Element in Modern Southeast Asian History," in *Essays on Indonesian and Malayan History* (Singapore: Eastern Universities Press, 1961), 11–12.

6. Examples of this genre include J. S. Furnivall, *Colonial Policy and Practice* (Cambridge: Cambridge University Press, 1948); Furnivall, *Netherlands India* (Cambridge: Cambridge University Press, 1944); Joseph Ralston Hayden, *The Philippines* (New York: Macmillan, 1945); Rupert Emerson, *Malaysia* (New York: Macmillan, 1937).

7. See Ronald Robinson, "Non-European Foundations of European Imperialism: Sketch for a Theory of Collaboration," in *Studies in the Theory of Imperialism,* ed. Roger Owen and Bob Sutcliffe (London: Longman, 1972); reprinted in *The Robinson and Gallagher Controversy* (New York: New Viewpoints, 1976).

8. There have been some efforts to fill these gaps in the historical literature, but much remains to be done. For Malaya, see, for example, Lim Teck Ghee, *Peasants and Their Agricultural Economy in Colonial Malaya, 1874–1941* (Kuala Lumpur: Oxford University Press, 1977); Shaharil Talib, *After Its Own Image: The Trengganu Experience, 1881–1941* (Singapore: Oxford University Press, 1984); Francis Loh Kok Wah, *Beyond the Tin Mines: Coolies, Squatters, and New Villagers in the Kinta Valley, Malaysia, c. 1880–1980* (Singapore: Oxford University Press, 1988).

9. Sukarno, in his 1946 Independence Day speech, stated that the proclamation of independence was a demand for an end to 350 years of colonial rule over "Indonesia." President Sukarno, "Sekali Merdeka, Tetap Merdeka!" in *Amanat Proklamasi, 1945–1950* (Jakarta: Inti Idayu Press, 1985), 3–4. Ba Maw began his Declaration of Independence of Burma (1 August 1943) by saying, "To-day, after more than fifty years of British occupation, Burma resumes her rightful place among the free and sovereign nations of the world. She proudly occupied that place throughout a very long stretch of unbroken history." Ba Maw, document 43 in *Burma: Japanese Military Administration: Selected Documents, 1941–1943,* ed. Frank N. Trager (Philadelphia: University of Pennsylvania Press, 1971), 164–65.

10. See, for example, Dr. S. W. Siswoyo, *Sejarah untuk SMA dan Sekolah yang Sederajat* (Jakarta: Penerbit Intan Klaten, 1979).

11. These examples are drawn from Lamberto C. Gabriel and Mila dela Cruz-Paragas, *The Philippines: Geography, History, and Government: An Analysis* (Manila: Sta. Teresa Publications, 1998); Florida C. Leuterio, *Phil-*

ippine History and Government: A Centennial Edition (Manila: St. Augustine Publications, 1998).

12. David Wyatt, *Thailand: A Short History* (New Haven: Yale University Press; Bangkok: Thai Watana Panich, 1984).

13. W. A. R. Woods, *History of Siam* (London: T. Fisher Unwin, 1926).

14. M. C. Ricklefs, *A History of Modern Indonesia since c. 1300*, 2d ed. (Stanford: Stanford University Press, 1993).

15. For "tropical Holland" see H. A. van Coenen Torchiana, *Tropical Holland—Java and Other Islands* (Chicago: University of Chicago Press, 1921). For Insulinde, see Annabella Forbes, *Insulinde: Experiences of a Naturalist's Wife in the Eastern Archipelago* (London: Wm. Blackwood and Sons, 1887); Isabel Anderson, *In Eastern Seas: With a Visit to Insulinde and the Golden Chersonese* (Boston: B. Humphries, 1934); Jules Sion, *Asie des moussons,* vol. 2, *Inde, Indochine, Insulinde* (Paris: A. Colin, 1929). For Nusantara, see B. H. M. Vlekke, *Nusantara* (1943; rev. ed., The Hague: W. van Hoeve; Chicago: Quadrangle Books, 1960).

16. Barbara Watson Andaya and Leonard Andaya, *History of Malaysia* (London: Macmillan, 1982), 7; emphasis added. The same phrase is also used in the 2d ed. (Basingstoke, Hampshire: Palgrave, 2001), on the same page.

17. See Keith Taylor, "Surface Orientations in Vietnam: Beyond Histories of Nation and Region," *Journal of Asian Studies* 57, 4 (November 1998): 949–78; Thongchai Winichakul, this volume.

18. See Paul H. Kratoska, "Imperial Unity versus Local Autonomy: British Malaya and the Depression of the 1930s," in *Weathering the Storm: the Economies of Southeast Asia in the 1930s Depression,* ed. Peter Boomgaard and Ian Brown, 250–73 (Singapore: Institute of Southeast Asian Studies, 2000).

19. See, for example, S. J. Tambiah, *World Conqueror and World Renouncer* (Cambridge: Cambridge University Press, 1976); F. K. Lehman, "On the Vocabulary and Semantics of 'Field' in Theravada Buddhist Society," *Contributions to Asian Studies* 16 (1981): 101–11; Soemarsaid Moertono, *State and Statecraft in Old Java: A Study of the Later Mataram Period, Sixteenth to Nineteenth Century* (Ithaca: Cornell University Southeast Asia Project, 1981); Robert H. Taylor, *The State in Burma* (Honolulu: University of Hawaii Press, 1987).

20. For summaries of the discussion on these points, see Carl A. Trocki, "Political Structures in the Nineteenth and Early Twentieth Centuries"; Robert E. Elson, "International Commerce, the State, and Society: Economic and Social Change," in *The Cambridge History of Southeast Asia,* ed. Nicholas Tarling, vol. 2, *The Nineteenth and Twentieth Centuries* (Cambridge: Cambridge University Press, 1992).

21. See for example, Roy Ellen, "On the Contemporary Uses of Colonial

History and the Legitimation of Political Status in Archipelagic Southeast Seram," and Maribeth Erb, "Contested Time and Place: Constructions of History in Todo, Manggarai (Western Flores, Indonesia)," both in *Journal of Southeast Asian Studies* 28, 1 (March 1997).

22. The literature on minorities is substantial, and most accounts deal with these issues. A useful introduction is *Southeast Asian Tribal Groups and Ethnic Minorities: Prospects for the Eighties and Beyond,* Cultural Survival Report 22 (Cambridge, Mass: Cultural Survival, 1987).

23. Typical in this regard is Victor Purcell, *The Chinese in Southeast Asia,* 2d ed. (Kuala Lumpur: Oxford University Press, 1980); although there are some generalizations relating to the entire area, the greater part of the book consists of chapters describing the Chinese in individual territories. Other country studies of the Chinese include Tsai Maw-Kuey, *Les Chinois au Sud-Vietnam* (Paris: Bibliothèque National, 1968); G. William Skinner, *Chinese Society in Thailand: An Analytical History* (Ithaca: Cornell University Press, 1957); Donald E. Willmott, *The Chinese of Semarang: A Changing Minority Community in Indonesia* (Ithaca: Cornell University Press, 1960); J. A. C. Mackie, ed., *The Chinese in Indonesia: Five Essays* (Hong Kong: Heinemann Educational Books, 1976); Charles A. Coppel, *Indonesian Chinese in Crisis* (Kuala Lumpur: Oxford University Press , 1983); and the work of Leo Suryadinata.

24. The 1990s brought a number of innovative studies, such as Thongchai Winichakul's *Siam Mapped: A History of the Geo-Body of a Nation* (Honolulu: University of Hawaii Press, 1994); Lenore Manderson, *Sickness and the State: Health and Illness in Colonial Malaya, 1870–1940* (Cambridge: Cambridge University Press, 1996), but as is true of the examples cited, most of these works remain bound to a single country. Two notable exceptions are R. E. Elson, *The End of the Peasantry in Southeast Asia: A Social and Economic History of Peasant Livelihood, 1800–1990s* (London: Macmillan; New York: St. Martin's, 1997); J. Thomas Lindblad, *Foreign Investment in Southeast Asia in the Twentieth Century* (London: Macmillan; New York: St. Martin's, 1998).

Part Two

CONSTRUCTING AND DECONSTRUCTING THE NATIONAL PAST

Chapter 6

MYANMAR HISTORIOGRAPHY SINCE 1945

Ni Ni Myint

THERE ARE SEVERAL MOTIVES that prompt writers to write histories. In Myanmar traditional histories began with the beginning of the present era and the appearance of the first Universal Monarch, Mahasamata. The first reason for writing this kind of traditional history was to describe how Buddhism reached Myanmar. Disregarding historicity, Mons of lower Myanmar, Bamars in the central plain, and Rakhines in the west, claimed that Buddhism reached their land during the lifetime of the Buddha, and invented several stories about it. The second reason was to establish the antiquity of each political center and chronicles vied with each other in claiming how old their respective capital cities were. The third reason was to connect the ruling dynasties with the first Universal Monarch, as Myanmar chronicles started their history from Mahasamata. The fourth reason was the intention that the chronicles would serve as a manual for kings. Myanmar chronicles are therefore a detailed and continuous register of events arranged in chronological order and revolving chiefly around Myanmar kings.

The chronicles were first written in the fifteenth century, a great age of Myanmar literature. The *Mahayazawingyi* (Great chronicle) was the first full-scale historical work in Myanmar. It marked the beginning of Myanmar historiography and its style was mostly narrative with a few discursive passages. The author, U Kala, to a large extent made use of literature, both verse and prose, although he did not consult the stone inscriptions. The *Mahayazawingyi* became a model for later chronicles and was the principal basis of the famous *Hman nan mahayazawindawgyi* (Glass palace chronicle). The compilers of the *Hman nan* consulted several Myanmar chronicles, Myanmar and Pali literature, local histories, and inscriptions; the result was a more up-to-date, enlarged, critical version of U Kala's chronicle. Later chronicles continued the account of the *Hman Nan*. The *Dutiya mahayazawindawgyi* (Second chronicle) dealt with events from 1821 to 1869. In 1905, U Tin, a learned scholar and son of an official, extended the account up to 1885 and renamed it *Konbaungset mahayazawingyi* (Great chronicle of the Konbaung period).

After 1905 new historical works began to appear. They came as part of the new nationalism that spread in Asia. For many Myanmar scholars of the period, the writing of history was both an act of faith and a patriotic duty. During the 1930s nationalist histories flourished in Myanmar, in the form of editing and reprinting the earlier royal chronicles or rewriting a few episodes in a popular style for young people. An example of the latter was *Myanmar thuyegaung myar* (Myanmar heroes), published in 1933. It consisted of biographical sketches of famous kings, written by journalist U Thein Maung. Also directed at youths and students were simplified abridgments of the royal chronicles by U Ba Than and U Ohn Maung that were intended as high school texts.

The historiography of Myanmar was greatly affected by the Second World War and the country's subsequent independence. One of the changes was in the word used for history. Traditionally, the term *yazawin* was used for court chronicles dealing with kings, and *thamaing* for popular accounts on the stories of pagodas and historic landmarks. *Yazawin* commanded greater respect and continued to do so in the colonial period. Until independence the epithet was still current, but the term *thamaing* came into use in 1948. Bohmu Ba Shin used *thamaing* to introduce a new approach to Myanmar history. His

Pyidaungsu Myanmar nainggandaw thamaing (History of the Union of Myanmar) added modern historical ideas to the traditional dynastic material to trace Myanmar history from the Stone Age to the attainment of independence.[1] Kyaw Thet's work of the same name, presenting a similar outline of Myanmar history from the prehistoric period to after independence, became a textbook and reoriented students to the new view of Myanmar history.[2] Bohmu Ba Shin and Kyaw Thet were professional historians, but many others outside the history profession, including politicians, writers, and doctrinaire authors drew upon their personal experiences and their political activities to present their views and versions of history. U Ba Pe's *Myanmar thamaing akyin gyok* (A brief history of Myanmar), Tekkatho Ne Win's *Hpetsit tawhlanye thamaing* (A history of antifascist resistance), and Thakin Chit Maung's *Bamarpyi naingganye hmattan* (Record of Myanmar politics), belong to the category of books that deal with various aspects of the struggle for independence.[3] Major Ba Thaung, writing under the pseudonym Maung Thuta, not only traced Myanmar history from the First Anglo-Myanmar War to the attainment of independence but also wrote about the armed forces and the national spirit in his *Bama tawhlanye thamaing* (The roots of revolution). Describing the scope of his own work, he wrote:

> The aim in this book is to describe the history of Myanmar Resistance, but in doing so, it will be necessary to include the history of the Myanmar independence struggle. In the same way in describing the history of Myanmar Resistance and the history of the Myanmar independence struggle, it will also be necessary to talk about the history of Myanmar nationalism.[4]

The nationalist motif in Myanmar historiography continued into the 1960s. Bamaw Tin Aung's *Koloni khit Myanmar nainggan thamaing* (Myanmar history during the colonial period) covered Myanmar history from ancient times to the period after independence, when the Antifascist People's Freedom League (AFPFL) held power. He observed that during the colonial period history was written by British historians from a British viewpoint, with a bias against the Myanmar people: "During the colonial days, the Department of Myanmar

History was the preserve of colonialist history scholars and the Archaeology Survey of Burma was not accorded as much attention and respect as a backyard kitchen garden."[5] In much the same way Maung Maung's meticulously researched *Myanmar naingganye khayi hnint Bogyokegyi Ne Win* (Burma and General Ne Win), which covered the period from the British annexation to the setting up of the Burmese Way to Socialism, was intended to remind the younger generation of the price that had to be paid for independence by recounting some of the main events and describing some of the participants in those events. During the course of Myanmar politics, the people as a whole, and the leaders of the movement, had to take risks and work hard. Many lives were sacrificed and much property lost during the struggle for independence. Maung Maung wanted his readers in the coming generation to realize that regaining and preserving independence had not been easy.[6]

In addition to the development of the nationalist theme in Myanmar historiography, some writers after independence attempted to express their views in an independent way. Foremost among them was Sagaing Han Tin, author of *Lounwa lutlattye thouh* (Toward total independence) and *Myanmar lutlattye thouh* (Toward independence for Myanmar), which relates historical events from before the First Anglo-Myanmar War until independence.[7] Before writing the latter work he had begun a series entitled *Myanmar nainggandaw hmattan* (Records of Myanmar), a collection of primary sources on modern Myanmar history because he felt that "records of the struggle of the anticolonial national liberation movement should be properly maintained."[8] Hence he had begun to compile them about twelve years earlier (around 1960). *Toward Independence for Myanmar* was written as an abridged version of *Records of Myanmar* while the latter work was still in progress.

Another trend in Myanmar historiography after independence was the weaving together of personal experiences and history, the most prominent exponent of which was Thakin Thein Pe, better known as Thein Pe Myint, author of *Tawhlanye karla naingganye atwe akyone myar* (Reminiscences of the Resistance period), *Sitatwin khayithe* (translated into English as *Wartime Traveler* by Robert Taylor, a well-known specialist on Myanmar), *Ashega newun htwet thih parma* (As the sun rises in the east), and *Ne yittaw khit haung* (Fall back old period).[9] Thein Pe Myint describes his technique: "I have employed the history of our struggle for independence as background scenery and as the plot in depicting the drama acted out by my characters."[10] *Reminiscences of the Resistance Period* is a good representative of his method of writing current history. Beginning with the Young Men's Buddhist Association (YMBA) and the dawn of the nationalist movement, the book describes the independence struggle and the agenda of the communists, the postindependence attempt at maintaining national unity, the AFPFL split, and the splintering of the Burma Communist Party (BCP).

Another writer in the same genre is Thakin Tin Mya, who translated his personal experiences in politics into a book entitled *Boun bawa hmar hpyint* (In this world of existence), which begins:

> I have decided to publish what I have encountered in the world of politics for twenty-two years, from 1938 to 1960, in its entirety, without omission, whether good or bad, as it was or as it has been to the best of my knowledge, for the record.[11]

He explained that he wrote it in the style of political literature, rather than academic history, in order to make it interesting for the general reader. A later work, *Thamaing takit thit khepyi* (The dawn of a new era), is a record of developments during the period of the Revolutionary Council (beginning in 1962).[12] Unlike his earlier work, it is not a history at all but an account of the ideology and political agenda of the Burmese Way to Socialism.

Some authors of historical works based on personal political experience focused on political parties. Just as Thakin Tin Mya's *Dawn of a New Historic Era* was on the Burma Socialist Programme Party (BSPP), the *Thakin Than Tun eih naukhsone nei myar* (The last days of Thakin Than Tun) was concerned with the final chapter in the history of the Burma Communist Party, including the assassination of Thakin Than Tun by his own men and the dissolution of the BCP. Since it was written by former members of the BCP's politburo, it drew upon their personal experiences to provide detailed information on Thakin Than Tun and the internal affairs of the BCP. The authors declared that in writing the book, they were not presenting a history of the party so much as a detailed account of the its latest developments so that the people might draw their own conclusions.[13]

Works on local history also made their appearance. Well-written local histories of two of the best-known cities came out during this period. The venerable U Thawbita, writing under the name Shwe Gaing Thar, brought out his *Ahnit tayar pyih Mandalay* (Mandalay centenary) in 1959. He noted that, as the book had been written to commemorate the centenary, he was "under the obligation to provide the most complete and exhaustive account possible." To fulfill this great responsibility, he had traveled abroad in his search for materials, as domestic sources were not quite sufficient.[14] Using both domestic and foreign sources, he provided an account of Mandalay from its founding to its reoccupation by the British after the Second World War. Similarly, U Thein Maung's *Yangon Yazawin Thamaing* (History of Yangon) chronicled Yangon from its founding to the postindependence period.[15] A third city, Pathein, was also the subject of a history, *Pathein Yazawin* (History of Pathein/Bassein), by U Marga.[16] In addition to these works by individual authors, various local authorities were entrusted with the writing of the history of various townships after 1973. Hence several local histories resembling the district gazetteers of the colonial period came out after 1982. Written by local historians and literary figures who obtained their information from the grassroots level, these histories were very accurate.

The writing of history as a collective enterprise extended beyond the field of local history. The history of the Dobama Asiayone (DAA, We Myanmar) organization, which played a vital role in the struggle for independence in the 1930s, was produced by a committee set up for that purpose in 1964. The committee began work in 1968 and completed its work in 1973. The history was a major project, with many members of the organization who had been involved in the movement, down to its lowest level, contributing their personal experiences. The committee worked to very strict standards, adopting the view that "each point mentioned be true as far as it is verifiable, that events are recounted without exaggeration, and that an objective approach be prevalent in our writing."[17]

In addition to freelance individual and group efforts to record and interpret the more recent past, the government in the postindependence period also tried to establish its own version of events. Foremost among these was U Thant's *Pyidawtha khayi,* begun in 1954 and completed in 1958, which traced Myanmar history from the fall of the Myanmar kingdom in 1885 to the period of AFPFL power. U Thant explains how he came to write the book:

> Although the Union of Myanmar became a sovereign nation on 4 January 1948, there is as yet no account of its contemporary history, no record of the political tides that swept over it during the struggle for independence, of the trials and tribulations of the Second World War, and of the Resistance movement. This was pointed out to me by Premier U Nu in 1954 and he directed me to write a book to fill in the gap. Following this instruction, I have collected relevant documents, books, speeches, and reports and using this material have written this book, *Pyidawtha khayi,* in my spare time. . . . The intention is to place the great effort made by the people of Myanmar in its true proportion and without any distortion, so that the people's power to accomplish may be fully appreciated and the destiny perceived for the nation remain clearly focused.[18]

Nevertheless, the internal unrest that began soon after independence, and the BCP's role in it, was presented from the AFPFL viewpoint only. In other words, the account supports the AFPFL government and its policies.

During the BSPP period, the party headquarters published its *Ludoh eih koun louk hset hsanye thamaing* (History of human productive relations) to convey the BSPP interpretation of history based on socialist principles. The *Aloke thamar asiayone thamaing* (History of labor unions) and *Taungthu lethamar asiayone thamaing* (History of peasant associations), also published by the party headquarters, traced the history of what the BSPP considered to be the two basic social classes, the workers and the peasants, in Myanmar.[19] Although socialist in orientation, the works also drew upon the nationalist spirit of the earlier phase of history writing. The following example indicates a leaning toward a nationalist point of view in relating past historical experiences:

> The peasants' uprising of 1930 gave an impetus to nationalist fervor. The momentum from this uprising led to the birth of the Dobama Asiayone, which would later become an intrepid force fighting for national liberation. Although the uprising could not wage a decisive battle against the British, it paved the way for the coming anticolonial movement, the anti-Fascist movement, and the battles in the struggle for national liberation, and it provided invaluable experiences and lessons.[20]

Achepya myanmar naingganye thamaing (An elementary history of Myanmar politics), commissioned in 1970 by the Central Organizing Committee Headquarters of the BSPP had the stated aim of making history, from prehistory to the twentieth century, easily available to the people.[21] The authors of this work expressed the view that they had taken care to avoid the extremes of a chauvinistic attitude, or a deprecatory tone, as was often the case with foreign historians, and that, since the scope of the work was immense, they had used the qualifier *elementary* to indicate its introductory nature.

This trend of interpreting history from a nationalist viewpoint has continued to the present day. During the period of the State Law and Order Restoration Council (SLORC), the predecessor of the present State Peace and Development Council (SPDC), a committee was appointed for the enhancement of dynamism in patriotic spirit and the dissemination of knowledge. Under the leadership of this committee, many historical articles and books have been written, edited, and published. Books like *Pyidwin thaunggyan hmu thamaing* (A history of insurgencies), *Htaun koeyar shihsetshih ayeakhin karla yetset kyangyouk hmu hpyit yat hman myar* (The truth about the Atrocities during the 1988 disturbances), *Tatmadaw thamaing* (A history of the armed forces), and Pe Kan Kaung's *Arnar thein thaw tatmadaw mahout par* (Not a government by authoritarian coup), express the viewpoint of the government on recent history, with an underlying patriotic theme.[22] While some of the works written to enhance patriotism are not heavily documented, the indispensable *History of the Armed Forces* (in five volumes) has drawn its material from the military archives, with its great store of documents, as well as personal interviews with prominent personalities, and is able to provide, for instance, detailed information on the role of the armed forces in the Resistance, including notifications and operation plans.

Academics have also contributed to the development of postindependence historiography. Htin Aung's *The Stricken Peacock: Anglo-Burmese Relations, 1752–1948* and *History of Burma,* written in English, reflected the Myanmar point of view and make good use of historical materials.[23] In his preface, he challenges the biased views of such Western scholars as Dorothy Woodman, E. C. Foucar, and John F. Cady. He accuses them of delivering ex parte verdicts based on false and fraudulent evidence, with no consideration for the Burmese point of view or Burmese sources of history.[24] It is not so easy, however, to generalize the views of the Myanmar people toward Western historians and their works, as there are different levels of accomplishment among Western historians and a great variety of different attitudes among Myanmar peoples. Nevertheless, there would be, on the whole, a negative attitude toward colonialism and perhaps also some questioning of the credibility of historians who do not know the Myanmar language and have not experienced Myanmar society and culture firsthand.

The History of Burma by Htin Aung uses Myanmar sources to give a brief history of Myanmar from ancient times to the AFPFL period. Written for a Western audience, his works were later translated into Myanmar. They were meant to present the Myanmar nationalist viewpoint and not to contribute to the serious study of Myanmar history. While Htin Aung relied mainly on the Myanmar chronicles, Than Tun made extensive use of lithic inscriptions and the data provided by archaeological excavations. His *Khit haung myanmar yazawin* (Classical Myanmar history), beginning with the Stone Age and ending with the Bagan period, was written for scholars and those seriously interested in history, and did away with the baggage of fables and legends that had burdened the Myanmar chronicles.[25] Than

Tun revised not only earlier histories but also his own, and his *Athit myin bamar thamaing* (A new look at the history of Myanmar) amends some parts of the earlier work on the strength of new findings in lithic inscriptions and archaeological investigations. He acknowledges the importance of correcting one's own mistakes, which was why he "points out the errors in [his own] earlier papers and describes how they might be corrected."[26] Than Tun also made extensive field trips all over the country to unearth hitherto unpublished historical materials, which resulted in the three-volume *Nehleh yazawin* (Historian on tour), published in 1968–69.[27]

In the field of ancient history, Bohmu Ba Shin also covered the period from the Stone Age to the time of King Anawratha of Bagan in his *Anawratha ayinga Myanmar nainggan* (Myanmar before Anawratha). Departing from the myths and legends and unfounded claims of classical Myanmar historians, the book uses all the evidence available to present a fresh approach, written from a researcher's point of view. Noting that foreign historians began Myanmar history from the time of King Anawratha, which they regarded as the beginning of historical times, Bohmu Ba Shin extends Myanmar history into prehistoric times.[28]

Myanmar archaeologists also contributed to the reconstruction of Myanmar prehistory. Based on findings from the cities of Beikthano (Vishnu City), Hanlin, Sriksetra, and Tagaung, the authors of *Sheyhaung Myanmar myodaw myar* (Ancient Myanmar cities) have reconstructed the social and cultural history of Myanmar two thousand years ago. In the preface, U Aung Thaw comments:

> The basis for writing history is a description of the social system and achievements of men. Archaeology can reveal the history of human culture. . . . In dealing with historical times and traditions, lithic or palm leaf inscriptions and archival records are sources to be relied on, though the degree of reliability might vary from source to source. In dealing with prehistoric times, however, ancient artifacts are the sole source from which deduction can be made.[29]

The Journal of Burma Research Society (1910–1980), also presented research-based articles on Myanmar history, literature, and culture. Similarly, the Burma Historical Commission, founded in 1955, published articles on history in the *Bulletin of the Burma Historical Commission.*

There are, in addition, many as yet unpublished postgraduate theses on Myanmar history covering such aspects as politics, society, economy, administration, foreign relations, religion, and culture. Based on systematic research and done under competent supervision, they are a valuable resource. U Thein Hlaing's *Nyaungyan Hset,* completed in 1997, and U Kyaw Win's *Taungu Hset,* completed in 1998, which are annotated editions of the chronicle *Mahayazawin thit* (New chronicle) and among the few theses to have been published, indicate the general standard of these works.

Documentary material is sometimes not adequate for the study of certain subjects or topics in history. Invariably one has to turn to oral traditions and oral history, although oral material has to be used with some caution. Later researchers have resorted to interviews to obtain supplementary material, but their style differs greatly from the incomparable style of Hmawbi Saya Thein, who introduced historical writings based on oral traditions to Myanmar. His *Pazat yazawin* (Oral history) contains many incidents that are not mentioned in the official chronicle *Konbaung hset yazawin* (Chronicle of the Konbaung period). The author claims that the many details about the life, personalities, and intrigues of the court are reproduced from the stories he heard from his elders, just as they have been related to him. He also writes that that his stories are bound to be at variance with official accounts and leaves it to the scholar to form his own opinion and to be judicious in the use of the materials he provides.[30]

Myanmar has a comprehensive collection of materials for the writing of history. These materials include estampages (rubbings) of lithic inscriptions in Myanmar and other languages such as Pyu, Pali, Mon, Thai, Chinese, and various Indian languages, from the fourth to the eighteenth centuries. Other sources available are the ink glosses in prints and negative form for the Bagan region, traditional manuscripts such as palm leaf manuscripts, some of which remain unpublished, as well as *Dhammathats* (traditional codes of law) and *parabaiks,* or folded paper manuscripts, which contain a wealth of material bearing on administrative, economic, social, and other matters. Then there are original documents of various organizations such as government departments, political parties, and associations; besides newspapers and periodicals, personal collections, print collections, and oral archives. Moreover, there are also microfilms of materials collected from outside Myanmar, mainly from the India Office Library and Records, the Public Records Office, and the Quai d' Orsay Archives.

This wealth of source material has provided the basis for outstanding recent research, including: *Taingyinthar lu myo myar ayeh hnint 1947 achegan upade* (The 1947 constitution and the nationalities), *Myanmar naingganye thamaing, 1958–1962* (Political history of Myanmar), and *Myanmar naigganye sanit pyaung karla, 1962–1974* (Myanmar's changing political system).[31] These nine volumes prepared by the Myanmar Historical Commission and the Universities Historical Research Center have been carefully written, with full documentation supplemented by and checked against personal interviews.

The special character of the writing of contemporary history is conveyed in the preface to *The 1947 Constitution and the Nationalities,*

> The span of time from World War II to the present is nearly half-a-century and for many people it is the time through which they have lived. The events and changes of this period constitute contemporary history. For all—elderly, middle-aged, as well as the young—the events of today gradually but inexorably fade from memory tomorrow. Only when these events have been set down shall we be able to use the lessons of our past in the building of our future.[32]

The evolution of the question of the future of the hill regions is traced, starting from the arrangements made for the hill peoples and ethnic minorities under the colonial administration, to postwar changes with the development of the nationalist movement and the resolution of the question of the hill peoples and ethnic minorities, through the Panglong Conference, up to the constitution-making process, as the independence of Myanmar became imminent.

Political History of Myanmar, 1958–1962, and *Myanmar's Changing Political System, 1962–1974,* written to provide a sense of continuity in the political history of Myanmar, trace political developments from the latter part of the AFPFL period up to the end of the Revolutionary Council. They deal in some detail with the development of factionalism within the AFPFL and the split of the AFPFL into the Stable and Clean factions; the establishment of a military caretaker government, which staged elections and handed over power to the Clean faction, which then won the elections; the further split of the Clean faction and the development of the movement of the ethnic minorities for greater federalism; the coup of 2 March 1962 and the establishment of the Revolutionary Council; the formulation of a socialist ideology by the Revolutionary Council and its application in the Revolutionary Council; and, finally, the handing over of power to the BSPP.

From the Konbaung period to British colonial rule, biography as a genre received scant attention. But during the British colonial period, Myanmar translations from foreign literature, including biographies of notable personalities, began to appear. One such example was *Aar nar shin Hitler* (Hitler the dictator).[33] After independence, there was an increase in biographical writings, the earliest and most notable among which were Thakin Kodaw Hmaing's *Saya Lun,* which aimed to foster the patriotic spirit, and *Ba Sein ei Ba Sein* (Ba Sein by Ba Sein), which featured the history of independence struggle and that of the Dobama Asiayone.[34]

Not surprisingly, General Aung San, generally regarded as the architect of Myanmar independence and the foremost leader in the struggle for independence, has been the subject of a number of biographical writings in the Myanmar language. Several works were published from 1943 to 1995, including collections of articles, some containing autobiographical sketches written by General Aung San himself.[35] Despite the number of publications, however, there is an obvious dearth of works that can be said to possess such features as comprehensiveness, validity, and inclusion of the relevant historical contexts. This was acknowledged by Lieutenant Thein Swe, the author of *Biography of General Aung San,* which appeared in 1951, who called for the establishment of a government committee to compile

an authoritative and prestigious biography of the general.[36] Though
such a committee was formed in 1947, it apparently never met and
the proposed authoritative biography was never written.[37] In 1977
the Department of Historical Research formed a team to begin com-
piling materials toward this biography. The project was then inherited by the Universities Historical Research Centre, which has
completed a draft biography.

Myanmar historiography since 1945 has been diverse, with various motivations, approaches, and styles. This is because there is not
only a general awareness of the importance of history in defining
Myanmar national identity but also a consciousness of the need to
establish group and individual identities within the context of national history. The establishment of the Burma Historical Commission in 1955 represented an effort on the part of the state to produce
an official version of national history, but since the commission, motivated by academic principles rather than political goals, has been
tardy in its work, no official national history has yet appeared. This
has encouraged the diversity of Myanmar historiography, a diversity that extends not only to outlook and approach but also to subject
matter. A more active political life and a greater consciousness of locality and ethnicity have resulted in a number of local histories and
histories of ethnic peoples where such histories are possible. Where
localized histories are not possible because of the lack of written materials, ethnological studies have taken their place.

Despite the diversity of Myanmar historiography, one of the main
trends since 1945 has been a nationalist outlook and approach. This
has resulted in a new emphasis being given to the anticolonial nationalist movement, which before 1945 was largely ignored or interpreted in different terms. A new dimension has therefore been added
to the writing of the colonial past that, in the hands of colonial historians, had merely concentrated on the activities and achievements of
the colonial authority.

The nationalist outlook has also provided the basis for some historical controversies. One of these pits the traditionalists, who give
greater valuation to traditional historiography and place credence on

the chronicles, against the academics, who, although not entirely rejecting the chronicles, drew upon a wider array of resources, including epigraphy. Despite the nationalist outlook and the placing of national history on the political agenda, there has only been an orientation toward, not a real construction of, national history. The diversity of Myanmar historiography since 1945 may thus be attributed to a number of factors, among them, a diversity of political, social, and intellectual orientations and the strong individualism of the Myanmar character.

Notes

The Myanmar historiography surveyed in this chapter has not been translated into English and hence is beyond the reach of those who do not know the Myanmar language.

1. Bohmu Ba Shin, *Pyidaungsu Myanmar nainggandaw thamaing* (History of the Union of Myanmar) (Yangon: Pyithu Ahlin Literature House, 1963).

2. Kyaw Thet, *Pyidaungsu Myanmar nainggandaw thamaing* (Yangon: Ava House, 1962).

3. U Ba Pe, *Myanmar thamaing akyin gyoke* (A brief history of Myanmar) (Yangon: Sarpay Beikman Press, 1958); Thekkatho Ne Win, *Hpetsit tawhlanye thamaing* (A history of antifascist resistance) (Yangon: Shumawa House, 1955); Thakin Chit Maung, *Myanmar pyi naingganye hmattan* (Record of Myanmar politics) (Yangon: Seinban Myaing Sarpay, 1976).

4. Maung Thuta [Major Ba Thaung], *Bama tawhlanye thamaing* (The roots of revolution) (Yangon: Guardian, 1967), 11.

5. Bamaw Tin Aung, *Koloni khit Myanmar nainggan thamaing* (Myanmar history during the colonial period) (Yangon: Pyithu Ahlin Press, 1964), 28.

6. Maung Maung, *Myanmar naingganye khayi hnit Bogyokegyi Ne Win* (Myanmar and General Ne Win) (Yangon: Asia Publishing House, 1969), 11.

7. Sagaing Han Tin, *Lounwa lutlattye thouh* (Toward total independence) (Yangon: Pinya Literature House, 1964), and *Myanmar lutlattye thouh* (Toward Independence for Myanmar) (Yangon: Pyithu Arnar Book House, 1975).

8. Sagaing Han Tin, *Myanmar lutlattye thouh,* 14.

9. Thein Pe Myint, *Tawhlanye karla naingganye atwe akyone myar* (Reminiscences of the Resistance period) (Yangon: Yamunnar Book Distribution,

1963), *Sitatwin khayithe* (Wartime traveler) (Yangon: Bagan Bookshop, 1953), *Marxism and Resistance in Burma, 1942–1945: Thein Pe Myint's* Wartime Traveler, trans. Robert H. Taylor (Athens: Ohio University Press, 1984), *Ashega newun htwet thih pamar* (As the sun rises in the east) (Yangon: Nant Thar Literature House, 1969), and *Ne yittaw khit haung* (Fall back old period) (Yangon: Soe Naing Sarpay, 1977).

10. Thein Pe Myint, *Ashega newun htwet, ka.*

11. Thakin Tin Mya, *Boun bawa hmar hpyint* (In this world of existence), vol. 3 (Yangon: Bagan Press, 1966), 16.

12. Thakin Tin Mya, *Thamaing takit thit khe pye* (The dawn of a new historic era) (Yangon: Sabai Aung Literature House, 1967).

13. Yebaw (Comrade) Mya, Yebaw Ba Khet, Yebaw Saw Hla, Bo Min Din, and Bo Tin Shein, *Thakin Than Tun ei nawkhsone ne myar* (The last days of Thakin Than Tun) (Yangon: Mya Yar Bin Sarpay, 1969), *kha.*

14. Shwe Gaing Thar [U Thawbita], *Ahnit tayar pyih Mandalay* (Mandalay centenary) (Yangon: Kyee Bwa Yay Press, 1956), 4.

15. U Thein Maung, *Yangon yazawin thamaing* (History of Yangon) (Yangon: Zwe Sarpay Press, 1963).

16. U Marga, *Pathein yazawin* (History of Pathein/Bassein) (Yangon: Zwe Sarpay Press, 1967).

17. Do Bamar (We Myanmar), *Do Bamar Asiayone Thamaing* (We Myanmar Association) (Yangon: Sarpay Beikman Press, 1976), 11.

18. U Thant, *Pyidawtha khayi* (Welfare state) (Yangon: Sarpay Beikman Press, 1961), *ka.*

19. Burma Socialist Programme Party (BSPP), *Ludoh eih koun louk hset hsanye thamaing* (History of human productive relations) (Yangon: BSPP, 1964), *Aloke thamar asiayone thamaing* (History of labor unions) (Yangon: BSPP Central Committee Headquarters, 1982), and *Taungthu lethamar asiayone thamaing* (History of peasant associations) (Yangon: Party News and Periodicals Section, BSPP Headquarters, 1982).

20. BSPP, *Taungthu lethamar asiayone thamaing,* 163.

21. BSPP, *Achepya myanmar naingganye thamaing* (An elementary history of Myanmar politics) (Yangon: BSPP Central Organizing Committee, 1970).

22. State Law and Order Restoration Council (SLORC), *Pyidwin thaunggyan hmu thamaing* (A history of insurgencies) (Yangon: Ministry of Information, News and Periodicals Enterprise, 1990), *Htaun koeyar shihsetshih ayeakhin karla yetset kyangyouk hmu hpyit yat hman myar* (The truth about the atrocities during the 1988 disturbances) (Yangon: Ministry of Information, News and Periodicals Enterprise, 1991), and *Tatmadaw thamaing* (A history of the armed forces), 5 vols. (Yangon: Ministry of Information, News and Periodicals Enterprise, 1994); Pe Kan Kaung, *Arnar thein thaw tatmadaw*

mahout par (Not a government by authoritarian coup) (Yangon: Ministry of Information, News and Periodicals Enterprise, 1996).

23. U Htin Aung, *The Stricken Peacock: Anglo-Burmese Relations, 1752–1948* (The Hague: Martinus Nijhoff, 1965), and *A History of Burma* (New York: Columbia University Press, 1967).

24. U Htin Aung, *Stricken Peacock*, vi.

25. Than Tun, *Khit haung myanmar yazawin* (Classical Myanmar history) (Yangon: Kalya Thukha Press, 1969).

26. Than Tun, *Athit myin bamar thamaing* (A new look at the history of Myanmar) (Yangon: Mya Kan Thar Sarpay, 1975), i.

27. Than Tun, *Nehleh yazawin* (Historian on tour) (Yangon: Nant Thar Press, 1968–69).

28. Ba Shin, *Anawratha ayinga Myanmar nainggan* (Myanmar before Anawratha) (Yangon: Swe Swe Maw Sarpay, 1975), 15.

29. U Aung Thaw, U Myint Aung, and U Sein Maung, *Sheyhaung Myanmar myodaw myar* (Ancient Myanmar cities) (Yangon: Ministry of Information, News and Periodicals Enterprise, 1993), preface.

30. Hmawbi Saya Thein, *Pazat yazawin* (Oral history) (Yangon: Hmawbi Saya Thein Gyi Bookshop, 1954), 1.

31. Universities Historical Research Centre (UHRC), *Taingyinthar lu myo myar ayeh hnint 1947 achegan upade* (The 1947 constitution and the nationalities), 2 vols. (Yangon: Universities Press, 1990), *Myanmar naingganye thamaing, 1958–1962* (Political history of Myanmar), 4 vols. (Yangon: Universities Press, 1991), and *Myanma naingganye sanit pyaung karla, 1962–1974* (Myanmar political system in change), 3 vols. (Yangon: Universities Press, 1990).

32. UHRC, *Taingyinthar lu myo myar*, preface.

33. Published in Yangon in 1936 by the Nagani Book Society.

34. Thakin Kodaw Hmaing, *Saya Lun* (Yangon: Aleinmar Sarpay, 1964); and *Ba Sein ei Ba Sein* (*Ba Sein* by Ba Sein) undated unpublished manuscript.

35. Works on General Aung San include:

1943   Mya Daung Nyo, *Yebaw thongeik athtoke patti* (Biographies of the thirty comrades) (Yangon: Bawathit Book Shop)

1945   Mya Daung Nyo, *Aung San Bathu lai?* (Who is Aung San?) (Yangon: Ye Ye Tauk Distribution).

1947   Tekkatho Hsu Myaing, *Bogyoke Zarti Gon* (The general's native glory) (Yangon: Shumawa Press).

1948   U Pu Galay, *Nga doh bogyoke ba-dwe-loke-kei-tha-lai?* (What did our general do?) (Yangon: Thudhamawati Press).

1951   Aung San et al., *Bogyoke Aung San: Athtoke patti* (General Aung San: A biography) (Yangon: National Press).

1956   Lieutenant Aye Maung, *Bogyoke Aung San* (General Aung San) (Yangon: Burma Translation Society).

1965   Aung Than, *Aung Than ei Aung San* (Aung San by Aung Than) (Yangon: Nay Soe Shein Press).

1967   Tekkatho Ne Win (Lieutenant Tun Hla), *Aung San Oo doh ah-hpae* (Father of Aung San Oo) (Yangon: Gyobyu Press).

1970   Aung Than, *Aung San mithasu* (Aung San's family) (Yangon: Udann Sarpay).

Mya Maw, *Bogyoke Aung San ei naing-gan-yai, sibwa-yai, luhmu-yai hnint sit-yai atwai akkaw mya* (Political, economic, social and military thoughts of General Aung San) (Yangon: Pwint Lin Sarpay).

1975   Myint Tun, researcher, *Bogyoke Aung San ei Amyo tho hloe-hwet khayi* (General Aung San's secret trip to Amoy) (Yangon: Chit Sayar Sarpay).

1982   Tekkatho Ne Win (Lieutenant Tun Hla), *Bogyoke Aung San ei lutlatyay kyoepan hmu hmattan* (Memoirs of General Aung San's struggle for independence) (Yangon: Ah Thine Ah Wine Sarpay).

1995   Min Swe (Laputta), *Bogyoke Aung San hnit kyun daw* (General Aung San and I), (Yangon: Bar Ya Tee Sarpay).

36. Thein Swe, *Biography of General Aung San* (Yangon: National Press, 1951), *kaw*.

37. U Aung Than, *Aung San by Aung Than* (Yangon: Chit Kyi Yay Literature House, 1969), 4. Aung Than is Aung San's elder brother. Since it was first published in 1965, this book has been reprinted four times.

Chapter 7

OUR ISLAND STORY

Economic Development and the National Narrative in Singapore

C. J. W.-L. WEE

OF ALL SOUTHEAST ASIAN POSTCOLONIAL societies, Singapore is unique in the way the People's Action Party (PAP) government has, since 1959, recreated the city-state for the central purpose of economic development. The now standardized historical narrative of commercial and industrial emergence reflects this concern, in which the usual divisions between precolonial, colonial, and postcolonial are weakened. Foregrounded instead is the PAP's paramount role in effecting the achievement of "happiness, prosperity, and progress for our nation," as stated in the 1966 National Pledge. This perspective, which set in after the 1965 separation from Malaysia, became entrenched as the economy took off, to use the Rostovian term of the 1970s. While Singapore's national narrative is as linear in its historical emplotment as one centered on the story of a precolonial past destroyed by the imperialists, and while it, like some other national narratives, legitimizes the present government, this nevertheless does not detract from its distinctiveness.

There seem to be two interrelated dominant narratives. The first has to do with a Whiggish telos of economic development, progress, modernity, and modernization since 1819—when a "[t]rading station was established by Sir Stamford Raffles under an agreement between the British East India Company and the Sultan of Johore and Lingga, and the Malay Governor of the Island," signifying the beginning of "modern" Singapore.[1] The second has to do with the communist-, leftist- and communalist-inflected 1950s, from which the Lee Kuan Yew–led faction in the PAP emerged the victor, to play the leading role in establishing the self-ruling State of Singapore. In this essay, I shall examine the first of the two interrelated narratives as the second is dominated and sometimes displaced by it. But I will first say a little about the latter by way of introduction.

The second narrative more narrowly pertains to a liberal- or neo-nationalist historiography, which foregrounds elite personalities, institutions, and ideas and often sees the making of the nation-state as an idealist venture in which the indigenous bourgeoisie lead their people from subjugation to freedom. It certainly is true that in Singapore the militant leftist-led initiatives were finally unable to develop a full-fledged nationalist liberation. And it is also true that the economic thrust of the moderates in the PAP, situationally created and planned, gained gradual hegemonic status, reducing the immediacy of many of the earlier sociocultural and political difficulties. Having said this, the relationship of Lee and the moderates with Lim Chin Siong and the militant leftists within the PAP, in the 1950s until the break in 1961,[2] should pluralize the moments of sociopolitical change as the postcolonial state was being formed so that we can see these historical moments as *confrontations* between the moderates, the leftists, the communists, and the "Chinese-speaking world" (itself not homogeneous in political opinion)[3] rather than as a *transition* from a colonial society to a modern, capitalist one. A pluralistic perspective suggests that the agency of political change was not located entirely in the moderates' hands, as it is made out to be, and that the national-political narrative of emergence did not start in 1959 with the PAP's first major election victory. We need not accept a progressivist or evolutionary set of presuppositions to measure the failure or success of Singapore as an independent city-state.[4]

A broader issue in the confrontation between the leftists and the moderate socialists is the clash of two related modes of left-oriented progress and the cultural logic of what it means to stage modernity. The idea of liberty, and liberation as autonomy, is fundamental to the project of modernity: both PAP factions subscribed to a common project possessing an overall sense of history's direction within which they both used a discourse on liberation from British imperial control. The moderates' triumph, though, led to the embedding of their version of the story of political freedom *within* the overarching colonialist story of Singapore's emergence as the most modern, albeit colonial, society in the region. It was clear by the late fifties that the PAP moderates were pro-independence but not anti-British. There was not a deep antipathy toward the benefits of colonial modernity. During the Cold War, the PAP chose the First World's capitalism and modernity, a choice seemingly vindicated by the events of 1989 and the apparent triumph of the neoliberal New World Order.

After 1965, and the loss of any possible Malaysian common market, the city-state was forced to industrialize, and it did so by letting in multinational corporations (MNCs). This seemed a natural extension of allowing the world into Singapore, as it had done during the colonial period, when being an entrepôt secured prosperity for the island. Industrial development was not seen as collusion with neocolonialist or imperialist forces, as other postcolonial leaders in the Afro-Asian world might have seen it.

What happens to the discourse and narrative of political liberation with the ascendance of the PAP? After all, the colonial state had maintained a laissez-faireism narrowly concerned with an economic conception of freedom. This clashed ideologically with the early Fabianism espoused by the PAP. In the end, however, they created an interventionist state that emphasized the more material aspects of "progress." That progress, it was argued, is best maintained by encouraging a liberal, international economic order rather than individual freedom or laissez-faireism within the city-state. A critical counterpart—a discourse on disciplinization—resulted. This paternalistic discipline resembled colonial paternalism; it could already be found in the Fabian variety of socialism, which, by the earlier part of the century, had been willing to do away with parts of traditional liberalism and its commitment to individual freedom for the sake of social efficiency.[5] There is more continuity with the colonial past of Singapore than might be expected. I will return to this later.

The PAP leadership has inherited certain intellectual frameworks in which there was a conflict between individualism and collectivism.[6] The colonial legacy helped determine the PAP's worldview and allowed some generalities about Singapore's place in the world to be perceived. What reinforced aspects of this worldview was the change in the global economy away from the stable economic formation of the immediate postwar world into something that resembled more the laissez-faire world under Pax Britannica. These two considerations, then, form the intellectual and sociopolitical context from which the narrative of Singapore's economic emergence arises—the cultural logic that undergirds the city-state's commitment to maintain its position within post-1989 global capitalism.

Becoming Modern: "Our Island Story"

Among all the newly independent states that emerged in the fifties and the sixties, Singapore must stand out in having an official history in which a white man, and an official of the colonialist East India Company at that, is its official "founder." What accounts for this historical representation of Singapore identity, and how does it relate to the struggle for independence?

First, a note on historiography and some methodological matters. It is now an orthodoxy that needs little additional justification that the analysis of narrative historiography entails attention to the intellectual context of past historical works.[7] What I am interested in here, however, is less the personal visions of various scholars and more the *subscribed public visions,* in relation to the political elites who have helped formulate the Singapore Story. Given how relatively short our past is—if we accept that modern Singapore indeed did commence in 1819, even shorter if dated from independence in 1965—this seems to be a more suitable and less grandiose scheme for analysis than studying individual authors on Malayan and Singapore history in depth. In any case, thinking through the recently written nationalist histories of postcolonial societies is scarcely the same thing as sorting out, as intellectual historian John Burrow has done, the question of "Victorian historians and the English past."[8] Further, I am less concerned with the facticity—though that is an important question—of who did what, and the cause of this or that, but more the cultural logic that drives an economistic vision of who we are.

In terms of the immediate past of anticolonial nationalist liberation —that bit of "freedom" from Victorian liberalism that must occupy center stage in any account of any struggle for independence, be it Tunku Abdul Rahman's Malaysia, or Jomo Kenyatta's Kenya—the question is, Who has set the historical agenda in Singapore? Historian Hong Lysa's answer here is simple: it is the first-generation PAP politicians. We therefore start first with them before proceeding to the academic historians.

In a study of S. Rajaratnam, Hong cites his signed account of internal party history ("PAP's First Ten Years") that appeared in the *PAP Tenth Anniversary Souvenir 1964*. Among the watershed events in this account are the 1961 defection of the party leftists and their internally conflicted stand against Merger with Malaysia, shown up, as Rajaratnam would think, as weak in the 1962 referendum that elicited a 71 percent majority for the PAP's position. Another threatening party was the mainland United Malay National Organization (UMNO). The ultras, as Lee Kuan Yew called them, were, he charged, inciting communalism. Rajaratnam's call then was to "instil in our people the conviction that they and their children have more to gain by way of peace, prosperity and happiness by being Malaysians than by remaining Malays, Chinese and Indian."[9] With separation, the term Singaporeans is used in place of Malaysians, but the national-collectivist logic of working through an Enlightenment-derived idea of equality is the same.

Hong draws the following trenchant conclusion about Rajaratnam's "template of Singapore history":

> More than 30 years after it was written, the understanding of the period has not moved one iota from Rajaratnam's rendition of it. Studies

of the period—whether by John Drysdale or Dennis Bloodworth, the two authors who were given privileged access to documents of the period and to the political leaders themselves—have only confirmed the story.... The plotting of the PAP story as Singapore's history has not been seriously challenged by professional historians or by former political actors, who were [thus] doubly defeated.[10]

Part of the reason for "fixing" history is that to the victors go the ability to entrench their account of the past. But there is more at hand. Hong goes on to note,

Rajaratnam's greatest fear for Singapore was the exploitation of racial cleavages—hence he stamps the coming of Raffles . . . as [Singapore's] genesis. This unprecedented homage to the colonial heritage . . . was a "proper use of history," because [quoting Rajaratnam] "the price of a more impressive genealogical table would be to turn Singapore into a bloody battleground for endless racial and communal conflicts and interventionist politics by the more powerful . . . nations from which Singaporeans had emigrated."[11]

I am interested here less in alternative narratives of the fifties and sixties than in the fear of communalism and communism, as elements considered to be inimical by the PAP leadership to a modern Singapore. Lee Kuan Yew himself, before he championed Confucian values, had no problem in incorporating English or British elements in the history that led to a new society. After all, as he told the UK Manufacturers Association and the Confederation of British Industries in Singapore on 7 February 1967, Raffles made possible his family's success in Singapore: "I inherited what you [in the process of decolonialization] have left me. In a way, it was not all created by you because my great grandfather [from China] did play a subsidiary role and so did my father and so did I myself. So we have left [the statue of] Stamford Raffles standing on his pinnacle outside the Victoria Memorial Hall. But for him, Singapore would still be a mudflat."[12] And thus the derivative source of Singaporean modernity is oddly acknowledged via a simultaneous disdain of, yet admiration for, English actions. In the 1980s a replica of the Raffles statue was erected on the spot by the Singapore River where he first landed. It now stands in front of the Victoria Concert Hall.

As Hong notes, in recent years the PAP leaders have tried, if indirectly, to extend the history of Singapore, as it were, to before 1819—to a time before colonial modernity made its presence felt— via the state's "Asian values" program, from the eighties until its cessation in the mid-nineties. By the early eighties there was an emphasis on the "hyphenated" Singaporean—Malay-Singaporean, Chinese-Singaporean—which seemed to fly in the face of the National Pledge's sentiment, "regardless of race, language, or religion." However, the logic, even in this case, was still a question of how we could develop an *Asian* rather than *Asianized* modernity[12] without being "Western," which in retrospect seemed implicit in accepting the Rafflesian version of modern Singapore's birth. While in the earlier years the PAP leadership seemed to accept the notion of modernization as a universal process, there was, by the late seventies, public fear that "Western decadence," if not checked, could actually jeopardize the modernization process. The criticism of Asian values as nothing more than collusion, corruption, and nepotism after the 1997 Asian economic crisis seemed only to confirm the wisdom in dropping the Asian-values rhetoric.

What underlies such questionings over the national self, and its plural or singular historical genesis, is the issue of what it means to be a modern, economically developed society. In postwar Singapore, communism and communalism were depicted as impeding effective development. Since there was no one racial identity, and thus no single nation upon which to safely erect a national identity, Lee and his colleagues had aimed to make industrial modernity the metanarrative that would frame Singapore's national identity and to create a Global City that, because of its trading links, could escape the constraints placed upon it by history and geography. Eventually, this dash to become modern significantly defined the city-state's identity both "in" and "out" of less modern Southeast Asia itself. The national as a category was to be *renovated* so that racial and cultural differences could be contained and to some extent homogenized for the leap into modernity.[14] The Asian-values debate and the "Asianizing" of Singapore identity[15] arose because, in the late seventies, a notion of universal cultural homogenization as an *inherent* part of modernization seemed an obstacle to economistic nation building.

The above represents experiments in how a distinctively Singaporean progressiveness may be grounded. The British industrial bourgeoisie had in the Victorian era proudly spoken of growth and improvement, and these became pertinent issues for the leaders of the new nation-state, and remain so. The inherited idea of progress was seen, broadly, as industrialization together with the associated political and socioeducational institutions of a "developed" and "free" society. The telos of the English Whigs' "Our Island Story,"[16] with its promise of representative government directed by a spirit of liberty—in the anticolonial, democratic-socialist version of it that the PAP made as their political platform—increasingly seemed uninvigorating to the PAP leadership in the face of cultural and leftist challenges. As Peter Osborne remarks, "Indeed, one might say that in its perpetual anxiety to transcend the present, modernity is everywhere haunted by the idea of decline."[17] In Singapore's case, while the anxieties of what "Asian" Singapore is and how its economic success can be sustained are hardly resolved, this need for progress has meant, generally, using the colonial past and the modernity the British brought to the island colony as its foundational national history. This updated colonial modernity authorized the blocking of "irrational" cultural identities and an alternative, more leftist modernity as elements of a national narrative that could help build a nation able to match up economically to the former imperial master. In the midst of such nation building, internal freedom became less of an issue.

Thus, we arrive at the cultural logic driving the Singapore historical narrative. E. J. Hobsbawm remarks, "Nations without a past are contradictory in terms. What makes a nation is the past, what justifies one nation against another is the past, and historians are the people who produce it."[18] While the essentializing functions of history and its connection with the discursive construction of nationalism have been much criticized, not least by Hobsbawm himself, still, as anthropologist Akhil Gupta puts it, "National identity appears to be firmly spatialized [in everyday life] . . . , becoming almost a 'natural' marker of cultural and social difference. . . . It is difficult to imagine what a state that is not a nation would look like and how it would operate in the contemporary world."[19] Singapore is precisely that "state that is not a nation," with a historical narrative based on the very imperative of being modern itself.

Raffles, Free Trade, and Economic Development

The following narratives have been generated by the acceptance of the first-generation PAP's historical agenda, an agenda that has a continuity with the accepted colonial history of Singapore's success as an entrepôt, later to become a modern city-state useful to global capitalism beyond what its small size would indicate. These narratives, which are largely accepted in Singapore, do not represent a conspiracy between historians and the PAP historical agenda, but more the way a certain vein of historical thinking has been naturalized. I do not make an attempt to cover comprehensively all recent historical writings. The object is to examine the way economic development is made a key part of what is now called the Singapore Story. Specifically, I will look at the national narrative as it is navigated from the economic laissez-faireism of the colonial period into the postindependence period, with a no longer minimally interventionist state that nevertheless supports the maintenance of a liberal and open international order necessary to Singapore's export-oriented industry (EOI) strategy.

First, it will be instructive to look at some of the potted histories we encounter in the official publication *Singapore: Facts and Figures* (later *Facts and Pictures*), put out by the Ministry of Culture and its successor incarnations. While it is important *not* to take the state to be a unitary entity, the several versions of this publication can be taken to be an acceptable expression of the "official" mind. Despite changes from edition to edition, there is a pattern to the way their brief histories are assembled. What can be initially noted is that despite the Asian-values debate of the 1980s and 1990s, the chronology of Singapore's genesis invariably begins in 1819.

The 1964 edition, issued the year before separation, does not offer a short history but only historical dates. Not surprisingly, the bulk of the dates focus on the events leading up to moments of self-rule in 1959 and the 1963 Merger.[20] Looking at the dates from the colonial period, we find a number that recur in all the editions I looked at:

- 1819: Trading station established by Sir Stamford Raffles under an agreement between the British East India Company and the Sultan of Johore and Lingga, and the Malay Governor of the island.
- 1824: Singapore ceded in full sovereignty by the Sultan to the East India Company. Population already over 10,000.
- 1826: Incorporated, with Melaka and Penang, as the Straits Settlements.
- 1830: Straits Settlements brought under the Presidency of Bengal of the East India Company.
- 1851: Transferred to the direct control of the Governor-General of India.
- 1867: Control transferred to the United Kingdom Colonial Office.

What is the significance of the above dates, clearly inherited from a colonial historiographical structure? We can surmise that some notion of the history of governance is being offered, significant in indicating both the importance of the island to the British, the bringers of order and commerce, and a colonial administrative structure that paradoxically made a separate independent state possible in the end.

The 1967 edition, published two years after independence from Malaysia, offers a brief history, and we can start to inquire if what is emphasized represents some of the aspirations of the newly independent city-state. While a "prosperous commercial centre flourished at Singapore in the 13th and 14th centuries," "[m]odern Singapore was born in 1819."[21] Further, "[h]er strategic position in the centre of an area rich in tropical produce, coupled with a free port policy, soon attracted traders and settlers to her shores. The first 40 years of her existence saw the most rapid increase in her trade and growth" (3). By the turn of the century, "Singapore was to inaugurate the modern Malaya of tin and rubber. Finance, promotion and organisation were provided from Singapore" (4). The core of the colonial island's identity was trade and commerce rather than anything specifically "cultural" provided for by the diverse immigrants or settlers.

By the 1976 edition of *Facts and Pictures* the economy has evidently taken off, and the brief history now indicates that the colonial Rafflesian project for Singapore has not faltered in the anxiety-causing post-Malaysian years but, indeed, has found fruition. The Suez Canal's opening in 1869 is explicitly mentioned, for it "shortened the trade route between Europe and Asia and freight charges decreased; as a result, Singapore's prosperity and progress gained momentum."[22] After the Second World War, "With peace restored and the pace of commerce resumed, Singaporeans [though such nomenclature is anachronistic] began to agitate in earnest for greater involvement in government" (27). The history concludes, "With political and labour stability, Singapore continues to grow in strength and dimension. It has consolidated its pre-eminence in commerce, finance and communications, while its manufactured goods have made impressive inroads into sophisticated world markets. As envisaged by Sir Stamford Raffles in 1823, Singapore has become 'the emporium and pride of the East'" (28). The 1986 edition has a chronology that stresses how well the PAP has functioned at the polls, thus underlining how the party is intrinsically part of Singapore's postwar history. Apart from that, the major innovation is a list of "Heads of Government," which starts off with "Col. William Farquhar (Resident and Commandant)" (1819–23); moves on to a period marked as "Internal Self-Government," which has Sir William Goode (1957–59), and then David Marshall and Lim Yew Hock as the only two chief ministers; followed by three entries for Lee Kuan Yew, first as prime minister in the last stretch of the period of internal self-rule (1959–63), then during the Malaysian period and thereafter.[23] If the publications previously had indicated continuity in the economic project, we now see a continuity in the form of governance in Singapore.

The 1998 version no longer lists the heads of government and restores a three-paragraph discussion of the pre-1819 history of the island. However, it may not be useful to read too much into this, as the early history of Singapore exists as a vague or semimythic narrative to do with Sang Nila Utama. The chronology retains the key colonial dates of the 1964 edition, and the PAP's electoral victories are listed.[24]

Now we can ask how the more scholarly histories compare with the official representations of the city-state's history. I begin with two narratives dealing with economic growth. The first is the late, distinguished historian Wong Lin Ken's "Commercial Growth before the Second World War."[25] Wong begins almost immediately by emphasizing Raffles's vision: "Raffles' initiative and foresight in the choice of Singapore and the enterprise of Asian and Western merchants had rescued Singapore from obscurity in history, turning it into the most successful Western enclave in South-East Asia developed almost wholly by untrammeled private enterprise" (41). His essay reminds us that globalization is scarcely a recent phenomenon, for the liberal markets that liberal imperial Britain supported allowed the backwater of Singapore to connect with the Western industrializing world:

> Singapore's entrepôt trade was global in character, and the two sides of the entrepôt trade were complementary, manufactures being paid for by the Straits produce. Thus, Singapore thrived as the intermediary for the trade between the advanced industrial economies and countries with lower levels of achievement. . . . Singapore was the example par excellence of a colonial port that had prospered on global trade because its overlord had the wisdom not to confine its trade for narrow imperial gain. (42)

Wong then traces the rise of Britain as the foremost naval and industrial power in the world, the rise of free trade, and the consequent decline of mercantilism. Open Singapore "could not have prospered in the earlier era of mercantilism" (47). The expansion of colonial rule also brought with it political order and the legal framework for private enterprise and international free trade. Private enterprise had been the engine of growth in pre–World War II Singapore; the laissez-faire colonial state had mainly provided laws and infrastructure for the port. The interwar years, unfortunately, saw a decline in free tradism, and even Great Britain resorted to imperial preference—a system Singapore actually did not benefit from. Wong's conclusion emphasizes the externally created modernity: "Pre-war Singapore was an alien creation. . . . it represented what could be achieved with private enterprise unfettered by indigenous customs and institutions, or governmental interference in trade. It started as the spearhead in the region of an expanding international system based on free trade and private enterprise" (63). This is a universal progressivism that disdains the local. Freedom in this era was the freedom of safe sea travel, and under this benevolent imperialism, the opportunities for "post-war Singapore nationalists to face new challenges with solid historical advantages" (63) actually were created. This is a view of nationalism that is appreciative of colonial rule.

How do the postwar years fit into the narrative of private enterprise and free trade? I now turn to another article in Ernest Chew and Edwin Lee's *A History of Singapore,* a major effort at plotting Singapore's history. Cheng Siok Hwa records that the 1940s "closed . . . with often well-founded expressions of anxiety regarding the prospects for the future development of entrepôt trade."[26] Growing economic nationalism and the desire to regulate foreign currency in the region were part of the causes for the question mark over entrepôt trade. Still, trade mattered and the Korean War raised primary commodity prices. Nonetheless, the new PAP government took on the equally new task of "economic development via industrialization based on the free-enterprise capitalist model" (187).

The Economic Development Board was established as a state agency in 1961 to encourage industrialization, and Singapore maintained an "open economy" that benefited from the boom conditions prevailing in the industrial West of the sixties. That is to say, foreign capital was encouraged into Singapore, and the state—more so than in British times—provided strong infrastructure in the form of basic services such as power and water supplies, "and more directly in aiding secondary industry—conducting research, upgrading industrial and vocational training" (186), and so forth. The real difference from the colonial laissez-faire era was that "[t]he Government also participated directly in the economy, establishing wholly owned and partly owned industrial and commercial ventures" (213). This state participation in the seventies "mitigated somewhat the preponderance of foreign investment vis-à-vis local investment in the economy" (214). Of course, external factors beyond the state's control—"such as the state of world trade, the international monetary system, inflation" (215), and so forth—directly affect Singapore's growth.

We can see that despite the difference that the pre– and post–World War II histories show, between the laissez-faireism of the colonial state and the more interventionist postindependence state, influenced by aspects of a democratic-socialist concern for the social and thus some form of collectivism, the assumption is one of strong continuity of a commercial, later expanded to an industrial, modernity free from too much irrational, local cultural baggage. This assumption gives us the core of the city-state's national narrative. While a laissez-faire colonial modernity had its limitations, it taught nascent Singaporeans that an international order committed to liberal free trade was, and continues to be, vital for Singapore's success.

Continuity is an explicit theme in Edwin Lee's "The Colonial Legacy,"[27] a de facto commentary on aspects of both Wong's and Cheng's work. This is clear from the opening paragraph of Lee's article: "From that date [1819], a new society was born at one of the nodal points in the maritime trade of the world. The British presided over every stage of its growth and development from the time of its birth to 1959, when the new creation was deemed ready to rule itself internally and to become fully independent in the 1963–65 period" (3). And with this thought, we also can see why the 1986 edition of *Singapore: Facts and Pictures* did not seem to have a difficulty setting up a list of heads of governments that could flow from the colonial period into the postindependence periods. Lee foregrounds very much the context of laissez-faire colonial rule: "The founding . . . owed a great deal to major reorganizations of the world's economic system" (3). The first was the increasing importance of the China trade, which led the British to look for a Southeast Asian base, and the second was the Industrial Revolution, which led to the demise of the mercantilist system of trade. Raffles, though an East India Company employee, "was a firm believer in free trade" (4).[28]

Like Wong, Lee also advances the idea of the externality of Singapore's modernity, along with a certain cultural philistinism: "The city was indeed a modern construction. Singapore, even in the days of British rule, lacked historical atmosphere and had few monuments erected. . . . Grace, elegance, and beauty were not altogether absent, but the emphasis was on the utilitarian and modern rather than the aesthetic or antiquarian" (40). In terms of governance, the British "set standards of justice, efficiency, and incorruptibility which in turn generated feelings of well-being, trust and confidence in the subject peoples" (41).

Does all this explain why democracy is emaciated in Singapore? Or why freedom is manifest mainly in the support for international free trade? Or even why colonial historiography becomes postcolonial historiography as a sort of memory of the present? While Lee doesn't directly answer these questions, an answer is implied in his thinking on irresponsible rule, which can be very "responsible" in a paternal fashion. One colonial example of such irresponsible rule is Lord Alfred Milner's South African "Kindergarten." Milner and his associates saw themselves as "British race patriots"[29] engaged in "the endless adventure of governing men."[30] Lee writes:

> One hundred and forty years or so of British rule have etched on the Singapore consciousness certain principles and values which have become part of the national ethos. Singapore today is a country where the responsibility of government is assumed as a sacred trust, where the prime minister sets the tone of public life as the colonial governor once did, where the rule of law prevails. . . . It is this combination of the spiritual and tangible aspects of our colonial heritage that makes it such a power for good. (42)

Committed irresponsible rule is now an intrinsic part of the city-state's democratic life.

Political scientist Chan Heng Chee's take on the historiography that Lee's article represents is less positive. She agrees that "colonial values and precepts . . . provided the original foundation to the [PAP] administration," and that these values "were soon modified or jettisoned to meet the demands of a dynamic post-colonial government engaged in the rapid transformation of society and a search for effectiveness." However, in the final analysis, "[t]his legacy favored the development of a paternalistic authoritarian government, a style which came to characterize the PAP government, and more surely, the Singapore Government."[31]

Chan's negative opinion on a colonialist mentality, however, only reinforces the fact that there is an overall consensus regarding a continuity from the colonial period in the progressivism entailed in the Singapore version of Our Island Story. The original constitutionalist direction of the British story, though, is recast so that it is economic development and the freedom of markets backed by the rule of law that "progresses" rather than individual freedom.

Freedom and Modernity, the Interventionist State, and the Free Market

What accounts, above all, for the particular historiographical trajectory outlined above is the desire to catch up with the former imperial master's modernity using their cultural as well as economic legacy.[32] Economic development is a supposedly culturally neutral way to achieve the modernizing goal that avoids the stirring up of communal differences. How this goal of catching up functions to motivate the historiography has at least two intersecting or overlapping dimensions to it. The first is the inherited sets of ideas within which Singapore to some extent still functions, even if not so strongly now as in the fifties through the seventies. The second is the nature of the world economic order within which the city-state came into its own and how that world parallels aspects of the Victorian world, in which free trade was important.

First, the question of some of the key ideas within the inherited British view of the world, especially as it relates to the kind of state formation and nation building that the PAP used. The break in cultural-intellectual continuity before and after independence obviously cannot be absolute. Problematic as terms such as *postcolonial* or *postcoloniality* are in defining any coherent or practical space, the term *postcolonial* is useful in two ways that Sangeeta Ray and Bill Schwarz suggest: first, as indicating "the strictly historical and sociological study of what happens after colonization," and second, in the way it "can be seen not merely as the political moment of the break from the colonial past but also as the philosophico-cultural departure [or lack thereof] from the larger homogenizing logic of European modernity."[33] The latter accounts for the irony of postcolonial Singapore as the fruition of a colonial project.

Let me begin with the idea of liberty and liberation. In Singapore's case, as discussed earlier, in place of the individual freedom of liberal England, the PAP government offered a redefined notion of freedom as economic freedom along with a strong emphasis on (a heavy-handed) collectivism, in a combination of both the postwar European welfare state idea and colonial authoritarianism.

The PAP was a democratic-socialist party; we need not take that commitment to a benevolent paternalism as completely sham, even given the accusations made by the Dutch Labour Party against the PAP in 1976 of repression and the suppression of the trade union movement and intellectual freedom, which led to the PAP's withdrawal from Socialist International.[34] The issue of freedom remains more complex. How do the exported values of democratic socialism fare in a colonial society that retained the marks of a Victorian laissez-faire heritage, in a Southeast Asia in the midst of the Cold War? The national narrative that later resulted is a local negotiation of the "freedom" concept so important to liberalism and the conflict between individualism and collectivism, which itself emerges from earlier British debates over state intervention. The result of this negotiation is a Singapore that has become an internally interventionist and paternalistic collectivism that is the strongest champion of the international neoliberal economic order in Southeast Asia. This is an ideologically conflicted position to take, though it has held together through the 1980s and until the 1997 Asian economic crisis. The "pragmatic" economic position the state generally takes ("it works") in large measure has offset the need for a rigorous sorting out of the situation's complexities.

What one should also note is that the PAP's pragmatic scrambling of British political-economic thinking is not unique. One need only think of the complex history of mid-Victorian liberalism itself as it threads its tortured way into the twentieth century. By the time it reaches Margaret Thatcher in the 1980s, liberalism's economistic free-market aspects are absorbed into something called the New Right of the Tory Party, becoming an odd admixture of authoritarianism, nostalgic and nationalistic imperial adventurism, privatization, and support for the free market.

As we now know all too well, while the collapse of the right in Western Europe should have seen the reemergence of social-democratic parties that might have countered the economic neoliberalism of previous regimes, this did not happen. Tony Blair's and Gerhard Schröder's victories instead have become a Third Way and a *Neue Mitte* (new center), which are, in Blair's own words at the Labour Party's 1998 Blackpool conference, "pro-business and pro-enterprise."[35] What is now left, in both senses of the word, is a need for that popular buzzword *governance*—meaning depoliticized systems of regulation—rather than the now old-fashioned (interventionist) *government*. The Blairite catchphrase "No rights without responsibilities" would work well in "authoritarian" Singapore.

The confusion of the combined parts of liberalism and some dissipating socialist elements in Blair's Third Way and Singapore's pragmatist developmental discourses can be reduced if we recall the debates that revolved around the limits of state intervention as it related to the conflict between individualism and collectivism in the decades before the First World War. Concepts or values such as individualism shift in meaning; the contexts and arguments that framed them mutate, while their polemical force suggest that the variety of meanings were not infinite.

There is often a conflictual relationship between economic and social thinking. A recapitulation of the vicissitudes of liberal and collectivist values will remind us, first, that liberalism and socialism have always had a checkered existence, and second, that the contradictory economistic, communitarian, and also historiographical navigation of the ideological terrain of free-marketeerism is not without its confused precedents.

The economic argument, then as now, was the strongest force against state intervention in the nineteenth century. The colonial manifestation of the laissez-faire economy in Singapore, we can recall, was very much an issue in the various Singapore narratives. While the classical economists variously had recognized the need for some state functions, the clear presumption was that the economy was a system that regulated itself better than through forms of direct control. Alfred Marshall (1842–1924) thought it obvious that "those tendencies of Socialism that are towards increased bureaucracy" must be fought against.[36] An implicit theory of social justice in which there were no grounds to deprive the successful individual of any part of his wealth to give benefits to others also supported the economic argument. The moral importance of character also figured in such arguments, as *self-reliance* became *self-development;* this is in Mill's *On Liberty* (1859), as it is in Spencer's *The Principles of Ethics* (1893, vol. 2).

Collectivism and *socialism* were simply not interchangeable terms in this period. The theorists of social reform did not necessarily espouse socialism, though this charge could always be laid at their door, given that socialism could refer to either the ideal of collectively pursuing the common good or, pejoratively, a radical conception of society that abolished property, marriage, religion, the family, and so on.

By the 1900s, though, it had become possible to apply moral arguments to the term *socialism,* and to speak of "moral socialists." Some consequently claimed that liberalism had transcended itself, and those who came to be called New Liberals dissociated themselves from socialism while arguing that they were only extending liberalism's principles. The so-called socialist revival of the 1880s had brought a new set of socialist arguments into public view, and the New Liberal political theory of the 1900s was a compromise between traditional liberalism and socialism. What was common to both traditional and new liberalism, however, was the commitment to the principle of liberty, whether it was freedom from tariffs or freedom for the individual to pursue his or her interests. However, just what that reform meant started to differ.

L. T. Hobhouse (1864–1929), the first professor of sociology at London University, argued in *Liberalism* (1911) that his version of New Liberalism entailed the idea of the common good, which justified the state's intervention in existing private property rights. "The outcome of this exercise," Stefan Collini observes, "is a theory of redistributive justice in the economic sphere which would certainly be recognized as 'Social-Democratic.'"[37] Hobhouse also had a relationship with Fabian socialism. While he approved of the Fabian recognition that the state was "simply the people organized for all purposes of self-help to which such collective action can be made adaptable,"[38] he came to be annoyed with the way Beatrice and Sidney Webb and George Bernard Shaw considered liberal values as outmoded sentimentality standing in the way of bureaucratic administration by the specialist in the name of social efficiency. The Webbs were to gain the reputation of being imperialists who looked to a national and militarist state to implement their moderate collectivism.

The truncated history above gives a sense of the desire for freedom as it related to issues of individualism and collectivism, even as they were being reworked by different political actors. Thereafter, there was a breach between the Liberal and the Labour Parties, with the latter gaining dominance.

Singapore's economy, as managed by the PAP, gained pace in a period where, once again, the economic argument dominated. As a result, liberty seemed less important than social efficiency through bureaucratic rule so as to maneuver Singapore's way in a world where the postwar economy of national control seemed to be weakening. Elements of Fabian bureaucratic technocracy were thus in place. Freedom and liberty were not allowed to stand, given the supposedly realist attitudes to the world, with consequences for the national narrative. The question that follows, then, is, What was the nature of the global economy during which the PAP aggressively pursued an EOI strategy in Singapore from the 1960s? This, too, reinforced the cultural logic of the economistic national narrative. I enumerate below a few of the changes taking place in the international economic arena.

There was the collapse of the Bretton Woods semifixed exchange rate regime and the OPEC oil crisis, both of which produced volatility in the major economies. U.S. involvement in the Vietnam War also created global and domestic (U.S.) instability. Manufacturers and financial institutions compensated for domestic instability by seeking wider outlets during the inflationary seventies, leading to large bank loans to the Third World. An acceleration in the internationalization of the financial markets took place via market deregulation in the late seventies, though other volatile currency markets were reined in by the Louvre and Plaza Accords in the eighties. There was Anglo-American de-industrialization and long-term unemployment in Western Europe, leading to the weakening of the welfare state that had promised security for all and had been (as a concept at least) a model for a number of postcolonial leaders. Japan began to compete with the West.

Finally, a "flexible" regime of accumulation developed, versus the more nationally rooted, standardized (or Fordist-Keynesian) mass production of the oligopolistic corporation, predicated upon a certain combination of labor practices, consumption habits, and technological innovation. A more complex world of MNCs evolved, along with smaller, more agile firms, and with them, the so-called New International Division of Labour. Increasingly, offshore finance mattered too. Companies set up factories outside their home country, often in developing ones with cheaper labor. If the advanced economies exported more to the rest of the world, significantly, "the Third World [also] began to export manufactures to the developed industrial countries on a substantial scale."[39]

The security of the postwar period, predicated upon national control, seemed weakened in the trend toward increased internationalization, though the General Agreement on Trade and Tariffs helped keep the world trading system open and with at least some calculable rules. Still, the postwar multilateral order is no longer with us. As two authors succinctly put it, "'Globalization' is a myth suitable for a world without illusions."[40] Singapore became a beneficiary of these changes. Its full takeoff occurred when the advanced economies became more uncertain of themselves and when transport and communications growth allowed small units like Hong Kong and Singapore to become viable hubs in the new flows of capital.

The result is a city-state that functions as an aggressive individual within the global free market, but within the country functions as a paternalistic, interventionist state supported by a bureaucratic technocracy. The Singapore state displays some aspects of collectivist behavior, as in the extensive provision of subsidized public housing, but that is done in order to maximize the country's ability *to compete* regionally and globally. And so, in practical ways, the reassessment of the social and intellectual legacies of British liberalism and socialism transpired in Singapore, as it seemed to be functioning in an international economic environment that had a resemblance to development of international manufacturing in the Victorian free-trade era.[41] The economistic national narrative becomes, in the end, less a history of our past and more a narrative that iconoclastically hurtles Singapore's citizenry forward into a utopian future.

I have contended that the national narrative of Singapore's emergence is one concerned with economic development. This is a narrative based on the teleology of a progressive modernity, but with limited scope for individual freedom.

The narrative itself draws from an older colonial narrative of Singapore's development from a trading station (a factory, in older parlance), to the premier entrepôt in British Southeast Asia, ruled over by a benevolent if also negligent colonial state through a laissez-faire economic regime. Independence allows an indigenous government to take over, but one that maintains the "best" traditions of Britannia and simultaneously adds on the state-interventionism that Fabian socialism advocated could remedy social injustices. This postcolonial state also proceeds with an intense modernizing process, while functioning within the assumptions, and later championing the liberal free-trade order, of the colonial era, now reconstituted into the neoliberal New World Order. This, I have argued, is a significant adaptation and mix of the values and prerogatives of classic liberalism and socialism: minimal intervention outside and maximal intervention within the nation-state.

The overwhelming presence of the Singapore Story, and the claims that successive PAP governments make about their role since the late 1950s in this story of Singapore's arrival, to some extent explains why there are no "subaltern" histories written in the nation.[42] The "masses"—the immigrants who came to the island—are represented in the history, but usually as the hard-working peasants who contributed to the larger success of the trading center, or as the self-help, individual success story.[43] Non-Singaporean scholars ask why Singaporean scholars are obsessed by the state; why, indeed, *Singaporeans* are obsessed by the state. The dominance of the Story and the annexation of the past for the future go to some extent toward answering those questions.

It can be argued that Singapore's national economic narrative is indicative of some of the pathologies involved in postcolonial state formation. The historical fever of the nineteenth century in Western Europe "invented," as Eric Hobsbawm puts it, national traditions to legitimate the imperial nation-state and give coherence to societies conflicted by the developments of the Industrial Revolution. Many postcolonial societies chose to follow the same path of historical invention in their national cultural formation. But the PAP chose another route: they saw that path of national invention as dated and instead were more attracted by the frenzied modernization that had marked the late-Victorian fin de siècle. The Singapore that resulted functioned within the zone of what Walter Benjamin has described as the homogeneous empty time of the capitalist present; the embrace of colonial modernity was thus the embrace of capitalist reification. In a way, this modernization followed the path that the Japanese had earlier trod.[44] And it would be a path that other Southeast Asian societies, who later wanted Asian Tiger status, would try to follow in the 1980s.

The 1997 Asian crisis has forced the city-state to liberalize its economy faster than it has wanted, with the result that the vision of

a high-tech future that Singaporeans have lived with for a generation—with the government saying that it is less able to protect its
citizens from global capitalism's ferocity—may now become a dys-
topian vision, as it has been for many locations less in tune with the
global economy. In a society in which the government has welcomed the promises of informational cyberspace—now an industry
in crisis, with the 2001 U.S. dot.com crash—and in a world in which
historical consciousness is still waning, one wonders what sort of
structures of temporality can exist to ground Singaporean identity.
Some have spoken of a "global postmodern" in which the advanced
world and the semiperiphery interpenetrate each other. But the
Asian crisis also patently shows that this does not mean there is no
longer a center or a margin, even if, in Asian Singapore's case, it has
been part of the West for some time.

Notes

Thanks go to Barbara Watson Andaya, Cheah Boon Kheng, and, especially, to Tan Liok Ee for their responses to an earlier version of this chapter.

In the text, the page numbers of sequential citations of certain sources
are given in parentheses.

1. *Singapore: Facts and Figures 1967* (Singapore: Ministry of Culture,
1967), 6. The same line appears virtually as the opening entry in sections entitled either "Historical Dates" or "Chronology" in every *Facts and Figures*
(later *Facts and Pictures*) publication thereafter.

2. The Barisan Sosialis was formed as a breakaway, or ejected, party in
September 1961.

3. See Dennis Bloodworth, *The Tiger and the Trojan Horse* (Singapore:
Times Books International, 1986) and "The Plen: What Singapore Would
Have Become," *Straits Times Interactive* (Singapore), 22 July 1997, <http://
www.asia1.com.sg/straitstimes>.

4. C. J. W.-L. Wee, "The Vanquished: Lim Chin Siong and a Progressivist National Narrative," in *Lee's Lieutenants: Singapore's Old Guard,* ed. Lam
Peng Er and Kevin Y. L. Tan (St. Leonards: Allen and Unwin, 1999), 169–
90. See also Loh Kah Seng, "Within the Singapore Story: The Use and Narrative of History in Singapore," *Crossroads* 12, 2 (1998): 1–21; T. N. Harper,
"Lim Chin Siong and the 'Singapore Story,'" in *Comet in Our Sky: Lim Chin*

Siong in History, ed. Tan Jing Quee and Jomo K. S. (Kuala Lumpur: Insan, 2001), 3–55. *The Singapore Story* is also the title of volume 1 of Lee Kuan Yew's memoirs, *The Singapore Story: Memoirs of Lee Kuan Yew* (Singapore: Times Editions, 1998).

5. In Singapore's particularist multiracial society, the state as the guarantor of freedoms gained would draw on existing institutions, such as the Emergency Regulations set out by the British, later transformed first into the 1955 Preservation of Public Security Ordinance and thereafter the Internal Security Act, and restrict what it takes to be the most dangerous aspects of autonomous human action.

6. The political-theoretical terms Liberalism, Individualism, and Collectivism, as they were used from the late nineteenth century to the First World War, were capitalized but have since acquired broader and more general usages.

7. Quentin Skinner, "Meaning and Understanding in the History of Ideas," *History and Theory* 8 (1969).

8. J. W. Burrow, *A Liberal Descent: Victorian Historians and the English Past* (Cambridge: Cambridge University Press, 1981), 4.

9. The text of "PAP's First Ten Years" is reprinted in *The Prophetic and the Political: Selected Speeches of S. Rajaratnam,* ed. Chan Heng Chee and Obaid ul Haq (Singapore: Graham Brash, 1987), 64.

10. Hong Lysa, "Making the History of Singapore: S. Rajaratnam and C. V. Devan Nair," in *Lee's Lieutenants,* 101. She refers to Bloodworth, *Tiger and the Trojan Horse,* and John Drysdale, *Singapore: Struggle for Success* (Singapore: Times Books International, 1984).

11. Hong, "Making the History," 104. She is quoting from a speech by Rajaratnam given in 1968.

12. Cited in Alex Josey, *Lee Kuan Yew* (Singapore: Donald Moore Press, 1968), 538.

13. C. J. W.-L. Wee, "The 'Clash' of Civilizations? Or an Emerging 'East Asian Modernity'?" *SOJOURN: Journal of Social Issues in Southeast Asia* 11, 2 (1996): 211–30.

14. Hong reinforces this point: "Rajaratnam's cosmopolitanism should be understood as a provocation to those he saw as advocating ethnic-based nationalisms in Singapore rather than as being the credo of a supra-national humanist, for his concern is unabashedly centred on Singapore as a nation and the politics that would ensure its survival." Hong, "Making the History," 106. Also see C. J. W.-L. Wee, "Contending with Primordialism: The 'Modern' Construction of Postcolonial Singapore," *positions: east asia cultures critique* 1, 3 (winter 1993): 715–44.

15. Raj K. Vasil, *Asianising Singapore: The PAP's Management of Ethnicity* (Singapore: Heinemann, 1995).

16. The phrase itself is probably from Alfred, Lord Tennyson's "Ode on the Death of the Duke of Wellington" (1852) and was in that context more militaristic than Whiggish: "Not once or twice in our rough island-story / The path of duty was the way to glory." Cultural items can have strange lives.

17. Peter Osborne, "Modernity is a Qualitative, not a Chronological, Category," *New Left Review* 192 (March–April 1992), 76.

18. E. J. Hobsbawm, "Ethnicity and Nationalism in Europe Today," *Anthropology Today* 8, 1 (Feb. 1992): 3.

19. Akhil Gupta, "The Song of the Nonaligned World: Transnational Identities and the Reinscription of Late Capitalism," *Cultural Anthropology* 7, 1 (Feb. 1992): 63, 73.

20. *Singapore: Facts and Figures 1964* (Singapore: Ministry of Culture, 1964), 11–13.

21. *Singapore: Facts and Figures 1967* (Singapore: Ministry of Culture, 1967), 6, 3 respectively.

22. *Singapore: Facts and Pictures 1976* (Singapore: Ministry of Culture, 1976), 26.

23. *Singapore: Facts and Pictures 1986* (Singapore: Ministry of Communications and Information, 1986), 19.

24. *Singapore: Facts and Pictures 1998* (Singapore: Ministry of Information and the Arts, 1998), 10–15.

25. Wong Lin Ken, "Commercial Growth before the Second World War," in *A History of Singapore,* ed. Ernest C. T. Chew and Edwin Lee (Singapore: Oxford University Press, 1991), 41–65.

26. Cheng Siok Hwa, "Economic Change and Industrialization," in Chew and Lee, *History of Singapore,* 181.

27. Edwin Lee, "The Colonial Legacy," in *The Management of Success: The Moulding of Modern Singapore,* ed. Kernial Singh Sandhu and Paul Wheatley (Singapore: Institute of Southeast Asian Studies, 1989).

28. This interpretation has come under question recently. See Anthony Webster, *Gentlemen Capitalists: British Imperialism in South East Asia, 1770–1890* (London: Tauris Academic Studies, 1998), 67.

29. Alfred Milner, "Credo," *Times* (London), 27 July 1925.

30. F. S. Oliver, *The Endless Adventure: Personalities and Practical Politics in Eighteenth-Century England* (London: Macmillan, 1930), 3. Oliver was an associate of Milner's.

31. Chan Heng Chee, "Political Developments," in Chew and Lee, *History of Singapore,* 176.

32. The acknowledged economic architect of Singapore, Dr. Goh Keng Swee, was conscious of the Victorian colonial economic legacy. See Tilak

Doshi and Peter Coclanis, "The Economic Architect: Goh Keng Swee," in *Lee's Lieutenants,* 24–44; Goh Keng Swee, *The Economics of Modernization* (Singapore: Asia Pacific Press, 1972), esp. p. 41, where he counsels readers to read Samuel Smiles, "a singularly odious Victorian character."

33. Sangeeta Ray and Bill Schwarz, "Postcolonial Discourse: The Raw and the Cooked," *ARIEL* 26, 1 (Jan. 1995): 150.

34. For details of the clash, see C. V. Devan Nair, comp. and ed., *Socialism That Works . . . The Singapore Way* (Singapore: Federal Publications, 1976).

35. *International Herald Tribune,* 28 Sept. 1998.

36. Alfred Marshall, *The Official Papers of Alfred Marshall,* ed. J. M. Keynes (London: Macmillan, 1926), 253.

37. Stefan Collini, *Liberalism and Sociology: L. T. Hobhouse and Political Argument in England, 1880–1914* (Cambridge: Cambridge University Press, 1979), 129.

38. L. T. Hobhouse, "The Career of Fabianism," *Nation,* 30 March 1907.

39. E. J. Hobsbawm, *Age of Extremes: The Short Twentieth Century, 1914–1991* (London: Abacus, 1995), 280.

40. Paul Hirst and Grahame Thompson, *Globalization in Question: The International Economy and the Possibilities of Governance* (Cambridge: Polity, 1996), 6.

41. Ibid., 31.

42. We could take Brenda S. A. Yeoh's *Contesting Space: Power Relations and the Urban Built Environment in Colonial Singapore* (Kuala Lumpur: Oxford University Press, 1996) as one historico-geographical attempt to do a subaltern-type history.

43. C. F. Yong, *Tan Kah-Kee: The Making of an Overseas Chinese Legend* (Singapore: Oxford University Press, 1989); C. F. Yong, *Chinese Leadership and Power in Colonial Singapore* (Singapore: Times Academic Press, 1992); Richard Lim, *Building a Singapore Bank: The O[verseas] U[nion] B[ank] Story* (Singapore: Overseas Union Bank, 1999); Lien Ying Chow, with Louis Kraar, *From Chinese Villager to Singapore Tycoon: My Life Story* (Singapore: Times Books International, 1992); Ho Rih Hwa, *Eating Salt: An Autobiography* (Singapore : Times Books International, 1991).

44. *The Japanese Trajectory: Modernization and Beyond,* ed. Gavan Mc-Cormack and Yoshio Sugimoto (Cambridge: Cambridge University Press, 1988); Marilyn Ivy, *Discourses of the Vanishing: Modernity, Phantasm, Japan* (Chicago: University of Chicago Press, 1995).

Chapter 8

HISTORY THROUGH THE EYES OF THE MALAYS

Changing Perspectives of Malaysia's Past

ABDUL RAHMAN HAJI ISMAIL AND
BADRIYAH HAJI SALLEH

> Malay histories were a sociocultural expression of the Malay society in the past.—Mohd. Taib Osman, *Bunga rampai: Aspects of Malay Culture*

ACCORDING TO SOCIOLOGIST Mohd. Taib Osman, the Malay historian was himself a participant of the culture about which he wrote.[1] He could not extricate himself from the subject about which he was writing, as he was deeply and constantly conscious of the sociopolitical worldviews current in his society. Thus myths and legends could not be completely separate from history. This perspective has not been understood by some scholars, such as J. C. Bottoms, who made the well-known statement: "History to the Malay has not until recently been either a science or an art, but an entertainment."[2] Bottoms was referring to some of the classical Malay histories, such as the *Sejarah Melayu* (*The Malay annals*) or the *Sulalatussalatin,* and other Malay historical writings of the fifteenth to nineteenth centuries. To the Malays, however, the true expression of history is perhaps possible only when embedded in the values and worldviews of the society of the time, with its own cultural sensibilities, all of which, Osman stresses, were a necessary part of writing about and understanding real events in history.

Here we will not indulge in arguments about what Malay historians in the past thought about history for it is clear that the meaning of history among the Malays has since changed and evolved. With the advent of Western influence, especially through education, the writing of history permeated different levels of Malay society and was no longer the prerogative of the royal courts, as was the case before the twentieth century. Historical themes have moved from focusing on the palace to the lives of ordinary people, although this process has taken a long time. Concomitantly, the objectives of history writing have changed too, from defending the legitimacy of *raja*s (rulers) and royal institutions to galvanizing the *bangsa* (national community)[3] in support of the nationalist struggle. Nor will we trace the changing trends in history writing among the Malays since the early days when it included "a pleasant hotch-potch of Court and port gossip," and hence was considered by some scholars as not really history in meaning and purpose.[4] Rather, the main focus is on history writing in Malay since 1945;[5] historical writings before 1945 are discussed to provide a necessary sense of continuity.

Traditional Malay Historiography

Early Malay histories existed in the form of oral tradition. In their efforts to affirm and explain their existence and that of the world around them, Malays related themselves to some "facts" or "events" located in the past. Their lives and values were constructed according to these facts or events, which their society generally held to be truths, even if they might be, in fact, anachronistic or fictitious. Hence, for example, it was not unusual for the majority of the people during that period not to rebel against their raja (at least not blatantly) because they believed implicitly that the raja was chosen by God and was bestowed with *daulat* (divine power).[6] This explains why the themes of early Malay histories were centered on the rajas. Such histories, written in the form of a *kisah* (story) or *hikayat* (story, history), such as *Hikayat Malim Dewa* or *Hikayat pelanduk jenaka,*[7] were not so much history as didactic stories that portrayed the Malay sociopolitical and cultural worldview of the period through the exploits of Malim Dewa, a supernatural hero with astounding powers, and the fabled mouse deer, who outwitted foes with clever strategies.

Real historical figures replaced fictitious ones when court historians began to write the genealogies of their masters. Some famous ones are: *Sulalatussalatin* (popularly known as *Sejarah Melayu*), *Hikayat Raja-Raja Pasai, Hikayat Patani,* and *Hikayat Merong Mahawangsa;* the genealogies of the rulers of Melaka, Pasai, Patani, and Kedah, respectively.[8] However, the style of writing remained the same as the real historical figures or events were still encapsulated within the sociopolitical and cultural worldview of the Malays of the time, so that the *Malim Dewa* characteristics still remained in the characters of the sultans or rajas of the real kingdoms or states. The rajas were usually connected to some legendary or fictitious heroes or kings; for example, they were not only likened to great kings from the past, such as Iskandar Zulkarnain (Alexander the Great), but were actually said to be their descendants. Indeed, many of the early *hikayat* and *salasilah/silsilah* (genealogy) explicitly stated that their objective was to exalt the raja by making his glorious lineage known. But, besides the intention of highlighting the importance of the ruling institution and its personalities, these histories were also written to serve as reminders or warnings to future generations of rulers that the mistakes of the past should not be repeated in the future. For example, as early as 1865 Raja Ali Haji, the author of *Tuhfat al-Nafis,* had made a clear statement that the aim of his book was to present a "perfect" historiography that could be "used."[9] Similarly, other works such as *Hikayat Siak* and *Salasilah Melayu dan Bugis* were written with functional objectives in mind.[10]

Although the writing of history in Malay continued to focus on the palace, as in *Misa Melayu, Riwayat Kelantan,* and *Hikayat Pahang,* two authors in the nineteenth and early twentieth centuries broke away from this norm to write about their personal experiences as well as about society at large.[11] For this reason, *Hikayat Abdullah, Kisah pelayaran Abdullah,* and *Kisah pelayaran Muhammad Ibrahim Munshi*[12] stand out as markers in the development of Malay writing, especially because they were not emulated by anyone else of the same period.

In 1918 history was brought to the ordinary people when it was introduced as a subject in the teacher-training program in the Melaka Teacher-Training College by R. O. Winstedt, then the assistant director of education of the Federated Malay States.[13] The history texts used then were, among others, the *Sulalatussalatin, Hikayat Hang Tuah,* and *Hikayat Abdullah.* Other hikayat-style books written in the twentieth century are *Hikayat Pahang,*[14] *Hikayat seri Kelantan,*[15] and other state and personality histories.[16] It was also Winstedt who, in collaboration with Daing Abdul Hamid bin Tengku Muhammad Salleh, introduced a nonhikayat history, *Kitab tawarikh Melayu* (Book on the history of the Malays), which differentiated history from legend.[1721] This kitab, which provided a very general history of the Malay world, became a school textbook. In 1925 Abdul Hadi bin Haji Hasan, a graduate of the Melaka Teacher-Training College, produced *Sejarah alam Melayu,* using *sejarah,* the term currently adopted to refer to history. The first in this three-volume series of textbooks was very general; it discusses the origins and characteristics of the Malays and other indigenous peoples of the Malay world throughout the Malay Archipelago while the history of the Malay Peninsula is the central theme of the second volume.[18] Another teacher, Buyong Adil, who graduated from the prestigious Sultan Idris Teacher-Training College, completed the series by writing volumes 4 and 5.[19] The *Sejarah alam Melayu* series, which was reprinted several times, remained in use as standard history textbooks in schools throughout the 1950s and 1960s.

The period after the First World War, especially the economic depression of the twenties and early thirties, stimulated increasing political awareness among the Malays and history writing began to acquire a different role. Some Malay writers from the establishment, that is from either the government services or the *istana* (palace), who had been educated in Malay or English schools, began to write histories that could instill awareness among the Malays concerning their position as one nation or bangsa.[20] There were also writers who felt that there was a need to educate society in general through providing knowledge of the histories of other nations, such as Turkey, India, China, and Japan in Malay, so that readers could broaden their horizons and learn about other parts of the world that could be emulated. In the early forties, the struggle for political unity, and a single political entity, among the Malays gathered momentum. This was clearly manifested in the nationalist writings of Ibrahim bin Haji Yaakob, Burhanuddin Mohd. Noor Al-Helmy, Ahmad Boestamam, Ishak Haji Muhammad, Zainal Abidin bin Ahmad (Za'ba), Harun Aminurrashid, among many others, which will be discussed below.

Malay Historiography:
The Independence Era (1945–1960s)

A convenient year to demarcate the period before and after World War II is 1945, as experiences from the war left an indelible effect on many countries in the world, and Malaysia is no exception. But 1945 was not an absolute starting point for changes or developments in that country, as many new trends had started evolving much earlier.[21] In the field of history, most of the writing produced before 1945 was by nonprofessional historians—that is, people who were not formally trained in the discipline. Not only did this trend continue after 1945, it in fact became more pronounced as nationalist leaders of social and political movements, said to be "in full bloom" and more aggressive after the Pacific War, became prolific writers.[22]

One example is Ibrahim Yaakob, whose *Melihat tanah air* recorded observations from his travels to several states in the peninsula.[23] Another is Burhanuddin Mohd. Noor Al-Helmy in *Perjuangan kita* highlighted the Malay nationalist struggle and, in particular, the part played by Parti Kebangsaan Melayu Malaya (the Malay Nationalist Party) in opposing the British attempt to create a Malayan Union in 1946.[24] Another book, *Asas falsafah kebangsaan Melayu,* published in 1951, traced the origin, basis, and nature of the Malay nation from the earliest times to the middle of the twentieth century.[25] Earlier, in 1947, his colleague, Ahmad Boestamam, explained the rationale for establishing the youth wing of the party, in his *Testament politik API* (Political testament of API). *Api* (lit., fire) was the acronym for the youth organization Angkatan Pemuda Insaf (Awakened Youth Organization).[26] In the next few years Ibrahim Yaakob published three more books on the history of the struggle for freedom by the Malay leftist movement, of which he was one of the most prominent members: *Sedjarah dan Perdjuangan di Malaya, Nusa dan bangsa Melayu,* and *Sekitar Malaya merdeka.*[27]

The struggle for independence continued to be the favorite topic among Malay writers in the fifties and sixties: for example Muhammad Yunus Hamidi's *Sejarah pergerakan-pergerakan politik Melayu Semenanjung* and Mukhtar Petah's *Bangsa Melayu menggugat dunia.*[28] Some authors began to write about leaders who had fought against the British during the early period of the latter's encroachment into the Malay states to uplift the fighting spirit of the Malays. Among the popular historical personalities were Dol Sa'id of Naning, Tok Janggut of Kelantan, and Dato Bahaman of Pahang. Dol Sa'id, who led the fight against the British in Naning in 1831 and 1832, became a favorite topic for several writers, such as Syahba (a pseudonym)[29] and Darus Ahmad.[30] Dato Bahaman, who fought against the British in Pahang, also became a favored topic.[31] This period thus saw not only growing admiration for local heroes of the past but also indicated Malay writers' consciousness of the function of history in inciting patriotism.

In response, readers engaged actively in discussions about how history should be treated. On a book by Abdul Talib bin Haji Ahmad about Dato Bahaman, one reader commented: "The attempt of historian Abdul Talib bin Haji Ahmad to start a new phase in the history of the motherland is an effort that should be appreciated and encouraged."[32] The reader's evaluation of Abdul Talib's book was based on an appreciation of the author's efforts in investigating his subject by researching into primary sources besides using interviews and other references. In comparison, earlier books about Dato Bahaman by other authors had, according to the reader, "raised questions concerning their historical contents" because they were "unsuitably written and not meticulous, at times insincere and at other times even 'belittling.'"[33] From this brief quote, one can already gauge the sensitivity and objectivity of the reader in raising methodological issues. The reader's comments as a whole reveal that he had very clear ideas about the aims of writing history; which should be to elevate local personalities such as Dato Bahaman, who had fought against the British as "national heroes" and legitimize the status of the land of their birth, in this case Pahang, as an independent state.[34] Written in the same spirit as *Sejarah Dato Bahaman* is Abdul Talib Haji Ahmad's *Darah mengalir di Pasir Salak,* about Dato Maharajalela and others who fought with him against the British in Perak in a series of events that ended with the murder of J. W. W. Birch, the first British resident,[35] and Haji Abdullah bin Amirah's *Riwayat hidup Tok Janggut dan peperangan di Kelantan,* about the anti-British struggle in Kelantan.[36]

Books about local heroes during the British period were complemented by writings on the glories of the Melaka kingdom and its personalities. Reminiscences of the past appeared to be a necessary part of the process of strengthening the morale of the Malays before, and in the first few decades after, Malaya's independence in 1957. Among the best-known examples are Abdul Samad Ahmad's *Tak Melayu hilang di dunia* and *Laksamana Tun Tuah,* Ahmad Bakhtiar's *Korban keris Melaka,* Darus Ahmad's *Perang Melaka,* Ali Aziz's *Zaman gemilangnya kerajaan Melayu Melaka* and Harun Aminurrashid's *Sultan Mahmud Shah Melaka.*[37] It was quite obvious that the Malays of the newly independent Malaya yearned to return to the period when Melaka was at the height of its glories.

Harun Aminurrashid experimented with a special way of instilling historical consciousness by writing a novel, *Panglima Awang,* based on historical facts he obtained from two essays, one in an English and one in an Indonesian newspaper.[38] The two essays, similar in content, were about a Malay seaman who was acclaimed as the first person to have sailed around the world for the simple reason that he had followed Ferdinand Magellan on the latter's historic trip. But Magellan did not complete the trip as he was murdered in the Philippines, and it was the Malay seaman, known as Enrique in the newspaper essays, who completed the journey. By rights therefore, Enrique should be recognized as the first person to have sailed around the world. Harun Aminurrashid suggested that it was Western prejudice that had denied Enrique that honor and proposed, "It is the duty of historians of the Malay race who have become independent to revise our history, which has been suppressed for about five centuries by Western colonialists, and it is most proper to trace the background of Enrique."[39] Harun's aim in writing *Panglima Awang* as a historical novel was to present history from the native point of view. The book describes the famous adventure as an imaginary trip by the seaman Awang, a common Malay name chosen to suggest that he could be any person who was an expert sailor.

Harun Aminurrashid was not alone in trying to imbue his society with a sense of history. Other historical novelists followed suit in their endeavor to "enrich the libraries of the Malay nation" with heroes who, according to Abdul Talib Ahmad, had "created history." From studying past events, the Malays could learn about "past weaknesses, shortcomings, stupidities, as well as the strength and weaknesses of the Malay nation at that time." History could provide the "guiding light" for the present, as well as future, generations.[40] For the same reasons, from the 1950s to the 1970s and even later, Malay society was inundated by stories of Malay heroes and kingdoms of the past, with stories about Hang Tuah, Hang Jebat, and Tun Biajid becoming particularly popular.[41]

History enthusiasts also broadened their scope of interest to district and state histories. There was a slew of books, such as Shaharom Hussein's *Tawarikh Johor,* Misbaha's *Mengkaji sejarah Terengganu;*

Zainal Abidin Daud's *Riwayat Tanjung Malim;* Haji Abdullah bin Musa's *Sejarah Perak Dahulu dan Sekarang;* Abdul Talib bin Haji Ahmad's *Riwayat Kinta;* and Asa'ad Shukri Haji Muda's *Sejarah Kelantan.* Buyong Adil, the most prolific and well-known writer of this genre, deserves special mention as his works covered the histories of almost every Malay state.[42] He started with the *Sejarah alam Melayu* series, continuing the work begun by Abdul Hadi Haji Hasan in the 1940s and taking it up to the 1980s, while his later works were based on references from other sources, such as the *Tuhfat al-Nafis* and books written by R. O. Winstedt.

Writing about the personal experiences of individuals was another way of bringing history to the general public. Conscious of living in historic times, Abdul Aziz Ishak, a politician and former Federal Minister, wrote *Riwayat hidup Tunku Abdul Rahman Putra* about the first prime minister of Malaya/Malaysia and the author's former superior in the government.[43] Mokhtar Petah chose to write about a revered leader of the Islamic Party of Malaysia who died in a road accident in 1964 in *Zulkifli Muhammad dalam kenangan*[44] while Anwar Abdullah focused on Dato' Onn Jaafar, the first president of the United Malay National Organization (UMNO), who quit in 1951 to form an alternative political party.[45] A politician who was also a journalist, Ahmad Boestamam, wrote about his colleagues in *Dr. Burhanuddin: Putera setia Melayu Raya* and *Dato' Onn yang saya kenal.*[46]

Ahmad Murad bin Nasruddin, a teacher, wrote *Nyawa di hujung pedang* and Abdul Aziz bin Zakaria wrote *Lt. Nor Pahlawan Gerila,* both books about Japanese atrocities in Malaya and the struggle against them.[47] In 1951 Ahmad Murad reissued a book, first published ten years earlier as *Cerita mata-mata hutan simpan,* a straightforward record of the experiences of a Malay forest ranger, Illias bin Ahmad, in the performance of his duties during the decades before the Pacific War. Besides Ahmad Murad, there was Abdullah Hussein, journalist and creative writer, who wrote a number of "true story" narratives about his personal experiences. Two of them, *Terjebak* and *Peristiwa,* narrated his experiences as a member of the Fujiwara Kikan in Malaya and Sumatra during the Japanese occupation.[48]

Though not trained as professional historians, these writers had, consciously or unconsciously, evolved together with the development of history writing. The most prolific among them were teachers, writers, and literary figures, who wanted to see the Malay language "returned" to its proper position as the country's national language and for Malay schools to be the national schools of the country upon its independence. Hence the 1950s and 1960s also saw several works on the history of Malay education, language, and literature, among them Mansur Sanusi's *Sejarah perkembangan pelajaran Melayu*[49] and Abdul Samad Ahmad's *Sejarah kesusasteraan Melayu*.[50] Darus Ahmad's *Pancharan Melayu,* Anas Haji Ahmad's *Sastera Melayu lama dan baru,* Harun Aminurrashid's *Kajian sejarah perkembangan bahasa Melayu,* Li Chuan Siew's *Ikhtisar sejarah kesusasteraan Melayu baru, 1830–1945,* and Abdullah Sanusi bin Ahmad's *Peranan Pejabat Karang Mengarang* were all part of the same growing writers' movement.[51] As these topics demanded more factual and verifiable accounts based on documented sources, the trend in the late 1960s moved increasingly toward writing history for the sake of knowledge, as an academic exercise to provide much-needed general and specific information. This movement strengthened as students trained at local Malaysian universities began writing in Malay after it became the medium of instruction.

History Writing in Malay by Professional Historians (1970s–1990s)

After 1970 the concept of, and approaches to, history writing among the Malays and others who wrote in Malay gradually changed. This change came about after Bahasa Malaysia, the national language, was used as the medium of instruction at the Faculty of Arts and Social Sciences at the University of Malaya in Kuala Lumpur; the National University of Malaysia, first in Kuala Lumpur then moved later to its present location in Bangi; and the School of Humanities and the Social Sciences of Universiti Sains Malaysia in Penang. The history departments of these universities trained historians to conduct research on local history. This was, in fact, not completely new, as history students of the University of Malaya in Singapore and the first few batches of students to graduate from its Kuala Lumpur campus had already started conducting research on local topics, except that they wrote in English.[52] The introduction of Malay as the medium of instruction in higher institutes of learning brought with it some new approaches to history writing.

Another change in history writing came after local academics and their students were influenced by the call to write history from a local point of view. This began with D. G. E. Hall's proposal in the 1950s that "history cannot be safely viewed from any other perspective until seen from its own,"[53] which sparked off an intense debate among Southeast Asian historians. In the 1960s the issue of centricity became the topic of a heated debate involving John Bastin, then professor of history at the University of Malaya, and his contemporaries.[54] The debate inspired revisionist interpretations of history that had been written before from a Western point of view.[55] After 1970 historical research in the three local universities, in the form of academic exercises and theses, were written not only largely in Malay but increasingly from a local point of view. The topics were broad and varied; from political organizations and personalities to administrative structures and institutions to socioeconomic developments and cultural history; moving from history from above to history from below; and ranging from macro- to microperspectives on the past. As students were encouraged to work on areas or topics they knew well, their work ranged over many different localities— from the history of kampungs (villages), small towns, and districts in various states in the peninsula, to that of Sabah and Sarawak, two states often neglected in earlier studies.[56] Some of the students' works were published but most were not.[57]

The local universities also produced non-Malay professional historians who were able to write in Malay. With the implementation of the National Education Policy, Malay, as the national language, had become the main medium of instruction at the primary level and the sole medium at the secondary level. By 1980 all local university students, especially in the arts stream, were proficient in the language. Thus non-Malay history students not only could write in Malay, they were able to stretch the variety of research topics to cover themes concerning non-Malay communities.[58] This was in tandem with the political sensitivities of a time when the integration of the country's plural population became very important and the role and presence of non-Malays needed to be acknowledged.

In 1987 Anwar Ibrahim, then the minister of education, made history a compulsory subject in secondary schools. This increased the number of students who majored in history in Malaysian universities, especially among those aspiring to be teachers. General interest in history also grew as historical examples and reminiscences about the grandeur of the past were quoted by politicians in their speeches and seminars or workshops—on the history of Malay culture, or the Malay language, or on individual states—were conducted by universities, the national archives, museums, and historical associations.[59] This resulted in numerous research papers, many of which were published as articles in journals, as chapters of books, or compiled as monographs.

The role of publishers and journals in popularizing history in Malay should also not be underestimated; in particular Pustaka Antara in Kuala Lumpur and Sinaran Brothers in Penang published many history books. Local universities and the Malaysian Historical Society have also made important contributions; for example, in 1972 the first volume of the journal *Malaysia dari segi sejarah* (Malaysia in history) was produced to replace its predecessor, *Malaysia in History,* while the University of Malaya came out with *Jernal sejarah* (Journal of history) to replace the earlier English version, *Journal of History.* The history department of the National University of Malaysia followed with the publication of its journal, *Jebat.* In 1982 the Malaysian Museum Society, whose members consisted mainly of local historians and archaeologists, produced its own journal, *Purba* (Antique), while in 1983 Universiti Sains Malaysia in Penang launched a bilingual journal, *Kajian Malaysia* (*Malaysian Studies*). Ten years later the history department of the University of Malaya produced another history journal, *Sejarah* (History), to replace its precursor *Jernal sejarah*. And in 1994 the School of Humanities of Universiti Sains Malaysia initiated *Jurnal ilmu Kemanusiaan* (Journal of Humanities), which frequently publishes articles and debates in Malay on Malaysian history and historiography. Articles published in these journals are varied; most are academic papers presented at conferences or seminars, some are parts of graduate theses, yet others are term papers or course essays.

The popularizing of history writing in Malay stimulated some debates on changing Malay values and worldviews. A critically acclaimed essay by Kassim Ahmad, a local Malay graduate, which analyzed the portrayal of two main characters in a Malay text, brought to light a different interpretation of the Malay concept of a hero, signaling the beginning of serious revisions of the concept of raja as ruler, his powers and daulat, the relationship between raja and *rakyat,* the Malay subject, and other key concepts in the Malay worldview.[60] The classical *Sulalatussalatin,* which used to be popular as literature, became an important historical text. Reinterpretations of such classics began to suggest that there was more reciprocity in the relationship between raja and rakyat, and the authority of the raja was not as absolute as previously believed.[61] The changing concept of Malay heroism was reflected in the choice of *Jebat* (from Hang Jebat, the antihero character in Malay folk love) as the title of the history journal of the National University of Malaysia.

In response to complaints from students and the general public about a lack of good history books in Malay, Dewan Bahasa dan Pustaka, the government publisher, has produced translations of several major works in English, such as D. G. E. Hall's *A History of South-East Asia,* R. Emerson's *Malaysia: A Study of Direct and Indirect Rule,* W. R. Roff's *The Origin of Malay Nationalism,* O. W. Wolters's *The Fall of Srivijaya in Malay History* and *Early Indonesian Commerce,* Leonard and Barbara Andaya's *A History of Malaysia,* Leonard Y. Andaya's *The Kingdom of Johor, 1641–1728,* as well as R. G. Collingwood's *The Idea of History* and E. H. Carr's *What Is History?*[62]

Political history and personalities have long dominated the interest of Malay historians, with political figures, religious leaders *(ulama)*, writers, and journalists the most popular topics of research. There are three books on Dato' Onn Ja'afar, the first president of UMNO;[63] and, biographies of Tunku Abdul Rahman Putra, the first prime minister of Malaya/Malaysia;[64] Ibrahim Yaakob, one of the founding members of the Kesatuan Melayu Muda;[65] Dr. Burhanuddin Al-Helmy, a well-known figure in the fight for a greater Malaysia through the concept of *Melayu Raya* (Greater Malay Nation encompassing the whole of the Malay Archipelago);[66] and, Ishak Haji Muhammad, journalist, writer, and politician,[67] have been published in the last few decades. Religious and literary figures have also been topics of interest; for example, Sayyid Syaikh Al-Hadi, well-known writer and publisher;[68] Raja Ali Haji, the author of *Tuhfat al-Nafis;*[69] Syaikh Tahir Jalaluddin, an early-twentieth-century Islamic reformer;[70] and Za'ba, teacher-writer-nationalist.[71] Another source for local history and religious personalities is *Pengasoh,* a periodical produced by the Kelantan Council of Islamic Affairs and Malay Custom. The biographies of twenty-seven ulama were selected from this periodical for publication in *Tokoh-tokoh ulama semenanjung Melayu* (Ulama personalities of the Malay Peninsula) by Ismail Che Daud in 1987.[72]

From the history of politics and personalities, the themes of historical works in Malay have broadened as scholars moved into debates about social movements and protests. Stories of ordinary kampong heroes, who were revered for their exploits and prowess, became part of the history of protest movements against the British after they were researched methodically using archival and library materials. Well-known examples are Abdullah Zakaria's work on anti-British movements in Perak, Jang Aisjah Muttalib on the Pahang War, and Timah Hamzah on the Terengganu protests.[73] Many historians have moved into more contemporary history, stimulated perhaps by the memorable stories told by the people who have lived through the events. The history of the Japanese occupation has, perhaps for this reason, attracted much interest;[74] so has the Malayan

Emergency,[75] and the Thirteenth of May Incident, on which there are two books, one of which is by Tunku Abdul Rahman, then prime minister of Malaysia.[76] By comparison, relatively less has been written on the economic depression of 1929 and the 1930s.[77]

On the history of Islam, Malay historians have preferred to write about religious personalities, such as prophets, caliphs, and ulama, who are held up as exemplary role models for readers.[78] Another area that has attracted interest is the history of Islamic education and reformist movements in Malaysia.[79] In addition, there are some works written specifically to refute or correct what authors felt was a misunderstanding about Islam; for example, in 1958 Abdullah Hamid Edrus wrote *Sejarah Nabi Musa,* based on the Qur'an, to correct what he believed to be fallacies portrayed in the Hollywood film *The Ten Commandments* and to prevent people, specifically Malays, from believing uncritically the movies they watched.[80]

Though historiography has attracted much less attention among local historians, there nevertheless have been some significant contributions. Interest in Malaysian historiography began with local professors, such as Khoo Kay Kim, formerly from the University of Malaya, who has written both in Malay and English about the development of history writing in the country,[81] and Muhammad Yusof Hashim, also formerly professor at the University of Malaya, who has produced several works more specifically in the area of Malay historiography. Using selected Malay texts such as *Hikayat Raja-Raja Pasai, Sejarah Melayu, Hikayat Aceh, Bustanus Salatin, Hikayat Siak, Hikayat Patani,* his *Persejarahan Melayu Nusantara* discusses how the indigenous peoples in this region wrote their history based on their worldview of society and civilization. Muhammad Yusof believes that the writing of history in Malay can, and should, be traced back to the tenth century, to the earliest "Malay" history, *Arjunawiwaha,* a Javanese historical epic about the Airlangga dynasty.[82] Muhammad Yusof delved further into Malay historiography by going to the philological roots of traditional writings for the states of Terengganu and Pahang in his *Terengganu Daruliman: Tradisi persejarahan Malaysia* and *Tradisi persejarahan Pahang.*[83] These works serve, to some extent, as a rejoinder to J. C. Bottoms's earlier views, generally regarded as a misconception by Malay scholars.

Later Malay writings are surveyed in Mohd. Yusof Ibrahim's *Pensejarahan Melayu, 1800–1960,* which analyzes the changes in historical interpretation and structure of historical writings over the years based on a classification of available works according to themes; such as ancestral history, biographies, religious history, socioeconomic and political history, and popular history published in newspapers and journals. According to the author, who teaches at Universiti Kebangsaan Malaysia, more than 160 historiographical works in Malay, which have yet to be classified, have been published and hundreds more collected by the Malaysian National Library.[84]

At Universiti Sains Malaysia the emphasis has been on introducing broader theories and methods in history through books that can help to overcome the shortage of undergraduate texts in Malay. This began with R. Suntharalingam's *Pengenalan kepada sejarah* and *Pensejarahan barat,* both intended for undergraduate students.[85] The focus on historiographical issues was sustained in two later publications, *Isu-isu pensejarahan* and *Alam pensejarahan dari pelbagai perspektif.*[86] The latter originated from a national seminar on historiography, organized by the history section at the Penang-based university, in which a broad range of issues was discussed: from the role of individuals in history, the nature of historical causation, and the role of women to the use of different historical perspectives in researching Malaysian history. Papers were written not only by historians but also by scholars from other disciplines, highlighting the awareness among local historians that interdisciplinary approaches can enrich history writing.[87] Other publications from Universiti Sains Malaysia have taken a broad thematic approach rather than one limited to Malay or Malaysian historiography, with books on nationalism, colonialism, violence in history, and a more recent volume on Malaysian history.[88] The emphasis in these volumes, which have drawn on the combined efforts of lecturers from several universities, has been on questions of meaning, interpretation, causation, and consequences in history, rather than on detailed descriptive accounts of events.

Concurrent with the development of history writing in Malaysia is the production of more history textbooks for schools. From the 1939 Federated Malay States Education Report, we learn that British education officers, unhappy with a situation in which different types of schools in the country were using a variety of history syllabi, tried to come up with a standardized history syllabus for all schools.[89] The syllabus drawn up by the colonial education department, not surprisingly, centered on European, especially British, personalities and events. Local history was given scant attention, with the history of the Malay States and Malay world treated only as an adjunct to the British Empire. This is reflected in the books published for use in Malay schools, from the prewar years to almost two decades after Malaya's independence. Even though the writers were themselves Malays, there was little sensitivity to the importance of teaching young children the history of the country or of the Malays. The aim of history textbooks written during this period was simply "to fill a small part in the vacuum of books of knowledge available in Malay."[90] Classical Malay texts, such as *Sulalatussalatin,* were used more as general reading materials than as history texts.

There was a slight change in the syllabus after 1959, when the purpose of history teaching in schools was more clearly defined. "Official" history, as determined by the Ministry of Education, was to have two principle objectives—to provide explanations of the past so that students would understand present problems better and to use past experiences to teach young children to be more tolerant of one another, thereby promoting integration of the multiethnic communities through the teaching of history in schools. The National Education Policy, as laid out in the Razak Report of 1956, addressed similar aims through the strategy of using Malay, the official national language, as the main medium of instruction in national and national-type schools.[91] At this juncture, there was more emphasis on the role of Malay as the national language than on the content of the history syllabus itself.

Many of the textbooks approved by the ministry, and other history books available in the market in the 1950s, were written with the syllabus of the various public examinations in mind.[92] At the primary level, the objectives of studying history were reduced merely to learning about major scientific discoveries, personalities, and events that would "inform children about famous people and also make them understand about famous discoveries that helped improve their lives."[93] At the lower secondary level, the syllabus focused more on the history of world civilizations than on Malaysian history.[94] The heart of the history curriculum was still not Malaysian history, which was introduced only at the upper secondary (i.e., Forms 4 and 5) and the pre-university (Form 6) levels, along with Southeast Asian History. The history of Malaya that was taught began chronologically from the Melaka sultanate and continued up to independence, in 1957.[95] In contrast to the kind of history being written for general consumption, the textbooks produced to meet the syllabus requirements of the public examinations were stiff and factual, a mechanistic inventory of names, dates, and events. Naturally, the teaching of history in the schools was also mechanical and uninteresting, with students more concerned with memorizing answers to standard examination questions from guidebooks that were plentiful on the market. Writing such books became a lucrative occupation for some historians, but history failed to be an attractive subject for school students.

The history syllabus for Malaysian schools was reviewed in 1987, when Anwar Ibrahim, then minister of education, declared that history was to be made a compulsory subject. The core of the new history syllabus was changed to center on the history of the Malays, considered to be the principle indigenous people of the country. This was a move closely tied up with political trends in the 1980s, during which many Malay academicians, sociologists, writers, and politicians participated in several seminars on the Malay language, Malay history, and civilization.[96] Malik Munip's *Tuntutan Melayu,* which argues that the history of the Malays, as the original indigenous people, should be the basis of national history is representative of the views of some Malay academicians who had written on such issues.[97]

The Ministry of Education subsequently invited professional historians, many of them from the local universities, to rewrite the syllabus, taking into consideration the political sensitivities of the time. The Melaka sultanate, considered to be the basis of Malay culture and system of government, became an important component of the new history syllabus, which also includes the history of other Malay kingdoms from the fifteenth to the nineteenth centuries, the British period followed by the large-scale immigration of Chinese and Indians, local struggles against colonialism, changes in the economy, the growth of a new nation-state, postindependence development and progress, and finally Malaysia in world affairs, highlighting the position of Malaysia in the modern world.[98] This new syllabus became the basis of history textbooks published in the 1990s.[99] From a more critical perspective, however, one could say that though Malaysia has become the focus of official history as taught in schools, most history textbooks still have not succeeded in giving us a truly autonomous local perspective, as defined by John Smail.[100]

Although history writing in Malay has grown tremendously, there are still many gaps to be filled. Political themes continue to dominate, followed by social issues, with most writings centered on the Malays. The social history of different ethnic communities, both in West and East Malaysia, in particular much of the history of the indigenous peoples of Sabah and Sarawak, is still not covered. Women's history, economic history, and the history of intellectual and cultural trends remains extremely scanty. Few historians want to research the history of the indigenous peoples because of the lack of primary sources, while many are still influenced by the idea that primary sources must always be in the form of written or recorded in documents. In the absence of such documents, the imagination of historians appears to be stunted and their confidence challenged. Many Malaysian scholars are still unwilling to experiment with the use of interdisciplinary approaches, such as those advocated by Western postmodernists. There is still insufficient debate about alternative methodologies of history writing. The Malaysian History

Society has encouraged the publication of good research but does not extend its role more aggressively beyond that. History has not yet become a matter of popular interest, stimulating the public to become part of a more lively and uninhibited discourse on the meaning and purpose of history for ordinary people. The writing of "history from below" is still the prerogative of those who are trained at the universities. History workshops, such as have become popular among "barefoot" historians in Europe,[101] have not yet spread to the Malay-speaking public in Malaysia.

Notes

1. Mohd. Taib Osman, *Bunga Rampai: Aspects of Malay Culture* (Kuala Lumpur: Dewan Bahasa dan Pustaka, 1988), 125.

2. J. C. Bottoms, "Malay Historical Works: A Bibliographical Note on Malay Histories as Possible Sources for the History of Malaya," in *Malaysian Historical Sources,* ed. K. G. Tregonning (Singapore: University of Singapore, Department of History, 1962), 38.

3. The term *bangsa* can mean nation as well as race, as it connotes a sense of community based on culture, language, and Islam (the religion of the people from the "Malay world").

4. Bottoms, "Malay Historical Works," 38.

5. The focus is on those works which were published in the Malay language, in contrast to other works published in English, Chinese, or Tamil.

6. The word *daulat* in Arabic originally meant empire but has a different connotation in Malay, where it means a supernatural power bestowed by God on a person, usually a ruler.

7. Pawang Ana and Raja Haji Yahya, *Hikayat Malim Dewa* (The story of Malim Dewa) (Petaling Jaya: Fajar Bakti, 1971); *Hikayat pelandok jenaka* (The story of the comical mouse deer), comp. Ahmad Murad Nasruddin (Singapore: Malaya Publishing House, 1955).

8. *Sulalatussalatin,* or *Sejarah Melayu,* is available in several versions, see *Sejarah Melayu, The Malay Annals,* comp. Cheah Boon Kheng, romanized by Abdul Rahman Haji Ismail (Kuala Lumpur: Malaysian Branch of the Royal Asiatic Society, 1998); *Hikayat Raja Pasai* (History of the kings of Pasai), comp. Russell Jones (Petaling Jaya: Penerbit Fajar Bakti, 1987); *Hikayat Merong Mahawangsa* (The Merong Mahawangsa chronicle), comp. Siti Hawa Salleh (Petaling Jaya: University of Malaya Press, 1970); *Hikayat*

Patani (The story of Patani), comp. Siti Hawa Salleh (Kuala Lumpur: Dewan Bahasa dan Pustaka, 1992).

9. Raja Ali Haji, *Tuhfat al-Nafis: Sejarah Melayu dan Bugis* (The precious gift: History of the Malays and Bugis). The text, romanized by Munis bin Ali from the Jawi manuscript, was published in *Journal of the Malaysian Branch of the Royal Asiatic Society* 10, 2 (1965): 1–379. This quotation from Muhd. Yusof Ibrahim, *Pensejarahan Melayu, 1800–1960* (Malay historiography) (Kuala Lumpur: Dewan Bahasa dan Pustaka, 1997), xiii.

10. *Hikayat Siak* (The story of Siak), comp. Muhammad Yusoff Hashim (Kuala Lumpur: Dewan Bahasa dan Pustaka, 1992); *Salasilah Melayu dan Bugis* (Genealogy of the Malays and Bugis), comp. Mohd. Yusof Md. Nor (Petaling Jaya: Penerbit Fajar Bakti, 1984).

11. Raja Chulan, *Misa Melayu* (Sacred Malay heritage) (Kuala Lumpur: Penerbitan Pustaka Antara, 1966), which describes Perak in the eighteenth century, was written in the 1830s by a member of its royal family. Written by Asa'ad Shukri, *Riwajat Kelantan* first appeared as a series of articles in the journal *Kenchana* (Gold) and was later published in book form as *Sejarah Kelantan* (Kelantan history) (Kota Bharu: n.p., 1962). See Muhd. Yusof Ibrahim, *Pensejarahan Melayu 1800–1960,* 11 n. 34; Khoo Kay Kim, "Local Historians and the Writing of Malaysian History in the Twentieth Century" in *Perceptions of the Past in Southeast Asia,* ed. Anthony Reid and David Marr (Singapore: Heinemann Educational Books for Asian Studies Association of Australia, 1979), 304 n. 29. Kalthum Jeram, *Hikayat Pahang* (Kuala Lumpur: Penerbit Fajar Bakti, 1980).

12. Abdullah bin Abdul Kader Munshi, *Hikayat Abdullah* (The story of Abdullah), first published in Jawi in 1847; English translation by A. H. Hill in *Journal of the Malaysian Branch of the Royal Asiatic Society* 28, 3 (1955). Abdullah bin Abdul Kader Munshi, *Kisah pelayaran Abdullah dari Singapura ke Kelantan* (The story of the voyage of Abdullah from Singapore to Kelantan) (Kuala Lumpur: Oxford University Press, 1967o); first published in Jawi in Singapore, 1838. Muhammad Ibrahim Munshi, *Kisah pelayaran Muhammad Ibrahim Munshi* (The story of the voyage of Muhammad Ibrahim Munshi) (Kuala Lumpur: Dewan Bahasa dan Pustaka, 1980); first published in Jawi in Johore Bahru, 1919.

13. R. O. Winstedt later became the director of education of the Federated Malay States and the Straits Settlements between 1916 and 1931. See Ramlah Adam, "Maktab Melayu Melaka" (Malay College of Melaka), (academic exercise, Department of History, University of Malaya, Kuala Lumpur, 1972), 19; Khoo Kay Kim, "Panji-Panji gemerlapan: Satu perbicaraan pensejarahan Melayu" (Glittering flags: Debate on Malay historiography), in *Historia: Essays in Commemoration of the Twenty-fifth Anniversary of the*

Department of History, University of Malaya, ed. Muhammad Abu Bakar et al. (Kuala Lumpur: Malaysian Historical Society, 1984), 181.

14. There are at least two versions of this unpublished chronicle in the National Archives of Malaysia; see Kalthum Jeram, *Hikayat Pahang* (Pahang history) (Kuala Lumpur: Penerbit Fajar Bakti), 1980.

15. See Mohd. Taib Osman, "Hikayat seri Kelantan" (History of Kelantan) (M.A. thesis, University of Malaya, 1961); Khoo, "Local Historians," 300–301.

16. Ibid., bibliog. index, 409–10.

17. John Bastin, "Sir Richard Winstedt and His Writings," as quoted in Khoo Kay Kim, *Pensejarahan Malaysia* (Malaysian historiography) (Kuala Lumpur: Kementerian Kebudayaan, Belia dan Sukan, 1975), 14.

18. Abdul Hadi Haji Hasan, *Sejarah alam Melayu* (History of the Malay world) (Singapore: Tiger Press for Federation of Malaya Education Department, 1952). No copies of volume 3 are available; see Cheah Boon Kheng, "Writing Indigenous History in Malaysia: A Survey on Approaches and Problems," *Crossroads: An Interdisciplinary Journal of Southeast Asia* 10, 2 (1997): 45.

19. Buyong Adil, *Sejarah alam Melayu,* vols. 4 and 5 were printed for the Education Department by the Malaya Publishing House in Kuala Lumpur in 1948; a reissue of vol. 4 (Singapore: Tiger Press, 1952) was also located. Buyong Adil's prolific contributions on the histories of the Malay states are discussed later.

20. For example, Dato Haji Ramly bin Abdullah (Toh Tan Dewa Paduka) wrote *Orang-Orang Melayu Perak darul ridzwan* (The Malays of Perak, the abode of grace) (Taiping: n.p., 1935).

21. For intellectual developments before 1945, see W. R. Roff, *The Origins of Malay Nationalism* (Kuala Lumpur: Penerbit University Malaya, 1974), 126–177 passim.

22. Firdaus Haji Abdullah, *Radical Malay Politics: Its Origins and Early Development* (Petaling Jaya: Pelanduk Publications, 1985), 73.

23. Ibrahim bin Haji Yaakob, *Melihat tanah air* (Surveying the motherland) (Kota Bharu: Al-Islamiyah Press, 1941).

24. Burhanuddin Mohd. Nor Al-Helmy, *Perjuangan kita* (Our struggle) (Penang: United Press, 1955).

25. Burhanuddin Mohd. Nor Al-Helmy, *Asas falsafah kebangsaan Melayu* (The philosophical foundations of Malay nationalism) (Bukit Mertajam: Pustaka Semenanjung, 1954).

26. See Ramlah Adam, *Ahmad Boestamam: Satu biografi politik* (Ahmad Boestamam: A political biography) (Kuala Lumpur: Dewan Bahasa dan Pustaka, 1994), 150–51.

27. Ibrahim Yaakob, *Sedjarah dan Perdjuangan di Malaya* (History and the struggle in Malaya) (Jogjakarta: Nusantara Publisher, 1951); *Nusa dan bangsa* (Land and nation) (Bandung: N.U. Alma'arif, 1951); *Sekitar Melaya Merdeka* (On Independent Malaya) (Jakarta: Kesatuan Melaya Merdeka, 1957). For the first book, Ibrahim used the pseudonym I. K. Agastja.

28. Muhammad Yunus Hamidi, *Sejarah pergerakan-pergerakan politik Melayu semananjung* (The history of Malay political movements in Malaya) (Kuala Lumpur: Pustaka Antara, 1961); Mukhtar Petah, *Bangsa Melayu menggugat dunia* (The Malay nation shakes the world) (Kuala Lumpur: Pustaka Aman Press, 1965). See also Zainal Abidin Daud, *Sejarah Malaya Merdeka* (The history of independent Malaya) (Melaka: Sentosa Store, 1957); Syed Abdullah bin Hamid al-Idrus, *Peristewa-peristewa siasah di Tanah Melayu* (Political events in Malaya) (Singapore: Qalam Publisher, 1962).

29. Syahba [pseud.], *Pesaka Naning* (Naning's heritage) (Melaka: Sentosa Store, 1951).

30. Darus Ahmad, *Dol Said: Pahlawan Naning* (Dol Said: The warrior of Naning) (Pulau Pinang: Sinaran, 1957). He also wrote *Raja Haji: Pahlawan terbilang* (Raja Haji: The distinguished warrior) (Pulau Pinang: Sinaran, 1957).

31. Abdul Talib bin Ahmad, *Sejarah Dato Bahaman Orang Kaya Semantan* (The history of Dato Bahaman, Orangkaya of Semantan) (Kuala Lumpur: Pustaka Garuda, 1961).

32. Comments by Salleh Muhammad in ibid., 9; originally published in *Berita minggu* (Weekly news), 8 January 1961. The criticism was specifically directed at a book entitled *Singgahsana Kerajaan Pahang: Tawarikh rengkas negeri kita dan siapa dan siapa di-Tanah Melayu* (The throne of Pahang: A concise history of our state and who's who in the Malay States), n.p., n.d.

33. Ibid., 8.

34. Ibid., 9.

35. Abdul Talib bin Haji Ahmad, *Darah mengalir di Pasir Salak* (Blood flows in Pasir Salak) (Kuala Lumpur: Pustaka Antara, 1961).

46. Haji Abdullah bin Amirah, *Riwayat hidup Tok Janggut dan peperangan di Kelantan* (The life of Tok Janggut and the wars in Kelantan) (Penang: Sinaran, 1957).

37. Abdul Samad Ahmad, *Tak Melayu hilang di dunia* (Malays will not disappear from the earth) (Kuala Lumpur: Dewan Bahasa dan Pustaka,1950), and *Laksamana Tun Tuah* (Admiral Tun Tuah) (Kuala Lumpur: Dewan Bahasa dan Pustaka, 1954); Ahmad Bakhtiar, *Korban keris Melaka* (Victims of the kris of Melaka) (Kuala Pilah: Abdul Ghani Abdullah, 1956); Darus Ahmad, *Perang Melaka* (The Melaka war) (Penang: Sinaran, 1960); Ali Aziz, *Zaman gemilangnya kerajaan Melayu Melaka* (The

golden age of the Malay kingdom of Melaka) (Kuala Lumpur: Pustaka Antara, 1965). Other writings that fall within the same category are: Harun Aminurrashid, *Sultan Mahmud Shah Melaka* (Sultan Mahmud Shah of Melaka) (Singapore: Pustaka Melayu, 1967); Buyong Adil, *Sejarah Melaka dalam zaman kerajaan Melayu* (The history of Melaka during Malay rule) (Kuala Lumpur: Dewan Bahasa dan Pustaka, 1973); Ismail Ambia, *Bendahara-Bendahara Melaka dan hulubalang-hulubalang Melayu* (The Bendahara of Melaka and other Malay warriors) (Kuala Lumpur: Dewan Bahasa dan Pustaka, 1967).

38. These two essays, both entitled "Sudut Sejarah" (History corner), were appended at the beginning of Harun Aminurrashid, *Panglima Awang* (Warrior Awang) (Singapore: Pustaka Melayu, 1959), 8–9. The names of the two newspapers where the articles were first published were not mentioned.

39. Ibid.

40. Abdul Talib bin Ahmad, preface to *Sejarah Dato' Bahaman,* 13.

41. For example, Syed Alwi bin Sheikh Al-Hadi, *Hang Tuah atau pahlawan Melayu* (Hang Tuah or the Malay hero) (Singapore: Donald Moore for the Eastern University Press, 1963); Darus Ahmad, *Pahlawan Melayu: Tun Tuah Hang Jebat* (Malay heroes: Tun Tuah Hang Jebat) (Penang: Sinaran, 1960); Mansor bin Abdullah, *Panglima Melayu: Panglima Hitam Tun Biajid, anak Hang Tuah* (Malay warrior: The black warrior Tun Biajid, son of Hang Tuah) (Penang: Sinaran, 1960); Ibrahim Mahmood, *Tun Biajid: Anak Hang Tuah* (Tun Biajid: Son of Hang Tuah) (Penang: Sinaran, 1966).

42. Shaharom Husain, *Tawarikh Johor* (History of Johore), 3 vols. (Singapore: Al-Ahmadiah, 1950); Misbaha, *Mengkaji sejarah Terengganu* (Studying the history of Terengganu) (Terengganu: Sasterawan Pantai Timur, 1955); Zainal Abidin Daud, *Riwayat Tanjung Malim* (History of Tanjung Malim) (Kuala Pilah: The Sentosa Store, 1955?); Haji Abdullah bin Musa, *Sejarah Perak dahulu dan sekarang* (History of Perak, past and present) (Singapore: Qalam Publisher, 1958); Abdul Talib bin Haji Ahmad, *Riwayat Kinta* (The story of Kinta) (Kuala Lumpur: Rusna, 1959); Shukri, *Sejarah Kelantan* (see above); Buyong Adil's works are listed below without English translations except where they diverge from the obvious: *Sejarah Johor* (Kuala Lumpur: Dewan Bahasa dan Pustaka, 1971); *Sejarah Selangor* (Kuala Lumpur: Dewan Bahasa dan Pustaka, 1971); *Sejarah Singapura: Rujukan khas mengenai peristiwa-peristiwa sebelum tahun 1824* (History of Singapore: With special reference to events before 1824) (Kuala Lumpur: Dewan Bahasa dan Pustaka, 1972); *Sejarah Pahang* (Kuala Lumpur: Dewan Bahasa dan Pustaka, 1972); *Sejarah Melaka dalam zaman kerajaan Melaka* (History of Melaka during the period of the Melaka kingdom) (Kuala Lumpur: Dewan Bahasa dan Pustaka, 1973); *Sejarah Sarawak* (Kuala Lumpur: Dewan

Bahasa dan Pustaka, 1974); *Sejarah Terengganu* (Kuala Lumpur Dewan Bahasa dan Pustaka: 1974); *Sejarah Kedah* (Kuala Lumpur: Dewan Bahasa dan Pustaka, 1980); *Sejarah Perak* (Kuala Lumpur: Dewan Bahasa dan Pustaka, 1981); *Sejarah Perlis* (Kuala Lumpur: Dewan Bahasa dan Pustaka, 1981); *Sejarah Sabah* (Kuala Lumpur: Dewan Bahasa dan Pustaka, 1981); *Sejarah Negeri Sembilan* (Kuala Lumpur: Dewan Bahasa dan Pustaka, 1981); *Sejarah perjuangan orang Melayu menentang penjajahan abad 15–19* (History of the anticolonial struggles of the Malays in the fifteenth to nineteenth centuries) (Kuala Lumpur: Dewan Bahasa dan Pustaka, 1983). He also wrote at least four history books for children, all published in Kuala Lumpur by Titiwangsa in 1976; *Turun seorang Syed* (A Syed descending), *Memeluk ugama Islam* (Embracing Islam), *Laksamana muda* (The young warrior), and *Negeri Melaka* (The state of Melaka).

43. Abdul Aziz Ishak, *Riwayat hidup Tunku Abdul Rahman Putra* (The life of Tunku Abdul Rahman Putra) (Kuala Lumpur: Pustaka Antara, 1955).

44. Mokhtar Petah, *Zulkifli Muhammad dalam kenangan* (Commemorating Zulkifli Muhammad) (Kota Bharu: Pustaka Aman, 1966).

45. Anwar Abdullah, *Dato' Onn* (Kuala Lumpur: Pustaka Nusantara, 1971).

46. Ahmad Boestamam, *Dr. Burhanuddin: Putera setia Melayu Raya* (Dr. Burhanuddin: A loyal son of Melayu Raya) (Kuala Lumpur: Pustaka Kejora, 1972); *Dato' Onn yang Saya Kenal* (Dato' Onn as I knew him) (Kuala Lumpur: Adabi, 1979).

47. Ahmad Murad bin Nasruddin, *Nyawa di hujung pedang* (Life on the tip of a sword) (Kuala Lumpur: Jabatan Penerangan, 1946); Abdul Aziz bin Zakaria, *Lt. Nor pahlawan gerila* (Lieutenant Nor, guerrilla warrior) (Kuala Lumpur: Dewan Bahasa dan Pustaka, 1959); *Cerita matamata hutan simpan* (Story of a forest reserve policeman) (Kuala Lumpur: Pejabat Karang Mengarang, 1951).

48. Abdullah Hussein, *Terjebak* (Trapped) (Kuala Lumpur: Dewan Bahasa dan Pustaka, 1965), and *Peristiwa* (The event) (Kuala Lumpur: Pustaka Antara, 1965). The writer was forced to join Fujiwara Kikan, the Japanese Secret Organization.

49. Mansur Sanusi, *Sejarah perkembangan pelajaran Melayu* (History of the development of Malay education) (Penang: Sinaran, 1955).

50. Abdul Samad Ahmad, *Sejarah kesusasteraan Melayu* (History of Malay literature), 3 vols. (Kuala Lumpur: Dewan Bahasa dan Pustaka, 1957–58).

51. Darus Ahmad, *Pancharan Melayu* (Malay light) (Penang: Sinaran,1957); Anas Haji Ahmad, *Sastera Melayu lama dan baru* (Old and new Malay literature) (Penang: Sinaran, 1963); Harun Aminurrashid, *Kajian*

sejarah perkembangan bahasa Melayu (A study of the history of Malay language) (Singapore: Pustaka Melayu, 1966); Li Chuan Siew, *Ikhtisar sejarah kesusasteraan Melayu baru, 1830–1945* (A comprehensive history of the new Malay literature) (Kuala Lumpur: Pustaka Antara, 1966); Abdullah Sanusi bin Ahmad, *Peranan pejabat karang mengarang* (The role of the department of writing) (Kuala Lumpur: Dewan Bahasa dan Pustaka, 1966). The Pejabat Karang Mengarang (department of writing), established at the Sultan Idris Teacher-Training College in Tanjung Malim, Perak, to train and encourage students to write, produced many of the prolific writers mentioned above.

52. See Jean M. Waller, "Departmental Research, University of Singapore, 1951–1961," and "Higher Degree Theses," *Malaysian Historical Sources,* ed. K. G. Tregonning, 70–77.

53. D. G. E. Hall, *A History of South-East Asia,* 4th ed. (Houndmills, Hampshire: Macmillan Education, 1981), xvi.

54. John Bastin, *The Western Element in Modern Southeast Asian History* (Kuala Lumpur: University of Malaya Press, 1961). See also John R. W. Smail, "On the Possibility of An Autonomous History of Modern Southeast Asia," *Journal of Southeast Asia History* 2, 2 (1961): 72–102.

55. A good example is R. Bonney, *Kedah, 1771–1821: The Search for Security and Independence* (Kuala Lumpur: Oxford University Press, 1971), which was still written in English.

56. For example, Maludin Abang Oreen, "Sejarah perkembangan politik Melayu Sarawak, 1946–19963: Ketegangan dan tindakbalas" (The history of Malay political development in Sarawak, 1946–1963: Tensions and reactions) (academic exercise, Universiti Sains Malaysia, Penang, 1983); Faimin Kamin, "Sejarah perkembangan parti-parti politik bumiputera di Sabah, 1961–1963" (The history of the development of Bumiputera political parties in Sabah) (academic exercise, Universiti Sains Malaysia, Penang, 1985). Complete lists of graduate exercises and dissertations can be obtained from all the local universities.

57. Universiti Sains Malaysia in Penang has published collections of some students' work as occasional papers; see *Tokoh-tokoh tempatan* (Local personalities), ed. Cheah Boon Kheng (Penang: Occasional Papers from the School of Humanities, Universiti Sains Malaysia, 1982), and *Penghijrah dan penghijrahan* (Immigrants and immigration), ed. Paul H. Kratoska (Penang: Occasional Papers from the School of Humanities, Universiti Sains Malaysia, 1982). University of Malaya has also published some of the students' essays in collections such as *Lembaran akhbar Melayu* (Pages from Malay papers) (Kuala Lumpur: Malaysian Historical Society, 1980).

58. Examples are: Foo Ah Hing, "Pertumbuhan penradikalan pelajar-

pelajar sekolah China di Malaya, 1930–1940" (The growth of Chinese student radicalization in Malaya) (academic exercise, School of Humanities, Universiti Sains Malaysia, Penang, 1985); Chan Moi, "Kerahan tenaga dan kesetiaan masyarakat Cina di Malaya, 1948–1960" (National service and the loyalty of the Chinese community in Malaya) (academic exercise, School of Humanities, Universiti Sains Malaysia, Penang, 1989).

59. For example, *Bengkel sejarah Melayu* (Malay language workshop), organized by the Dewan Bahasa dan Pustaka, 1984; *Seminar sejarah dan kebudayaan Melayu Perak* (Seminar on the history and culture of Malays at Perak), organized by the Association of Perak Malays, Selangor, 1987; *Seminar sejarah dan kebudayaan Pahang* (Seminar on Pahang history and culture), organized by the Ministry of Culture, Arts, and Tourism, Kuala Lumpur, 1993; *Seminar sejarah dan masyarakat Sabah* (Seminar on the history and society of Sabah) held in Kota Kinabalu, 1981.

60. Hang Jebat rebelled against the raja to seek justice for his friend Hang Tuah who was wrongly punished by the raja. Tuah, who gave his unquestioning loyalty to the raja, became Jebat's antagonist and killed him when ordered to do so by the raja. The debate centered on who the real Malay hero was, Hang Tuah, the admiral who gave his absolute loyalty to the sultan, or Hang Jebat, who spoke up for justice. Kassim Ahmad, *Characterisation in Hikayat Hang Tuah: A General Survey of Methods of Character Portrayal and Analysis and Interpretation of the Characters of Hang Tuah and Hang Jebat* (1966); Malay ed., *Perwatakan dalam hikayat Hang Tuah* (Kuala Lumpur: Dewan Bahasa dan Pustaka, 1973).

61. Abdul Rahman Haji Ismail, "Kewibaaan mutlak raja Melayu dan kesetiaan mutlak rakyat kepada raja: Satu penilaian semula tentang lunas perhubungan raja-rakyat masyarakat Melayu traditional" (The absolute power of Malay kings and the absolute loyalty of the rakyat to their rulers: A reassessment of the principles of relationship between raja and rakyat in traditional Malay society), *Kajian Malaysia* 3, 1 (1985): 32–57, and "Sejarah Melayu: Antara sejarah dan dakyah" (The Malay Annals: Between history and propaganda), *Kajian Malaysia* 3, 2 (1985): 25–35.

62. For example, W. R. Roff, *Nasionalisme Melayu,* trans. Ahmad Boestamam (Kuala Lumpur: University of Malaya Press, 1975); E. H. Carr, *Apakah sejarah?* (What is history?), trans. Abd. Rahman Haji Ismail (Kuala Lumpur: Dewan Bahasa dan Pustaka, 1984); R. G. Collingwood, *Idea sejarah* (The idea of history), trans. Muhd. Yusof Ibrahim (Kuala Lumpur: Dewan Bahasa dan Pustaka, 1985).

63. Anwar Abdullah, *Dato' Onn* (Petaling Jaya: Pustaka Nusantara, 1971); Shaharom Hussain, *Biografi perjuangan politik Dato' Onn Ja'afar* (Biography of the political struggles of Dato' Onn Ja'afar) (Petaling Jaya: Fajar

Bakti, 1985); Ramlah Adam, *Dato' Onn Ja'afar: Pengasas kemerdekaan* (Dato' Onn Ja'afar: The originator of independence) (Kuala Lumpur: Dewan Bahasa dan Pustaka, 1992).

64. Aziz Ishak, *Riwayat hidup Tunku Abdul Rahman* (The life of Tunku Abdul Rahman) (Kuala Lumpur: Pustaka Antara, 1955).

65. Bachtiar Djamily, *Ibrahim Yaakob pahlawan Nusantara* (Ibrahim Yaacob, Nusantara warrior) (Kuala Lumpur: Pustaka Budiman, 1985).

66. Ahmad Boestamam, *Dr. Burhanuddin putera setia Melayu Raya* (Dr. Burhanuddin, loyal son of Malaya) (Kuala Lumpur: Pustaka Kejora, 1972); Ramlah Adam, *Dr. Burhanuddin al-Helmy: Suatu kemelut politik* (Dr. Burhanuddin al-Helmy: A political crisis) (Kuala Lumpur: Dewan Bahasa dan Pustaka, 1996).

67. Abdul Latiff Abu Bakar, *Ishak Haji Muhammad, penulis dan ahli politik sehingga 1948* (Ishak Haji Muhammad, writer and politician until 1948) (Kuala Lumpur: University of Malaya Press, 1977).

68. Talib Samad, *Syed Syeikh Al-Hadi, sasterawan progresif Melayu* (Syed Syeikh al-Hadi, progressive Malay journalist) (Kuala Lumpur: Dewan Bahasa dan Pustaka, 1992).

69. Abu Hassan Sham, *Puisi-puisi Raja Ali Haji* (The poems of Raja Ali Haji) (Kuala Lumpur: Dewan Bahasa dan Pustaka, 1993).

70. Haji Bachtiar Djamaly, *Syeikh Tahir Jalaluddin* (Kuala Lumpur: Dewan Bahasa dan Pustaka, 1994).

71. Adnan Hj. Nawang, *Za'ba dan Melayu* (Za'ba and the Malays) (Kuala Lumpur: Berita Publishing, 1998).

72. Ismail Che Daud, *Tokoh-tokoh ulama semenanjung Melayu* (Ulama personalities of the Malay Peninsula) (Kota Bharu: Majlis Ugama Islam dan Adat Istiadat Melayu Kelantan, 1987) (Kelantan Council of Islamic Affairs and Malay Custom)

73. Abdullah Zakaria Ghazali, "Agama dan kebangkitan anti-British di Tanah Melayu" (Religion and anti-British uprisings in the Malay Peninsula) in *Tamadun Islam di Malaysia* (Islamic Civilization in Malaysia), ed. Khoo Kay Kim (Kuala Lumpur: Historical Association of Malaysia, 1980); Jang Aisjah Muttalib, *Pemberontakan Pahang, 1891–1895* (The Pahang rebellion) (Kota Bharu: Pustaka Aman Press, 1972); Timah Hamzah, *Pemberontakan tani 1928 di Trengganu: Satu kajian ketokohan dan kepimpinan Haji Abdul Rahman Limbong* (The 1928 peasant revolt in Trengganu: A study of the personality and leadership of Haji Abdul Rahman Limbong) (Kuala Lumpur: Dewan Bahasa dan Pustaka, 1981).

74. Haron Tarip, "Peranan penghulu dalam zaman Jepun di Johor, 1942–1945" (The role of the Penghulu during the Japanese period in Johore) (academic exercise, School of Humanities, Universiti Sains Malaysia,

Penang, 1982); Muhammad Isa Othman, *Pendudukan Jepun di Tanah Melayu, 1942–1945: Tumpuan di negeri Kedah* (The Japanese occupation of the Malay Peninsula: Focus on the state of Kedah) (Kuala Lumpur: Dewan Bahasa dan Pustaka, 1992); Mat Zin bin Mat Kib, "Persatuan bekas buruh paksa dan keluarga buruh jalan Keretapi Maut Siam-Burma, 1942–1946, persekutuan Tanah Melayu" (Association of ex-conscript laborers of the Death Railway between Siam and Burma and their families in the Federation of Malaya) (academic exercise, School of Humanities, Universiti Sains Malaysia, 1988).

75. Jenny Chan Siew Lee, "Johor semasa darurat, 1948–1960" (Johore during the emergency) (graduate exercise, history department, Universiti Sains Malaysia, 1986–87).

76. Abu Bakar Hamzah, *Ilham 13 Mei* (Inspiration from 13 May) (Kota Bharu: Bintang Emas, 1970); Tunku Abdul Rahman Putra, *Sebelum dan selepas 13 Mei* (Before and after 13 May) (Kuala Lumpur: Utusan Melayu, 1969).

77. Abdul Rahman Taib, "Zaman meleset, 1929–1933: Kesannya ke atas orang Melayu Melaka" (The Depression: Its impact on the Malays in Melaka); Koh Ai Kian, "Kemelesetan ekonomi tahun, 1929–1933, di Malaya: Satu tinjauan sejarah melalui akhbar-akhbar Bahasa Inggeris" (The economic depression in Malaya: A historical survey through English newspapers) (academic exercises, history department, Universiti Kebangsaan Malaysia, Bangi, 1974 and 1989, respectively).

78. Abdullah Basmeh, *Abu Bakar al-Sidiq* (Singapore: Qalam Publisher, 1951); Haji Muhammad Arif Abdul Kadir al-Natly, *Sejarah hidup Imam Syafie* (Biography of Imam Syafie) (Penang: Persama Press, 1952).

79. See Abdul Halim bin Mat Diah, *Pendidikan Islam di Malaysia* (Islamic education in Malaysia) (Kuala Lumpur: ABIM, 1989); Abdul Rahman Haji Abdullah, *Gerakan Islam tradisional di Malaysia: Sejarah dan pemikiran jemaah Tabligh dan Darul Arqam* (Traditional Islamic movements in Malaysia: The history and thinking of the Tabligh and Darul Arqam) (Kuala Lumpur: Penerbitan Kinta, 1992).

80. Abdullah, *Gerakan Islam*, 61.

81. For example Khoo, *Pensejarahan Malaysia,* and "Local Historians."

82. Muhammad Yusoff Hashim, *Persejarahan Melayu Nusantara* (Malay historiography in Nusantara) (Kuala Lumpur: Teks Publishing, 1988), 16.

83. Muhammad Yusoff Hashim, *Terengganu Daruliman: Tradisi persejarahan Malaysia* (Terengganu, the Abode of Faith: The tradition of Malaysian historiography) (Kuala Lumpur: Dewan Bahasa dan Pustaka, 1991), and *Tradisi pensejarahan Pahang* (The tradition of Pahang historiography) (Petaling Jaya: Tempo Publishing, 1992).

84. Mohd. Yusof Ibrahim, *Pensejarahan Malayu, 1800–1960* (Malay historiography) (Kuala Lumpur: Dewan Bahasa dan Pustaka, 1997).

85. R. Suntharalingam, *Pengenalan kepada sejarah* (Introduction to history) (Kuala Lumpur: Marican and Sons, 1985), and *Pensejarahan barat* (Western historiography) (Petaling Jaya: Fajar Bakti Publisher, 1987). Similar in intent is Muhd. Yusof Ibrahim, *Pengertian sejarah* (The meaning of history) (Kuala Lumpur: Dewan Bahasa dan Pustaka, 1986).

86. *Isu-isu pensejarahan: Esei penghargaan kepada Dr. R. Suntharalingam* (Historiographical issues: Essays in honor of Dr. R. Suntharalingam), ed. Abu Talib Ahmad and Cheah Boon Kheng (Penang: Universiti Sains Malaysia Press for the School of Humanities, 1995). *Alam pensejarahan dari pelbagai perspektif* (The world of historiography from various perspectives), ed. Badriyah Haji Salleh and Tan Liok Ee (Kuala Lumpur: Dewan Bahasa dan Pustaka, 1996).

87. See, for example, Haron Daud, "Pensejarahan masyarakat Melayu dalam perspektif kepercayaan dan pemikiran" (Historiography of Malay society within the perspectives of its beliefs and thinking), in Badriyah and Tan, *Alam pensejarahan,* 175–209.

88. *Nasionalisme: Satu tinjauan sejarah* (Nationalism: A historical survey), ed. R. Suntharalingam and Abdul Rahman Haji Ismail (Petaling Jaya: Penerbit Fajar Bakti, 1985); *Kolonialisme di Malaysia dan negara-negara Lain* (Colonialism in Malaysia and other countries), ed. Cheah Boon Kheng and Abu Talib Ahmad (Petaling Jaya: Penerbit Fajar Bakti, 1990); *Kekerasan dalam sejarah: Masyarakat dan pemerintah* (Violence in history: Society and state), ed. Qassim Ahmad (Kuala Lumpur: Dewan Bahasa dan Pustaka, 1993); *Sorotan terpilih dalam sejarah Malaysia: Esei sumbangsih kepada Dr. Cheah Boon Kheng* (Select forays in Malaysian history: Essays in honor of Dr. Cheah Boon Kheng), ed. Mahani Musa and Tan Liok Ee (Penang: Universiti Sains Malaysia Press for the School of Humanities, 2000).

89. Commission on Higher Education in Malaya, *Report of the Commission Appointed by the Secretary of State for the Colonies to Consider Higher Education in Malaya,* Sir William McLean, chairman (London: Colonial Office, 1939), 51.

90. Zainal Abidin bin Abdul Wahid, *Tawarikh manusia dan kemajuan: Ilmu tawarikh bagi darjah VI* (History of man and development: History for Standard VI) (Kuala Lumpur: Dewan Bahasa dan Pustaka, Kementerian Pelajaran Persekutuan Tanah Melayu, 1961).

91. In 1956 Abdul Razak Hussein, who later became the first deputy prime minister and the minister of education, chaired the Education Committee, which formulated a new education policy for the independent Federation of Malaya. For the report that became the basis of the National

Education Policy, see Federation of Malaya, *Report of the Education Committee, 1956* (Kuala Lumpur: Government Printers, 1956). National-type school uses Malay as the medium of instruction for all subjects.

92. These public examinations, following British tradition, were used to weed out students at successive levels; from the end of primary to the first year of secondary school, from lower to upper secondary, from completion of secondary to pre-university, and thence to university levels. See Federation of Malaya, *Report of the Education Committee*, pars. 75–80.

93. See, for example, *Kesah-kesah hari ini: Sejarah rendah federal untok sekolah-sekolah di Malaysia, buku 3* (Stories for today: Malaysian elementary federal history schools, book 3) (Kuala Lumpur: Federal Publications, 1968).

94. See, for example, Hussein Ahmad, *Sejarah menengah baharu: Malaya dalam tawarikh dunia* (New history for secondary schools: Malaya in world history) (Kota Bharu: Pustaka Aman Press, 1965).

95. See, for example, Shamsuddin Mohd. Yusoff, *Kursus ulangkaji tawarikh Tanah Melayu* (Revision course for history of the Malay Peninsula) (Kuala Lumpur: Pustaka MAHA Bookstore, 1967); Hussein Ahmad, *Sejarah Asia* (Asian history), for Form 6, Certificate of Higher Education (Kota Bharu: Pustaka Aman Press, 1975).

96. For example, Pertemuan Dunia Melayu, 1982 (meeting of the Malay world), held at the Dewan Bahasa dan Pustaka, Kuala Lumpur.

97. Malik Munip, *Tuntutan Melayu* (Malay demands) (Kuala Lumpur: Sarjana Enterprise, 1981), 20–22. For a discussion of the term *indigenous* in Malaysian history writing, see Cheah Boon Kheng, "Writing Indigenous History in Malaysia. A Survey of Approaches and Problems," *Crossroads: An Interdisciplinary Journal of Southeast Asian Studies* 10, 2 (1997): 33–81.

98. See, for example, Ministry of Education (Malaysia), *Sejarah Malaysia tingkatan 5: Kurikulum bersepadu sekolah menengah* (History of Malaysia for Form 5: Integrated curriculum for secondary schools) (Kuala Lumpur: Dewan Bahasa dan Pustaka, 1992), 126.

99. See, for example, Norani Salleh, *Sejarah sekolah menengah atas* (History for upper secondary schools) (Petaling Jaya: Penerbit Fajar Bakti Publisher, 1993).

100. John R. W. Smail, "On the Possibility of an Autonomous History of Modern Southeast Asia," *Journal of Southeast Asian History* 2, 2 (1961): 77–78.

101. See Roger Fletcher, "History from Below Comes to Germany: The New History Movement—The Federal Republic of Germany," *Journal of Modern History* 60 (1988): 563.

Chapter 9

DIALOGUE OF TWO PASTS

"Historical Facts" in Traditional Thai and Malay Historiography

KOBKUA SUWANNATHAT-PIAN

SINCE THE 1960s, INTEREST IN the field of Southeast Asian historiography has been on the increase. It can be stated confidently that one main factor contributing to this healthy interest is an acute awareness among historians of the value and fruitfulness of the traditional "histories" written or recorded by indigenous writers. These local histories, be they Javanese *babad,* Malay *hikayat* or *sejarah,* Burmese *yazawin,* or Thai *phongsawadan* or *tamnan,* are now accepted as essential sources on the sociopolitical development of Southeast Asia in general and the relevant Southeast Asian states in particular.[1] From academic work produced since the 1960s on the development of historiography in Thailand and Malaysia, it is evident that the contribution of traditional histories to modern history writing in both countries cannot be overstated.

In Thailand, *prawatsat,* the Thai term for history in its modern academic sense, only appeared at the beginning of the twentieth century. The traditional words denoting records of the Thai past are *tamnan, phongsawadan,* and *chotmaihet.* These records reflect the Thai understanding of their past in the context of their social, political, and religious worldview, which was totally different from that of the West and from Western concepts of history. Symbolically, with the introduction of the word *prawatsat* in the reign of King Vajiravudh (1910–25), Thailand accepted the Western concept of history. Thai historiography can thus be divided into two principal genres: the traditional consisting of tamnan and phongsawadan, which prevailed before the coming of Western colonialism to mainland Southeast Asia, and modern history writing of the prawatsat period, beginning roughly in the early twentieth century.

The historiography of the Malay Peninsula went through a somewhat similar experience. Until British intervention in the Malay states in 1874, the most popular and respected genre of history writing was hikayat or salasilah. It was the appearance of historical works written by the early colonial scholar-administrators that pushed aside these local histories and replaced them with the "scientific" and "rational" history written by specialists in the affairs of the Malay Peninsula. Until the twentieth century, indigenous histories were often dismissed as fairy-tale nonsense whose value, if any, lay mainly in their literary contributions. Indeed, a distinguished local scholar in the field of Malay literature considers literature and traditional history to be inseparable.[2] The resurgence of national pride and scholarly appreciation of the value of the indigenous wisdom contained in these traditional works has restored them to their proper place as an integral part of the search for a Malaysian sociopolitical identity.[3]

It is worth mentioning that traditional historical works in both Malaysia and Thailand on the whole reflect the principal characteristics of the historical writing of the period. Works in the genres of phongsawadan/tamnan and hikayat/sejarah generally belong to the chronicle style of writing history, a style that pays little attention to the accuracy of historical facts or events as they "actually occurred," or to rationality as understood within Western concepts of reason and logic, or to the idea of proof and evidence in the context of scientific knowledge. In other words, this indigenous genre of recording history implicitly rejected the characteristics that have been held to be important in the Western style of history writing since the nineteenth century. Instead, chronicle-style history placed a high premium on the practical value of history to a society, to the well-being of individuals in the afterlife, to order and harmony within the community, to the preservation of the sociocultural heritage that was regarded as essential to the survival of a society, and to the perpetuation of the esteemed sociopolitical order of the time. Often, in order to achieve these objectives, extraordinary happenings that cannot be accepted by those trained in scientific reasoning are paraded as indisputable proofs for the validity of the dos and don'ts that individuals are required to uphold at all costs. More often than not, phongsawadan and hikayat concentrate on the history of kings or of the ruling elite; on dynasties and their activities in war and peace; on royal etiquette and ceremonies; and the sociocultural values of the society in question. In sum, the theme of the chronicles in both countries centered on the palace. For example, the principal aims of the *Sejarah Melayu* (Malay annals) were to prove beyond doubt the illustrious line of the Melaka-Johore rulers, who claim to have descended from the most blessed Iskandar Zulkarnain and to preserve, at all costs, the great tradition of the Melaka sultanate, regarded as the very core of Malay identity.[4]

It is important to note that the chronicle was regarded as an effective instrument in strengthening or upholding the dignity and good name of the court, in both domestic politics and external relations. Furthermore, such literary efforts were normally meant more to mirror the sociopolitical designs of particular rulers or power centers than to record the actual situation within a given time frame. For instance, the *Sejarah Melayu* proudly records that in the reign of the great Sultan Mansur Shah, the emperor of China "fell sick and was stricken with chloasma [liver spots] all over his body." This incurable skin condition arose because "the raja of Melaka sent 'obeisance'" and the only cure the court doctor could prescribe required the Chinese emperor to drink the "water used by the raja of Melaka for washing his feet and [to] bathe in that water."[5] In somewhat the same vein, the *Phongsawadan krung si Ayutthaya* (Ayutthaya chronicles) *(Phanchanthanumat Version)* records that Ayutthaya claimed to be suzerain of sixteen tributaries at the time King U Thong founded Ayutthaya as the new power center of the Thai world, around 1350.

The same phongsawadan proceeds to list the names of the sixteen polities under Ayutthaya's suzerainty, which included Melaka.[6] The fact that Melaka had yet to be founded by Parameswara/Iskandar Shah effectively rules out the veracity of such a claim.

It is evident that neither the story of the Chinese emperor's queer illness, and the even queerer mode of treatment, nor the wild claim of Ayutthaya can find authentic historical evidence in their support. However, it is also evident that the historical value of both episodes lies in reading the sociopolitical messages Ayutthaya and Melaka were sending out in support of their respective declarations of greatness, with the strongest signals possible for the prevailing political atmosphere of the time. A quick survey of selected versions of the hikayat/sejarah or the phongsawadan would further support the view that the more concerned the traditional ruling elite was of what they perceived to be essential to the sociopolitical well-being or survival of the order against menacing challenges, the more conscientiously would they depict the purported grandeur of their respective polities.

The *Sejarah Melayu,* written in the seventeenth century under the supervision of the Bendahara, the prime-ranking nobleman of the land, reflects a serious attempt to depict the unrivaled greatness of Melaka during the reign of the Palembang-Melaka dynasty. One scholar has commented that the writer of the *Sejarah Melayu* preoccupied himself with information concerning the Malay ethos, which was apparently employed as a mechanism to confirm and further emphasize the strength of Melaka and its heritage in the eyes of his contemporaries.[7] The same scholar quotes an episode involving the Seri Nada Diraja, who declined a royal favor to become the ruler's son-in-law after the fall of Melaka to the Portuguese, a crucial time for the survival of the Malay sultanate, as a clear example of the determination to maintain the dignity and greatness of the throne even in its most precarious hour. By recording the Sri Nada Diraja story, the *Sejarah Melayu* takes pains to emphasize that, regardless of the physical and political weaknesses of individual kings, the sacred traditions of the Palembang-Melaka dynasty were not to be compromised.

Another pre-nineteenth-century work, the *Hikayat Hang Tuah,* likewise glorified the greatness of the Palembang-Melaka dynasty and its sultanate through an emphasis on the divine origin of its founder. According to the *Hikayat Hang Tuah,* the glory and splendor of Melaka was second to none. Hang Tuah, the legendary Malay warrior who epitomized all that was great and wholesome in the Malay ethos, emerged victorious against the challenges of the Javanese and the Majapahit empires, and also captured the admiration of the Ayutthaya court, providing through his heroic stature further evidence of the greatness of Melaka.[8]

There can be no dispute that the traditional chronicles of Malaysia and Thailand were written within the same sociocultural wavelength and speak the same ideological language. Yet, as sources on Malay-Thai relations, the hikayat/sejarah and the phongsawadan clearly differ, so much so that they often become the cause of conflicting interpretations and analyses. It is my aim to bring out some of the more significant differences and probe into the meaning of some conflicting "historical facts" in the hope that others will join in this discussion to arrive at more fruitful conclusions. Based on a rough survey of the leading chronicles written in Thai and Malay, I have classified their dialogue[9] on the historical facts concerning Malay-Thai relations into two main categories, sociocultural and political.

Sociocultural Dialogue

After the arrival of British colonial agents at the close of the eighteenth century, negative responses to the sociocultural differences between the two neighbors increased. Buddhist Siam was often pitted against the Islamic Malay states; each was suspicious and contemptuous of the other. The *Hikayat seri Kelantan,* for example, harbors a barely concealed contempt toward its northern neighbor, Siam. Even though "Negeri Siam" is described as a powerful state with a number of tributary rulers under its wing, Siam is nevertheless still regarded as inferior to Kelantan because of its religion and culture. The ruler of Kelantan, Sultan Abdullah, is quoted as expressing contempt for his more powerful neighbor when it is reported to him that the king of Siam wants to take his (the Kelantan sultan's) wife, the legendary Puteri Saadong, as his (the Siamese king's) own: "The Siamese are indeed infidels; they do not know proper etiquette; they even want to marry the wives of others."[10] The feelings of the mythical ruler of Kelantan was echoed in the sentiments expressed by the sultan of Perak who, though hard pressed on all sides in 1818, nevertheless refused to send tribute to Bangkok because "I am a king of the ancient race. I am he who holds the Dragon Betel Stand and the Shellfish which came out of the sea, which came down from Bukit Siguntang. . . . I am the oldest of all the kings in this part."[11]

At a glance, it may seem surprising that the Thais appear to be immune to the seemingly deep-rooted negativism and culturally superior sentiments entertained by the Malays against them. There is no direct record of deprecating sociocultural episodes concerning the Malays in the phongsawadans written during the Ayutthaya period (1350–1767). From the Thai sociocultural perspective, Malay tributaries are recorded simply as being required to present tribute to Ayutthaya at regular intermissions.[12] Thai official documents of the early Bangkok period, however, do register suspicion toward the Malay states within its sphere of influence. For example, in a royal decree sent to the governor of Nakhon Si Thammarat (Ligor), Bangkok reminded the governor that he should be alert to the dishonesty of the Malays, who were in the habit of "conspiring" against Siam.[13] Nonetheless, on the whole, Bangkok appeared to have accepted the fact that Siam and the Malay states were socioculturally different. Bangkok made a real concession to the fact that Kedah, which had raised the flag against Bangkok authority, shared no sociocultural attitudes with the Thais. By implication, Kedah's action against the Siamese authority could not be seen as a direct refutation of the king's moral superiority.[14] Thus, Bangkok saw the sociocultural differences, based on religion, in a totally different light from the Malays.[15] Thais were neither better nor worse than Malays because of their religion. If anything, these differences made them equal in sociocultural terms and therefore deserving of due consideration.

The Malay concept of kingship, and the legitimacy of the king's power to rule, as put forward by the *Sejarah Melayu, Hikayat Hang Tuah,* and *Hikayat Merong Mahawangsa,* stressed the concept of the divine right to rule. Various versions of the phongsawadan written during the Ayutthaya period likewise give prominence to the concept of divine kingship. However, after the fall of Ayutthaya in 1767, Thai kingship and the related concept of legitimacy gave more weight to the principle of personal merit as prescribed by Buddhist teachings. Thus the moral superiority of a ruler no longer depended on his illustrious lineage but rested squarely on his moral attainment, his *bun-baramii.* Actually a great number of Malay hikayat/sejarah written after the 1699 regicide also register this shift from birthright to the personal merit principle.[16] It is therefore not surprising that the Bangkok kings were insensitive to the sultan of Perak's attachment to his unblemished genealogy and his strong objection to Bangkok's claim to the implicit moral superiority of the Bangkok court over the Perak king's ancient seat of power. At this juncture, it is clear that they were not speaking the same ideological language, a good example of Malay-Thai sociocultural disparity.

Sociopolitical Dialogue

For those who have had the opportunity to examine the traditional indigenous histories of the Malay states and of Siam, it is evident that they provide conflicting accounts of Malay-Thai relations. Thai and Malay sources hardly agree on any version of the same events, particularly those dealing with their early contacts, later diplomatic relations, and rivalry or conflicts between the two.

EARLY RELATIONS

It is generally agreed that Malay-Thai relations have their roots in the fourteenth century, when the founder of Melaka and of the

Palembang-Melaka dynasty landed on the island of Singapore, then a Siamese outpost in the Malay Archipelago. While the Siamese claimed suzerainty over Melaka and most of the Malay Peninsula, it is quite obvious from the accounts of both sides that Siamese suzerainty was either challenged outright or only implicitly tolerated by Melaka. This situation arose from the inability of the Thai ruling elite to accept the emergence of Melaka as another independent sociopolitical center within what Sukhothai and Ayutthaya regarded as their sphere of influence. According to the *Sejarah Melayu,* the conflict led to repeated wars between Melaka and Ayutthaya throughout the fifteenth century. Histories on both sides recorded that there was prolonged conflict.

Melaka-Ayutthaya hostility was caused, according to the *Sejarah Melayu,* by the refusal of Sultan Mudzaffar Shah to send a "letter of obeisance" to Ayutthaya, as he demanded. The *Sejarah Melayu* tells of two serious Siamese attacks during the reign of Sultan Mudzaffar Shah and the *Phongsawadan krungsi Ayutthaya (Luang Prasert Version)* concurs that in year 1455 Ayutthaya sent an army to conquer Melaka.[17] The Malay source in fact narrates in detail the two attacks by the Siamese that failed in the face of superior strategies employed by the Malay leaders, Tun Perak and Paduka Raja. To demonstrate further Melaka's superior spiritual power, the *Sejarah Melayu* boasts of the spiritual prowess of a sayyid who sent a magic arrow that killed Chau Pandan, a Siamese prince who was in Ayutthaya preparing for the third attack on Melaka.

The phongsawadan is silent on these episodes referred to by the *Sejarah Melayu.* Though a few phongsawadan written or revised during the Ayutthaya period do state that King Borommatrailoknat sent an army to conquer Melaka, it does not report the outcome of the mission, from which one can safely assume that the war against Melaka did not achieve its objective.[18] Thus the claim made by the *Sejarah Melayu* appears accurate, at least as far as one war was concerned. It is also likely that Ayutthaya did not send any more armies to suppress Melaka after this; the reason being that Ayutthaya was very much preoccupied with its lengthy armed conflict with Lan Na to the point that the king decided to move his headquarters to Phitsanulok to be closer to the trouble area. By this time, it is clear that Melaka was much further down the list of political priorities in Ayutthaya's grandiose scheme of preeminence in mainland Southeast Asia. The question nevertheless remains: Why should the *Sejarah Melayu* take so much trouble to elaborate on dangers that did not actually exist? One immediate answer is surely that, whatever the reason, it had less to do with the actual sociopolitical scenario at the time and more to do with Melaka-Johore's requirements in the seventeenth century, when the text was written.

There are many accounts, recorded in the hikayat, of family ties in Malay-Thai relations. Best known among these are the accounts in the *Hikayat Merong Mahawangsa* and *Sejarah Melayu*. The former tells of the family ties between Kedah and the other three power centers that apparently were more powerful or more prestigious than Kedah, namely Perak, Pattani, and Ayutthaya. The *Hikayat Merong Mahawangsa* claims that the founder-rulers of the other three states were Kedah princes sent out by its ruler to found new states of their own. By implication, therefore, Kedah claimed to be of equal, if not higher, political status than Perak, Pattani, and Ayutthya. The *Sejarah Melayu* proudly refers to an offspring from the marriage between Tun Telanai and a Siamese noble lady, Otang Minang, who later became Laksamana Tun Ali Haru at the court of Melaka. These apparent efforts at consolidating relations with Siam were politically motivated—to increase the prestige of the Malay state and to affirm to the contemporary audience that intimate relations with Siam were part of the traditional practice. There is no such account of close family ties in any of the traditional Thai sources until the Bangkok period, when such ties existed as a result of measures taken by Bangkok.

DIPLOMATIC RELATIONS

It appears that after 1455, with the exception of the last few years before the fall of Melaka, there was a notable improvement in Ayutthaya-Melaka relations. Sultan Mudzaffar Shah took the initial steps to cultivate diplomatic relations with his powerful northern neighbor. *The Sejarah Melayu* records in detail the preparation of what was apparently the first emissary bearing a letter of goodwill to the Siamese court. Tun Telanai, son of the Paduka Raja who had outmaneuvered Awi Dichu, a Thai general of the second military attack on Melaka, was selected as the envoy with the requisite diplomatic credentials. The *Sejarah Melayu* is particular about the contents of the letter. It was to be "neither a letter of obeisance, nor one of greetings nor one of friendship." Yet to prove the sincerity of the Melaka court, the letter was to be borne "in procession by elephant," a mark of the honor given to the importance of the letter and its recipient.[19] Ayutthaya reciprocated the gesture of peace and diplomacy. Tun Telanai acquitted himself commendably; he became a favorite at the Siamese court and was presented with a Siamese noble lady as a wife. Ayutthaya also reciprocated by sending a letter of friendship to the sultan, borne in an elaborate procession to the ship, from where it was carried in another grand procession to the audience hall. The *Hikayat Hang Tuah* confirms that good relations also obtained during the reign of Sultan Mansur Shah. Hang Tuah proved his prowess and diplomatic skill to the satisfaction of the Siamese king, who also granted Hang Tuah the distinctive privilege of presenting himself to His Majesty in accordance with the etiquette of the Melaka court.[20]

Strangely enough none of these events are recorded in the traditional chronicles of Ayutthaya. However, a Dutch official of the Dutch East India Company at the Ayutthaya factory by the name of Jeremias van Vliet, who wrote a book in the seventeenth century on the history of the Siamese kingdom, talks at length of the reign of King Ramathibodi II (1492–1529/30). He narrates that during this reign "many [such] kings and princes from Patani, Kedah, Perak etc. came to visit and fall at his feet. They submitted willingly to his domination."[21] It can reasonably be surmised that diplomatic and friendly relations existed between the two power centers at least until the reign of Sultan Mahmud Shah. There were obvious reasons for the willingness of Ayutthaya to accept the friendly offer of Sultan Mudzaffar Shah and his successors. The second half of the fifteenth century was filled with a series of wars and conflicts between Ayutthaya and Lan Na in the north and Ayutthaya and Kampuchea in the east. Ayutthaya would surely have appreciated some order and peace with its southern neighbor and thus was probably more than happy to oblige the Melaka sultan.

In the context of diplomatic relations, many accounts in the Malay chronicles betray both the Malay ruling elites' frustration at the unequal relations with Siam and their determination to restructure the situation in accordance with the order they desired. For example, the *Hikayat seri Kelantan,* in the story about Puteri Saadong (mentioned above), employs Islam as an explanation for the moral superiority of Kelantan over Buddhist Siam. The *Hikayat Merong Mahawangsa* explains the origin of the *Bunga emas dan perak* (gold and silver flowers) tribute to Siam as a symbol of a once close family tie, while another Kedah source portrays said tribute as a tradition that arose from the appreciation of the Kedah ruler for the assistance rendered by the governor of Ligor, when the former was facing a most dangerous threat from Tenasserim. According to the second account, the gold and silver flowers presented to the court of Siam were nothing more than a symbol of friendship and appreciation on the sender's part.[22] Only the *Hikayat seri Kelantan* and contemporary foreign sources agree that the gold and silver flowers were indeed the symbol of the tributary relations practiced among Southeast Asian polities.[23]

If the Bangkok kings were unaware of, or unimpressed by, the pedigree of the Malay rulers, the same cannot be said of their royal predecessors of the Ayutthaya period. There is at least one item of evidence of Ayutthaya's efforts to strengthen its prestige and its moral and political credentials in the language easily understood by its Malay neighbors. John Struys, one of the few contemporary Dutch writers on Ayutthaya, tells of the grand title of the king of Siam, which included the title Paduka Sri Sultan and stated that he was "of the Race and offspring of the great Alexander," among his other illustrious origins.[24] A French account also confirms the superior position of the Siamese court as claimed by the Thai chronicles. Abbey Tarchard, who was one of the members of the French diplomatic mission to the court of King Narai (1644–88), describes the hierarchy of the audience in the Throne Hall, thereby confirming the wide political power and influence of Siam in the seventeenth century: "There are three sorts of princes at the court of Siam; the first are princes of the Cambodian royal blood and other kingdoms tributary to the king of Siam. The second are the princes of Laos, Chiengmai and Banca who have been captured in war and some others who have put themselves voluntarily under the protection of the king. The third are those whom the king has raised to the rank of prince."[25]

RIVALRY AND CONFLICT

In spite of the desire to be at peace with their northern neighbor, Melaka and other power centers in the Malay Peninsula found themselves often at crossed swords with the court of Siam. It is obvious that Malay chroniclers took pains in recording these events in detail while their counterparts, the scribes in the service of the Siamese court, appear to be less concerned over the same events. The *Sejarah Melayu,* as mentioned earlier, narrates with great pride the successes of Melaka over the invading Siamese army and fleet while only one of these events appears in the Thai chronicles. The same chronicle mentions the inglorious retreat of the Thai army under the Raja of Ligor from Pahang during the reign of Sultan Mahmud Shah of Melaka (1511–29). It also records the rivalry between Melaka and Ayutthaya over the suzerainty of Pahang, which continued unabated after the fall of Melaka. During the reign of Sultan Alauddin Riayat Shah (1529–64) of Ujung Tanah (Johore), the Malay ruler who was the successor of Mahmud urged the Raja of Pahang, who had been sending the gold and silver flowers to Ayutthaya "on a regular basis" together with a "letter of obeisance," to discard his tributary status. Bendahara Paduka Tuan of Johore urged His Highness of Pahang to unilaterally upgrade his relations with Ayutthaya from the tributary to the "friendship" level.[26] According to the *Sejarah Melayu,* the attempt was flatly rejected by the Phra Khlang of the Siamese court. About this time, the phongsawadan talks about a tributary mission sent by Kedah that was well received by Ayutthaya.[27] It is clear that one of the main causes of friction in the relationship between Ayutthaya and Melaka-Johore originated from Melaka-Johore's desire to undermine the political influence of Ayutthaya within the Malay world, an overlapping sphere of influence claimed by both Siam and the Palembang-Melaka sultanate.

The *Hikayat seri Kelantan* begrudgingly narrates how Kelantan was forced to surrender to the Siamese army because of famine. "It was God's wish" that Sultan Abdullah of Kelantan swallow his pride and sue for peace on Siamese terms. Yet, according to the same Malay source, the King of Ayutthaya soon fell victim to the moral superiority of Puteri Saadong. He became ill after being struck by her chewed-up betel nut. To recover from this illness, the king had to agree to send Puteri Saadong back to Kelantan.[28] The meaning of the story is clear. In spite of its military might, Siam was no match for the spiritual superiority of the Malay center. One of the causes of rivalry and conflict, from the Malay perspective, is here presented in the form of a struggle between Siamese physical strength and Malay spiritual might, with the latter emerging victorious.

Conversely, Thai chronicles appear more interested in recording tributary missions from around Southeast Asia to the Siamese court, including those from the Malay world. From the Thai perspective, these missions were the undisputed evidence of the kingdom's moral and physical greatness as understood in the context of the Buddhist sociopolitical worldview. None of them found their way into the Malay chronicles, or at least not in the form of a Malay tributary mission to the Siamese court.[29] For example, the *Phanchanthanumat Version* of the *Phongsawadan krung si Ayutthaya* records the following missions sent to Ayutthaya by the various centers:

- In 1592 Kedah sent a tributary mission to King Ekathosarot and was presented to the king at his war headquarters at Kamphangphet.[30]
- In 1659 the Laksamana Paduka Raja of Johore sent an emissary bearing precious gifts of diamond and emerald rings to King Prasat

Thong, apparently as a diplomatic move to cement Ayutthya's goodwill in the event Johore encountered hostility from Jambi.[31]

• In the same year, a mission of friendship came from the regnant queen of Aceh with a diamond ring; the diamond was said to be the size of "an unpeeled tamarind fruit" and worth "ten tamrung-weight of gold."[32]

Other sources also report on various missions of friendship and tribute to the Siamese court of about the same period. For instance, Dutch documents of the seventeenth century state that in 1609 an emissary was sent from Taungoo (Burma) to Ayutthaya, bearing a big ruby ring to the Siamese king, in search of friendship and assistance. A Dutch document of 1640 stated that Pattani and Johore missions arrived in the Siamese capital, the former bringing the customary gold and silver flowers and the latter bringing "some tributary gifts." Another Dutch record mentions that in 1642 there was a diplomatic mission from Lan Chang (Laos) to Ayutthaya.[33] These reports lead to the conclusion that at the very least Ayutthaya in the seventeenth century was regarded by the Malay Archipelago states as powerful and that its goodwill deserved to be cultivated.

Most of the accounts of Malay dignity and moral superiority, as portrayed in the *Sejarah Melayu* and other hikayat, are reflections of the political situation at the time the works were written or compiled.

It should be noted that there exists a wide gap in the reports of Melaka's relations with Ayutthaya, between the *Sejarah Melayu* and the *Hikayat Hang Tuah,* on the one hand, and those written after the nineteenth century, on the other. While insisting on Melaka's superiority and greatness, the *Sejarah Melayu* and the *Hikayat Hang Tuah* are careful in their portrayal of Siam, a powerful and potential enemy to Melaka in the fifteenth century but a diplomatic and friendly neighbor of Johore in the seventeenth century.

Other Malay traditional histories of the nineteenth century, in their attempts to illustrate the superiority of the respective Malay power centers, take more directly undiplomatic, or less subtle, shots at their northern neighbor, and even downgrade the significance of the gold and silver flowers. This can be explained from the fact that, first, these histories were mostly compiled or written during a period of strong Malay consciousness, which coincided with the prevailing anti-Siamese historiography. Second, after 1909, Bangkok relinquished its political role in the Malay Peninsula to Britain. Thus a contemporary Malay pride in their own heritage and the freedom, as well as possibly indirect but influential colonial encouragement to demonstrate such sentiment, gave birth to the somewhat mythical-historical negativism and deprecation of the Thai-Malay relations.

On the Thai side, the almost absolute silence on Melaka affairs can be explained in the context of Ayutthya's preoccupation with the affairs of the north, that is the Lan Na and Lan Chang kingdoms, which were then crucial to the security and undisputed position of Ayutthya in the Thai world. It was only during the Bangkok period that Siam made a series of serious attempts to organize the south in accordance with its sociopolitical requirements. Thus the various phongsawadan of the period, particularly during the reign of King Rama III (1824–51), prominently record the affairs of the Malay states within Bangkok's sphere of influence in great detail.[34]

There has been sensitivity on the Thai side regarding the availability of documents in the Thai national archives since the 1960s. Most of the official documents concerning the Malay states in the Thai national archives from the time of King Chulalongkorn have been categorized as "secret and confidential." This means that the official permission of Thai authorities is required on a case-by-case basis for particular documents to be available for study. Similarly, in Malaysia documents in the national archives concerning Malay-Thai relations after World War II are strictly off limits. The mutual sensitivity displayed on both sides is a refreshing change from the nineteenth century, when the histories were blatantly employed whenever a mud-slinging campaign was required.

The dialogue found in the Thai-Malay traditional histories can be considered a simultaneous dual conversation. First, traditional Thai and Malay histories endeavor to talk to each other, each presenting their divergent nuances on the same topics. These nuances were heavily colored by the domestic sociopolitical requirements of the time the work was being recorded; each was impregnated with its own sociopolitical agenda. Second, these histories are simultaneously a series of conversations between the past being recorded and the contemporary sociopolitical sentiments of the author's time, thought by him to be relevant to the well-being or survival of his society.

In conclusion, the dialogue of the two pasts tells us a great deal about traditional sociopolitical relations between the two power centers, as well as about the individual centers themselves, at particular times. Those particular times are the times the works were being composed, and not really the times when the events concerned were supposed to have taken place. That the recorded events might or might not have happened was of less significance in traditional Malay-Thai perceptions of the past. What was more significant was the message these histories were intended to convey to their targeted audience. Traditional histories, at least as far as Siam and the Malay Peninsula were concerned, were less about historical facts, or events that actually occurred, than about *perceived facts,* as seen and understood by the elite to hold immense value to the society as a whole. In our attempt to understand and appreciate traditional histories from the intention of the writers, we as historians must accept this basic value of our professional forefathers. Without the required understanding and appreciation, present-day scholars may never be able to fathom the wisdom of these histories. And what a tragic situation that would be for us all.

Notes

1. An outstanding work on the subject is *Perceptions of the Past in Southeast Asia,* ed. Anthony Reid and David Marr (Singapore: Heinemann Educational Books for Asian Studies Association of Australia, 1979). On the immense value of traditional historical sources to an understanding of the past see Anthony C. Milner, *Kerajaan: Malay Political Culture on the Eve of Colonial Rule* (Tucson: University of Arizona Press, 1982); and Nidhi Aeusrivongse, *Prawatsat Rattanakosin nai phraratcha phongsawadan krung si Ayut-*

thaya/Bangkok History in the Ayutthaya Chronicles (Bangkok: Association of Social Science of Thailand, 1978).

2. Ismail Hussein, *The Study of Traditional Malay Literature with a Selected Bibliography* (Kuala Lumpur: Dewan Bahasa dan Pustaka, 1974), 12.

3. See, for example, Muhammad Hassan Dato' Kerani Muhammad Arshad, *Al-tarikh salasilah negeri Kedah* (History of Kedah) (Kuala Lumpur: Dewan Bahasa dan Pustaka, 1968), xv, in which the writer recalls that it was Malaysia's first prime minister who urged him to appreciate the importance of history books written by "our own people" (pentingnya buku-buku sejarah tanah air kita [yang] ditulis oleh ahli-ahli sejarah dari anak negeri kita sendiri).

4. The title of the text is *Sulalat us-Salatin*, in Malay *Pertuturan Segala Raja* (Genealogy of the rulers), which more than makes clear its intention. According to the text, it was composed at the royal command of Sultan Alauddin Riayat Shah, a member of the Palembang-Melaka dynasty in the seventeenth century, who said: "It is my wish that the treasury shall make a chronicle setting forth the genealogy of the Malay Rajas and the ceremonial of their courts, for the information of my descendants who come after me, that they may be conversant with the history and derive profit therefrom." C. C. Brown, tr., *Sejarah Melayu; or, Malay Annals* (Kuala Lumpur: Oxford University Press, 1976), 1. This is comparable to the *Phongsawadan khrung si Ayutthaya, the Luang Prasert Version,* also written during the seventeenth century at the order of the ruling monarch and aimed at updating the records of palace-centric history.

5. Brown, *Sejarah Melayu,* 87. The same story was repeated in the Raffles 18 version; see *Sejarah Melayu/Malay Annals,* MS Raffles no. 18, comp. Cheah Boon Kheng (Kuala Lumpur: Malaysian Branch of the Royal Asiatic Society, 1999), 173.

6. *Phraratcha phongsawadan krung si Ayutthaya, the Phanchanthanumat and Phra Chakraphatdiphong Versions* (Bangkok: Khlang-witthaya, 1964), 2, 502. It is important to remember that Ayutthaya's claim to suzerainty appears only in versions of the phongsawadan written or revised after the fall of Ayutthaya. The most reliable version, the *Phongswadan krung si Ayutthaya, the Luang Prasert Version,* puts forward no such claim. See *Phongsawadan krung si Ayutthaya, the Luang Prasert Version* (Bangkok: Khlang-wtthaya, 1972), 443. Conversely, Phra Phonnarat, a well-known royal chronicler of the First Reign (1782–1809) claims in *Chulayutthakarawong,* that Ayutthaya is the suzerain of twenty-four principalities.

7. Virginia Matheson, "The Concept of Malay Ethos in Indigenous Malay Writings," *Journal of Southeast Asian Studies,* 10 (1979): 351–71.

8. Kassim Ahmad, comp. and annot., *Hikayat Hang Tuah* (The story of

Hang Tuah) (Kuala Lumpur: Dewan Bahasa dan Pustaka, 1975), esp. chs. 1, 7, 8. The author of the work is unknown but it is generally accepted that it was written after 1641. It tells of the greatness of Melaka and its rulers through the adventures of Hang Tuah, the top warrior of Melaka.

9. The term *dialogue* is employed here in a liberal manner; the main thrust of the analysis is on the "conversation" between the written records in Malaysia and Thailand but there are also other levels of dialogue taking place simultaneously; between two authors with different agenda—whether this agenda is "national," "local," or simply political—and between the author in the present and the past he is dealing with.

10. "Patutlah orang Siam bangsa kafir, tiada tahu cara bahasa; anak bini orang pun hendak ambil buat anak bini kepadanya." Mohd. Taib Osman, "Hikayat seri Kelantan" (History of Kelantan) (M.A. thesis, University of Malaya, 1961), 55–57.

11. Raja of Perak to governor of Penang, 27 August 1816, quoted in Barbara Watson Andaya, *Perak: The Abode of Grace* (Kuala Lumpur: Oxford University Press), 21.

12. *Phraratcha phongsawadan krung si Ayutthaya, Phanchanthanumat Version,* 13, 310, 392.

13. Chotmaihet Reign 2, JS 1173, order, Ministry of Kalahom to governor of Nakhon Si Thammarat, 1813.

14. Documents Reign 3, Tongtra Chao Phraya Akkramahasenabodi to Chao Phraya Yommarat, JS 1201/1839; see also Kobkua Suwannathat-Pian, *Thai-Malay Relations* (Singapore: Oxford University Press, 1988), 55–56.

15. King Rama III, for example, described the differences between the two peoples as that between oil and water, which "cannot be made into one"; he thought the Kedah Malays would be better administered by their own leader rather than a Thai since the former better understood his people. Documents, Reign 3, Tongtra Chao Phraya Akkramahasenabodi to Chao Phraya Yommarat, JS 1201/1830.

16. See, for example, Raja Ali Haji ibn Ahmad, *Tuhfat al-nafis* (Kuala Lumpur: Oxford University Press, 1982); Raja Chulan, *Misa Melayu* (Sacred Malay heritage) (Kuala Lumpur: Pustaka Antara, 1962). Both are works of post-1699 authors who had witnessed a fundamental change in the Malay political understanding of kingship and the ruler's position vis-à-vis the people.

17. Brown, *Sejarah Melayu,* 56–60; Cheah, *Sejarah Melayu,* 136–41; *Luang Prasert Version,* 448.

18. Though none of the Ayutthayan chronicles talks about the outcome of the war against Melaka, some chronicles revised or written after the Ayutthaya period record that the Siamese succeeded in suppressing Melaka.

See Phra Phonnarat, *Chulayutthakarawong* (Bangkok: Kurusabha, 1992), 333. The reason for the additional information is explained below.

19. Brown, *Sejarah Melayu,* 60–61. For Mudzaffar Shah's explicit specifications, see Cheah, *Sejarah Melayu*: "Kehendak kita, sembah pun jangan, salam pun jangan, surat kasih pun jangan" (142–43). The contents of the letter written by the Bendahara Paduka Raja summed up Melaka's desire to let bygones be bygones and to be at peace with Ayutthaya.

20. Kassim Ahmad, *Hikayat Hang Tuah,* 416–17.

21. Jeremias van Vliet, *The Short History of the Kings of Siam,* tr. Leonard Andaya (Bangkok: Siam Society, 1975), 68.

22. Muhammad Hassan, *Al-tarikh salasilah negeri Kedah,* 20–22.

23. Osman, "Hikayat seri Kelantan," 110–11; see also Tomé Pires, *The Suma Oriental of Tomé Pires (1512–1515) and the Books of Francisco Rodrigues,* trans. A. Cortesão (London: Kraus Reprint, 1967); *The Dutch Documents (1608–1620; 1624–1642)* trans. Nantha Suthakun (Bangkok: Krom Silapakon, 1970), 144–45.

24. John Struys, *The Voyage and Travels of John Stuys through Italy etc.* (London, 1684) as quoted in J. Kemp, *Aspects of Siamese Kingship in the Seventeenth Century* (Bangkok: Social Science Review, Thailand, 1969), 32.

25. Guy Tachard, *Voyage de Siam des pères jésuites envoyez par le roy aux Indes et à la Chine* (Paris, 1686), 230–33.

26. Brown, *Sejarah Melayu,* 190–91.

27. *Phanchanthanumat Version*, 310.

28. Osman, "Hikayat seri Kelantan," 57–60.

29. Many tributary missions are recorded in the *Sejarah Melayu,* but only when they were missions from other Malay states to Melaka—for example, the Kedah mission during the reign of Sultan Mahmud, during which time the ruler of Kedah was given the *nobat,* or regalia for Malay kingship (131), and a tributary mission from Pattani, when the latter was given "the drum of sovereignty" and the "robe of honours" by the ruler of Melaka (146).

30. *Phanchanthanumat Version*, 310.

31. Ibid., 392. For the historical background of this period, see Leonard Y. Andaya, *The Kingdom of Johor, 1641–1728* (Kuala Lumpur: Oxford University Press, 1975). Quoting a Dutch document as his source, Andaya also states that Jambi likewise sent a yearly tribute of the gold and silver flowers to Ayutthaya during this period.

32. *Phanchanthanumat Version,* 392.

33. Nantha Sutakun, *The Dutch Documents,* 16, 256, 282. Vliet talks of the emissaries sent by King Prasat Thong of Ayutthaya (1629–56) to Aceh and Arakan "to establish peace with Their Majesties." Vliet, *Kings of Siam,* 95. He also refers to the good services of Kedah in persuading Pattani to

come to terms with Ayutthaya and assume the tributary relations that Pattani had rejected when Prasat Thong came to power.

34. See, for example, Prince Damrong-rajanubhab, *Phraratcha phongsawadan krung Rattanakosin, Reign 2* (Bangkok: Kurusabha, 1962); Chao Phraya Thipakorawong, *Phraratcha phongsawadan krung Rattanakosin, Reign 3* (1961) and *Reign 4* (Bangkok: Kurusabha, 1972).

Chapter 10

THE SCRIPTING OF SINGAPORE'S NATIONAL HEROES

Toying with Pandora's Box

HONG LYSA AND HUANG JIANLI

THE NINTH OF SEPTEMBER 1999 is a landmark in the history of currency in Singapore. On that day, a new series of notes was issued, featuring the portrait of Yusof Ishak, the first president of the independent republic of Singapore,[1] the first time that a historical personage has graced either its dollar bills or postage stamps.[2] However, the significance of this development goes beyond the world of numismatics and philately. It can be regarded as one of a number of statements and measures that the government has been adopting in the 1990s that signify the official emphasis on a Singapore history germinating from the fifties and sixties. Concomitantly, to make the scripting of such a history more concrete and inspirational as the basis for a national identity and for constructing an ethos of nationhood, some key personalities of the period, who remain in favor with the powers that be, have been projected as possible national heroes

Critics who make sweeping condemnations of Singapore politics as being wholly manipulated by the People's Action Party (PAP), the dominant party in power since 1959, and caricature its people as either voiceless and helpless or bribed into silence, grossly underestimate the continual state efforts in presenting the narratives for a cultural-moral order in response to both changing conditions in the capitalist world economy, into which Singapore is firmly embedded, and the repositioning by those at the margins in engaging with the hegemonic narrative.[3] While the first phase of nation building from self-rule to the seventies has been centered discursively on the trope of survival by rising above adverse historical conditions and burdens, the economic confidence reached since the eighties has given rise to discourses on culture and history as the basis of a Singaporean nationhood, particularly in light of the view that economic growth had intensified the consumerist orientation in the society, with a greater emphasis on individual selves. "To the PAP government, individualism, with its emphasis on difference, tends to produce a sense of hyper-subjectivity at the expense of commonality with others, implying an unwillingness to make self-sacrifice for the social good."[4]

Religious knowledge was introduced with great fanfare in schools by 1982 to counteract this, but was quietly phased out in 1988, in the wake of the arrests of Catholic activists who were critical of what they considered the social injustices ensuing from the capitalist system as it worked out in Singapore, and who themselves eschewed the professional careers and middle-class pursuits that their educational attainment entitled them to.[5] Cultural values, eased in to replace the religious and moral ones around 1998, referred to the communitarianism of Asian traditions, defined as "placing society before self." Prime Minister Goh Chok Tong's declaration that "we are a people . . . from at least three different ancient civilizations. These deep roots endow us with rich values and traditions" is representative of the *Asian values* discourse.[6] In the sixties and seventies, such pronouncements would have been criticized by the authorities as primordial, antimodern, chauvinistic, and militating against a multiracial society. In the early nineties, the ancient empires of the "ancestors" (China, India, and the early trading empires of the Malay Archipelago) were introduced into the school history syllabus, in order that a distance be kept from what was regarded as decadent Western cultural, social, and political trends, while drawing on the economic and scientific pursuits of the free-market system, of which the United States was the world leader.

In 1991 eight statues of Chinese legendary heroes, donated by a food manufacturing company, were placed in a public sculpture park as part of the celebrations of twenty-five years of independence.[7] At the official unveiling, Goh noted that these heroes, though Chinese in origin, embodied virtues like patriotism, filial piety, loyalty, righteousness, and benevolence that "transcended racial boundaries." He called for the Malay and Indian communities in Singapore to similarly represent their heroes, culture, and values, which would, when located together, "clearly illustrate that despite our racial and cultural diversity, Singaporeans are united, and share similar basic moral values and virtues."[8] The newspaper coverage included an educator and artist's suggestion that "home-grown" Malay personalities such as Singapore's first head of state, Yusof Ishak, nineteenth-century scribe Munshi Abdullah, and philanthropist Hajah Fatimah could be honored by the Malay community, while the president of an Indian cultural society proposed Narayan Pillai (a businessman who arrived in Singapore with Stamford Raffles and built a temple in South Bridge Road) and Thiru Valluvar ("a philosopher poet who wrote 1,700 stanzas on different virtues").[9] Members of the two communities on the other hand wrote to the newspapers in the following days suggesting verses from the Qur'an, and Mahatma Gandhi. To date, however, there have been no additions to the Chinese legendary heroes at Sculpture Park.

The Heroic Enterprise:
From Negating History to Spotting Heroes

Prasenjit Duara has argued that the nation as a collective subject, whose ideal periphery exists only outside itself, is poised to realize its historical destiny in a modern future. Its narrative defines the framework of its self-understanding and thus represents the site where very different views of the nation, and the cultural-moral order that it embodies, contest and negotiate with each other. Various social actors develop and deploy narratives to redefine the boundaries and identities of a collectivity with multiple identifications. Thus even while closure is successfully achieved by some, it unravels with time as the voices of those on the outside, or on the margins, of the narrative then seek to reorganize counternarratives.[10] An examination of the move on the part of the government to identify national heroes, one aspect of the rescripting of Singapore history taking place in the nineties, underlines Duara's point on the need to view national identity as founded upon fluid relationships and brings out the paradoxes, ironies, and ambivalences in the idea of a Singaporean nationhood.

By and large, Singapore has done without officially declared national heroes. This absence has not been much of an issue hitherto. In fact, the government has taken pride in its eschewing of personality cults, basing its legitimacy instead on a de-personalized rationality and efficiency. The closest that one can find to public statuary, for example, would be a statue of Sir Stamford Raffles, the East India Company official, on the bank of the Singapore River, reputedly where his first footsteps were made, marking the postcolonial government's recognition of that moment as the founding of modern Singapore. However, from the mid-nineties, there have been official calls for identifying national heroes. This has not been a simple task. At the core of this enterprise is the teleology of Singapore as a sovereign state. Without a populist, revolutionary nationalist movement, and denying a precolonial indigenous society, where would one look for candidates to be adulated as national heroes? Singapore has no counterparts to Aung San of Burma or Sukarno of Indonesia,[11] nor were its independence leaders inclined to claim a glorious precolonial past. They chose instead to regard the Chinese-majority colonial entrepôt and naval base, which they took over, as a conglomeration of migrants with historical ancestries that had to be forgotten if they were to constitute the citizenry of a new nation. It was only in 1999 that Prime Minister Goh Chok Tong himself mused, "A country needs national heroes. Some of the first-generation leaders who fought for our independence and built up Singapore can be conferred the stature of our national heroes. We shall do so at an appropriate time."[12]

While Goh did not specify any such leaders, nor the "appropriate time," the name of Lee Kuan Yew, who was prime minister from 1959 to 1990 and has been senior minister since, immediately comes to mind; the difficulty with officially conferring such recognition on him is that he is still active in politics. Nevertheless, the creed of these heroes-in-waiting, "the founding fathers" of the nation, based on values such as meritocracy, fairness, pragmatism and integrity in governing Singapore could be the guiding ethos for Singaporeans. Goh Chok Tong's speech on national heroes falls into the current phase of legitimizing the state's moral order, the culmination of an unprecedented intense concentration on the part of the government in the nineties on making the PAP's struggle for predominance in the fifties and sixties a cornerstone of Singaporeans' social memory.

This process is not without its ironies and limits, despite the overwhelming command of institutional and financial resources on the part of the state, as can be seen from some earlier instances. In 1997 the deputy prime minister, Brig. Gen. Lee Hsien Loong, announced the launching of the national education campaign, after expressing his shock at the ignorance of the young in Singapore about the country's history, in particular about the turbulent decade before 1965, the year Singapore was declared independent after its expulsion from Malaysia.[13] Addressing schoolteachers, Lee declared: "The Singapore Story is based on historical facts. We are not talking about an idealized legendary account or a founding myth, but an accurate understanding of what happened in the past, and what this past means for us today. . . . It is objective history, seen from a Singaporean standpoint."[14] In July 1998 a mammoth multimedia national education exhibition called The Singapore Story: Overcoming the Odds presented the argument that in the pre-independence years the battle against the insidious threats of communist subversion, as well as communal and religious chauvinism, was won, resulting in the successful emergence of Singapore as a multiethnic nation.[15] Clearly, the Singapore Story had found its closure: ending in the country's sustained economic success that has become the basis of legitimacy of the PAP's monopoly in government over almost forty years.

If Singapore students had little awareness of the country's recent past, it was not for lack of interest but because hitherto such knowledge was considered neither desirable nor essential.[16] The national education project of 1997 was not simply a case of making the effort to appreciate the contributions of the older generation; it bespeaks the leadership's conviction that the immediate past could and should be spoken of. Undoubtedly, official narratives of the Malaysian period, when Singapore was part of the federation (1963–65), could be expected to invite critical response from Malaysian leaders; similarly, a triumphal PAP story would open the wounds suffered by the party's opponents in the country itself. But these are now considered history—spent forces whose grievances could no longer instigate subversion, debate, and dissent against the story, as personalized in Senior Minister Lee Kuan Yew's two-volume memoir documenting his own legacy, the first volume of which was issued in 1998, on his seventy-fifth birthday. Reportedly, a team of researchers had assisted him in this task, ferreting out documents and papers from archives in Singapore, Britain, Australia, and the United States, apart from also being given access to Lee's personal correspondence.[17]

The autobiographical narrative of heroism on the part of the first "national" Singaporeans is situated at the conjuncture between national history and the global economy, the latter producing among Singaporeans a segment who are encouraged to invest, work, and live overseas to develop a second economic "wing" with, simultaneously, the encouragement of highly mobile "foreign talent" to Singapore to propel its information technology and banking industry, in particular.[18] The ensuing dislocation and relocation may loosen the notion of citizenry and strain the social fabric as able Singaporeans become cosmopolitan, while those less so regard the foreign entrants into the domestic employment market as rivals, sentiments accentuated during the severe economic downturn of 1997–98. More pertinent, national history, with its emphasis on national heroes, has a critical place in suggesting rootedness, precedence, and inspiration. The majority of these men who, by their own account, overcame worse odds than those faced in the present were, ironically, not born in Singapore, but in Malaya, China, Ceylon, India, constituting the "original" foreign talent.

Interim Heroes, Mutating Pasts

Before the arrival of what is deemed the appropriate time for iconizing individuals among the PAP's old guard as national heroes, Singaporeans have been offered a few persons who may turn out to be interim figures. Among those Goh's government has singled out for their bravery during the Second World War were Col. Lim Bo Seng and Lt. Adnan Saidi, although it was acknowledged that they were not quite national heroes, having been tortured and killed during the Japanese occupation for defending Singapore for the British, "so they cannot compare with freedom fighter José Rizal, whom the Filipinos regard as the father of the modern Philippines."[19] Since national heroes are configured by their constituents to be the epitome of the virtues and commitments of the geo-body that claim them, and their heroisms are often displayed against those labeled historical enemies, Singapore's entry into the newly formed Federation of Malaysia in 1963 and its subsequent expulsion from it has made the choice of the war heroes serving under different flags as interim national heroes even more problematic. Not only was Adnan defending Singapore for the British as a lieutenant in the Royal Malay Regiment, he is also not the exclusive property of Singapore. In late 1999 the Malaysian defense ministry announced that it was producing a film to portray the bravery of "a Malay soldier, Lieutenant Adnan Saidi, who was killed in a battle with Japanese troops in Singapore during World War II." The film was shot entirely in Malaysia, where his eldest son, who was invited to the launching of the production, resides. Adnan had led a Royal Malay Regiment platoon in the final stand against Japanese shock troops who crossed the Terbau Straits into Singapore from Johore in the final days of the Malayan campaign.[20] The ministry hoped to evoke patriotism among the younger generation of Malaysians, and the film was screened in conjunction with the forty-third Merdeka (independence) Day celebrations in 2000.[21]

The interwoven history of Singapore and Malaysia, and their acrimonious separation has resulted in generally tense official relations, with the leadership on both sides invoking nationalist sentiments by demonizing one another. That Adnan has been made a role model and an inspiration for the Malaysian armed forces would reduce his suitability as a national hero in Singapore. The fracas over claims on the heritage of the legendary P. Ramlee (1929–1973), whose films had won several awards in various Southeast Asian film festivals held in the fifties and early sixties, also indicates the exclusivity of Malay national heroes to either Singapore or Malaysia, but not both, even when the heroes predated both these nation-states. The Singapore minister of information and the arts was quoted in the Malaysian tabloid *Harian Metro* as claiming in his speech when opening the P. Ramlee exhibition in May 1999 that Ramlee's films would not have been possible without the support of various parties in Singapore. To this, his Malaysian counterpart responded that P. Ramlee is Malaysia's asset, a "Malaysian citizen who had contributed to the development of the music and film industry that was centered in Singapore at that time." Apparently, the Singaporean minister had quoted from a booklet presented by the Singapore Film Commission and the Shaw Organization cinema group, in which Yusnor Ef (Ramlee's friend and colleague, a film critic and a former president of Perkamus, the Singapore association of Malay artistes) had written, "There would be no P. Ramlee without Singapore."[22]

Another set of individuals who have been conferred some degree of qualified recognition as inspirational personae are the Chinese self-made millionaire philanthropists who donated unstintingly to the cause of education. Foremost among these men are Tan Kah Kee and Tan Lark Sye. Both, like Adnan, operated in pre-independent Singapore but were hitherto linked with the communist cause by the state: Tan Kah Kee professed admiration for Mao and chose to live in Communist China after the Second World War, while Tan Lark Sye had his Singapore citizenship papers revoked in 1963 on the grounds that he had "actively and persistently collaborated with an active antinational group of communists."[23] Hence recent public references to both men have been singularly focused on their munificence toward education, especially the building of schools and the provision of scholarships. Their politics as understood by the state is left unmentioned, as is the context of Singapore's anticolonial history. Singapore's heroes are thus in limbo—an intermediate state of simultaneous exposure and suppression, of being made known and yet not fully understood.

Arguably this situation is not remarkable; history is complex and ambiguous, and national heroes, by the very nature of the roles they are made to serve are simplified characters, seldom without skeletons that are scrupulously locked in the closet. However, the aspects that are unspeakable in the case of the Singapore heroes mentioned above are no less than the very elements that constitute their worldview, the raison d'être of the deeds that are deemed heroic. Stripped of these crucial elements, individuals like Lim Bo Seng, who received his colonel rank from the Kuomintang,[24] as well as Adnan, Tan Kah Kee, and Tan Lark Sye have no place in Singapore's past, nor the shaping of it. They are simply brave or civic-minded individuals who happened to function in Singapore.

The suppression of the political contexts and beliefs of Singapore's public figures, who even if still alive are no longer politically active, marks their marginalization vis-à-vis those who were in the political party that triumphed in 1959, and further, who remained with the ruling party rather than leaving for the breakaway Barisan Sosialis group in 1963. It is not surprising that those who lost out in the political contest to succeed the colonial power have been sidelined by those who were victorious. What is less usual perhaps is the degree of their marginalization, since the PAP has been in power since 1959, and historiographical revisions grow more and more remote with the deaths of key leaders who became PAP opponents, such as Lim Chin Siong, T. T. Rajah and James Puthucheary. Lee Kuan Yew's memoirs thus hardly face any domestic interlocutors.[25]

In the fifties the Chinese-educated component of the PAP was viewed as ultimately dangerous by the English-educated leadership, led by Lee Kuan Yew, but indispensable to win over the newly enfranchised Chinese-speaking majority of the electorate. In public history they have been dubbed communists and communalists. So potent have these labels been that whether these individuals were really communists seems to be all that matters to posterity. The Chinese-educated communist-chauvinists of the fifties and sixties are sorted into two groupings in the PAP rhetoric: the hangers-on, who expected the left to triumph and so stood to benefit personally for backing the winners, and the dedicated, morally upright men of principle, who were wedded to the communist ideology. The latter have been complimented for setting the high standards of personal behavior and commitment that the PAP moderate leadership understood they had to match, and better. This tribute was paid, on his death, to Lim Chin Siong,[26] the leader of the leftist Chinese-educated PAP faction (and to no other named individual from that period in history) by none other than Lee Kuan Yew.[27]

In tracking the genealogy of Singapore as a nation-state, the PAP leadership seeks to strengthen its mantle by claiming a vast middle ground, marginalizing those cast on the right as weaklings who looked to the patronage of the British, and those on the left as communists in the shadow of the Chinese Communist Party, and hence also as chauvinists in the plural society of Singapore. It thus virtually declares a monopoly on being national-minded, and before independence "national" was understood to mean merger with Malaya. The past configured this way is very much alive in Singapore. It lives on in the ruling party's handling of its present-day political opponents, who are cast as reincarnations of earlier antinational forces: they are either enamored of Western political systems and universalistic ideas of human rights, or communists, Marxists, or chauvinists—labels whose negative resonance has been amplified by reinforcement through national education, in which the latter grouping, especially, is featured as fearsome threats to nationhood.

However, while *communist* and *chauvinist* remain lethal labels, they have been removed from certain individuals, though not due to the discovery of new historical sources that reveal the "truth," or because of a change in the fundamental thinking of the regime in power, resulting in the overturning of the previous official historiography. In 1998 Nanyang Technological University announced the endowment of the Tan Lark Sye Professorship, to be filled by international scholars in Chinese language and culture, a move seen by a Nantah alumnus from the first graduating class as a positive gesture toward the Chinese community as "many members regard him [Tan] as a hero and are still grateful to him."[28] In a newspaper interview the nephew of this millionaire communist-chauvinist, and a past president of the Chinese Chamber of Commerce and Industry in 1999, claimed that his uncle, the largest single individual donor to Nanyang University, was so successful in business that he could not have been a communist:

> *Straits Times:* Your late uncle Tan Lark Sye is enjoying a comeback in the media, with even a professorship named after him now. How do you feel about it?
>
> *Tan Eng Joo:* Whatever incident there might have been in the past, Tan Lark Sye *was* the founder of Nanda [Nantah]. So it is very nice and appropriate that he be remembered with a professorship at Nanyang Technological University. Because he contributed so much to Chinese schools and was active in the Chinese chamber, he was faulted for being a Chinese chauvinist, which sort of connected him to China, and China at that time was communist. But Tan Lark Sye was an out and out capitalist. That he could be communist is unthinkable. Now that is understood a little more, and it is clearing up a little, as I knew it would.[29]

Tan Kah Kee's nephew Tan Keong Choon, also a past president of the chamber, responded similarly in a *Straits Times* interview to the "rehabilitation" of his uncle's name by emphasizing that for years "Some people mistook him to be a communist or a communist sympathizer, but he was neither. He had simply focused his energy to help China and win a place for ethnic Chinese in the world, by contributing to education here and in China. This was not valued in the beginning. But now, it is recognized that there is a need to revive the Tan Kah Kee spirit—this spirit of contributing to society."[30]

With the clarification of the "misunderstanding," that the two men were actually selfless champions of Chinese education rather than communists, both men have become fit for emulation in public discourse, for their enterprise and public spiritedness. A PAP member of Parliament who considers himself to be the voice of Chinese-educated Singaporeans has castigated young Singaporeans as materialistic, self-centered, and lacking in humility and has prescribed the emulation of heroes such as Tan Kah Kee.[31] Recalling the tycoon-philanthropist image and erasing the communist label have made them suitable as heroes, while leaving intact if not reinforcing the association of "communists" with villains, a scripting within which those so labeled remain trapped. In a rare interview published in 1996, Lim Chin Siong himself had denied flatly that he was a communist, a move that scholar Wee Wan Ling has surmised was made in order to claim a place in the history of Singapore's process of achieving independence.[32] The government, however, pointed to the number of Malayan Communist Party members who inserted an obituary for Lim in the Chinese newspapers, and to a letter issued by the Barisan Sosialis denouncing Lim as an "anti-people, anti-communist traitor"[33] when he was freed from detention under the Internal Security Act and resigned from the party in July 1969.

The communist-noncommunist conundrum fits into the PAP's Singapore Story paradigm and does away with the need to explore the widespread appeal of communism, and the inspirational impact of 1949, in the anticolonial context of Southeast Asia. It effaces the credibility of all those who were caught up in those revolutionary times, confining them into the categories of those who were manipulated, and the manipulators—diabolical proxies who served Beijing. Tan Kah Kee's and Tan Lark Sye's posthumous rehabilitation and transformation from communists to communitarians, effected collaboratively between the state in search of local role models, and the scions of the families lending their weight as people who would know the "truth" about their forebears, perpetuates a pop-up storybook dimension rather than a historically complex appreciation of their human agency.

Simply a War Heroine

Even when the subject is still living, representations of him or her in a simplistic monochrome may yet go unchallenged. A notable feature of the way the PAP leaders have distinguished themselves from their opponents of the fifties and sixties is in the consistent and unflinching moral judgments made of the latter, without reference to the political setting of the time. Thus, those who favored a more prolonged path to constitutional devolution to be granted by the colonial government have been cast as self-serving and lacking in courage and vision.[34]

Among the individuals who belonged to what is usually depicted as the archetype of this—the Progressive Party—is Elizabeth Choy, who has been given much official attention as a war heroine while that part of her public life after the war years is not spoken of. Choy, who was captured and tortured by the Japanese for giving aid to British prisoners of war, was selected to embody the collective hardship of the Japanese occupation. As part of the National Education activities, the Singapore History Museum curated an exhibition on her life entitled Elizabeth Choy: A Woman ahead of Her Time. The highlight of the exhibition was the display entitled Japanese Occupation —Canteen Operator and Internee, showing a replica of her prison cell at the Kempeitai (Military Police) headquarters. The exhibition portrayed her as an ordinary, kindhearted school teacher who, before the war, had not participated in any anti-Japanese activities and who happened to help the interns at the military hospital.[35] Indeed, an earlier biography, Elizabeth Choy: More than a War Heroine,[36] is likewise a hagiographic account, painting her as too good and politically naive to be a politician, a tack that the museum exhibition followed faithfully. Choy and other war heroes were the subject of a locally produced Mandarin serial drama, The Price of Peace, which starred the most popular local actors and swept the local television awards.[37] Choy is regularly invited to talk at schools and junior colleges, where her frailty (because of age; she was born in 1910) adds to the poignancy of her retelling of the Japanese tortures inflicted on her. As a female survivor, her heroic status is differentiated from that of Lim Bo

Seng and Adnan, whose heroism was centered precisely on their death by torture.

However, Elizabeth Choy's public life is more than that of a war victim who lived to tell her story. She ran as an independent candidate for the municipal elections in 1950 (and lost), was an unofficial member of the Legislative Council in 1951, was prominent in the women's auxiliary of the Singapore Volunteers' Corps, and ran for the Legislative Council elections in 1955 under the Progressive Party banner (and lost). The British saw in her a potential symbol of Commonwealth harmony, and she was presented to the Queen. Clad in a resplendent cheongsam for that occasion, she was one of the symbols of the colonial power's attempts to maintain continuing links with its multifarious subjects, soon to be citizens of new nation-states. But without an awareness of this requisite political context, the garments she wore are just museum exhibits showcasing the high fashion of an earlier time, with a few visitors most struck by how svelte the wearer must have been to get into them. Almost nothing of her larger public profile in the postwar years or her political concerns is hinted at in the configuration of Elizabeth Choy as war heroine. The colonial power had courted her as among those it would like to work with in the decolonization process as she and her party, mainly comprising privileged, English-educated professionals, were in favor of retaining the closest of relationships with Britain and considered the PAP then to be too radical and populist. Reduced in stature to a political naiveté, and thus rescued from political castigation, the heroic subject herself has not ventured in her public statements to go beyond the physical ravages of the war years.

A National Treasure:
Revealing or Reiterating the Silences?

A more recalcitrant candidate, Pan Shou, did not in the end observe the silences requisite in his elevation from brigand to national treasure. Pan was rendered stateless in 1958, stemming from his involvement in Nanyang University, of which he was secretary-general for five years. His Singapore citizenship was subsequently reinstated in 1983, and from then on he was feted nationally and internationally for his artistic and poetic attainments; receiving the Singapore Cultural Medallion in 1986 for excellence in calligraphy and, finally in 1998, at age eighty-seven, being granted an honorary doctor of letters degree by Nanyang Technological University.[38] His rehabilitation and rise to national prominence was tinged with official patronage. In 1991 Pan was commissioned to write a seventy-character poem in classical Chinese to congratulate the newly elected prime minister, Goh Chok Tong,[39] and to pen in 1994, a four-character calligraphic tribute, which was presented to Senior Minister Lee Kuan Yew. He later penned a piece with the single character *shi* (lion), which graces the entrance to the Singapore Art Museum, and the Chinese name of the Ministry of Information and the Arts, at the request of the minister, for its new premises.[40]

Pan Shou did not let the irony of his life pass without remarking in an interview with the Chinese press that was suppressed until after his death in 1999: "I was then a brigand; later I became a national treasure."[41] In the acceptance speech for his honorary degree, he did not refrain from making a politically sensitive call for the reinstatement of the university's name to Nanyang University. The vice-chancellor immediately responded that this would not do justice to the reputation that the institution had built up in the last seventeen years in the field of technology. This view was shared by the minister of education, who added that the university nevertheless should treasure the feelings that Pan had expressed, "as well as the Nantah spirit of self-help and hard work amid adversity."[42] The *Straits Times* editorialized that reverting to the name Nanyang University would likely

revive issues that marked a turbulent period in Singapore's early efforts at nation-building. This is not to argue for a moment that there is anything anti-national in the Nantah spirit. However, it may perhaps be best not to resuscitate sentiments that were modified and molded into the national consensus of today. What NTU does, in name and function, is to retain Nantah's guiding spirit of self-help, endeavor and enterprise, while combining these with academic pursuits that answer Singapore's needs in the context of its multi-racial society.[43]

Like Tan Lark Sye and Tan Kah Kee, Pan was rehabilitated by the state in the 1980s. However, a 1996 comment—"Pan Shou is Singapore's most celebrated calligrapher, . . . not many people know of his pivotal role in the founding of Nantah"[44]—signaled the end of that period of "forgetfulness" maintained by the years of silence that Pan and others kept, following the high-level, vocal, and public condemnation of their administration of Nanyang University. In July 1959 the newly elected PAP government had publicized the recommendation of a commission, set up by its predecessor, that the university's standards were unacceptable.[45] Chief among the reasons given was that its organization and administration was "not consistent with that of a modern educational institution of the university type."[46] In particular, it was thought that the secretary-general, Pan Shou (then known as Pan Kuo Chu), who had held the position since the university's inception and served as the main channel of communication between the executive council and the university council, lacked "training in academic affairs," and was "one of the factors which have retarded the development of the Nanyang University on sound academic lines."[47] The PAP government then proceeded immediately to seek a second opinion by setting up another review committee, which finished its task by November 1959. Its findings more or less paralleled that of the previous commission and were released only in February 1960.[48] However, in January the Chinese-language edition of *Petir,* the weekly publication of the PAP, had already openly called on Nanyang University authorities to get rid of incompetent officials and charged that "personal friends were being dragged in to hold office."[49] Shortly after, Pan submitted his official resignation, claiming that while the private university of only four years old undeniably had many defects, they were not those "as reported by the press." He also vigorously refuted the "erroneous impression" that "personal influence has played an important part during the past four years in the appointment of general and teaching staff."[50]

Denied citizenship status and hence a passport in 1958, Pan "turned from an animal into a small bonsai plant."[51] He was to be found only on weekends at a Chinese bookstore, which was the gathering point of the Chinese-educated, leisurely writing calligraphy and giving his works away. In 1965 he was invited by the Chinese Chamber of Commerce to write the inscriptions on the memorial for the victims of the Japanese occupation. On the day of the unveiling he found that his entire composition, which hit out widely against war, Japanese butchery, imperialism, and colonialism, was mysteriously omitted. It was nearly twenty years later, in 1984, that this calligraphic piece and the mystery of its disappearance was finally revealed in a local scholarly journal, and the work was later included in a 1995 exhibition of his art.[52] By this time his public persona was that of a national treasure, one who keeps "the torch of Chinese culture and tradition in Singapore burning bright," without which Singapore society would be considerably weakened. Now considered "an outstanding example of a great calligrapher and poet whose works are Chinese in form but Singaporean Chinese in essence," Pan's "patriotic spirit" was held to be exemplary. Furthermore, Pan was honored as "a great teacher," who although serving as the secretary-general of Nanyang University for only five years, left behind a legacy "which saw 21 batches of students graduating from the university before it merged with the former University of Singapore."[53]

The parallel rehabilitations of Chinese culture, Pan and Nantah, were initiated in the mid-eighties, when the scope of the Speak Mandarin campaign, launched in 1979, was extended to an appreciation of Chinese language, culture, and values. In 1992 the Nanyang Technological Institute, which occupied the premises of the former Nanyang University, was transformed into the Nanyang Technological University (Nanyang Ligong Daxue), and became known by the Chinese acronym Lida (Technological University). The term Nantah, which had hitherto stood for Nanyang University, was officially adopted as the shortened form after the prime minister urged the transfer of the Nanyang University alumni register from the combined National

University of Singapore to the Nanyang Technological University. Nantah hence became an official code for the commitment to support Chinese education and culture, as defined by the government.[54]

The essentializing of Nanyang University into a symbol of community spirit and perseverance had been given full vent with the republication in the Chinese press of Tan Lark Sye's speech during the official opening ceremony in 1958, at which the British governor of Singapore was present. Written by Pan and delivered by Tan in the Hokkien dialect, the speech was an expansive and inclusive declaration calling for "cultural interaction among various local races so as to promote interracial friendship and to strengthen interracial cooperation," and decrying the extension of political parties into schools. The medium of learning at Nanyang University would be both Chinese and English, while Malay- and Indian-language courses would be introduced in the future, and the university would be open to "all brotherly races that have for generations lived here."[55] Pan Shou added credence to the claims made in Tan's speech of forty years ago, hitherto overwhelmingly displaced by the dominant rhetoric that the university was a hotbed of communism and chauvinism, with his recollection that the Nanyang crest itself vividly symbolized multi-racialism. According to Pan, he designed the crest with the help of his daughter. It comprised a yellow star, representing Nantah, and yellow, blue, and red rings, representing the Chinese, Malays, and Indians. The rings were interlocked, standing for racial harmony.[56]

Tan Lark Sye's and Pan's argument, in the fifties and sixties, that the university was the victim of politics was thus ironically revived in the mid-nineties, with Pan's careful omission of the early years of PAP rule, in order to recast the government in the role of champions of Nantah in its reincarnated form, as the living embodiment of the Nantah pioneering spirit, as well as in the role of patron of Pan Shou. Whether the national treasure himself was revealing or reiterating the silences in Singapore's history, or perhaps doing a bit of both, is ambivalently sustained in the following narrative of Nantah's early history:

In 1959, the Lim Yew Hock government decided not to recognize Nantah's degrees, thus dealing a mortal blow to the fledging university. The official explanation was that Nantah's education standards were below par, but the fact that the Chinese students and the Chinese community were openly critical of the government must have also influenced the decision. The 50s and early 60s were turbulent years in Singapore's history. Banned by the colonial government, the communists channeled their resources to infiltrate the unions and the Chinese students. Since Nantah was regarded as the pinnacle of Chinese education, it was not surprising that the government should view it with suspicion. Moreover, only a thin line separated the passion for Chinese education and Chinese chauvinism. Invariably the proponents of Chinese education were tarred with the same brush as the chauvinists. . . . Pan insisted Nantah had sought to recruit the best lecturers. What problems it faced in the early days were typical teething ones encountered by any new university.[57]

Swan Song of a Heroic Ghost?

Living heroes are obviously potentially problematic. Pan Shou and his supporters had undoubtedly sought and encouraged the rehabilitation of his status as a Chinese cultural personality.[58] His son's testimony added weight to the portrayal of Pan as a loyal Singaporean who was the victim of colonialism and its lackeys, with the PAP government appearing in the narrative only in 1983, when his citizenship was restored:

> Father knows that the Lim Yew Hock government was biased against Chinese education and Nanyang University. Like a faithful servant of the British Empire, [Lim] guarded against the existence of Chinese culture outside China. . . . The Lim Yew Hock government's ugly jealousy toward Nantah and my father was soon revealed. Soon after the official opening ceremony, my father's citizenship was canceled. My father's passport was confiscated. . . . It was only twenty-five years later that the Singapore government of the People's Action Party returned my father's citizenship to him.[59]

However, the history of Pan's involvement in Nanyang University and its closure after twenty-five years of existence remained painfully embedded as the defining events of his life in Singapore,

surfacing publicly in the weeks surrounding his controversial convocation address. In an interview, which he did not want published
at the time, he lamented "the premature death" of the university
and called himself "a first-class criminal" who had failed Nantah,
contrary to the public acclaim he was being accorded.[60] On Pan's
death, the reporter published the interview as a final tribute. Pan's
unexpected confession quickly elicited a "clarification" from the
president of the Chinese Calligraphy Society of Singapore, who
stated that it was the colonial government that had deprived Pan of
his citizenship and labeled him a brigand, and that it was the PAP
government that had valued him as a national treasure.[61] The
clarification thus reversed the transformation contained in Pan's
ironic observation, from being the outcome of a complex historical
process to a neat periodization mediated by righteous leaders and a
happy ending to a fulfilled life. Any suggestion of Pan being a bitter
Nanyang University loyalist was suppressed. It was a scramble to
slam down the lid of Pandora's box.

The Pan Shou chronicle can be read as one possible culmination
of the vicissitudes of history writing in Singapore, from a willful rejection and negation of history to a scripted celebration of the past
within the span of forty years. However, Pan's stubborn recollection
made the connection between the two treatments of the past as two
sides of the same coin and exposed the chasm between the historical
and the new-design Nantah and Chinese intellectuals,[62] so thinly
papered over by the honors given to him. Baring his painful past,
splinters of which are also lodged in those who take pride in being
Chinese-educated Singaporeans—who look to the fifties and sixties
and especially the Nanyang University as their point of identification, and who await recognition for their historical cause—Pan gave
voice at the Nantah convocation, and in its aftermath, to this hitherto
carefully muted constituency, which had been consigned to the
margins of the nation-building enterprise, at the border between the
struggle for national independence and the battle against chauvinism and communism.

Elizabeth Choy and the English-educated professionals have been absorbed into the political mainstream; the forgetting of her postwar past perhaps simply reduces the richness of the texture of the Singapore Story. Pan's persistent memory, however, challenged the supposedly unproblematic conferment of the title of national hero, the hegemony of national history, and the reduction of marginalized historical actors to the nation's "other," which is the damnation of political defeat and disempowerment—on the very convocation podium that was meant to mark his forgetting.

Notes

This essay has benefited from the research assistance of Leander Seah Tze Lin and from interviews on Pan Shou given to Huang Jianli by Ho Chee Lick and Choo Yam-Wai, who of course are not responsible for the views and interpretations expressed. Hong Lysa's appreciation to Vani S for sharing her wavelength.

1. A biography of Yusof Ishak (1910–1970) was launched at the Currency 21 Exhibition introducing the new currency series. Melanie Chew, *A Biography of a President: Yusof bin Ishak* (Singapore: Singapore National Printers, for Board of Commissioners of Currency, 1999), esp. ch. 9, "A Hero's Passing." See also Huang Jianli, "The Head of State in Singapore: An Historical Perspective," in *Managing Political Change in Singapore: The Elected Presidency,* ed. Kevin Tan and Lam Peng Er (London: Routledge, 1997).

2. Portraits of Queen Elizabeth, and earlier of her father, King George VI, were standard features of stamps, banknotes, and coins in the Straits Settlements, of which Singapore was a part.

3. See Chua Beng Huat, *Communitarian Ideology and Democracy in Singapore* (London: Routledge, 1995), ch. 1.

4. Ibid., 26.

5. Ibid., 31.

6. Loh Kah Seng, "The Use of History by Singapore's Political Leaders since Independence" (B.A. Hons. thesis, Department of History, National University of Singapore, 1995–96), 20. Goh's speech was reported in the *Straits Times,* 21 Jan. 1996. The *Asian Values* rhetoric emphasized the perceived superiority of traditional family and social structure as well as the "work hard save hard" ethic of Asians in comparison to Westerners.

7. The food company, Tee Yih Jia, commissioned the one-million-dollar statues from China under a government scheme granting tax exemption to

those who donate sculptures to the nation. They were of Qu Yuan, Guan Yu, Hua Mulan, Yue Fei, Wen Tianxiang, Zheng He, and Lin Zexu, all heroic figures from the pages of China's imperial history.

8. "Come Up with Your Models Too, PM Urges Malays and Indians," *Straits Times,* 19 Sept. 1991. Goh noted that Muslims did not as a rule capture human forms in sculpture, "but there may be other creative ways of presenting their legendary heroes or certain aspects of their culture, such as calligraphic rendering of certain values."

9. Ibid.

10. Prasenjit Duara, "Historicizing National Identity, or Who Imagines What and When," in *Becoming National: A Reader,* ed. Geoff Eley and Ronald Grigor Suny (New York: Oxford University Press, 1996), 151–69.

11. Studies on the making of official heroes as privileged sites of collective national imaginings in Southeast Asia include Klaus H. Schreiner, "The Making of National Heroes: Guided Democracy to the New Order, 1959–1992," in *Outward Appearances: Dressing State and Society in Southeast Asia,* ed. Henk Schulte Nordholt (Leiden: KITLV Press, 1997), 259–90; Timothy P. Barnard, "Local Heroes and National Consciousness: The Politics of Historiography in Riau," *Bijdragen tot de taal-, land-, en volkenkunde* 153, 4 (1997), 509–26 and Glen May, *Inventing a Hero: The Posthumous Re-Creation of Andres Bonifacio* (Quezon City: New Day, 1997).

12. "Old Guard Fighters Are National Heroes: PM," *Straits Times,* 12 May 1999. The death of old guard stalwart E. W. Barker, the long-serving minister of law, and PAP member of Parliament (1963–88) on 12 April 2001 occasioned a commentary by Irene Ng, a *Straits Times* journalist, that as one of the founding fathers of modern Singapore, "surely he deserves to be remembered as a hero?" *Straits Times,* 3 June 2001. See also comments by another reader in the *Straits Times,* 6 June 2001, and response from the Board of Commissioners of Currency, 8 June 2001, on featuring "other national leaders and heroes" on future currency designs.

13. Loh Kah Seng, "Within the Singapore Story: The Use and Narrative of History in Singapore," *Crossroads* 12, 2 (1998): 1–2.

14. *Straits Times,* 20 May 1997.

15. Ministry of Information and the Arts, "The Singapore Story: Overcoming the Odds," CD-ROM, Singapore, 1998.

16. A number of the old guard, the first generation of PAP leaders who were retired from politics in the 1980s, had made this point. Veteran Ong Pang Boon, who had served from 1959 variously as minister of home affairs, minister of education, minister of labor, and environment minister, retiring in 1984, described this amnesia as symptomatic of "a parvenu society where if one was not successful, they would be forgotten and neglected.

Thus, the old guard, once they retire, were often regarded as 'losers.' Their contributions would be buried and forgotten." *Straits Times,* 5 Oct. 1980; cited in Sai Siew Min and Huang Jianli, "The 'Chinese-Educated' Political Vanguards," in *Lee's Lieutenants: Singapore's Old Guard,* ed. Lam Peng Er and Kevin Y. L. Tan (Sydney: Allen and Unwin, 1999), 163.

17. Lee Kuan Yew, *The Singapore Story: Memoirs of Lee Kuan Yew* (Singapore: Times Editions, 1998), and *From Third World to First: The Singapore Story, 1965–2000* (Singapore: Times Editions, 2000). Lee asserted that the thoroughness was paramount, as his credibility would be impaired should his points be shown to be weak or false. *Straits Times,* 12 Sept. 1998. The notable omission is the Malaysian archives.

18. "Vital to Stay Open to Talent," *Straits Times,* 26 Nov. 1998.

19. "Old Guard Fighters Are National Heroes: PM," *Straits Times,* 12 May 1999.

20. "KL to Make Patriotic Film on War Hero," *Straits Times,* 13 Nov. 1999.

21. Described as "a war epic . . . which depicts the bravery of Malay soldiers against the might of the invading Japanese army during World War II," the movie was voted best film of the year and a "Special Jury Award for the education value in the film towards inculcating patriotism" at the fifteenth Malaysian Film Festival in August 2001; *Star,* 6 Aug. 2001. On the Singapore side, the National Archives of Singapore spearheaded the launching of a 4.8 million SD multimedia museum at Bukit Chandu, Pepys Road in February 2002 to commemorate the bravery of the Malay regiment and Lt. Adnan Saidi. *Straits Times,* 27 Dec. 2001.

22. *Straits Times,* 2 Mar. 1998; 6 May 1999; 7 May 1999. The issue of whether P. Ramlee is a Singaporean or Malaysian cultural hero is complicated by the issue of intellectual property. Many of the rights to his films belong to the film company, Shaw Brothers. UMNO Youth (United Malay National Organization) had announced plans to form a committee to recover the artistic works and the rights to his films. According to the Malaysian information minister, the Copyrights Act provides that works produced in a country become the right of that country and other countries have no right over them.

23. Sai and Huang, "'Chinese-Educated' Political Vanguards," 147.

24. That Lim Bo Seng saw himself as a Chinese national fighting for Kuomintang China was pointed out by George Yeo, minister of information and the arts, in his speech ("Being Chinese: Keeping the Culture without the Politics") at the official opening of the Chinese Heritage Center in 1985. Yeo argued that this qualification was necessary when honoring Lim as a "national or proto-national hero" for "there was no republic of Singapore in the fifties and early sixties." *Straits Times* 19 May 1985. This sensibility is absent in the

didactic function to which Lim has been assigned; a huge portrait of him is displayed at the Singapore Armed Forces Training Institute library, as an example for Singaporeans of a soldier who put the defense of the country before family, a freedom fighter who believed that the latter could not exist before the former. Denise Gan Eunne-Ru, "Public History in Singapore in the 1990s: The Second World War" (B.A. Hons. thesis, Department of History, National University of Singapore, 1997–98), 11.

25. Except perhaps from Lee Siew Choh, former leader of the Barisan Sosialis, who has written to the press (see for example his letter in the *Straits Times,* 16 June 1997) to challenge official accounts. But without documents to substantiate his case, nor corroboration from other political actors of the period, his account has been cast as biased and groundless. More recently an ailing Lee Siew Choh has announced that he is writing his memoirs as "somebody has to say something about the untruths propagated by the PAP because so many people have been deceived." *Straits Times,* 16 June 2001. For a discussion on the use of "classified information to limit a researcher's access to information and knowledge in "Asian democracies," see Nirmala PuruShotam, "The Possibilities of 'Asian' Intellectuals," *Items* 52, 4 (Dec. 1998): 86.

26. For more on Lim, the only other PAP leader whose stature could rival that of Lee Kuan Yew in the 1950s, see C. J. W.-L. Wee, "The Vanquished: Lim Chin Siong and a Progressivist National Narrative," in *Lee's Lieutenants,* 169–90.

27. Lee's letter of condolence to Lim's wife, dated 8 February 1996, reads: "I have just read that Chin Siong died of heart attack on Monday 5 February. I got on well with Lim Chin Siong from the time we first met in 1954. He was a shy, soft-spoken, modest, serious man, and a hard worker. He fought tenaciously for his beliefs and for his side. The only way we, the non-communists, could counter his attacks was to match his determination, tenacity and stamina. I was sad to hear that he has died at a relatively young age. My wife and I send our condolences to you and your two sons. We hope they will live up to the promise that their father showed and would have achieved had he been on the non-communist side." *Straits Times,* 9 Feb. 1996.

28. *Straits Times,* 24 Apr. 1998. The first Tan Lark Sye Professorship lecture, "The Rise of Ethnic Chinese Business in East and Southeast Asia," was delivered by Yen Ching-Hwang on 4 August 2000. Nantah was the acronym for Nanyang University. For a brief history of Nanyang University's merger with the University of Singapore to form the National University of Singapore, and the subsequent setting up of the Nanyang Technological University, see Sai and Huang, "'Chinese-Educated' Political Vanguard," 162–63. See also Edwin Lee and Tan Tai Yong, *Beyond Degrees* (Singapore: Singapore University Press, 1996).

29. *Straits Times,* 1 Jan. 1999.

30. *Straits Times,* 13 Nov. 1998.

31. Member of Parliament Peh Chin Hua's speech, reported in "What Will Become of Them?—Young and Mobile," *Straits Times,* 13 Oct. 1999.

32. C. J. W.-L. Wee, "Vanquished," 174.

33. *Straits Times,* 26 Feb. 1996.

34. S. Rajaratnam has branded the conservative camp of Singapore politics in the 1950s as "the Progressives and their feeble leaders." Even though these comments were made in 1964, the PAP leadership has not changed its views on the matter. Rajaratnam's article "PAP's First Ten Years" has been republished in *S. Rajaratnam: The Prophetic and the Political,* ed. Chan Heng Chee and Obaid ul Haq (Singapore: Graham Brash, 1987), 26–64.

35. Gan, "Public History in Singapore," 44–47.

36. Zhou Mei calls Choy "a living saint" (the title of a chapter in her book)—caring, trusting, sacrificial, full of integrity, devoted to social work but politically naive. Zhou, *Elizabeth Choy: More than a War Heroine* (Singapore: Landmark Books, 1995). "The Political Naiveté" is the title of a chapter that argues that Choy had no idea what she was going into when she ran for elections, except that she was fueled by a sense of service. An interview with the press given when Elizabeth Choy turned ninety-one gave a similar account of her life but with a suggestion that Mrs. Choy, having met the then young lawyer Lee Kuan Yew, had perhaps sensed that "Singapore had found a new political leader" and decided to turn her back on politics, remaining a school teacher from 1955 till her retirement in 1975. *Sunday Times,* 1 Jul. 2001.

37. The television serial was produced at the suggestion of Foong Choon Hon, the senior director of culture and community affairs with the Singapore Chinese Chamber of Commerce and Industry, who expected that young people following the series would "ponder over issues such as whether there would be any Lim Bo Sengs and Tan Kah Kees if Singapore should ever be occupied by an enemy." "Choy's Remarkable Life on Show," *Straits Times,* 1 Nov. 1997. The Lim Bo Seng story is most recently retold yet again in "Heroes," in Chinese opera style, with the orthodox storyline of an anti-Japanese hero who made great personal sacrifices unchanged. See comments by Chua Soo Pong, director of the Chinese Opera Institute, who wrote the script in *Straits Times,* 10 Feb. 2000.

38. Pan received the following accolades: 1985 Salon des Artistes Français Gold Prize; 1986 Singapore Government Cultural Medallion; 1991 Officer des Arts et des Lettres; 1994 Government of Singapore Meritorious Service Medal; 1997 ASEAN Cultural Medal; 1998 honorary doctorate, Nanyang Technological University. See Pan Shou, *Pan Shou shiji*

(Collection of Pan Shou's poems) (Singapore: Singapore Cultural Studies Society, 1997), back cover; Pan Soo Yeng, "A Poet Is Happy—Remembering Pan Shou," *Straits Times,* 18 Aug. 1997.

39. *Lianhe Zaobao,* 1 May 1991.

40. "The Legacy of Pan Shou," *Straits Times,* 25 Feb. 1999.

41. *"dangnian shi qiangdao, houlai chengle guobao."* Quoted in Li Huiling, "Pan Shou de Nanda leihen" (Pan Shou's lament on Nantah), *Lianhe Zaobao,* 6 March 1999.

42. *Lianhe Zaobao,* 27 Aug. 1998, available in the Chinese Library of the National University of Singapore within a loosely organized set of photocopies on writings and news clippings about Pan Shou (the original publication details are often incomplete; hereafter cited as NUS Pan Shou Collection) 125. The issue is likely to remain alive. At the celebrations of NTU's twentieth anniversary, its president, who had announced his imminent retirement in 2002, noted that while reversion to the use of the name Nanyang University would not happen soon, he was confident that it would "take place in a decade." *Lianhe Zaobao,* 3 July 2001; *Today,* 9 July 2001.

43. "NTU Lives Up to Name" *Straits Times,* 28 Aug. 1998.

44. This observation is made by the *Straits Times* in its introduction to the translation of an interview conducted with Pan by Pang Cheng Lian, secretary of the Singapore Chinese Clan Associations Working Committee, originally published in Chinese in *Yuan* (Origins) 34 (1996): 26–31, a quarterly published by the federation. On Pan's recollection of his involvement in the founding of Nanyang University and its early years, see "He Was There When Nantah Needed a Head—Pan Shou's Pivotal Role in University's Setup," *Straits Times,* 28 Nov. 1996.

45. The findings of the Prescott Commission, appointed by the Lim Yew Hock government in January 1959 and comprising five internationally respected academics, was submitted in March but made public only in July 1959. The PAP won the elections on 30 May 1959; the first class, of four hundred students, was to graduate at the end of the year. The commission stated that it could not "in good conscience recommend the recognition of the university's degrees." "Nanyang: No Recognition," *Straits Times,* 23 July 1959.

46. S. L. Prescott et al., *Report of the Nanyang University Commission 1959* (Singapore: Government Printing Office, 1959), 5, paras. 2.1, 2.2.

47. Ibid., 6, para. 2.7; "Nanyang: No recognition," *Straits Times,* 23 July 1959.

48. *Report of the Nanyang University Review Committee,* presented to the Legislative Assembly on 6 Feb. 1960, Misc. 1 of 1960. This committee, headed by Gwee Ah Leng, was appointed on 23 Jul. 1959 and submitted its

report on 20 Nov. 1959. See also *Straits Times,* 10–11 Feb. 1960; *Nanyang Siang Pau,* 10–11 Feb. 1960.

49. "*Petir* Attack on Nanyang Varsity," *Straits Times,* 11 Jan. 1960.

50. *Straits Times,* 3 Feb. 1960; *Nanyang Siang Pau,* 2 Feb. 1960.

51. Pan Soo Yeng, "Fuqing de shi" (My father's poems), article dated as Nov. 1996, in NUS Pan Shou Collection, 30; see also Li, "Pan Shou de Nanda leihen."

52. See the various references in NUS Pan Shou Collection, 46–47, 57–58, 91, 96. See also Pan, *Pan Shou shiji,* 590–92; and Foong Choon Han, ed., *The Price of Peace: True Accounts of the Japanese Occupation* (Singapore: Asiapac, 1997), 340–44.

53. The minister of information and the arts himself paid Pan this tribute at the launch of the latter's collection of poems. See "Nantah Grads Playing 'Major Role' in S'pore," *Straits Times,* 19 Aug. 1997.

54. The complexities of Nanyang University's history in Singapore's political development may yet surface in public discourses. In August 2000 the NTU Chinese Society Drama group presented *A Nantah Story,* a play on conflicting views between a husband and wife, both Nanyang University graduates, and their daughter's attempt to comprehend the "Nantah spirit."

55. Full speech reprinted in *Lianhe Zaobao,* 3 June 1995, available in NUS Pan Shou Collection, 100–102. The republication of this speech after a lapse of forty years is yet another cautiously calibrated step in the rehabilitation of Chinese culture, Pan, and Nantah. See also Pan, *Pan Shou shiji,* 580–84; and Wang Ruming, ed., *Chen Liushi bainiandan jinian wenji* (Commemorative volume on the hundredth anniversary of Tan Lark Sye's birth) (Singapore: Nantah Company/Hong Kong Nantah Alumni, 1997), 199–201.

56. *Lianhe Zaobao,* 3 June 1995, in NUS Pan Shou Collection, 100. This claim was repeated in *Lianhe Zaobao,* 14 Nov. 1996 and again in the *Straits Times,* 28 Nov. 1996.

57. Pang, "When Nantah Needed a Head."

58. On the year long process of restoring Pan's citizenship in 1982–83, the use of the alternative name Pan Shou instead of Pan Kuo Chu, and the help of Tan Siah Kwee, the president of the Chinese Calligraphy Society of Singapore, in approaching the minister of home affairs and other PAP leaders, see Chen Shenggui (Tan Siah Kwee), "Pan Shou: Yiduan weiceng gongkai de wangshi" (Pan Shou: A hitherto undisclosed matter) *Lianhe Zaobao,* 20 Mar. 1999.

59. Ironically, Pan Soo Yeng was then writing in 1996 about this citizenship restoration within the context of analyzing a 1986 poem composed by his father while he was visiting the site of the old Nanyang University, lamenting the run-down condition of the place. Pan Soo Yeng, "Fuqing de shi," 29–30.

60. Li, "Pan Shou de Nanda leihen."

61. Pang, "When Nantah Needed a Head."

62. Chew Cheng Hai, director of the Nanyang Technological University Center of Chinese Language and Culture, highlighted the chasm by declaring that "traditional monolingual Chinese intellectuals, like Pan Shou, are disappearing from the scene" and the new "Chinese intellectuals" and "Chinese elite" are products of the modern bilingual system and have good command of English in addition to in-depth understanding of Chinese language, art, and culture. See *Straits Times,* 28 Mar. 1999. Prime Minister Goh Chok Tong had first raised the issue of the need for a Singapore Chinese cultural elite in his national day speech in August 1997. Following the announcement of a new syllabus permitting more students to study the Chinese language as a school subject at a higher level, a seminar was organized by the Hwa Chong alumni to discuss the role of Chinese intellectuals. This discussion became the largest and most open debate on the topic in Singapore for four decades. See *Straits Times,* 2 Mar. 1999.

Part Three

SHIFTING BOUNDARIES, MOVING INTERSTICES

Chapter 11

WRITING MALAYSIA'S SOCIAL HISTORY FROM THE ECCLESIASTICAL RECORDS

Abu Talib Ahmad

Few works in Malaysian historiography fall within the field of social history, a field that can be broadly understood to include the history of class formations, social relations, and class conflicts as well as studies of fringe groups, in addition to the more conventional themes of demographic history (birth, marriage, divorce, internal and external migrations) and related topics in economic and cultural history. Apart from a few pathbreaking studies on the peasantry in colonial Malaya, little work has been done on class studies, in particular the formation and rise of the middle class. Published works have tended to focus on a few highly selective topics such as education, both secular and religious. And though there has been a fair amount of interest on the evolution of a plural society, with separate studies of the Chinese, Indians, and Malays, including groups that originated from the Netherlands East Indies, no comprehensive demographic history of Malaysia has yet been written.

A corpus of invaluable studies pertaining to various aspects of the country's history and culture was undertaken by British scholar-officials. However, this does not seem to have stimulated further research in, or alleviated the depressing state of, social history research in this country. The general lack of interest in social history among local scholars and researchers is, to some extent, due to the widely held perception that there are vexing problems in the sources. But in fact there is a multitude of source materials available, ranging from those deposited in European archives (Portuguese, Dutch, or British) to local sources deposited at the National Archives of Malaysia and its regional branches. Thus it would be possible, for instance, to write a comprehensive demographic history of Malaysia beginning from the nineteenth century, or even earlier, up to the present. But such a mammoth task would necessitate closer collaboration efforts among local historians, which is rather limited at the moment. Fortunately there has been a noticeable surge of interest in social history among Malaysian academics in recent years, notably in women's history, history "from below," of the laboring classes including prostitutes, and, to a lesser extent, of marginalized groups such as the Orang Asli (original people). It is also interesting to note that scholars from the social sciences have contributed significantly to our understanding of various aspects of Malaysia's social transformations by incorporating materials from intensive archival research into their work.

Research on Malaysia's Social History since 1957

Social history tends to be treated in popular history books within the confines of chapters on topics such as the development of education or the evolution of a plural society. The few works on Malaysia's social history, which have been published since 1957, remain obscure and inaccessible to the general reader. In addition, there are a number of unpublished theses, academic exercises, long essays, or term papers left to gather dust in departmental or university libraries. This section surveys the various categories of work by local scholars—studies by prominent academics, studies published for popular consumption, or short studies by undergraduates—as all can contribute colorful additions or useful insights into local social history.

As stated earlier, there is no comprehensive demographic history of Malaysia from the pre-Melaka period to the present. But several studies of Malaysia's population have been undertaken by geographers and social scientists that focus on the diverse ethnic components of Malaysia's plural society. Strictly speaking, many of these studies do not quite fall within the parameters of social history. Nevertheless, they can be extremely useful, especially when they deal with the nineteenth and twentieth centuries, or the British colonial period.[1] Our understanding of Malaysia's Indian society, for example, has been enhanced through studies by historians, such as Rajeswary Ampalavanar, as much as by as nonhistorians like P. Ramasamy.[2]

Studies of the Chinese are varied, covering different aspects of Chinese society, both in the Malay Peninsula and East Malaysia. J. D. Vaughan's invaluable classic, first completed in the nineteenth century, was reissued in 1994, reflecting the great interest in the Peranakan or Straits Chinese.[3] Local scholars have undertaken studies of Chinese in particular states,[4] or Chinese education and Chinese politics,[5] while Chinese secret societies have attracted the interest of mostly non-Malaysian scholars.[6] There are also a few studies devoted to the Chinese working class in general, or with specific reference to particular groups, such as the tin miners of Kinta Valley.[7] Studies of Chinese immigration have generally tended to begin with the British period, overlooking the earlier patterns of migratory movements of people during the Srivijaya period and after, and the kind of accommodation between locals and nonlocals that began long before the emergence of what is, today, termed the plural society.

Not many studies of the social history of the Malays have been published. Of these, Khoo Kay Kim's *Malay Society: Transformation and Democratization,* a collection of previously published articles, is useful for an understanding of the political and social changes in Malay society since the nineteenth century.[8] Shaharil Talib's examination of Malay elites and peasants in Terengganu, from the late nineteenth century to the Japanese conquest, is a highly acclaimed study that complements very well an earlier pioneering study of the peasantry in Perak by Lim Teck Ghee.[9] Malays were also involved in secret societies during the second half of the nineteenth and first quarter of the twentieth century, whether on their own or in cohort with Chinese secret societies, particularly in Penang.[10] There are no studies of Malays in relation to land issues on a countrywide scale but the study by Nazri Abdullah on Malay reservation land in the Federated Malay States is an important contribution to the field.[11]

Malaysia dari segi sejarah (Malaysia in history), the journal of the Malaysian Historical Society, has devoted some of its issues to immigration and immigrants, but more useful to our understanding of the changing formation of Malay society are the studies that focus specifically on groups that came from Indonesia, such as the Javanese in Selangor, Seberang Perai, and Parit Jawa (Batu Pahat), the Banjarese in the Krian district, and the Bawean community in the Malay peninsula—all of whom were classified in earlier censuses as Malaysians.[12] On the other hand, there are very few studies that focus on the Arabs and their descendants; or the Syeds (Sayyids), who are also of Arab descent;[13] or the Pakistanis and Afghans, who have assimilated into the local population, for example in Terengganu.[14] There is a similar lacuna in our understanding of the Indian Muslims, also known as Jawi Pekan/Peranakan, although an account of the Merican clan, descendants of the famous Kapitan Kling, written by one of its members, and the study of the Indian Muslims of Penang by Helen Fujimoto have gone some way toward redressing it.[15] As social history, however, none of the above studies can match the sophistication of John Butcher's study of the British in Malaya.[16]

Neglected in these studies are the multitudes of Orang Asli, which did receive considerable attention from non-Malaysian scholars during and after the Japanese occupation. Studies of these groups of marginalized Malaysians, both in peninsular and East Malaysia, have remained the preserve of cultural anthropologists.[17] Where they are included in historical studies, they appear to be incidental to the larger themes of the Emergency and the communist insurrection. A recent study has shown the serious problems that these people have faced in coming to terms with the modern world since the nineteenth century—for example slavery, economic exploitation, and conversion to a new religion.[18]

Though few local historians have written works based on class analysis, Lim Teck Ghee's study of the peasantry in the Krian district in Perak, Shaharil Talib's discussion of the experiences of peasants on the east coast of the Malay peninsula, and Cheah Boon Kheng's analysis of the peasant robbers in Kedah during the first quarter of the twentieth century are indicative of the potential of writing social history, as yet untapped, that is grounded in an analysis of class structures and relations.[19] The publication of *The Underside of Malaysian History: Pullers, Prostitutes and Plantation Workers* (1990) and Leong Yee Fong's study of labor in Malaya (1999), further indicate growing interest in this kind of social history among Malaysian and non-Malaysian scholars.[20] Equally useful are the contributions of scholars who come from other disciplines, such as political science, economics, and anthropology/sociology—for instance, Loh Kok Wah's study of the Chinese working class, including squatters, in Perak, Ishak Shari's analysis of development and underdevelopment among the peasantry in Kelantan, Shamsul Amri's fascinating account of developmental politics at the local level, and Zawawi Ibrahim's thought-provoking insights on the Malay working class.[21] Other disciplines that have contributed to our understanding of Malay society include work done in the arts, such as drama and folk theatre, as well as literature. For example, Muhammad Haji Salleh and Siti Hawa Salleh are known for their penetrating analyses of Malay literature while Wazir-Jahan Karim, a cultural anthropologist, has examined various facets of Malay society relating especially to women.[22]

For the Japanese occupation, Paul Kratoska's *The Japanese Occupation of Malaya: A Social and Economic History* is exceptional in devoting a significant portion of its contents to social history, making it the most comprehensive, and arguably the best, account of the occupation available.[23] Kratoska's excellent discussion covers a variety of themes, such as education and propaganda, currency and banking, estates and mining, as well as rationing and food production, distinguishing it from Cheah Boon Kheng's earlier work, which focused mainly on the roots of political conflicts planted during the Japanese occupation.[24] Kratoska was meticulous in his research methodology, using not only historical materials located in Malaysia, Singapore, Britain, and the United States but also drawing on oral history, to enable a refreshing interpretation and, more important, to set a benchmark for any future study of the occupation.

This is not to say that other studies of the Japanese occupation by local researchers have not been up to the mark. Rather, these studies are less comprehensive, being more focused in their geographical coverage and the kinds of documents consulted and giving social history only a small part in the overall narrative. Several fall more within the realm of local or regional studies. For instance, Mohamad Isa Othman has covered Kedah quite well, including the political changes caused by the change of administration from the Malayan military administration to the Siamese midway through the occupation, Japanese control of the local economy, the resultant social rumblings among locals, and anti-Japanese resistance. Mohamad Isa's study, originally part of an M.A. thesis, depends heavily on records kept in the National Archives in Kuala Lumpur and its Alor Setar branch, in particular the State Secretariat Series.[25] Similarly, a study of Terengganu by Abdullah Zakaria Ghazali is very much an administrative study of this east coast state during the Japanese and Thai interlude. Abdullah did, albeit briefly, raise some interesting issues, such as the Japanese treatment of Islam, religious elites, and the sultan, and the reaction of the Terengganu elites to the transfer of the state's suzerainty to Thailand. Abdullah has also indicated the importance of documents originating from the Terengganu state secretariat, which are kept in the Kuala Terengganu branch of the National Archives.[26]

Ghazali Mayudin's study of Johore is another significant contribution to the historiography of the occupation.[27] This is also very much an administrative history, emphasizing the limited success of efforts undertaken by the Malayan military administration to solve various socioeconomic issues that had arisen in Johore. Of particular interest is the discussion of the plight of the Johore civil servants, who were greatly affected by various wartime measures, including salary cuts and retrenchments, which made them very much dependent on food supplied or subsidized by the government. Meanwhile not much attention has been paid to the social history of this period in East Malaysia, although the work of younger scholars such as Ooi Keat Gin on Sarawak has looked at this period from the perspective of both the colonizers and the colonized.[28]

My own interest in this period covers both political and social history, especially in relation to the Malay masses and exploring the exciting potential of using oral history. Of particular interest to me is the social crisis that bedeviled the Malay masses and how that crisis in turn affected political change during, and immediately after, the occupation. One particular aspect is changes in marriage and divorce patterns. In the state of Johore, I have found a marked increase in divorces in the big towns, smaller towns, and rural villages during this period. This was due to socioeconomic factors as much as the nature of the Japanese presence that restricted the power of the religious elites, rendering them ineffective as arbiters of religious morality among Malay Muslims. The increased rate of divorce caused considerable concern among the religious elites themselves, some of whom suggested specific measures to curb it and a host of other related social problems. But these steps were ineffective in curbing the trend, which continued until the Japanese surrender. On rereading the sources, I became increasingly doubtful of the capacity of conservative religious elites to come up with effective solutions for those difficult times. And even if they had done so, I am equally doubtful of their ability to have them implemented under the rule of the samurai. I am also intrigued by the collaboration with and loyalty to the British among the Malay elites, and by the confusions created by these emotive issues within the spectrum of Malay nationalists and intelligentsia.[29]

I have pointed out earlier that the work conducted in our local universities is very much hidden from the view of the Malaysian general public. As a first step toward publicizing work done by humanities students at Universiti Sains Malaysia, the editors of *Jurnal ilmu kemanusiaan* (Journal of the humanities), published by the School of Humanities, have published a list of all academic exercises and long essays submitted to various disciplines within the school between 1973 and 1993.[30] Looking through this lengthy list, one is struck by the variety of themes that have commanded student interest. They include aspects of social and economic history as well as cultural practices, some of which are no longer in existence. Some of this work has been revised for publication in the journal itself or in *Kajian Malaysia* (Malaysian studies), another journal based at Universiti Sains Malaysia, or as occasional papers.[31] Equally exciting is the variety in the themes of academic exercises completed by University of Malaya and Universiti Kebangsaan Malaysia students, who have relatively better access to the National Archives in Kuala Lumpur. To the credit of the history department at Universiti Kebangsaan Malaysia, seven of their academic exercises have already been published as monographs.[32] Among them, Ghazali Mayudin's *Johore semasa pendudukan Jepun, 1942–1945* (Johore during the Japanese occupation) and Timah Hamzah's *Pemberontakan tani 1928 di Terengganu* (The 1928 peasant rebellion in Terengganu), have become part of reference materials used in undergraduate teaching at local universities. Similarly, a few of the better academic exercises produced by the University of Malaya have been published as monographs,[33] while more have been revised for publication as articles in *Malaysia in History* and the department's own *Jurnal sejarah* (Journal of history). Recently, a few master's theses from the history department of the University of Malaya have also been published, for example a study of Brunei history and another of Malaysia-Vietnam relations in the postwar period.[34]

Term papers and course essays by undergraduates and upper secondary students, which utilize oral history in addition to archival materials, can also provide invaluable information on local social histories. The School of Humanities of Universiti Sains Malaysia has, since 1982, published three anthologies of such work that provide invaluable information on local conditions, local leaders and personalities. In *Penghijrah dan penghijrahan* (Immigrants and immigration),[35] we read about Tay Hooi Soo, Malaya's first Chinese district officer; Panglima Salleh, the famous peasant robber of Kedah; and lesser-known personalities, such as Haji Uthman Haji Senik, a mufti of Pahang before and during the First World War. There is more social history in *Tokoh-tokoh tempatan* (Local leaders), with studies of the arrival of Javanese, Bawean, and Banjarese immigrants in various parts of Johore, Perak, Penang, and Klang; estate food supply and distribution before and during the occupation; and a Hakka community in Selayang, Selangor. *Pendudukan Jepun di Tanah Melayu, 1942–1945* (The Japanese occupation of Malaya) contains essays on socioeconomic life in a particular state, district, or village and on food rationing, as well as personal accounts of former Death Railway laborers, a group marginalized from the current national narrative.

The Malaysian Historical Society has published some of the better essays from its competitions. Despite their limited length, these essays provide a valuable source of information, especially on the history of small towns or villages like Beserah in Pahang and details from the socioeconomic life of ordinary people, adding additional flesh to the bare bones of our social history and highlighting aspects so often overlooked in standard accounts.[36] The society has recently indicated renewed interest in publishing undergraduate work, while the *Journal of the Malaysian Branch of the Royal Asiatic Society* is publishing prize-winning work from the Sheppard Memorial Essay Competition. Many Malaysian scholars have recognized the need for more local-level studies before a broader, more comprehensive, social history can be attempted. Social history not only provides a counterbalance to the current overemphasis on political history, it also offers room for more actors, especially those on the margins, to be projected onto the center stage of the national historical narrative.

Records of the States' Religious Departments (Ecclesiastical Records)

One type of documents that may be particularly valuable for researchers interested in social history relating to Malay Muslims are those originating from the various states' Islamic religious affairs departments and the associated offices of senior officials in the Islamic bureaucracy, such as the muftis and *kathis*. For the sake of convenience I will call this group of materials ecclesiastical records.

Ecclesiastical records are available from the second decade of the twentieth century onward for the three states of Johore, Kelantan, and Pahang; for the others, a large part of the documents were destroyed while others have survived as appendices to reports or correspondence, necessitating more time and effort to track them down. For the districts of Parit Buntar (Perak), Hulu Langat, Tanjung Karang, and Sabak Bernam (all in Selangor) there is a small collection of documents that originated from the offices of the district kathis, including those dated before the occupation, which are kept at the National Archives in Kuala Lumpur. However due to haphazard cataloguing these materials are unfortunately unavailable for perusal by interested researchers.

In Johore there was, by the 1880s, a semblance of a religious bureaucracy, although it was not until 1895 that a religious affairs department was instituted after a major reorganization of the state bureaucracy. It was known as the Ecclesiastical and Education Department and was on par with other government departments.[37] In 1906 the education section became a separate department but the original name was retained for both since the same individual headed both the religious and education departments. The ecclesiastical department was vested with jurisdiction over matters relating to Islamic religion, including religious education, and was headed by a president, who was, in the department's early days, often a member of the Johore aristocracy. Under the president there was a hierarchy of officials, including the chief kathi and the mufti; below them were the district kathis, the imam of Johore Bahru, and other imams. The records of this department, which are kept at the Johore Bahru branch of the National Archives, come from both the religious department (Pejabat Agama Johore) and the Office of the Johore Chief Kathi (Kathi Besar Johore), which also includes records of the district kathis. The major collection of the former is catalogued under the J/UG 7 series while that of the latter is listed under the J/KAD 2 series.[38] More than 95 percent are in Jawi, either handwritten or typed, and available to researchers. These documents cover a wide range of topics: marriage, divorce, and reconciliation; religious teachings, Friday prayers, and sermons; and a variety of reports pertaining to the Malay Muslims of Johore as well as Singapore. It is not quite clear when the religious elites first began to compile these reports. In the Johore Bahru archives, 1916 is the earliest for both the J/UG 7 and J/KAD 2 series. However, there are very few files for the second and third decades, as the major concentration of the records relates more to the 1930s, the occupation years, and stretches to 1967.

In Kelantan and Pahang there appears to be a different setup in the Islamic bureaucracy. For Kelantan, the Kelantan Council of Islamic Religion and Malay Customs (Majlis Agama Islam dan Istiadat Melayu Kelantan; MAIK) was established in December 1915 as an autonomous entity, theoretically separate from the state government. MAIK was given the legal authority to counsel and assist the Kelantan ruler on all matters relating to the Islamic religion and Malay customs, which created the grounds for conflicts between the religious elites and the sultan, as shown in a recent study.[39] The interference of British officials in matters affecting Malay customs and Islamic religion further complicated matters at times and made a mockery of the professed official policy of noninterference in such matters. Since its inception, MAIK had issued annual reports as well as various other reports regarding the Malay Muslims and other matters pertaining to Islam in Kelantan. Other offices—for example, the Ketua Penyelia Agama (chief religious supervisor), Office of the Mufti and Kathi Courts, and district kathis (as in the districts of Pasir Putih and Kota Bharu)—also issued annual reports as well as a variety of other documents, although most of them cover the postwar or post-1957 period.[40]

As for Pahang, a religious council, which was actually a committee of the State Council, was given the responsibility for religious affairs. It was headed by a senior member of the Pahang aristocracy. From the 1920s and until the late 1950s it was headed by Tunku Sulaiman Sultan Ahmad Muadzam Shah, the Tunku Besar Pahang. Hence the files from this department are listed as the Tunku Besar Pahang

(TBP) files. Since the 1930s, the office of the TBP had issued various reports and documents relating to Islam and Muslims in Pahang and we have more such documents for the wartime and postwar period. All of them have been microfilmed and are available in the National Archives in Kuala Lumpur. The TBP files also include reports submitted by district kathis on various issues affecting Muslims and Islam, in particular on tithe collection and religious education. As for the other states, such as Selangor and Perak, prewar documents of a similar category are incomplete, with some appearing as appendices to other reports or correspondence. However, for the postwar period we do have more records from the various states' religious affairs departments, deposited at the National Archives in Kuala Lumpur.

The Ecclesiastical Records and Social History

The ecclesiastical records basically relate to local history, thus offering possible alternatives to the current emphasis on national political history, or perhaps fresh interpretations. Writing of local or regional histories is in fact not a new trend in Malaysian historiography. Since the early twentieth century such histories have been undertaken, albeit in the fashion of the court chroniclers of earlier times.[41] In the 1960s this trend was continued by amateur historians like Buyong bin Adil, Misbaha, Abdul Samad Ahmad, and Asa'ad Shukri, names that are familiar to most students of Malaysian history. Buyong Adil was the most prolific and the best known in this group. His works include histories of all thirteen states that formed the Malaysian federation, as well as Singapore. Some of these amateur histories are rather short while others, such as those relating to Terengganu and Pahang, are longer. In continuing the tradition of court historiographers and British scholar-officials, Buyong's studies are basically political histories that dwell at length on the pre-British period while the period after 1945 up to the seventies or eighties is treated in just a few pages.[42] For the pre-British period, chronicles were an important source for Buyong's study; for early Kedah, for example, he merely copied large chunks from the

Merong mahawangsa (Kedah annals). Much more substantial are the later state histories written by professional historians—for example, Shaharil Talib's book on Kelantan, Muhammad Isa Othman's work on Kedah, and the collaborative study on Pahang by Aruna Gopinath and Muhammad Yusof Hashim.[43] These studies used a range of sources but do not really fit into the social history mold outlined earlier.

The ecclesiastical records are still very much neglected in Malaysian historical research, although many researchers are aware of their existence. Thomas F. Willer, for example, took note of various government documents, including reports issued by the Pejabat Agama (Religious Office; Ugama in the old spelling system), but his use of these materials was rather limited.[44] That some Malaysian undergraduates and graduate students were aware of these documents is evident from studies undertaken since the early seventies at local universities.[45] Most of these studies relate to the administration of Islam and there is as yet little effort to utilize these materials to reconstruct the social history of Malay Muslims for any particular state or period. Up to the nineties, undergraduates were still utilizing the ecclesiastical records to write institutional or administrative histories.[46] In fact, these materials offer more than just materials for administrative history, especially for the thirties and the occupation period. They tell us in great detail about the social life of Malay Muslims, the issues that the conservative religious bureaucracy had to grapple with before, during, and after the Second World War, a time of rapid socioeconomic and political transformations.

A case in point are the records of the J/UG 7 and J/KAD 2 series, which are still in good condition and extremely well organized.[47] In 1969 Hapipah Endot, a University of Malaya undergraduate, had consulted these materials for her academic exercise, and Fawzi Basri referred to the Johore ecclesiastical records for his study of the Johore religious department.[48] Ismail Mohamad Talib of Universiti Kebangsaan Malaysia also referred to these records in his study, conducted in the early 1990s, of the Johore ecclesiastical department, from its inception until the occupation.[49] These studies still remained within the category of administrative history. Ghazali Mayudin, from Universiti Kebangsaan Malaysia, made a very limited attempt to use the Johore ecclesiastical records for nonadministrative history in his study of the occupation period in Johore, for which the main documentary evidence came mainly from the files of the Johore state secretariat and the office of the Menteri Besar (chief minister).[50]

It was only in the mid-nineties that the significance of the J/UG 7 and J/KAD 2 series in relation to the social history of the Malays during the Japanese occupation was realized. In 1994 Kosnan Bukhiran, a final-year history student from Universiti Sains Malaysia, made selective references to these materials to write a term paper on Muar during the occupation. Kosnan found scattered figures on divorce for the Muar district in the J/KAD 2 series.[51] A colleague of his, Shamsuddin Abdul Kadir, who consulted some documents from both the J/KAD 2 and J/UG 7 series for a longer study of the occupation period, provided useful insights on the religious life of Malay Muslims under Japanese rule, despite overlooking certain important materials in the files he had access to.[52]

Constraints of time and finances made it difficult for undergraduates to undertake the tedious job of thoroughly perusing these materials, which I have been able to do, with extremely fruitful results. From my own research at the Johore archives from mid-1995 to the end of 1997, the ecclesiastical records promise enormous possibilities for writing Malaysia's social history, particularly at the state level. One aspect that I was struck by was the high incidence of divorce in Johore due to reasons that I have outlined earlier. But beyond patterns of marriage and divorce, these records also offer invaluable insights on the Japanese response toward Islam and the religious elites and the reaction of these elites to the religious and moral decadence of the *ummah* (community of believers). In short, for a study on the social history of the Malay Muslims from the turbulent 1930s to the equally turbulent 1950s, these documents can provide invaluable insights not to be found in other types of documents.

The MAIK documents, too, are very much underutilized. Abdullah Haji Hassan had consulted the Kelantan ecclesiastical records, including those issued by MAIK, the kathi's office, and the *shariah*

("Islamic law" courts).[53] However Abdullah's commendable study falls mainly within the framework of administrative history, though some of the materials he consulted could definitely be used to reconstruct a social history of Malay Muslims in Kelantan. This was shown by another researcher, Haryati Hassan, who consulted these records extensively for a thesis on Malay prostitution in Kelantan in the first half of the twentieth century. Among the more interesting documents used by Haryati were the MAIK annual reports, statutory declarations or statements made by prostitutes to MAIK officers, police reports, and reports compiled by MAIK enforcement officers.[54] Haryati was heavily influenced by the discipline of sociology in the way she used these documents. Nevertheless, we have for the first time a historical study of Malay prostitution in what is arguably the most conservative of the Malay states.

Haryati identified the many prostitution "nests" in Kota Bharu as well as small towns like Pasir Mas and Bachok. Despite constant official harassment, the Kota Bharu "prostitute colony" kept shifting back and forth within such "famous" localities as Lorong Kubur, Lorong Gajah Mati, Padang Garong, and Jalan Hamzah, as well as between Kota Bharu and smaller towns. As for the clients, they comprised married Malay Muslims as well as Chinese and Indian laborers, who patronized prostitutes for different reasons. Despite the constant raids by both MAIK enforcement officials and the police, prostitution centers continued to exist, and in some cases prostitutes received protection from certain police personnel. The tough anti-prostitution laws suffered from poor implementation, rendering them ineffective. Haryati shows us that the origins of prostitution in Kelantan must be looked at from the broader socioeconomic history of the state and as part of the changing values among the Malay population, which were a direct result of the tremendous social and economic changes taking place in the state due to increasing capitalist penetration from the beginning of the twentieth century. This kind of social history certainly merits more in-depth study for Kelantan, even if it means looking again through the files that Haryati has already used, as well as for the other states.

The Pahang ecclesiastical records are the least consulted of the materials of this type. Other than the study on the Islamic administration of Pahang mentioned earlier—for which the Pahang records were not used to reconstruct a social history, whether of the 1930s, the war years, or the postwar period—I am unaware of any other study that has used these documents. Though they may not be as detailed or comprehensive as the Johore or Kelantan records, nevertheless the Pahang ecclesiastical records still shed much-needed light on the plight of Malay Muslims and the nature of religious education in various districts in the state. The TBP documents also provide population statistics for the districts of Bentong and Raub, apart from indicating how the Japanese were using Islam and the religious elites for nonreligious purposes.

Although the Johore, Kelantan, and Pahang ecclesiastical records are the most complete among such records available thus far, these documents are by their very nature limited to one particular ethnic or religious group, Malay Muslims. These reports provide us with some views of the emerging Malay Muslim dilemma toward the evolving plural society for the 1930s. They also show an overwhelming preoccupation of the religious elites (presumably of the Kaum Tua, or older group) on the question of what constituted a good Muslim. As the arbiter and protector of religious and social values, the religious elites sought to enforce values that were being eroded by the rapid socioeconomic changes taking place since the early thirties. Elsewhere we get glimpses of the conservative posture of these elites—for instance, on the increasing freedom and the opening of more economic opportunities for Malay Muslim women during and after the Japanese occupation.

Apart from social history, another significant aspect of these records is what they reveal of the dynamics of the religious bureaucracy in the various states. Thomas Willer has shown us the subtle interference of British officials in matters relating to Islamic religion and Malay customs in Kelantan and Terengganu.[55] But we do not yet know enough about the extent of Japanese interference in similar matters during the occupation and how far Japanese interference differed from the British colonial period. The Pahang, Kelantan, and Johore records have shown the ingenious way in which Japanese officials manipulated and subverted Islam, the religious elites, and mosques and *suraus* (prayer houses) as part of a grand strategy of winning a war in Southeast Asia in which neither Islam nor Malay Muslims had any vested interest. It is only by looking further into this aspect that we can comprehend the rationale for the regular attendance of Japanese officers at religious council deliberations, as in Pahang, Johore, and even Kelantan. Why would non-Muslims be involved in matters relating specifically to Islam and Malay Muslims other than for social and political control? We also have much information on the way the religious elites reacted to Japanese rule, and how in the end they too became an intrinsic part of the Japanese mechanism of social and political control in occupied Malaya vis-à-vis Malay Muslims.[56]

Apart from the Japanese occupation years, the ecclesiastical records could provide some important clues to understanding how Malay Muslims adjusted to the process of modernization, or more aptly perhaps, to Westernization, for a longer span in Malaysian history. The period from the early thirties to the mid-sixties is a time of considerable economic, social, and political change. The crisis of the mid-thirties, followed by the occupation and then by the emergency, caused dislocations among the local population. To what extent were the religious convictions of Malay Muslims, and consequently their social values, affected by these crises? I have attempted to provide some answers based on a reexamination of the Johore ecclesiastical records.[57] What is required is a larger study on Malay Muslims in other states in Malaya, and for such a study the ecclesiastical records and other similar records for all the states would be nearly indispensable.

I am quite aware of the inadequacy of these records and the necessity of supplementing them with other types of records (for example, the district files for Bentong, Temerloh, and Kuantan complement the TBP records very well). Equally important are the departmental files kept at the National Archives in Kuala Lumpur and at its various branches, as well as records kept within, or outside, Malaysia. For many issues affecting Malay Muslims during periods of rapid social and political transformations, the ecclesiastical records are a gold mine, with the Johore records the most complete among them. It is impossible to obtain, for example, divorce figures for Malay Muslims for the whole of Malaya during the entire occupation, for a host of reasons, including the wanton destruction of such records by various parties. Thus the figures that are available for Johore are invaluable and can serve as a general indicator for such phenomenon at the national level. But, in the final analysis, the kind of source materials discussed in this essay may result in yet another type of local history, even if it falls more clearly within the realm of social history, if we are unable to locate issues emerging at the local levels to a broader picture of social history at the national level.

Notes

1. One example is Zaharah Haji Mahmud, "The Evolution of Population and Settlement in the State of Kedah," in *Darulaman: Essays in the Linguistic, Cultural, and Socio-Economic Aspect of the State of Kedah,* ed. Asmah Haji Omar (Kuala Lumpur: University Malaya Publishers, 1979), 120–53.

2. Rajeswary Ampalavanar, *The Indian Minority and Political Change in Malaya, 1945–1957* (Kuala Lumpur: Oxford University Press, 1981); P. Ramasamy, *Plantation Labour, Unions, Capital, and the State in Peninsular Malaysia* (Kuala Lumpur: Oxford University Press, 1993).

3. J. D. Vaughan, *The Manners and Customs of the Chinese of the Straits Settlements* (Petaling Jaya: Fajar Bakti, 1994). A recent work by a Malaysian scholar is Tan Chee Beng, *Chinese Peranakan Heritage in Malaysia and Singapore* (Petaling Jaya: Fajar Bakti, 1993).

4. Examples are John M. Chin, *The Sarawak Chinese* (Kuala Lumpur: Oxford University Press, 1981); Daniel Chew, *Chinese Pioneers on the Sarawak Frontier* (Singapore: Oxford University Press, 1990); Danny Wong Tze-ken, *The Transformation of an Immigrant Society: A Study of the Chinese of Sabah* (London: Academy Press, 1998).

5. For example, Tan Liok Ee, *The Politics of Chinese Education in Malaya, 1945–1961* (Kuala Lumpur: Oxford University Press, 1997); Oong Hak Ching, "Masalah komuniti Cina dan proses dekolonisasi di Semenanjung Tanah Melayu, 1942–1957" (The problems of the Chinese commu-

nity and the decolonization process in the Malay peninsula), *Malaysia dari segi sejarah* (Malaysia in history) 24 (1996): 56–69.

6. Well-known examples are Leon F. Comber, *Chinese Secret Societies in Malaya, 1800–1900* (New York: Lotus Valley, 1959); M. R. Wynne, *Triad and Tabut: A Study of the Origin and Diffusion of Chinese and Mohamedan Secret Societies in the Malay Peninsula, A.D. 1800–1935* (Singapore: Government Printing Office, 1941); Wilfred Blythe, *The Impact of Chinese Secret Societies in Malaya* (London: Oxford University Press, 1969).

7. Leong Yee Fong, *Labour and Trade Unionism in Colonial Malaya: A Study of the Socio-Economic and Political Basis of the Malayan Labour Movement, 1930–1957* (Penang: Universiti Sains Malaysia Publishers, 1999); Loh Kok Wah, *Beyond the Tin Mines: Coolies, Squatters, and New Villages in the Kinta Valley, c. 1880–1980* (Kuala Lumpur: Oxford University Press, 1988).

8. Khoo Kay Kim, *Malay Society: Transformation and Democratisation* (Petaling Jaya: Pelanduk Paperbacks, 1991).

9. Shaharil Talib, *After Its Own Image: The Trengganu Experience, 1881–1941* (Kuala Lumpur: Oxford University Press, 1984); Lim Teck Ghee, *Peasants and Their Agricultural Economy in Colonial Malaya, 1874–1941* (Kuala Lumpur: Oxford University Press, 1977). An important addition is *Masyarakat Melayu Abad ke-sembilanbelas* (Malay society in the nineteenth century) (Kuala Lumpur: Dewan Bahasa dan Pustaka, 1991), a collection of papers from a conference organized by the history department of Universiti Kebangsaan Malaysia (National University of Malaysia).

10. See Mahani Awang Musa, "Malay Secret Societies in Penang, 1830s–1920s," *Journal of the Malaysian Branch of the Royal Asiatic Society* 72, 2 (1999): 151–82; Zainol Jusoh, "Kongsi gelap Melayu Bendera Merah dan Bendera Putih di Pulau Pinang, 1890–1940" (The Red Flag and White Flag Malay Secret Societies in Penang), *Jurnal ilmu kemanusiaan* (Journal of humanities) 2 (1995): 44–67.

11. Ahmad Nazri Abdullah, *Melayu dan tanah: Tumpuan khusus kepada tanah Simpanan Melayu* (Malays and land: A focus on Malay Reserve Lands) (Kuala Lumpur: Media Intelek, 1985).

12. Khazin Mohd. Tamrin, *Orang Jawa di Selangor: Penghijrahan dan penempatan, 1880–1940* (The Javanese in Selangor: Migration and resettlement) (Kuala Lumpur, Dewan Bahasa dan Pustaka: 1984); Rahmat Saripan, "Pembangunan sosio-ekonomi kaum tani Parit Jawa, 1870–1900" (The socioeconomic development of the peasants of Parit Jawa) *Jebat* 14 (1986): 49–64; Muhamad Rosli Jambari, "Masyarakat Bawean: Tinjauan ringkas mengenai sejarah kedatangan, kehidupan dan institusi sosial mereka di Tanah Melayu" (The Bawean community: A brief survey of their migratory history, life, and social institutions in Malaya), *Malaysia in*

History 19, 2 (1976): 37–42; Ahmad Sukardi Aziz, "Notes on the Javanese in Kampung Jawa and Kampung Baharu, Simpang Empat, Seberang Perai," *Malaysia in History* 21, 2 (1978): 65–70.

13. Omar Farouk Sheik Ahmad, "The Arabs in Penang," *Malaysia in History* 21, 2 (1978): 1–16; Mahayudin Haji Yahaya, "Latarbelakang sejarah keturunan sayid di Malaysia" (The historical background of the descendents of sayyids in Malaysia), in *Tamadun Islam di Malaysia* (Islamic civilization in Malaysia), ed. Khoo Kay Kim (Kuala Lumpur: Malaysian Historical Association, 1980), 60–73.

14. Zakaria bin Haji Abdul Rahman, "Masyarakat Kabul di daerah Besut, Terengganu" (Kabul society in Besut, Terengganu), *Malaysia dari Segi Sejarah* (formerly *Malaysia in History*) 14 (1985): 75–89.

15. Rogayah Eusoff, *The Merican Clan: A Story of Courage and Destiny* (Kuala Lumpur: Times Books International, 1997); Helen Fujimoto, *The South Indian Muslim Community and the Evolution of the Jawi Peranakan in Penang up to 1948* (Tokyo: Tokyo University of Foreign Studies, 1989).

16. John G. Butcher, *The British in Malaya, 1880–1941: The Social History of a European Community in Colonial Southeast Asia* (Kuala Lumpur: Oxford University Press, 1979).

17. Juli Edo, *Tradisi lisan masyarakat Semai* (The oral tradition of the Semais) (Bangi: University Kebangsaan Publishers, 1990); Iskandar Carey, *Orang Asli: The Aboriginal Tribes of Peninsular Malaysia* (Kuala Lumpur: Oxford University Press, 1976); Wazir-Jahan Karim, *The Belief System of the Ma(k) Batisek of Pulau Carey, Malaysia* (London: British Library, 1977).

18. Mahani Musa, "Orang Asli di Tanah Melayu: Satu evolusi hubungan dengan pemerintah dan masyarakat luar dari akhir abad ke-19 hingga 1960-an" (The Orang Asli in Malaya: The evolution of relations with the rulers and outside society from the end of the nineteenth century to the 1960s), *Jurnal ilmu kemanusiaan* 3 (1996): 40–70.

19. Lim, *Peasants and Their Agricultural Economy;* Shaharil Talib, "Peasant Anger through the Ages: An East Coast Malay Peninsular Experience," *Malaysia in History* 28 (1985): 15–24; Cheah Boon Kheng, *Peasant Robbers of Kedah, 1900–1929: Historical and Folk Perceptions* (Kuala Lumpur: Oxford University Press, 1988).

20. Peter J. Rimmer and Lisa M. Allen, ed., *The Underside of Malaysian History: Pullers, Prostitutes, Plantation Workers* (Singapore: Singapore University Press for the Malaysia Society of the Asian Studies Association of Australia, 1990); Leong, *Labour and Trade Unionism.*

21. Loh, *Beyond the Tin Mines;* Ishak Shari, *Pembangunan dan kemunduran: Perubahan ekonomi luar bandar di Kelantan* (Development and underdevelopment: Rural economic change in Kelantan) (Kuala Lumpur:

Dewan Bahasa dan Pustaka); Shamsul Amri Baharuddin, *From British Rule to Bumiputra Rule: Local Politics and Rural Development in Peninsular Malaysia* (Singapore: Institute of Southeast Asian Studies, 1986); Zawawi Ibrahim, *The Malay Labourers: By the Window of Capitalism* (Singapore: Institute of Southeast Asian Studies, 1998).

22. Muhammad Haji Salleh, *Sajak-sajak sejarah Melayu* (Malay historical poetry) (Kuala Lumpur: Dewan Bahasa dan Pustaka, 1981); Muhammed Haji Salleh, *Sulalat al-Salatin ya'ni Pertuturan segala raja-raja* (Genealogy of rulers) (Kuala Lumpur: Yayasan Karyawan, 1997); Siti Hawa Salleh, *Hikayat Merong Mahawangsa* (The Merong Mahawangsa chronicle) (Petaling Jaya: University of Malaya Press, 1970); Wazir-Jahan Karim, *Women and Culture: Between Malay Adat and Islam* (Boulder: Westview, 1992).

23. Paul Kratoska, *The Japanese Occupation of Malaya, 1941–1945* (London: Hurst, 1998).

24. Cheah Boon Kheng, *Red Star over Malaya: Resistance and Social Conflict during and after the Japanese Occupation, 1941–1946* (Singapore: Singapore University Press, 1983).

25. Mohamad Isa Othman, *Pendudukan Jepun di Tanah Melayu, 1942–1945 (tumpuan di negeri Kedah)* (The Japanese occupation of Malaya [focus on Kedah]) (Kuala Lumpur: Dewan Bahasa dan Pustaka, 1992).

26. Abdullah Zakaria Ghazali, *Pentadbiran tentera Jepun dan Thai di Terengganu, 1942–1945* (The Japanese and Thai military administration in Terengganu) (Petaling Jaya: Universiti Malaya Publishers, 1996).

27. Ghazali Mayudin, *Johor semasa pendudukan Jepun, 1942–1945* (Johore during the Japanese occupation) (Bangi: History Department, Universiti Kebangsaan Malaysia, 1978).

28. Ooi Keat Gin, *History of the Japanese Military Occupation of Sarawak, 1942–1945, from the Perspective of the Experience of the European Community* (Penang: Universiti Sains Malaysia Publishers, 1997), and "Pendudukan Jepun dan kaum Cina di Sarawak" (The Japanese occupation and the Chinese community in Sarawak), in *Sorotan terpilih dalam sejarah Malaysia: Esei-esei sumbangsih kepada Dr. Cheah Boon Kheng* (Reflections on Malaysian history: Essays in honor of Dr. Cheah Boon Kheng), ed. Mahani Musa and Tan Liok Ee, 187–212 (Penang: Universiti Sains Malaysia Publishers, 2000).

29. Abu Talib Ahmad, "The Impact of the Japanese Occupation on the Malay-Muslim Population," in *Malaya and Singapore during the Japanese Occupation,* ed. Paul Kratoska, 1–36 (Singapore: JSEAS Special Publication Series, no. 3, 1995), "Marriage and Divorce in Johor among the Malay-Muslims during the Japanese Occupation, 1942–45," *Journal of the Malaysian Branch of the Royal Asiatic Society* 71, 2 (1998): 63–90, "Research on Islam and Malay-Muslims during the Japanese Occupation of Malaya, 1942–45,"

Asian Research Trends: A Humanities and Social Science Review (Tokyo: Center for East Asian Cultural Studies for UNESCO [Toyo Bunko]), no. 9 (1999): 81–119, "The Malay Community and Memory of the Japanese Occupation" in *War and Memory in Malaysia and Singapore,* ed. Patricia Lim Pui Huen and Diana Wong (Singapore: Institute of Southeast Asian Studies, 2000), 45–89.

30. "Latihan Ilmiah/Academic Exercises, Pusat Pengajian Ilmu Kemanusiaan, Universiti Sains Malaysia, 1973–85" *Jurnal ilmu kemanusiaan* 1 (1994): 102–31; "Latihan Ilmiah/Academic Exercises, Pusat Pengajian Ilmu Kemanusiaan, Universiti Sains Malaysia, 1985–93," *Jurnal ilmu kemanusiaan* 2 (1995): 117–40.

31. Examples are Azhar Raswan Dean Wan Din, "Pengeluaran dan perdagangan padi dan beras di negeri Kedah dari pendudukan Jepun hingga pentadbiran tentera Thai, 1942–1945" (Production and trade in padi and rice in Kedah from the time of the Japanese occupation until the Thai military occupation), *Kajian Malaysia* 10, 2 (1992): 40–62; Sokma Abdullah, "Adat istiadat pendaraan di kalangan masyarakat Melayu di Melaka" (Fertility rites among Malays in Melaka), *Kajian Malaysia* 11, 1 (1991): 124–49; Ismail Md. Isa, "Pekan Cina (Alor Setar): Penubuhan dan perkembangannya" (Chinatown [Alor Setar]: Its origins and developments), in *Isu-isu pensejarahan: Esei penghargaan kepada Dr. R. Suntharalingam* (Issues in historiography: Essays in honor of Dr. R. Suntharalingam), ed. Abu Talib Ahmad and Cheah Boon Kheng (Penang: Universiti Sains Malaysia, 1995), 250–64.

32. Ghazali Mayudin, *Johor semasa pendudukan Jepun;* Md. Salleh Md. Ghaus, *Politik Melayu Pulau Pinang, 1945–57* (Penang Malay politics); Nabir Haji Abdullah, *Maahad Il Ihya Assyarif Gunung Semanggol, 1934–1959* (The Maahad Il Ihya Assyarif in Gunung Semanggol) (Bangi: Universiti Kebangsaan Malaysia, 1976); Osman Mamat, *Darurat di Terengganu, 1948–1960: Beberapa aspek sosial dan ekonomi* (The emergency in Terengganu: Some social and economic aspects) (Kuala Lumpur: Dewan Bahasa dan Pustaka, 1981); Sabri Haji Saad, *Madrasah Al-Ulum Al-Syari'ah Perak, 1937–77: Satu kajian pendidikan Islam* (The Al-Ulum Al-Syari'ah religious school of Perak: A study of Islamic education) (Kuala Lumpur: Dewan Bahasa dan Pustaka,1983); Timah Hamzah, *Pemberontakan tani 1928 di Terengganu* (The 1928 peasant rebellion in Terengganu) (Kuala Lumpur: Dewan Bahasa dan Pustaka, 1981); Zulkipli Mahmud, *Warta Malaya: Penyambung lidah bangsa melayu, 1930–1941* (Warta Malaya: The defender of the Malay race) (Kuala Lumpur: Dewan Bahasa dan Pustaka, 1983).

33. One example is Badriyah Haji Salleh, *Kampung Haji Salleh dan madrasah Saadiah-Salihiah, 1914–1959* (Haji Salleh Village and the Saadiah-

Salihiah religious school) (Kuala Lumpur: Dewan Bahasa dan Pustaka, 1984).

34. Danny Wong Tze-ken, *Vietnam-Malaysia: Relations during the Cold War, 1945–1990* (Petaling Jaya: University of Malaya Press, 1995); Jatswan Singh Sidhu, *Sejarah sosio-ekonomi Brunei, 1906–1959* (Brunei's socioeconomic history) (Kuala Lumpur: Dewan Bahasa dan Pustaka, 1995).

35. Paul Kratoska, ed., *Penghijrah dan penghijrahan: Kumpulan esei sejarah Malaysia oleh pelajar-pelajar USM* (Immigrants and immigration: A collection of essays on Malaysian history by USM students) (Penang: Universiti Sains Malaysia School of Humanities, Occassional Paper no. 1, 1982); Cheah Boon Kheng, ed., *Tokoh-tokoh tempatan: Kumpulan esei sejarah Malaysia oleh pelajar-pelajar USM* (Local leaders) (Penang: Universiti Sains Malaysia School of Humanities, Occasional Paper no. 2, 1982); Paul Kratoska and Abu Talib Ahmad, ed., *Pendudukan Jepun di Tanah Melayu, 1942–1945: Kumpulan esei sejarah Malaysia oleh pelajar-pelajar USM* (The Japanese Occupation in Malaya) (Penang: Universiti Sains Malaysia School of Humanities, Occasional Paper no. 4, 1989).

36. Khoo Kay Kim, ed., *Esei-esei sejarah Malaysia: Peraduan mengarang esei, 1980–1981* (Essays in Malaysian history: Essay competition) (Kuala Lumpur: Persatuan Sejarah Malaysia, 1982).

37. M. A. Fawzi Mohd. Basri, "Perkembangan dan peranan jabatan agama Johor, 1895–1940" (The development and roles of the Johore religious department), *Malaysia in History* 18, 1 (1975): 10–21.

38. A small number of files from this department can also be located in the Menteri Besar (Johor) series or even at the Kuala Lumpur National Archives.

39. On differences in the Islamic bureaucracy of various states, see Thomas Frank Willer, "Religious Administrative Development in Colonial Malay States, 1874–1941" (Ph.D. diss., University of Michigan, 1975).

40. Abdullah Alwi Haji Hassan, *The Administration of Islamic Law in Kelantan* (Kuala Lumpur: Dewan Bahasa dan Pustaka, 1996).

41. For instance, Muhammad Said Sulaiman, *Hikayat Johor dan tawarikh al-Marhum Sultan Abu Bakar* (Chronicle of Johore and history of the late Sultan Abu Bakar] (Singapore: Malayan Publishing House, 1930); Muhammad Hassan Muhammad Arshad, *Al-tarikh salasilah negeri Kedah* (History of Kedah) (Penang: Jelutong Press, 1928).

42. See, for example, Buyong bin Adil, *Sejarah Pahang* (History of Pahang) (Kuala Lumpur: Dewan Bahasa dan Pustaka, 1984) and *Sejarah Terengganu* (History of Terengganu) (Kuala Lumpur: Dewan Bahasa dan Pustaka, 1982).

43. Shaharil Talib, *After Its Own Image;* Muhammad Isa Othman, *Politik tradisional Kedah* (Traditional politics in Kedah) (Kuala Lumpur: Dewan

Bahasa dan Pustaka, 1990); Aruna Gopinath and Muhammad Yusof Hashim, *Tradisi pensejarahan Pahang darul makmur, 1800–1930* (The historiographical tradition of Pahang) (Petaling Jaya: Tempo Publishing, 1992).

44. Willer, "Religious Administrative Development."

45. Notable examples are: Abdul Khalil Haji Hashim, "Struktur dan fungsi pentadbiran hal ehwal ugama Islam di negeri Kedah" (Structure and function of the administration of Islamic affairs in Kedah) (academic exercise, University Malaya, 1970); Hapipah Endot, "Pentadbiran pejabat ugama Johor dan peranannya dalam masyarakat Islam" (The administration of the Johore religious department and its function in an Islamic society) (academic exercise, University of Malaya, 1969); Mohd. Fadzil Haji Abdul Malik, "Pentadbiran agama Islam di negeri Pahang" (The administraion of Islam in Pahang) (academic exercise, University Malaya, 1971).

46. An example is Zuriati Zahari, "Sejarah penubuhan majlis agama Islam dan Adat Istiadat Melayu Kelantan (MAIK) serta peranannya dalam pendidikan dan keagamaan, 1946–1956" (History of the establishment of MAIK and its function in educational and religious matters) (mini-thesis for course on documents in Malaysian history, History Section, School of Humanities, Universiti Sains Malaysia, 1998–99). A mini-thesis is a research paper of approximately 10,000 words in replacement of the much longer academic exercise.

47. Both series contain a substantial number of files in good condition and conveniently indexed to assist the researcher.

48. Hapipah Endot, "Pentadbiran Pejabat Ugama Johor"; M. A. Fawzi Mohd. Basri, "Perkembangan dan peranan jabatan agama Johor."

49. Ismail Mohd. Talib, "Sejarah perkembangan jabatan agama Johor, 1895–1940" (The history of the development of the Johore Religious Department) (academic exercise, History Department, Universiti Kebangsaan Malaysia, 1996–97).

50. Ghazali Mayudin, *Johor semasa pendudukan Jepun.*

51. Kosnan Bukhiran, "Pendudukan Jepun di Johor, 1942–1945: Tinjauan sejauhmana pentadbiran tentera Jepun mengubah corak kehidupan seharian penduduk di bandar dan di kawasan luar bandar" (Japanese occupation of Johore: A survey of the extent to which the Japanese military administration affected the daily life of the local people living in towns and rural areas) (term paper for course on Japanese occupation of Southeast Asia, History Section, School of Humanities, 1994).

52. Shamsuddin Abdul Kadir, "Tinjauan keadaan ekonomi dan sosial di Johor, 1942–1945" (A socioeconomic survey of Johore, 1942–1945), (mini-thesis for course on documents in Malaysian history, History Section, School of Humanities, 1995).

53. Abdullah Alwi Haji Hassan, *Administration of Islamic Law*.

54. Haryati Hassan, "Pelacuran di kalangan wanita Melayu Kelantan dari 1900 hingga 1941" (Prostitution among Malay women in Kelantan from 1900 to 1941) (M.A. thesis, History Department, University of Malaya, 1998).

55. Willer, "Religious Administrative Development."

56. Itagaki Yoichi, "Some Aspects of the Japanese Policy for Islam under the Occupation with Special Reference to Nationalism," in *Papers on Malayan History*, ed. K. G. Tregonning (Singapore: Malaya Publishing House, 1962); Itagaki and Kishi Yoichi, "Japanese Islamic Policy: Sumatra/Malaya," *Intisari* 2, 2 (1966?): 11–23; Abu Talib Ahmad, "Japanese Policy towards Islam in Malaya during the Occupation: A Reassessment," *Journal of Southeast Asian Studies* 33, 1 (2002): 107–22.

57. Abu Talib Ahmad, "Japanese Policy."

Chapter 12

TOWARD AN AUTONOMOUS HISTORY OF SEVENTEENTH-CENTURY PHUKET

Dhiravat na Pombejra

When Reverend John Carrington presented his detailed observations on Phuket and its environs to members of the Siam Society early last century, he described it as "one of the most beautiful and enchanting spots in the world."[1] Well known nowadays as a tropical holiday destination, Phuket has had a long and often turbulent history. That history first received attention on its own merit, not just as a small part of the history of Siam, in an essay by Colonel G. E. Gerini, a contemporary of Carrington's.[2] The island of Phuket, variously labeled Jonsalam, Oedjangh Salangh, or Junkceylon by Westerners from the sixteenth to the eighteenth century, was formally part of the Siamese kingdom and subject to the capital city's commands and demands. Phuket's governors were directly appointed by Siamese rulers in Ayutthaya, Thonburi, and Bangkok, and it often came under the overall administrative control of the governors, or "viceroys" of Ligor (Nakhon Sithammarat). At no time was it ever an independent sultanate like Pattani or a semi-independent regional center like Ligor. So is it justifiable to think of an *autono-*

mous history centered on Phuket? Is the division between periphery and center more of a hindrance than an aid to our understanding of the past? Are there enough sources on salient elements of local politics and society to write an autonomous history of Phuket?

A preliminary answer to the first, and most important, question is that it is justifiable to consider Phuket as an economic and social entity with a limited autonomy. It was difficult for the capital to control Phuket, like many of Ayutthaya's more distant *huamuangs* (provinces), though this does not mean that it was populous or politically significant enough to merit autonomous historical attention on its own as a state or even statelet. Economically, Phuket was part of the larger Indian Ocean trading network, not just a link between Ayutthaya and trade in the Bay of Bengal and the Malay Archipelago. Tin would have been bought up in Phuket's small seaports even if there had been no capital city or administrative center at Ayutthaya. Therefore, the history of Phuket can be considered to have a limited autonomy in relation to the "national" history of Thailand, but it arguably may be closer to a local history than a sociologically sophisticated autonomous history, as John Smail envisaged.[3]

In researching and writing this essay, I continually encountered problems of balance and perspective. The Dutch, French, and English sources would pull the narrative toward one European nation or another, while Siamese sources would attract attention toward Ayutthaya.[4] In writing the history of seventeenth-century Phuket it is hard to avoid the view from the company ship's deck and the high gallery of the trading house because the overwhelming majority of the sources available are European. Similarly, the larger picture of court politics bearing down on "provincial" politics cannot be eliminated from the analysis. Nevertheless, seventeenth-century Phuket certainly deserves more than just a few entries for Oedjangh Salang or Junkceylon. By focusing on the resources and interests of traders, both local and foreign, the history of Phuket can be seen to be more than merely a small adjunct of Ayutthayan history or a footnote in company history. This essay is a step *toward* such a history.

The Setting

In his study of Phuket, Gerini commented that by "reason of its position on the old sea route to Further India that crossed the Bay of Bengal further to the north, and then skirted the West coast of the Malay Peninsula for its whole length down to the Straits, Junkceylon could certainly not escape becoming well known to the early navigators, at least by existence, if not by name."[5] Gerini links the island to the prominent port of Takola (Takuapa) and the mainland Siamese provinces of Ligor and Phangnga. The island of Phuket is indeed so close to the mainland that the isthmus linking it to continental Siam was, in the seventeenth and eighteenth centuries, only covered at high water. This geographical factor may well have been crucial to Phuket's commercial significance, since the area around Takuapa was a tin-producing region too.

Located on the southern frontier of the Siamese kingdom, Phuket is geographically very close to the Malay Archipelago. According to a late-eighteenth-century source, the inhabitants of Phuket in general spoke Malay "from their intercourse with that people"; hence the island's Malay name of Ujong Salang, later corrupted by Europeans into Jonsalam or Junkceylon.[6] The precise meaning of Salang or Thalang is unclear but in Malay *ujong* means point or cape, emphasizing the island's ambiguous relationship to the mainland. Had Phuket's inhabitants in the past thought of it exclusively as an island, the word *pulau* (island) would have been used instead. However, the Kedah chronicle *Merong Mahawangsa,* which dates from around the end of the eighteenth century or the early nineteenth century, does refer to Phuket as Pulau Salang.[7]

A French archival document, dating from November 1686, portrays the island as a wild, sparsely populated place with "impenetrable jungle full of tigers, wild elephants, and rhinoceroses" and scattered hamlets and villages, the largest of which was referred to as a town.[8] Another early description by Thomas Bowrey, an Englishman, also emphasizes the wildness of Phuket but mentions that there were three seaports: "Bangquala" (Bangkhli? on the southwest coast),

"Buckett [Phuket]," and "Luppoone [Liphon?]," all of which were deemed "very excellent roads [roadsteads]," except that the entrances to the rivers were very shallow.[9] Seventeenth-century Phuket, then, was a densely wooded island with only one settlement meriting the label *town,* where the governor resided. Though there were "well-cultivated plains abounding with rice fields in the middle of the island," and the rice grown was of an "excellent sort," there was "scarcely enough to subsist with the whole year." Fish and coconuts were plentiful but not "cattle or fowls" and other foodstuffs, including salt, had to be brought in from elsewhere.[10]

The population of seventeenth-century Phuket numbered "perhaps six thousand persons adult and child" and occupations consisted "solely in cutting wood, sowing rice, and digging the ground in order to find the entrails of tin which is the greatest wealth of the country."[11] Bowrey describes the population as consisting mainly of "natural Syamers" (by which he probably meant Siamese), intermingled with Malays, some "sea-gypsies," and some "saletters" or "saleeters," who were "a race distinct from those who lived on the mainland" and one among several groups of *orang laut* (sea gypsies) who roamed the seas of the Malay Archipelago.[12] The writer of the French document found "nothing beautiful, good, rare, nor curious in this place" apart from its tin and was unimpressed by its inhabitants, whom he found "a little wild" or "less polite than those in other areas of this kingdom of Siam." Bowrey, however, found the Siamese of Phuket to be "for the most part a very civil good humoured people" but portrayed the Malays as a "resolute" but "roguish sullen ill-natured people" who often robbed foreigners.[13] This perception was probably due to the fact that the Malays, as seafaring traders, were potential rivals in the tin trade.

Bowrey unequivocally categorizes Phuket as a place that "wholy belongeth to the Kinge of Syam and he hath a govenour here whom the natives entitle Radja, vizt. Kinge, as indeed he is a vice-kinge to the great King of Syam."[14] From the Siamese side, the *phra thammanun* in the Three Seals Code refers to "Thalang" as one of the provinces under the direct supervision of the *samuha phra kalahom,* or minister in charge of military affairs.[15] As the division of provinces into those controlled by the samuha phra kalahom and the *samuha nayok*, or minister in charge of the civilian wing of the administration, probably occurred during King Phetracha's reign (1688–1703),[16] it is not clear what the system before that was. According to Gerini, Phuket was nominally under Ligor for much of the early to mid-Ayutthaya period. But later, territories such as Phangnga (including Phuket) and Songkhla were put under the direct rule of Ayutthaya.[17] Communications between Phuket and Ligor, a first-rank province of the Ayutthaya kingdom, had never been easy in spite of the existence of ancient overland trade routes across the peninsula. The shift of authority over the southern provinces and tributaries from Ligor to Ayutthaya not only demonstrated a desire to clip Ligor's wings but also reflected the efforts of the capital to increase its share of the tin trade. But in the seventeenth century Ligor still retained some measure of authority over Ayutthaya's southern provinces. It would probably be correct to say that during most of the seventeenth century the administration of Phuket was in the hands of governors appointed by the capital, though we cannot be sure whether these governors were under the supervision of the samuha phra kalahom. From Dutch sources, it seems that the governors were directly appointed by the king but the Dutch may have been given such information to stress the king's personal involvement in the appointments and reassure them of the ruler's seriousness in solving any problems that arose on the island.

Phuket and Tin in the Trading World of the Indian Ocean

Phuket was a port frequented by merchants from the many nations involved in the Indian Ocean and Malay Archipelago trade. It was important to Ayutthaya as one of the few ports that Siam possessed on the Bay of Bengal, apart from Mergui/Tenasserim, Trang, and Phuket's neighbor Bangkhli. Trade to and from Indian destinations, whether Asian or European, was mainly via Mergui, but by the sixteenth century Phuket had indisputably become a port of note in Southeast Asia, mentioned by early Western writers such as Pinto, Fitch, Linschoten, and Barker.[18] Phuket's "greatest wealth" and principal attraction to seafaring traders was tin, which abounded in the southern part of the Kingdom of Siam. George White observed in 1679 that "this whole tract of land betwist Legoore & Tenasseree" was "almost one intire inexhaustible mine."[19] Apart from Ligor and Phuket, other places involved in the tin trade mentioned in Western documents included Chaiya, Phunphin, Chumphon, Takuapa, and Bangkhli.

Phuket's geographical and economic significance in relation to its neighboring tin-producing areas should also be noted. The Europeans saw the Malay Peninsula as a huge tin-rich region with many local rulers to negotiate with, or to cow into submission. Some of them were sultans, others were *rajas* or "viceroys," while yet others were mere "governors." The local chiefs or governors, who were subject to the court of Siam, theoretically had to be approached through Ayutthaya, but this was not always necessary. The East India Companies, "country traders," and Asian traders alike perceived the maritime world of Southeast Asia more in terms of commodities and ports than in terms of kingdoms or empires; especially in the case of ports or regions situated far away from royal or imperial centers. Central powers had little direct control over the day-to-day running of business in these faraway places.

Simon de La Loubère's compendious account of Siam, written around 1688, mentions that all the tin in the kingdom belonged to the king, "and he sells it as well to strangers as to his own Subjects, excepting that which is dug out of the Mines of *Jonsalam* on the Gulph of *Bengal*: for this being a remote Frontier, he leaves the inhabitants in their ancient Rights, so that they enjoy the Mines which they dig, paying a small profit to this Prince."[20] This is important as it means that the tin in Phuket was not part of the Crown's monopoly and local inhabitants had a certain degree of autonomy as far as the sale of their tin was concerned.

We do not know when tin was first mined in Phuket. Gerini,

showing a bias toward the importance of early Indian seafaring traders and settlers in Southeast Asia common to many scholars of his time, speculates that "Indu traders and colonists" were the likely pioneers.[21] As for the amount of tin obtainable annually from the mines of Phuket, in 1682 Aarnout Faa the Dutch *opperhoofd* (factory head) was told by a certain "Moor" who had been trading in Phuket that 1,000 to 1,200 *bahar* (58–70 tons) of tin could be got from Phuket and its dependencies. Faa believed that more could be obtained if only the "thieves' dens" and "secret shelters" could be closed down or eliminated.[22] He also tells us that tin from Phuket and adjoining areas was transported "principally to Tenasserim, Aceh, Bengal and Pondicherry,"[23] confirming George White's earlier account (1679) that the Indian market was of greatest importance, although tin produced in Siam was sometimes sold to Japan and China.[24]

Writing at roughly the same time as White, Bowrey recounts that he traded blue and white calicoes, iron, steel, knives and scissors, small "Cushion carpets" (small-sized carpets or rugs), sugar, soap, and other goods in exchange for tin, "which doth here passe very currant for ready moneys."[25] Faa's "Moor" contact told him, in 1682, that the French had just bought 450 to 500 bahar of tin from Phuket and had sold poor-quality blue and white *salempuris* (medium-quality textile from South India), sugar, Manila tobacco, and ironwork. But the Phuket market was a limited one, due no doubt to the small population and relatively small amount of shipping traffic that came to the island and its dependencies. Bowrey was certain that twenty bales of Indian chintz and calicoes would be enough for half a year "for the whole country."[26]

Bowrey, the first Westerner to describe how trade was carried on at Phuket, begins by relating that the currency used in Phuket was not minted silver coinage but tin money. The tin was melted into small lumps, or "puttas," and "pass[ed] very currant provided they be of their just weight allowed by statute." A large lump of tin was worth seven English pennies. If the foreigner brought in silver or gold, the "rich men" of Junkcelyon would "trucke with us for tinne and give some advance, 10 or 15 per cent, upon the moneys."[27] The foreigner who arrived in Phuket would normally leave his ship in the roadstead of "Banquala" (Bangkhli), and go to the town, about four or five miles upriver by boat. There the *syahbandar* (harbormaster) and "the king's secretary," together with some others, came to meet the foreigners and obtain information on the merchandise brought into Phuket and the arms in the visitors' possession. All answers were "written downe in the king's booke, as also the commander's name, and sent up to Luppoone [Liphon] (the place of the Radja's residence)."[28] There everything was reported in detail to the governor and his council, consisting of around ten to twelve officials.[29]

If the governor found the information acceptable, as was obviously the case for Bowrey, the "commander" of the visiting ship would be transported up to "Luppoone" by elephant on "a very tedious day's journey" through wild terrain. When they reached Luppoone they were lodged at a place specially allotted to them by the governor. This was a "temple of idols" (*wat*) where there were "2 or 3 tombs of the deceased vice-kings adjoyninge therunto." The governor sent them provisions and prepared food, "very decently dressed after the Syam manner," and the syahbandar and a few others sat down to eat with the foreigners.[30] The next morning they were sent for to be presented to the governor and answer more questions posed by the governor and his council. The most important, in Bowrey's case, centered on whether they had the king of Siam's "Phyrmane [*firman,* or decree]." If they did not have a firman or *tra* (license) the governor was within his rights to claim 10 percent "custome" for all goods on board their ship, "although he knoweth very well that the English nation in general is free from all such duties in the kingdome of Syam and all the provinces & isles thereto appertaineinge." Bowrey knew that the right to toll-free trade had been granted to the English East India Company by King Narai in 1674–75, and believed that the governor would not have dared take any customs duty from the English even though he claimed that "the Kinge of Syam hath given him this island for soe many years."[31] Negotiations were directed at getting the English to give the governor something "considerable" as a "present," and precondition for his cooperation in the sale of their goods. The English gave the governor presents to the value of 100 or 120 pieces of eight while two of the governor's council, plus the syahbandar of "Banquala," had to be "piscashed" with a few pieces of fine calicoes or chintz each. After the negotiations, the Englishmen were feasted royally for a couple of days. The governor even "beats the gunge [gong]" (a call to attention) for the people of Phuket to buy the Englishmen's goods, "before which they dare not buy any."[32]

Whatever autonomy Phuket had, then, was an economic and commercial autonomy. It was a part of the trading world of the Indian Ocean and the wider international trade system, with a role primarily in intra-Asian trade. Its political autonomy was similar to that of other similar areas distant from the capital. Ayutthaya could appoint or replace the so-called rajas (governors) of Phuket but it could not always control what went on in Phuket.

Resistance to Dutch Attempts to Exert Monopoly

European involvement in the tin trade of the Malay Peninsula led to greater interest in Kedah, Perak, Phuket, Bangkhli, Ligor, and the surrounding areas, including Chaiya, Phunphin, and Chumphon, resulting in conflicts with local powers and longer-established groups. The Europeans thought in terms of export monopolies or binding contracts with kings and local governors, or failing that, permission to settle and trade. Such monopolies would have excluded other foreign traders who had been regular visitors to the tin ports of the peninsula before the arrival of the Europeans.

The Dutch East India Company (VOC) saw the usefulness of buying up tin in the Malay Peninsula quite early in its involvement in Southeast Asia's trade. In 1639 the VOC sent an expedition to Phuket and Bangkhli, among other places, with Orlando Thibault as commander.[33] After the Dutch captured Melaka from the Portuguese in January 1641, it became a foothold from which to expand trading activities in the peninsula. As tin was to be the key commodity in the Melaka trade, the VOC "sought to monopolize the tin production of the area by signing treaties with the Sultan of Kedah on 18 June 1642, the head of JunkCeylon (Phuket) on 18 March 1643, and with the Governor of Bangery [Bangkhli] on 1 January 1645."[34] The Dutch concentrated on negotiating monopoly contracts with local Malay rulers as it proved impossible to prohibit Melaka from continuing its trade with the Coromandel coast generally, and the tin trade carried on by Indian merchants specifically. They were also unable to impose any strict control over the tin and textiles trade in the Malay Peninsula, largely because Asian merchants still retained access to the Sumatran port of Aceh. The Dutch attempted to restrict Asian (notably Bengal-based) shipping through an embargo on all Asian shipping in the "tin ports" and Aceh, and later through a system of issuing selective passes to Asian vessels, but such policies did not appear to eliminate the company's rivals in the tin ports.[35]

The history of the VOC's dealings in Phuket and Bangkhli after 1643 was one of frustration. There were many problems, including low production of tin, loss of part of the textile consignment brought to Phuket to be sold in exchange for tin, and poor sales of cloth because many local inhabitants, ruined by continuous exploitation, had fled. However, the main problem seems to have been unstable conditions on the island itself. There were raids on Phuket by "Johorse Saletters" (orang laut from Johore?) the previous year, leading to twenty-four people from the island, and "not a few" people from the neighboring area of Bangkhli, being spirited away. The Johoreans also attacked the pearl fishers of Pulau "Mottia," or "Mabangers." The people of Phuket were said to be very embittered by these attacks and wanted revenge.[36]

Administratively, too, things were unsettled. In 1645 the king had summoned the governor of Phuket to Ayutthaya for the fourth time, to answer for his unwillingness to come up to the court, as well as various other alleged faults.[37] As it was a "Ligor Mandarin" who summoned Phuket's governor to report to Ayutthaya, it is clear that Phuket was still under the administrative control of Ligor. The VOC report of October 1645 says that Ayutthaya appointed a new governor of Ligor in 1645, who vexed the people of Trang, Phuket, and Bangkhli with so many demands for the taxation of fruit trees and agricultural produce that many ran away.[38]

The letters of the governor of Phuket to Governor van Vliet of Melaka in 1644 and 1645 show that he was acting quite independently. There is no mention of the court at Ayutthaya, and the governor received gifts in his own right, very much as any local raja might have done. He sent van Vliet gifts of tin, ambergris, and a rhinoceros horn, and acknowledged the receipt of gifts from the VOC, consisting of red damask, other cloth, jewelry, a musket, and a Japanese "*comptoirken* [writing desk]." He also asked the company to supply him with rarities such as two birds of paradise and two mother-of-pearl "*hoorns*."[39] This is one indication of how the governors of Thalang and Bangkhli viewed the VOC.

Another indirect way of uncovering local reactions to the VOC is to examine the text of a contract-treaty concluded between the company and the governor of Bangkhli in January 1645. The governor promised to deliver to the VOC all the tin annually mined in Bangkhli and to forbid local inhabitants, merchants included, from purchasing cloth brought in by foreign vessels. The penalties for locals who did not sell their tin to the company were specified as follows: the first offense would result in the confiscation of half the tin, the second in confiscation of all the tin plus the *perahu* (boat), and a third would mean enslavement of the offender as well as confiscation of the tin, the vessel, and "all goods." Half the confiscated tin and other goods would go to the king, and the other half to the company. *King* presumably meant the king of Siam, indicating that Ayutthaya had enough hold over Phuket and Bangkhli for the governors to agree to send confiscated articles to the capital. The governor of Bangkhli further promised to help ensure that all payments to the company were prompt and the Dutch lodge well protected. In the event that a VOC employee committed theft, assault, rape, or murder, the governor would not judge him but wait for the opperhoofd's annual visit to hand the offender over to that company official.[40] The contract, a series of obligations demanded by the Dutch and concessions granted by the governor of Bangkhli, favored the Dutch, and Governor van Vliet naturally wanted to revive the Phuket-Bangkhli office of the VOC in anticipation of benefits accruing from the contract.

Until the early 1650s, Phuket's relations with the VOC appear, at least on the surface, to have been quite peaceful, even though there must have been some misgivings on the part of local officials who realized the Dutch wanted to extract as much tin as they could. The governor-general reported, in December 1651, that the tin miners in Phuket were busily occupied and the company's resident there was confident of being able to deliver a "good quantity of tin" to Melaka. But tin was not to be expected from Bangkhli, where the "regent" had recently usurped the authority of the governor of Phangnga, another famous tin-producing area.[41] This showed that local unrest was never far from the surface. Indeed, the actual amounts of tin obtained from Phuket and environs was often disappointing. In January 1652 it was reported that Melaka got only a hundred bahar of tin from Phuket and in January 1654 the company's tin trade at Phuket was described as being of little significance.[42]

The troubled political situation in Phuket and its environs was such that the court at Ayutthaya could apparently do little when the governor of Bangkhli took over Phangnga, as these areas were then under the authority of Ligor. In 1652–53 the prince of Ligor divided the island administratively into two sections, as a result of which the old governor—the popular Okkhun Phet, who had previously ruled the whole island—lost administrative power over the more populous half of the island, where the VOC lodge stood. This part of the island was given over to an official who was "a great drunkard," causing great dissatisfaction among the local people. It was decided to appeal to Ayutthaya directly for a return to the original administrative arrangement. The Phuket mission to Ayutthaya went by way of Tenasserim so that it would not have to pass Ligor. The Dutch, siding with Okkhun Phet, saw fit to accommodate the Phuket mission in a freeman's vessel based in Melaka, a fact that Batavia realized was not going to please the Ligor governor.[43]

Until 1654 Okkhun Phet had yet to return from Ayutthaya. The

VOC general letter of 7 November 1654 concluded that the Dutch had suffered "for some time" in Phuket from the effects of an "unstable government" but hoped that when Okkhun Phet, "a friend of the company," was restored to his former full governorship, he would ensure peaceful trading for the Dutch and a good amount of tin yearly.[44] But friends proved fickle and the Dutch encountered a big problem in February 1655, when the company's "friend," Okkhun (now Okphra) Phet, broke the terms of the VOC-Phuket contract that gave the Dutch a monopoly over the tin in Phuket. He was selling his tin in exchange for Coromandel textiles even though the contract with the Dutch forbade any dealing in Indian cloths, which the Dutch themselves wanted to monopolize in their trade with Phuket and Bangkhli.[45]

In 1655–56 the Dutch bought 125 bahar of tin from Phuket, again considered to be a small amount. But the amount of tin bought at Kedah was even lower, a mere twenty-nine bahar, owing to competition from other foreign traders.[46] Another reason the Dutch failed to obtain more tin in Phuket was corruption within the ranks of company employees; for example, in 1656 Jan van Groeningen, a VOC merchant, was recalled from Phuket on account of private trading.[47] Sometimes, the Dutch were fairly successful; for example, in December 1656 the vessel *Cleen Batavia* brought a thousand bahar of Phuket tin to Melaka, a figure more in accordance with Dutch expectations of the Phuket tin trade.[48]

Local resentment at the VOC's monopolistic policies soon exploded. In 1658 the VOC factory and patrol boat at Phuket were seized by Malays, angry at their exclusion from the tin trade and Dutch insistence on their right to search all Malay vessels. The VOC general letter of 14 December 1658 recounts that "some foreigners . . . among whom were three Makassarese *hadjis* burnt down the VOC factory," and killed some company employees. The opperhoofd and a few others were severely injured but escaped. Total losses suffered by the company, including assets consumed by fire or taken by the attackers, amounted to over twenty-two thousand guilders. The Dutch suspected their former "friend" Okphra Phet to be behind this incident, because he did not punish the offenders, allowing them to flee to

Kedah.[49] The VOC factory at Phuket was closed in 1660, though VOC vessels continued to trade at Phuket regularly. This incident needs to be seen in the wider context of Malay resistance to Dutch monopolistic practices in the region. In 1651 twenty-seven Dutchmen were killed and the VOC factory destroyed in Perak, where resentment against the Dutch had been mounting steadily since the 1640s. In 1652 a Dutch envoy was seized at Kedah. In all three cases Dutch demands for redress from local rulers met with no success.[50]

The VOC general letter of 14 December 1658 tells of King Narai's anger and regret over the incident in Phuket, and of the king's order to Okphra Phet to put to death all the guilty people in this affair. But Batavia was skeptical that the governor would actually do so.[51] In 1659 a letter written by Jan van Rijck in Ayutthaya mentions that the king of Siam had sent two commissioners down to Phuket via Ligor, accompanied by an official from Ligor, to help clear up the matter of the murder of the Dutchmen in Phuket. Okphra Phet was summoned to Ligor to account for his actions, but he stood in such credit there that the VOC's complaints against him did not carry much weight.[52] Van Rijck reported two years later that the three commissioners who had been sent to Phuket stayed there a whole year without achieving anything. When they finally returned to Ayutthaya in June 1661, they brought with them Okya Ligor and Okphra Phet, together with three Malays accused of the murder of the VOC employees.

The governor of Ligor was excused from punishment on account of his old age, but the governor of Phuket and the three "delinquents" were "bound in five parts of the body," tortured, and interrogated. The governor of Phuket was found innocent of any wrongdoing, according to the testimony given by the three men, who were found guilty and handed over to the VOC to be punished. The accomplices of the three were not caught, as they had fled to Kedah. Flight to Kedah was a common option for those who found themselves in difficulties in Phuket. King Narai sent Okphra Phet back as governor to Phuket, with a stern injunction that, on pain of death, he was to look after the Dutch nation on Phuket as if they were "the apple of his eye," ensuring that they enjoyed a "free unhindered commerce," and came to no harm from the doings of "evil people."[53] Despite the king's injunctions, Okphra Phet was sufficiently far away from Ayutthaya to act contrary to them, as he appears to have continued to be more sympathetic to the Malays than to the Dutch.

Nevertheless, the VOC's objective in the 1660s and early 1670s was still to obtain tin export monopolies at Ligor, Phuket, and Bangkhli. Nicolaas de Rooij, the Dutch opperhoofd in Ayutthaya between 1669 and 1672, wrote in October 1670 that King Narai was unlikely to grant a monopoly to the VOC in Phuket and Bangkhli because he wanted as many foreign traders as possible to trade in his realm.[54] The tin of peninsular Siam was obviously important to the king himself. Through his agent in Ligor, the king took regular tributes in tin while his trade minister (the *chaophraya phrakhlang*) also had an interest in the tin commerce of the area. With the return of the English East India Company, there was yet another European nation keen to lay hands on some of the tin. The Japanese mestizos resident in Ayutthaya transported the tin from Ligor to the capital, while the Moors took tin from the west coast of Siam to India via Mergui. The Malays also took part in the tin trade of the Phuket-Bangkhli area. The monopolistic policy of the Dutch was thus in conflict with existing trading interests in the region's tin trade.[55]

According to George Vinal Smith, the VOC's tin trade at Ligor, which had begun promisingly enough, had declined by the 1660s owing to English and Chinese competition, as well as to the monopolization of the trade by local officials. The VOC petitioned the king for an export monopoly of the tin at Ligor and at Phuket and Bangkhli and in 1671 King Narai granted the Dutch a monopoly at Ligor. For more than a decade after that "the Dutch usually had effective support from the king or his officials" in maintaining this monopoly, which meant that Ligor was the main supplier of tin for the company.[56] But the VOC's attempts to control the tin market of the whole peninsula did not succeed because there was too much competition from the English and Muslim traders, and also because the Siamese monarch refused to grant the company a monopoly in other tin centers, particularly Phuket.

In 1670 Nicolaas de Rooij had succeeded in getting two *tra* (licenses) from King Narai that excluded all Asiatic ("Indian") nations from the tin trade at Phuket and Bangkhli and also at Ligor, through the help of one Gosia Zacharias, an Armenian merchant living in Ayutthaya. De Rooij decided to bypass the chaophraya phrakhlang because the latter, having a personal interest in the tin trade, was unwilling to further the company's affairs in this matter. Zacharias was able to obtain the licenses for the company because he was, at that time, "very much in favor with this king and his grandees." But de Rooij himself was wary of placing too much confidence in the power of these tra and counseled the governor-general that it was better to cultivate the favor of local dignitaries, especially at Phuket and Bangkhli. But this proved difficult. In the case of the company's monopoly at Ligor, the situation seemed extremely promising because the king even excluded himself from the trade, reserving only the right to claim his annual tribute.[57]

Just after the Dutch obtained a tra for exclusive tin trade at Phuket, the VOC sloop *Dolphijn* was seized by Malays in April 1671 in the Bangkhli River. The ship was burned and most of the people on board killed. The Dutch protested to the Siamese court, whereupon Ayutthaya sent an official to Phuket to summon the governor to the capital,[58] a standard reaction unlikely to succeed in obtaining satisfaction for the Dutch. In de Rooij's November 1672 report as outgoing opperhoofd, he referred to various difficulties, including bloodshed and murder, that had accompanied the company's trade in the Phuket and Bangkhli area. Once again, in one whole year it had been possible to obtain only a hundred bahar of tin there. Furthermore, the overhead costs of maintaining a blockading vessel meant that there was more loss than profit for the company, all this despite the VOC having obtained a tin monopoly in this area.

The trouble partly stemmed from Dutch attempts at forcing local officials and inhabitants to sell them tin at a price far lower than what they could obtain from other foreign traders coming to Phuket and Bangkhli. The Dutch blockade also hurt the inhabitants of the island of Phuket at the most basic level as imported foodstuffs such as rice, salt, and other goods were not reaching the islanders. De Rooij was of the opinion that this was the real reason why the Dutch were so hated by the inhabitants of Phuket and Bangkhli.[59] The VOC's prospects of conducting a thriving tin trade at Phuket and Bangkhli, as De Rooij pointed out, were not good as long as the company insisted on uncompetitive prices. In the past the Dutch were able to buy tin for thirty to thirty-five *realen* (rials) per bahar, but times had changed as Bengal and Coromandel Moors were willing to pay fifty-four realen for a bahar of tin at Tenasserim, a port quite close to Phuket. It was not surprising, therefore, that the people of Phuket resented the Dutch and their demands. King Narai might agree to the company's terms but the king's subjects in Phuket were living in a "distant and desolate land."[60]

More Conflicts and Turbulence

One salient factor in the tin trade of Phuket at this juncture was the participation of the so-called Moors and the Hindu merchants of India. The Moors seemed especially prominent in Siam, and at the Ayutthaya court, in the 1660s and 1670s. De Rooij's November 1672 report mentions Dutch dealings with a certain Benjaen Radja Ram (probably a Hindu merchant) and a Persian known as Aqa Muhammad Astarabadi or Okphra Sinaowarat.[61] Another VOC document, the report of Steven Claarbout on his trade at, and blockade of, Phuket in 1673, tells us how the Dutch had, between 8 and 10 January 1673, set fire to several houses, including that of a certain Intgie Lilla, a Kedah Malay, near Bangkhli. Claarbout insisted on personally inflicting reprisals on Intgie Lilla for some earlier deed by the Kedahans against the Dutch because he did not trust the Siamese authorities at Phuket and Bangkhli, accusing the governor of Bangkhli of "seeming to love [the Dutch] with the mouth but the Kedahans with the heart."[62] The administrators of Phuket and Bangkhli thus had to balance the interests of the Malays, the Indians, and the Dutch all the time in their work.

According to Bowrey, the Dutch blockade at Phuket and Bangkhli continued for several years, until 1675, during which they maintained "a ship of sixteen or twenty guns and two or three sloops to cruise about this island." The VOC tried, through this blockade, to obtain a monopoly of Phuket's tin trade. But, in Bowrey's words, "by their too much presumption and encroachinge (as theire usuall way is in every place they do gett footinge in) they utterly lost it."[63] Bowrey relates how on one occasion when a ship from Aceh slipped past the Dutch blockade, the Dutch seized the ship when she was nearly fully laden with goods, claiming that, being Acehnese, it was an enemy vessel. The local Malay inhabitants refused to tolerate such high-handedness and took the Acehnese vessel by force from the Dutch. In the fight that ensued, a Dutchman fired a musket and killed two of the Phuket inhabitants, who decided to avenge themselves. They mustered a force of two hundred men, overpowered the Dutch, "cutt them off every man and pulled theire sloop in pieces, which so squashed the Dutch designes over this place that they went away with theire ship and other sloope and never molested Janselone any more."[64]

The VOC immediately launched protests to the king of Siam while the governor of Phuket sent a full account of events to the court of Ayutthaya. Bowrey was with the governor when the latter received a tra from the king, who, "incensed" at the Dutch, ordered the Phuket authorities to arm themselves and all three seaports on the island against any further actions by Dutch sloops in the area. Failure to comply with these belligerent orders would result in the execution of the governor, his chief counselors, and the three syahbandars. The governor and his counselors were only too happy to carry out the king's orders with great alacrity.[65]

The Dutch perspective on this incident is provided by Governor Balthasar Bort of Melaka, who in 1677 complained that not only was no action taken against those who had inflicted "murder and damage" on the Dutch, but the governors of Phuket and Bangkhli had become "more insolent and petulant." Worse, the whole of the trade was taken from the Dutch while Phuket still traded with Indian, Javanese, and other foreign merchants. The Moors took tin from Phuket and brought in considerable amounts of Indian textiles. Bort observed bitterly that 600 bahar of tin was exported annually from Phuket, without any regard to the "dominion and jurisdiction" claimed by the VOC in Melaka over the island.[66] Bort's comments clearly indicate the powerlessness of the company to impose a monopoly over the Malay Peninsula's tin-producing areas. What is also striking is that Phuket and Bangkhli were classified as territories under the jurisdiction of Dutch Melaka, rather than as provinces or dependencies of Ayutthaya. The economic importance of Phuket took precedence over its political or administrative status within the Siamese kingdom. Again, the monopolistic ambitions of the VOC conflicted both with the commercial ambitions of elements at the court of King Narai and with the way trade had been carried on for several generations at Phuket.

Dutch documents dating from the mid-1670s are full of references to conflicting commercial and political interests within the Siamese court. The main rivalry was that between the incumbent phrakhlang minister, Chaophraya Kosathibodi (Lek), or Kosa Lek, and the leading Persian official at the court, Okphra Sinaowarat, or Aqa Muhammad. Kosa Lek and Aqa Muhammad clashed most obviously when their commercial interests conflicted. In 1676 Aqa Muhammad helped the VOC to get rid of Okphra Phet, the old governor of Phuket, who fought tenaciously to retain his post but failed against the powerful Aqa Muhammad. Two Indian Muslim brothers, Mohammed Beg and Ismael Beg, were made governors of Phuket and Bangkhli in mid-1676, appointments that reflected Muslim influence at the Siamese court and Moorish ambitions to increase their share of the tin trade on Siam's west coast.[67]

In Bowrey's version, Mohammed Beg was appointed governor of Phuket because King Narai wanted to have "an austere man" who would be "fitter to governe this island" than the old governor Okphra Phet. But the two Indians could not assert any lasting control over Phuket and Bangkhli as their administrations grated on local sensibilities and, more important, ran counter to local commercial interests. During a visit in 1677, Bowrey found that "the most eminent men, both Syamers & Malayars," had many complaints against the governors and there was loud murmuring from local inhabitants, who felt "tyrannized over" as they had to endure great hardships in carrying out public works for the capital. The Siamese were, in addition, aggrieved that their local elite, "councellors, secretaries, shabandares, bandarees &c, men of antient standinge and choice men of all the countrey," had all been replaced by Chulias (Indian Muslim merchants from the Coromandel, India).[68] Tension and trouble in the area reached a climax when the new governors, along with over seventy Moors and Chulias, were massacred by Malays and Siamese, who, apart from chafing under their administration, strongly resented the Moors' attempt to divert all the export of tin from the Phuket and Bangkhli area to Mergui. Mohammed Beg's and Ismael Beg's administrations came to an end because they had wanted to make the tin trade an exclusive preserve of their fellow Moors, who could then buy up tin at Mergui and ship it to Indian and Persian destinations.[69]

The state of near anarchy in Phuket was real enough for the king, and other elements at court, to use it as an excuse to turn down repeated requests from the VOC to return to Phuket. Even though Batavia had a low estimation of Phuket as a potential profit-making trading outpost, the VOC still hoped to trade there. On the other hand, the king and his courtiers had their reasons for keeping the Dutch out of Phuket.[70] In 1679 King Narai, through the phrakhlang minister, wrote to Governor-General Rijckloff van Goens that some Kedah Malays, and some bandits, had been causing trouble in the Phuket region. The Kedah "enemies" had attacked Phuket and Bangkhli, had caused great damage to the people there, and could well create difficulties for the company's ships. As the king was then preparing his subjects in Ligor and "Ternaso" (Tenasserim) to help the people of Phuket resist another expected attack from the Malays of Kedah, it was impossible for him to allow the Dutch to return there just yet.[71] Kedah and Kedah Malays who regularly traded in Phuket and Bangkhli were thus frequently involved in local politics. At the same time, Phuket had a role to play in Siam's relations with its Malay dependency of Kedah too. In 1681 Batavia learned that the governor of Phuket had, with support from his master, the king of Siam, attacked Kedah in order to bring the Malay sultanate back to obedience, that is to send the *bunga mas dan perak* (golden and silver flowers of tribute) to Ayutthaya.[72]

The 1680s saw the entry of yet another European player, the French, who were very interested in obtaining a tin export monopoly at Phuket, as the Dutch already had an export monopoly of tin at Ligor while the English had monopolies of sorts at Chaiya, Phunphin, and Chumphon. In September 1680 the French East India Company sent a vessel to Phuket, which returned with enough tin to make the journey profitable despite a devastating smallpox epidemic on the island a few years earlier.[73] Though the French carried on "small-scale" intermittent trade with Phuket, their company was in constant financial trouble in Asia while trade with Phuket did not prosper as hoped. After 1683 things improved when King Narai accepted King Louis XIV's letter enabling the French company to draw up a contract with the Siamese court, securing a pepper monopoly and the right to buy goods brought into Siam by junks from China and Japan. King Narai, however, resisted both French and Dutch requests to cede Junkceylon to them.[74]

Meanwhile, the Siamese court had repeatedly given evasive answers to Aarnout Faa, the Dutch opperhoofd, who was seeking permission for the VOC to reestablish itself in Phuket. The Dutch were increasingly wary of both English and French competition in the tin trade of Phuket, which was still believed to be considerable, except that much of it was sent to Tenasserim.[75] The English were also pressing the Ayutthaya court for trading privileges in Phuket, but without success, while the French were still exploring more trade possibilities in and around Phuket between 1683 and 1688.[76]

French hopes of a more flourishing tin trade at Phuket may have increased in the late 1680s as King Narai, toward the end of his reign, appointed French governors for Phuket. This trend had started, probably around 1682, with the appointment of "Brother René" Charbonneau, who was in the service of the Siam mission of the Société des Missions Etrangères. According to Dutch sources, Charbonneau was ordered by King Narai to allow all incoming vessels to Phuket to enjoy "free trade" there, an order he faithfully carried out.[77] Charbonneau, one of the more remarkable characters in seventeenth-century Siamese history, was one of those rare Europeans who married and settled down in Ayutthaya till his death, at age eighty-three, in 1730.[78] He must also have been a good administrator gifted at human relations, as Phuket and Bangkhli were notoriously unruly communities subject to attacks by pirates and Malays. He managed to survive where the two Moorish governors, Mohammed and Ismail Beg, had perished.

In 1685 Chevalier de Chaumont negotiated a commercial treaty with the Ayutthaya court that gave the French the port of Songkhla (Singora) and a tin monopoly at Phuket, but Paris was not satisfied with Songkhla, as they wanted a more strategic location for a depot. Songkhla was deemed to be too far away from Ayutthaya, while Phuket and Ligor were not attractive enough.[79] Nevertheless, when the French decided to head back for Siam after withdrawing to Pondicherry in late 1688, their choice was Phuket. Opposing viewpoints on the wisdom of going to Phuket in 1689, with a force of 332 men "to frighten the Siamese into a reconciliation by a show of force," delayed the departure of the expedition until early April 1689. In the end, the "expedition" proved to be an anticlimax, as "strictly nothing was gained" and "noone was sure that Phuket had even been reached."[80] The objective of freeing some French missionaries held in Ayutthaya was not attained and the French mission at Phuket suffered difficulties and neglect after 1688.[81]

With reduced Dutch interest and the end of the French adventure, Phuket was no longer the target of European East India Companies for the rest of the seventeenth century. But during this time and until the first half of the eighteenth century, its tin continued to attract Malays, Moors, Chinese, and European country traders who still visited Phuket from time to time, a pattern that was to continue into the time of Captain Francis Light.[82]

Phuket was a province of the Ayutthaya kingdom, with commercial significance on an international level. Its tin trade gave Phuket a certain commercial autonomy while the great distance of the island from the capital afforded its governors considerable political autonomy at times. In the early part of the seventeenth century the local governors, though nominally under the supervision of Ligor, seemed to have considerable freedom of action, as demonstrated in the direct contract-treaties between Phuket and Bangkhli and the Dutch. Competition over Phuket tin intensified later in the seventeenth century as more European players entered the fray. Their monopolistic intentions threatened patterns of local and regional trade that had existed for generations, resulting in resistance and, sometimes, violent conflicts. The local elite, from the king and his ministers in Ayutthaya to the governors and his councillors in the province, had their own interests in the tin trade. Phuket's geographical location and sociocultural links with the Malay Archipelago, in particular Kedah, added yet another dimension to its commercial and political connections.

Ayutthaya had to intervene several times in the administrative affairs of Phuket during the seventeenth century, at times attempting to impose more direct control over Phuket and Bangkhli but with variable success. The Phuket governor Okphra Phet was often able to act quite independently of Ayutthaya during the earlier parts of King Narai's reign. The violent rejection of the Chulia governors of Phuket and Bangkhli appointed by King Narai in the mid-1670s reflected the power struggles at the court but, from a local perspective, it showed how far the resistance of local inhabitants could go. The later appointment of Frenchmen to governorships in Phuket and Bangkhli showed the extent to which French influence at the Ayutthayan court had grown during the 1680s.

The scarcity of primary documentary sources may diminish hopes for a truly autonomous history for seventeenth-century Phuket, for which we do need local sources to give the people of premodern Phuket a distinct voice and more reliable data on social structures and local culture. But, as this chapter has attempted to show, we can still read between the lines of the European sources to discern the local concerns and interests of Phuket traders and governors during the seventeenth century. And from the surfacing of tensions into violent conflicts, we can discern when the dissatisfaction of Phuket's inhabitants against their governors or the monopolistic policies of the VOC had reached what for them were intolerable levels.

Notes

A longer version of this chapter has appeared as "Towards a History of Seventeenth Century Phuket" in *Recalling Local Pasts,* ed. Sunait Chutintaranond and Chris Baker (Chiang Mai: Silkworm Books, 2002).

1. John Carrington, "Montone Puket (Siam) Malay Peninsula," *Journal of the Siam Society* 3, 1 (1906), reprinted in The Siam Society, *Old Phuket* (Bangkok: The Siam Society, 1986).

2. G. E. Gerini, "Historical Retrospect of Junkceylon Island," in *Old Phuket* (Bangkok: Siam Society, 1986; orig. in *Journal of the Siam Society* 2, 2 [1905]).

3. John R. W. Smail, "On the Possibility of an Autonomous History of Modern Southeast Asia," *Journal of Southeast Asian History* 2, 2 (1961): 72–102.

4. The sources consist of French archival sources, documents of the Dutch United East India Company (VOC) and English East India Company, as well as accounts written by Westerners during the seventeenth century as well as Siamese and Malay sources, which are more scarce in direct references to Phuket.

5. Gerini, "Historical Retrospect," 22.

6. Ibid., 61–62.

7. *Sjeik Abdullah en de bloemen: Hikayat Merong Mahawangsa,* trans. H. M. J. Maier (Amsterdam: Meulenhoff, 1978), 8–10, 36–37.

8. Archives Nationales, Paris (henceforth AN), CI 23, f. 116.

9. Thomas Bowrey, *A Geographical Account of Countries round the Bay of Bengal, 1669–1679,* ed. Sir Richard Carnac Temple, Hakluyt Society, 2d series, no. 12 (Cambridge: Hakluyt Society, 1905), in India Office Records (henceforth IOR), Mss Eur D782, 131.

10. Gerini, "Historical Retrospect," 62–63.

11. AN, CI 23, f. 116.

12. IOR, Mss Eur D782, 131.

13. AN, CI 23, f. 116 verso; IOR, Mss Eur D782, 131.

14. IOR, Mss Eur D782, 131.

15. Gerini, "Historical Retrospect," 36–37; Krom Sinlapakon (Fine arts dept.), "Phra Thammanun," in *Ruang kotmai tra sam duang* (Bangkok: Krom Sinlapakon, 1978), 83.

16. Manop Thawonwatsakun, *Khunnang ayutthaya* (Bangkok: Thammasart University, 1993), 99–104.

17. Gerini, "Historical Retrospect," 25–29.

18. Ibid., 34–38.

19. IOR, E/3/40, no. 4696 and G/21/7A, George White to Robert Parker and Council, 15 Nov. 1679, 18–32; also in *Records of the Relations between Siam and Foreign Countries in the Seventeenth Century* (Bangkok: Vajirana National Library, 1915), vol. 2, 421–28.

20. Simon de La Loubère, *A New Historical Relation of the Kingdom of Siam*, trans. A. P. (Kuala Lumpur: Oxford University Press, 1969), 94.

21. Gerini, "Historical Retrospect," 22.

22. A unit of weight, one bahar was equivalent to 3.0 *piculs,* or approximately 130 English pounds. Algemeen Rijksarchief, The Hague, VOC Archives (henceforth VOC), VOC 1377, Aarnout Faa to Governor-General (G-G) and Council, 10 Dec. 1682, f. 519 verso–520; see also La Loubère, *New Historical Relation,* 14.

23. VOC 1377, Faa to G-G and Council, 10 Dec. 1682, f. 519 verso.

24. IOR, E/3/40, no. 4696, George White (1679).

25. Ibid.

26. VOC 1377, Faa to G-G and Council, 10 Dec. 1682, f. 519 verso; IOR, Mss Eur D782, 134.

27. IOR, Mss Eur D782, 132.

28. The place called Luppoone was probably Ban Liphon, in Northern Phuket.

29. IOR, Mss Eur D782, 132–34.

30. Ibid.

31. Ibid. On the grant to the East India Company, see John Anderson, *English Intercourse with Siam in the Seventeenth Century* (London: Kegan, Paul, Trench, Trübner & Co. Ltd, 1890), 116–17.

32. Ibid.

33. *Generale missiven der gouverneurs-generaal en raden aan Heren XVII der Verenigde Oostindische Compagnie* (henceforth *GM*), ed. W. Ph. Coolhaas (The Hague: Rijks Geschiedkundige Publication, 1960), letter of 18 Dec. 1639, 68–69.

34. Leonard Y. Andaya, *The Kingdom of Johor, 1641–1728* (Kuala Lumpur: Oxford University Press, 1975), 106.

35. Dianne Lewis, *Jan Compagnie in the Straits of Malacca, 1641–1795* (Athens: Ohio University Press, 1995), 18–20; Om Prakash, *The Dutch East India Company and the Economy of Bengal, 1630–1720* (Delhi: Oxford University Press, 1988), 230–31.

36. VOC 1158, *Verbael* (by Johan Verpoorten) of Oct. 1645, fs. 139–40.

37. Ibid., f. 140.

38. Ibid., fs. 140, 152.

39. Ibid., fs. 141–141 verso.

40. Ibid., fs. 142–43.

41. *GM* II, letter of 19 Dec. 1651, 518.

42. *GM* II, letter of 24 Jan. 1652, 572;. *GM* II, letter of 19 Dec. 1654, 690–91.

43. *GM* II, letter of 31 Jan. 1653, 648.

44. *GM* II, letter of 7 Nov. 1654, 752.

45. *GM* III, letter of 24 Dec. 1655, 20.

46. *GM* III, letter of 1 Feb. 1656, 47.

47. *GM* III, letter of 4 Dec. 1656, 93; letter of 17 Dec. 1657, 161.

48. *GM* III, letter of 31 Jan. 1657, 126.

49. *GM* III, letter of 14 Dec. 1658, 220.

50. Lewis, *Jan Compagnie,* 22–23.

51. *GM* III, letter of 14 Dec. 1658, 245; letter of 16 Jan. 1660, 294.

52. VOC 1230, Jan van Rijck and Enoch Poolvoet to G-G, 27 Nov. 1659, f. 239 verso; *GM* III, letter of 16 Dec. 1660, 326.

53. VOC 1236, Jan van Rijck and Council to G-G and Council, 7 Oct., 1661, f. 675.

54. *GM* III, letter of 25 Jan. 1667, 543.

55. On the Siamese crown's trade activities in the seventeenth century, see Dhiravat na Pombejra, "A Political History of Siam under the Prasatthong Dynasty, 1629–1688" (Ph.D. thesis, London, 1984), 312–13; Dhiravat, "Crown Trade and Court Politics in Ayutthaya during the Reign of King Narai, 1656–1688," in *The Southeast Asian Port and Polity,* ed. J. Kathirithamby-Wells and John Villiers, 127–42 (Singapore: Singapore University Press, 1990). For a general view of commercial activity in this period, see Anthony Reid, *Southeast Asia in the Age of Commerce 1450–1680,* vol. 2, *Expansion and Crisis* (New Haven: Yale University Press, 1993), esp. chs. 1, 2, 4.

56. George Vinal Smith, *The Dutch in Seventeenth-Century Thailand* (De Kalb, Ill.: Northern Illinois University, 1977), 67.

57. Dhiravat, "Political History of Siam," 314; also VOC 1278, Nicolaes de Rooij and Jan van der Spijck to G-G, 25 Nov. 1670, fs. 2116 verso–2117.

58. Dhiravat, "Political History of Siam," 315.

59. VOC 1290, Nicolaes De Rooij, report, 20 Nov. 1672, fs. 245 verso–246.

60. Ibid., fs. 247 verso–248.

61. VOC 1290, De Rooij, report, 20 Nov. 1672, fs. 248 verso–261; on the "Moors" in Ayutthaya, see Dhiravat, "Political History of Siam," 292–94, 325–30; Ibn Muhammad Ibrahim Muhammad Rabi, *The Ship of Sulaiman,* trans. John O'Kane (London: Routledge and Kegan Paul, 1972), 97–106.

62. VOC 1294, Steven Claarbout's report on his trade at, and blockade of, Phuket (Feb. 1673?), fs. 653–60 verso.

63. IOR, Mss Eur D782; see also *GM* III, letter of 13 Nov. 1673, 882.

64. Ibid., 138–39.

65. Ibid., 139–40.

66. As quoted in Lewis, *Jan Compagnie,* 23.

67. VOC 1322, Dirck de Jonge to G-G and Council, 2 Nov. 1679, f. 407; *GM* IV, letter of 13 Feb. 1667, 157–58; Dhiravat, "Political History of Siam," 327–28.

68. IOR, Mss Eur D782, 140–42.

69. *GM* IV, letter of 13 Feb. 1679, 283; Dhiravat, "Political History of Siam," 337.

70. See Dhiravat, "Crown Trade and Court Politics."

71. VOC 1350, King of Siam to G-G and Council, 1679, fs. 487–88; see also Dhiravat, "Political History of Siam," 336–37.

72. *GM* IV, letter of 29 April 1681, 439.

73. Michael Smithies, *A Resounding Failure: Martin and the French in Siam, 1672–1693* (Chiang Mai: Silkworm Books, 1998), 20–22.

74. Ibid., 23–24.

75. VOC 1377, Faa to G-G Council, 10 Dec. 1682, fs. 518 verso 519; *GM* IV, letter of 19 March 1683, 536, 538.

76. Smithies, *Resounding Failure,* 29, 79.

77. *GM* IV, letter of 19 Feb. 1684, 661; letter of 18 March 1685, 7896; La Loubère, *New Historical Relation,* 91.

78. Dhiravat, *Court, Company, and Campong* (Ayutthaya: Ayutthaya Historical Study Centre, 1992), 49.

79. E. W. Hutchinson, *Adventurers in Siam in the Seventeenth Century* (London, 1940), 119–20.

80. Smithies, *Resounding Failure,* 119–20.

81. Dirk Van de Cruysse, *Louis XIV et le Siam* (Paris, 1991), 484; Dhiravat na Pombejra, "Ayutthaya at the End of Seventeenth Century: Was There a Shift to Isolation?" in *Southeast Asia in the Early Modern Era,* ed. Anthony Reid (Ithaca: Cornell University Press, 1993), 267; Adrien Launay, *Histoire de la Mission de Siam, 1662–1881* (Paris: Anciennes Maisons Charles Douniol et Retaux, 1920), vol. 2, *Documents historiques I,* 97.

82. See D. K. Bassett, "British 'Country' Trade and Local Trade Networks in the Thai and Malay States, c. 1680–1770," *Modern Asian Studies* 23, 4 (1989): 625–43.

Chapter 13

CONTINUITY AND CONNECTEDNESS

The Ngee Heng Kongsi of Johore, 1844–1916

P. Lim Pui Huen

One Sunday morning I attended a graveside ceremony in Johore Bahru's oldest Chinese cemetery, a ceremony organized by the Chinese Association of Johore Bahru and attended by the leaders of the Chinese community.[1] The grave, however, was not the final resting place of a deceased person but of a secret society, the Ngee Heng Kongsi (Yixing Gongsi).[2] As I watched the smoke rise from the incense and candles, I was intrigued by the thought that for more than eighty years people had come to this spot every year to pay their respects to an empty grave. The grave obviously holds some meaning not only for those present but also for the whole Johore Chinese community, as it can be observed that the ritual performed contributes to the sense of community and its sense of heritage. What was the Ngee Heng Kongsi and what role did it play in the history of the Chinese in Johore?[3]

In doing research on local history, I am struck by how particular landmarks provide the connection to the past and how history is localized through man-made structures such as buildings, bridges, and monuments, or natural features in the local landscape.[4] Every locality has such landmarks, each with its own history and connections to the community. History becomes more real and meaningful when the past is related to the people's own experience and knowledge. Local history, therefore, not only provides us with local knowledge but also with continuities to the past and a connectedness between the elements that make up that past. However, the value of local history does not lie in deepening the sense of heritage, no matter how enriching that may be, but in offering the possibility that by highlighting the particular we may illuminate the whole, and thereby gain some insight that we cannot perceive from the more distant and broader perspective of the larger picture.

In an earlier work, I discussed the continuities embedded in the physical landscape, but in this chapter I shall focus on the continuities in the social landscape of Chinese associations and in the cultural landscape of religious practices and traditions.[5] Woven into these continuities is yet another kind of connectedness—that between the Malays and the Chinese, an interaction and accommodation between the two communities—that began when the Chinese first settled in Malaya.

One of the features in the local landscape is a road in Johore Bahru named after the Ngee Heng Kongsi, one of the brotherhoods commonly referred to as secret societies, partly because of the secrecy in which their operations were shrouded and partly because they went underground after they were suppressed. However, in Johore the Ngee Heng Kongsi did not have a clandestine image but was instead given a legitimate place in society and, although it was eventually proscribed in 1916, it has left behind a legacy that is still discernible today. A study of the Ngee Heng Kongsi therefore provides an opportunity for examining the two themes of continuity and connectedness in local history.

Secret societies, called *hui* (or *hoe, hoey, huey, wui*), had their origins in China, where they appeared in times of hardship and weak administrative control when discontented men from the lowest strata of society were drawn together by a combination of mutual need and rebellious resentment of authority. Unfortunately these gangs easily descended into criminal violence. Under the disintegrating Qing dynasty, these secret societies found an environment ripe for disaffection while foreign rule by the Manchus provided them with a legitimate revolutionary cause. When the Chinese started migrating to Malaya in large numbers, they brought their social organizations, including these hui, with them and their history forms the underside of the history of the Chinese in Malaysia.

There is considerable literature on these secret societies, much of the older material having been written by colonial officials, who had to manage a large and growing immigrant population and who tended to see secret societies as part of the "Chinese problem."[6] They were interested in the nature of these hui and their history and organization and were fascinated by the exoticism of their symbolic language and elaborate rituals. However, research by scholars such as sociologists Mak Lau Fong[7] and David Ownby[8] has examined the social conditions that produced these organizations and enabled them to flourish. More recently a volume edited by David Ownby and Mary Somers Heidhues has brought together a multidisciplinary collection of papers on the social and economic functions of secret societies as well as their more well known criminal and political activities.[9]

The China Origins

It is generally known that such brotherhoods have always lurked in the background of Chinese history and that the harsh environment of the Qing dynasty strengthened their appeal. These groups drew their inspiration from two traditions that are still prevalent in popular culture today:

- The idea of sworn brotherhood derived from well-known tales from the *Romance of the Three Kingdoms,* in which the three heroes—Liu Bei, Guan Yu, and Zhang Fei—swore brotherhood with each other. Since Guan Yu, deified as Guangong, the god of war, is regarded as the epitome of courage in war and loyalty in comradeship, he is the tutelary deity of secret societies.
- The higher loyalty of a fictive relationship (in the stories translated as *Outlaws of the Marsh* or *The Water Margin*) was idealized over the real relationship of kinship and lineage.

These traditions form the backdrop to the practice of ritual brother-hood, with its obligations of absolute and unquestioned loyalty, rein-forced by elaborate and frightening rituals and blood oaths, which have always been the cornerstone of the organization of secret societies.

The Tiandihui became the dominant brotherhood in South China and was known by several names, including Tiandihui (Heaven and Earth Society), Sanhehui (Society of the Three Unities), and Hung-menhui (Hung League). The first two refer to the trinity of heaven, earth, and man in Chinese cosmogony, from which the anglicized name Triad Society is derived. The last is drawn from the name Hongwu, reign title of the first Ming emperor, who is venerated as the symbolic founder of the brotherhood, and the character *hong* or *hung* was adopted as its "family name."[10] According to tradition, its founders belonged to the famous order of fighting monks of the Shao-lin monastery in Fujian so frequently featured in kung fu movies.[11] The monks had helped the Qing emperor defeat a rebel tribe but the emperor became fearful of their military prowess and ordered the monastery to be destroyed. His troops set fire to the buildings, and the five monks who survived the flames swore an oath of brother-hood to avenge the monks who died. This foundation myth is deeply rooted in Chinese history and legend while its rituals, beliefs, and symbolisms are based on Taoist and folk beliefs. When deteriorating social conditions led to resistance against the Manchus, the Tiandihui adopted the slogan *Fan Qing fu Ming* (Resist the Qing and restore the Ming) as its rallying cry and the brotherhood spread rapidly throughout Fujian and the neighboring provinces. In the nineteenth century migration to Southeast Asia became an option and one such record of dispersal to Malaya is dated 1813.[12]

There are therefore two factors relating to the appearance of the brotherhoods in Malaya, one as a natural consequence of immigra-tion and the other as a result of Manchu persecution. Since the word *hui* refers to all forms of Chinese associations, *secret societies* has usu-ally been used in the literature. I have also used the term *brotherhoods* where applicable, as ritual brotherhood is the most distinguishing feature of these organizations.

The Malayan Background

Secret societies in Malaya were found among not only the Chinese but the Malays, Indians, and Siamese.[13] They were initially not illegal, as the disturbances they created were directed at each other rather than against the government. In the beginning they promoted cooperation between members, controlled investment and labor recruitment, maintained law and order, and acted as intermediaries between Malay and British authorities through the Kapitan China system. But as their activities against law and order increased, their operations drew the concern of the British authorities. By the 1820s secret societies had become a serious threat to law and order, especially when it was discovered that they had considerable military resources under their command[14] and their activities extended over Malaya, the Dutch East Indies, and Borneo.

The Chinese secret societies had certain characteristics in common:

- They originated from the Tiandihui.
- They had splintered into many groups under different names, the most prominent being the Ghi Hin, the Ghi Hok, and the Hai San.
- They tended to draw on men from the same dialect group or place of origin.
- Their leaders were made Kapitan Chinas to draw them into a system of indirect control.
- They competed for the rich profits of the tin mines and revenue farms.[15]
- They frequently clashed violently with each other (witness the riots in Melaka in 1848, in Singapore in 1854, and in Penang in 1867).[16]
- Their conflict became more significant when they became involved in Malay politics, as in the Larut Wars (1862–73) and the Selangor Wars (1862–65).

Officials in the Straits Settlements had pressed for measures to control the secret societies. The Dangerous Societies Suppression Ordinance was passed in 1869, following the Penang riots, but did not have enough teeth to be effective and final control only came with the Societies Ordinance of 1889. This was followed by similar legislation in the Malay states, although not in Johore until 1916.

The Ngee Heng Kongsi in Johore

What we know about secret societies in Malaya is based on studies of their activities in the Straits Settlements (Penang, Singapore, Melaka) and the Federated Malay States (Perak, Selangor, Negri Sembilan, Pahang), but information on the Ngee Heng Kongsi of Johore is to be found in works of economic history, mainly through the work of Carl A. Trocki on the growth and development of pepper and gambier agriculture.[17] Ngee Heng is the Teochew dialect rendition of Ghi Hin, the name of the brotherhood in Hokkien, which identifies it as the Teochew offshoot of the Tiandihui.[18] The term *kongsi* is usually used to refer to any firm or partnership, or to any group or society in a very broad sense. Wang Tai Peng defines it as "a form of open government, based on an enlarged partnership and brotherhood."[19] This synthesis of partnership and sworn brotherhood, he says, was uniquely Chinese, and partnership (in the sense of membership) together with sworn brotherhood was certainly applicable to the Ngee Heng in Johore.

The history of the Ngee Heng Kongsi is an integral part of the history of the Chinese in Johore, which in turn is an integral part of that state's economic history. It is well known that when Temenggong Daing Ibrahim wished to develop Johore after receiving sovereignty over it by the treaty of 1855 with Sultan Ali, he had few resources at his command.[20] However, he had observed the success of pepper and gambier cultivation in Riau, from where his father had brought the first Chinese planters to Singapore. The Chinese cultivators were predominantly Teochew and when the temenggong opened Johore to the Chinese, the Ngee Heng gained a dominant position among them. Johore then consisted of vast tracts of dense jungle, and rivers were the only means of access into the interior. The temenggong therefore devised a system by which the agricultural pioneer, called the *kangchu* (master of the river), was given a grant called a *surat sungai* (river document), which permitted him to cultivate land on the banks of rivers and tributaries. This became known as the kangchu system, which has been well documented. Johore and Singapore formed one economic and social unit in the nineteenth century; pepper and gambier production as well as trade was an important part of this connection and, through them, so were the secret societies.

It is usually assumed that secret societies came to Malaya in the wake of Chinese migration, and certainly by 1824, only five years after Singapore was founded, the Tiandihui was already well established, with a membership of several thousand.[21] By 1830 it had become the strongest and most dangerous of the three brotherhoods active in Singapore.

The drift toward Johore was a natural consequence of its proximity to Singapore, but in the 1840s the move northward was also caused by the growing shortage of land. When land registration was introduced in Singapore, the cultivators objected to paying quit rent and in 1846 the Ngee Heng commanded four thousand of its members to relocate to Johore in protest, the first record of a substantial migration of Chinese to Johore.[22]

The Pioneering Period under Tan Kee Soon

Chinese sources, however, put a more political complexion on the move. According to an article by Lee Xing, the secret organization Hungmenhui survived the defeat of the Taiping Rebellion, went underground, and reemerged as the Yixing/Ghi Hin.[23] Its members fled, first to Taiwan and then to Riau and Singapore. Their bitter rival, the Hokkien Ghi Hok, was also in Riau and the two brotherhoods often collided violently. However, only the Ngee Heng had appeared in Johore, because Sultan Abu Bakar, son of Temenggong Daing Ibrahim, permitted only one secret society to function in Johore.[24]

Lee Xing tells us that the Ngee Heng at first enjoyed freedom of action in Singapore, but when the government began to curb its activities, its leaders felt that it was time to make a move. As a matter of fact, Lee's sense of dating is in error because the Taiping Rebellion took place between 1850 and 1864 and the Ngee Heng under Tan Kee Soon (1803–1857) was in Johore by 1844. Nevertheless, he has connected the Ngee Heng's arrival in Malaya to Manchu suppression in China, and its move to Johore to changing British policy toward secret societies. In other words, Lee has highlighted the Ngee Heng factor in the migration of the Chinese to Johore. The Ngee Heng did not follow the Chinese to Johore but led them there.

Tan Kee Soon settled in Johore after obtaining a surat sungai for Sungai Tebrau. He established a pepper and gambier settlement called Tan Chukang at Kangkar Tebrau that, located upriver in deep jungle, was reminiscent of the bandits' marshy lair in the stories of *The Water Margin*. Chinese sources do not describe Tan Kee Soon as a planter or agricultural pioneer but as a *yishi,* a righteous man who resisted the Manchus.[25] In other words, he was what we would today call a political dissident and as such he would have had military capabilities, which would have been an asset to Sultan Abu Bakar during the crucial period when the latter was still in the process of establishing his authority over Johore. Lee Xing explains:

> After some years when Muar disobeyed the Sultan, Tan Kee Soon raised an army and went to pacify Muar. Thus the Sultan came to love and trust him. And he was commissioned by the Johor government to be responsible for the police force. Since he was the leader of the Ngee Heng, the government specifically permitted their open activities. This is the reason why the Ngee Heng of Johor was different from that of Singapore.[26]

Lee could be referring to the occasion when Sultan Abu Bakar raised a force of four hundred men against Muar in 1857.[27] His statement also reveals something about the relationship between the sultan and the Ngee Heng. He mentions the sultan's trust in Tan Kee Soon while other Chinese sources refer to his "devotion and loyalty to the palace."[28] Hence, we can conclude that Tan had a personal relationship with the sultan and that loyalty combined with martial resources were valuable assets to the sultan in the early period of his reign, when he lacked a properly constituted police force. Since Tan Chukang predated the treaty of 1855 and the founding of Johore Bahru, Tan Kee Soon through his powers as kangchu and Kapitan China was the only authority among the Chinese, so that Tan Chukang was to all intents and purposes the center of local government.

The suggestion that the Ngee Heng had provided military assistance to Sultan Abu Bakar at a critical time in Johore's history is quite plausible on two counts if we examine the Johore rulers' relations with Sultan Ali. The first relates to their jurisdiction over Johore. Temenggong Daing Ibrahim held traditional rights over the territory, but prior to 1855 its sovereignty rested with Sultan Ali. In this ambiguous situation, both sides competed for the extraction of gutta percha and other jungle produce. When pepper and gambier cultivation was introduced, it became clear to Sultan Abu Bakar, the temenggong's son, that the Chinese population should come under his control through Chinese loyal to him, not merely for the revenues they produced but also to prevent Chinese loyal to Sultan Ali from entering Johore. A brotherhood like the Ngee Heng, with its combination of muscle and moral authority, provided an effective barrier against infiltration and was the best means of ensuring that the scattered Chinese population remained loyal to him.[29] The second relates to the troubled situation in Muar, which was not included in the 1855 treaty. As a result, it went through an uneasy period before it was eventually incorporated into Johore territory in 1877. During that time there were clashes between the two sides, including the Jementah War of 1879, when Sultan Abu Bakar would have been glad to have experienced fighters on his side.[30] Although we have no evidence to support this supposition, I would argue that the Chinese were very likely to have given him military support.[31]

Although the Ngee Heng had established itself in Johore, it was not as yet recognized by the Johore government while other brotherhoods were not far behind in attempting to gain a foothold in the rivers. None of them were recognized, as Thomas Church, the resident councillor of Singapore, had warned Temenggong Daing Ibrahim about the dangers they posed. In a letter to Colonel Orfeur Cavenagh, governor of the Straits Settlements, the temenggong wrote:

Being fully aware of the evils resulting from these societies, and the great hindrance they offer to the due administration of justice and the proper government of Countries in which they are allowed to exist, I did everything in my power to carry out the suggestions of Mr. Church; but not withstanding all the means adopted by me I found that endeavors were constantly and often successfully made by the heads of Secret Societies in Singapore to establish branches in Johor.[32]

He would, he added, continue to prevent the establishment of secret societies in Johore.

In 1859, when this letter was written, some thirty surat sungai had been issued, and when the temenggong died, in January 1862, the number had increased only by nine. Sultan Abu Bakar was impatient to open up more jungle for development, but increasing the number of pepper and gambier concessions would bring more Chinese into the state and aggravate the problem of control. The sultan was no doubt aware that secret societies had been involved in the politics of other Malay states and, in the uneasy relationship with Sultan Ali, the last thing he needed was for the brotherhoods to enter the equation on the other side.

Official recognition of the Ngee Heng came in 1865, a date documented by court records in the Johore Archives, which refer to an edict of 1282 A.H. (1865 A.D.).[33] The Kanun Kangchu (Law of the Kangchus) also includes a clause forbidding the kangchu from starting "any Society other than the Ghi Hin [Ngee Heng] in accordance with the provisions of the Order issued in the time of the late Ruler."[34] The reference to an order issued by Temenggong Daing Ibrahim appears to contradict his letter to Cavenagh and suggests that the Johore rulers had quietly pursued an independent policy toward the Ngee Heng.

While policing functions were needed under frontier conditions, by 1858 Mohamed Salleh bin Perang, better known as Dato' Bentara Luar, had been put in charge of supervising the pepper and gambier plantations and the collection of revenue. Well before Chinese-speaking British officials were appointed, Mohamed Salleh, who had learned to read and write Chinese and was able to communicate directly with the cultivators in Teochew, had become the chief Johore official dealing with the Chinese. The Ngee Heng was still needed since the Chinese population continued to increase, but the death of Tan Kee Soon in 1857 started the process of transformation within the organization.

From a quasi-military revolutionary brotherhood based in rural Kangkar Tebrau, the Ngee Heng became an organization of kapitans, kangchus, and revenue farmers based in the state capital, Johore Bahru. The expansion of pepper and gambier planting continued and in time spread all over Johore. Since the sultan required all Chinese to be members of the Ngee Heng, its influence spread throughout the state wherever kangchu settlements were formed and this became a means by which the sultan's authority was carried to remote areas of Johore. In this way, the sultan brought all Chinese under one system of political and economic control and extended his authority over his state. The history of the Ngee Heng continues as the history of pepper and gambier cultivation and the development of the kangchu system, which has been thoroughly described elsewhere. It only need be mentioned that the kangchus were initially agricultural pioneers who held the grants to their rivers but, around 1860, there was a reorganization of the system and the surat sungai was increasingly issued to merchants, who became known as *tuan sungai* (owners of the river). The kangchu was instead issued with a *surat tauliah* (letter of authority) to work the river on behalf of the owner. The sultan's intention was to draw in more investment, but the effect on the Ngee Heng was to subordinate the kangchu to the merchant, and the pioneer agriculturist gradually gave way to the *towkay* (boss or merchant).

The Rise of the Merchants under Tan Hiok Nee

Tan Kee Soon was succeeded by his adopted son, Tan Cheng Hung, as kangchu and Kapitan China in Tebrau. But he was succeeded by Tan Hiok Nee (1827–1902) as leader of the Ngee Heng. The latter was twenty-six when he obtained his first surat sungai in 1853; he eventually held nine such grants, which made him the largest holder of kangchu concessions. He started life as a cloth merchant who gained the friendship of Sultan Abu Bakar and his family and by 1866 had established himself as a prosperous pepper and gambier trader in Singapore.[35] A map of 1887 shows that he owned several plots of land in the center of Johore Bahru, where he started a market and also owned many shops and houses.

Probably in 1870 Tan Hiok Nee was appointed Major China of Johore, an office that is listed in the *Straits Calendar and Directory, 1874.* He is shown as being assisted by an assistant treasurer, a head clerk, and a head inspector. The directory also names him as one of the two Chinese members of the Council of State. There is also a reference by Sultan Abu Bakar to "our subordinate Tan Yeok Nee"— all of which suggests that the office of Major China was seen as a part of the government.[36] Johore seemed to have followed the Dutch model of instituting the office of Major China and incorporating it into the government structure.[37] As far as can be ascertained, he was the only Chinese appointed to the office of Major China in Malaya, and since Johore already had two kapitans, it is very likely that he was appointed to a higher position above them. While no surviving records indicate his responsibilities, there must have been two aspects to his duties. The first relates to matters within the Chinese community, the settlement of disputes, and the maintenance of law and order. These were not easy tasks, given that the Chinese community was by no means homogeneous and the Major China would need to strike a balance between the interests of his dialect group and that of the whole Chinese community, for which he was responsible.[38] The second relates to matters between the Chinese and the Malay authorities and would have included the enforcement of regulations governing pepper and gambier planting.[39]

Like Tan Kee Soon, Tan Hiok Nee was also a Teochew and a man whom Sultan Abu Bakar trusted. He was a trader and his commercial contacts and diplomatic skills were more suited to the continued prosperity of Johore. Mohamed Salleh bin Perang had been appointed chief of police and policing responsibilities were now carried out by Johore officials. The Ngee Heng had become less an organization of agriculturists and even less an organization of political dissidents; rather, it was becoming an organization of merchants who financed the plantations and operated the profitable revenue farms. The kangchu system was important for Johore's agricultural produce but was even more important for the revenues generated as part of what were called kangchu rights. These rights included not only the right to cultivate land but also the right to operate highly profitable monopolies for the sale of opium, spirits, and pork, and the operation of gambling houses and pawnshops. Revenue farmers, who were often leaders of the Ngee Heng, were granted these kangchu rights and there was keen competition to "farm" any urban area where there was a sizable Chinese population. Chinese sources write of the kangchu in somewhat awestruck terms as "the king of the river" and tend to overlook the exploitation and profiteering from human misery that lay on the underside. As revenues from pepper and gambier gradually declined, revenue farming became the main source of revenue and the kangchu and revenue farmer were locked into one economic system. Tan Hiok Nee was the most important revenue farmer in Johore in addition to the kangchu rights he held in his concessions. Since his various enterprises made him one of the wealthiest men in Johore, it is even possible to deduce that he was one of Sultan Abu Bakar's financiers.[40]

As a consequence of revenue farming, Johore was drawn into the network of revenue farmers who formed powerful syndicates that controlled large blocks of such farms in Malaya and the surrounding region. In 1870 Tan Hiok Nee joined two Singapore merchants, Tan Seng Poh and Cheang Hong Lim, to form what was perhaps the most powerful syndicate of them all, the Great Opium Syndicate, which until the death of Tan Seng Poh in 1879, controlled the combined opium and spirit farms of Johore, Singapore, Melaka, and Riau.[41] Economic advance in Johore, as in other places, rode on the back of revenues raised from human failings, namely gambling and opium.[42] Given the importance of revenue farming in the economy of Johore and its connections with pepper and gambier planting and trade, the relationship between these Singapore merchants and the Ngee Heng is one that needs to be further explored.[43]

With his position as Major China, as head of the Ngee Heng, and as partner in the Great Opium Syndicate, Tan Hiok Nee held in his hands all the levers of wealth and power available to a Chinese. Then, inexplicably, he gave up his connection with Johore, probably in the 1880s after the Great Opium Syndicate came to an end. He retired to Singapore, where his magnificent mansion was completed in 1885.[44] Eventually he returned to China, one of the few migrants who made good overseas and returned to end their days in their native village.

The Declining Years under Lim Ah Siang

Tan Hiok Nee was succeeded by another Teochew, Lim Ah Siang (1853–1917). In Chinese sources, Lim is referred to as the Second Brother, which is the second most senior in rank within the Johore Ngee Heng and the equivalent of vice president in the secret society hierarchy. Perhaps he was second in rank and not first because Tan Hiok Nee was still a towering presence in nearby Singapore. Tan had retired as Major China but, I suspect, one does not retire from a brotherhood. Tan Kee Soon and Tan Hiok Nee had personal relationships with the sultan but Lim Ah Siang is only described as a friend of the Mentri Besar (Chief Minister). He was by no means the most prominent Teochew in Johore at the time. Although Kapitan Tan Cheng Hung had dropped out of sight after selling off his concessions and Kapitan Seah Tee Heng had died in 1884 with no new kapitan having been appointed, the latter's son, Seah Ling Chai, had taken over his father's kangchu concessions, pepper and gambier business, and revenue farms. In addition, he held shares in eight rivers in his own right and was the manager of the Johore Pepper and Gambier Society. Seah Ling Chai was therefore the most prominent towkay in Johore but the Ngee Heng passed him over for an unknown young man. The mostly likely reason was that Tan Hiok Nee was still running the Ngee Heng from Singapore and only needed an assistant, not a business rival in charge. From available documents we see that Lim Ah Siang only began to rise to prominence in the 1890s, after he became head of the Ngee Heng. In 1896 he obtained timber concessions for east Johore and for Endau. By then he was also a revenue farmer for Kota Tinggi and had been granted kangchu rights in his concessions. In Johore Bahru he is best remembered for opening up a kampong at Stulang, in the eastern part of the city, called Kampong Ah Siang and old-timers can still remember the gambling house he built on stilts over the sea.[45]

After the Great Opium Syndicate ended, the opium-farming syndicates passed into the control of different groups of Chinese merchants at different times. For Johore, it meant that the control of its chief source of revenue was in the hands of merchants in Singapore and Penang, a situation the government could not accept with equanimity. In 1886, in a strategy masterminded by the Mentri Besar Dato' Jaafar bin Mohamed, the Johore government, acting through Dato' Jaafar and two Johore Chinese intermediaries, Seah Ling Chai and Seah Jim Kui, bought some shares in the current syndicate.[46] However, this was to last only from 1886 to 1888, after which the Johore farms reverted to the syndicates, as before.

Tan Hiok Nee had withdrawn at a time when Johore was standing at the peak of its progress under the rule of Sultan Abu Bakar. The economy was healthy, with good prices for pepper and gambier, and production continued increasing to meet rising demand in Europe and North America. Plantations continued to be opened up, pushing further eastward toward Sedili, but good prices also attracted other states to embark on plantations, reducing Johore's share of the market.

For the Ngee Heng, however, it was the beginning of the slide downhill. The administrative structure of government was well established and was managed by a core of able and experienced officers led by Dato' Jaafar bin Mohamed. The Johore government was able to provide adequate police protection and its judicial system was able to mediate in disputes so that the power of the Ngee Heng was automatically reduced. The office of Major China no longer had the same significance and Tan Hiok Nee's position was never replaced. Besides, the fate of the Ngee Heng, which was so closely tied to pepper and gambier cultivation, began to decline as the Chinese role in commercial agriculture gradually diminished with the diversification of the economy. Coffee was introduced in 1881 and enjoyed some initial success. But the chief significance of coffee planting was that it marked the entry of European plantations into Johore. The rise of rubber planting in the early twentieth century was accompanied by drastic falls in the prices of pepper and gambier, so that rubber was to become the main commercial crop. The end of pepper and gambier planting finally came in 1917, when the Kangchu Rights (Abolition) Enactment abolished the kangchu system.

The Suppression

British officials had pressed for legislation to suppress the secret societies and in 1869 they succeeded in enacting the Dangerous Society Ordinance. However, it was limited in its effectiveness as it only gave the government powers to register but not to suppress the brotherhoods. Possibly the attempt on Chinese Protector W. A. Pickering's life in his own office, by a Teochew carpenter instigated by the Ghi Hok, finally shook the government to action. As a start, the 1869 ordinance was amended in 1882 to give it more bite by allowing the registrar of societies to refuse to register a society. However, it was only in 1890 that suppression came with the enactment of the Societies Ordinance, after which similar legislation was adopted in the Malay states, except in Johore. When Governor Sir Cecil Clementi Smith asked Sultan Abu Bakar to follow suit, his reply in 1891 was a defense of the Ngee Heng and his policy. The Ngee Heng, the sultan said, was "a recognized institution established under his patronage." It was permitted to function on the conditions that

- it was the only Chinese society to be permitted in Johore;
- it was to be a friendly society;
- it would be responsible for the behavior of its members individually and collectively;

- all Chinese should be eligible as members;
- all Kapitan Chinas and kangchus must become members.

Although the Ngee Heng was initially a Teochew organization, it was required to accept all Chinese, and in this way the Chinese were integrated into one system of control and brought under the sultan's patronage, as he had declared. In effect it became the sultan's agent in the task of controlling a large immigrant population. The Ngee Heng, he told Sir Cecil, was under the direct control of the government and under his protection, and one that had been of "vast use and benefit to my Chinese population." The sultan therefore resisted suppression and told the governor, "I do not agree with you that it is always to the advantage of a State to suppress them."[47]

Sir Cecil tried again in 1892, this time conveying two resolutions passed by the Chinese Advisory Board in Singapore, one of which pertained to the suppression of secret societies. In reply, the sultan wrote, "I am still of the opinion that the existence of this Society in its present form is a guarantee of the peace and good behavior of the greater bulk of the Chinese population of my country."[48] However, Sultan Abu Bakar was able to delay, but not prevent, the inevitable. He died in 1895 and in 1910 his son Sultan Ibrahim was prevailed upon to accept a general Advisor (equivalent to British advisor). British officials were anxious to bring Johore in line with British policy in the other Malay states. By 1914 a Chinese protectorate had been set up and D. G. Campbell, the general advisor, stated in the *Johore Annual Report 1914* that secret societies had been the cause of much disturbance and crime and that in the absence of an officer expert in Chinese language and customs, the government was frequently obliged to seek the assistance of the Ngee Heng for the suppression of other secret societies and for the detection of crime and the arrest of criminals. He added in the same report, "The time has however now come when the Government should attempt to deal with these societies directly and not through an unofficial Chinese organization, and I hope that during the current year a new policy may be initiated."

The new policy was not long in coming. In 1915 the Societies Enactment was passed and the *Johore Annual Report 1916* carried a brief statement: "The largest Chinese Society, the Ngi Hin, was dissolved during the year without trouble." Lim Ah Siang's final duty for the Ngee Heng was to sign a bond for $30,000 for the winding up of the Kongsi, which was required for the settlement of the Ngee Heng's liabilities and the disposal of its properties.[49]

The Legacy

Even though the Ngee Heng Kongsi first took root in Tebrau, it is in Johore Bahru that its legacy is most visible. Tan Hiok Nee and Lim Ah Siang, the kapitans and the kangchus, were leaders of the community in the traditional mold. They took the lead in providing for the welfare of the community—they built schools and temples, maintained cemeteries, provided for the sick and indigent, and donated generously for these purposes. In the same way, the Ngee Heng Kongsi functioned like a traditional social organization and was active in providing for the social and religious needs of the Chinese. It promoted the building of the Ancient Temple of Johore (Roufu Gumiao) and also established a cemetery on the land around their lodge, which is still popularly referred to as Kongsi Shan (Kongsi cemetery). In 1913 its leaders joined with other Chinese to found the Foon Yew School, with Wong Ah Fook as chairman and Lim Ah Siang as his deputy.[50] Some of the institutions the Ngee Heng founded still exist today.

Lim Ah Siang died soon after executing the bond and it was his successor, Lin Jin He, who had to manage the disposal of the Ngee Heng's assets.[51] Lin spent $5,000 on building a tomb not far from their lodge, into which the leaders of the Ngee Heng deposited all their ritual and sacred objects, including their ancestral tablets. The tombstone carries only two characters, Ming Mu, meaning Ming Tomb. The ancestral tablets and the words on the tombstone are a throwback to the Tiandihui's founding myth, to the monks who died in the burning of the Shaolin temple, and to the survivors' aim of restoring the Ming. The balance of the $30,000 was donated to Foon

Yew School to establish an endowment fund. A condition of the donation was that the school would perform rituals of ancestor worship at the Ming Tomb during *Qingming*, the annual festival of remembrance. A contemporary account of this event has been written by Wong Hei Chor, the first secretary of the school committee, as part of the history of the school.[52] Foon Yew is the only Chinese school in Johore Bahru and has now grown to comprise six campuses serving a total elementary and middle school enrollment of more than twenty thousand. Generations of students who have passed through the school are familiar with this part of the school's history and carry with them a memory of the Ngee Heng.

Ever since, this ritual of remembrance has been faithfully carried out. Once every year for more than eighty years, senior members of the Chinese community have gathered at this symbolic tomb to honor a promise made when a secret society was proscribed. I was with Carl Trocki in 1985 when he observed one of these occasions. He has written about this "forlorn spot" in the overgrown grass.[53] I attended the Qingming ceremony at the Ming Tomb again in 1999 and found the place much changed. A paved road had been constructed and the surroundings landscaped and attractively planted with trees and shrubs. The attendance this time was even more impressive than that in 1985. It included the chairman and members of the Foon Yew School Committee and its headmaster as well as the president of the Chinese Association of Johore Bahru and the presidents of the five *bang* associations, currently the key traditional organizations of the Chinese community in Johore Bahru.

The Chinese Association of Johore Bahru was the organization the Chinese founded after the Ngee Heng was suppressed. Contrary to the British attitude, the Ngee Heng was perceived by the Chinese to represent the needs and interests of the community as a whole. Even today, Chinese opinion views its suppression as a matter of British policy. In 1922, to fill the gap left by its demise, Lin Jin He, the last head of the Ngee Heng, led other Chinese in founding the Chinese Association of Johore Bahru.[54] After World War II, Wong Shee Fun, one of the founders, revived the association and emerged as its new leader.[55] One of his first tasks was to arrange for the purchase of land and the construction of its present building. Active at both the national and state levels, Wong led the association to a larger view of its responsibilities. For example, it encouraged Chinese to apply for citizenship when Malaya achieved independence. The association maintains an active interest in traditional areas of Chinese concern such as education, religion, and culture, apart from organizing seminars and discussions on contemporary affairs for public education. One of the association's most important public services is to act as a registry of Chinese marriages.

The term *bang* refers to subethnic identities among the Chinese and the five bang associations in Johore Bahru referred to earlier cater to the five main subethnic groups in the state. There are a few other traditional social organizations but they do not have the same weight in the social life of the community:

Guangzhou Huiguan (est. 1878) for the Cantonese
Qiangzhou Huiguan (est. 1883) for the Hainanese
Fujian Huiguan (est. 1920) for the Hokkien
Tongyuan She (est. 1927) for the Hakka
Teochew Eight Districts Association (est. 1934) for the Teochew

Each of the above is an independent organization, and the Chinese Association of Johore Bahru is not a federal entity. The latter draws its leadership from the bang associations, and there is a healthy movement of people between the Chinese Association and the bang associations, with an implicit rotation of leadership. They cooperate closely with each other and appear to have a good understanding of what falls within their respective jurisdictions. The bang associations are proud of their close-knit relationship, the *wu bang jingsheng* (spirit of the five bangs), which allows them to assist and support each other but still retain their separate identities. This spirit of cooperation between the various bangs is another legacy that can be traced back to the Ngee Heng.

The Ancient Temple of Johore Bahru dates from the 1860s and is the oldest Chinese building in the city. Despite recent renovations, the temple is a small, modest structure. Although the Johore Chinese population in the nineteenth century was predominantly Teochew, it is a tribute to the wisdom of Tan Hiok Nee and other Teochew leaders that the temple was intended as, and remains, a center of worship for the entire Chinese community. It does so by honoring the patron deities of the five bangs. Johore Chinese have avoided the pitfalls of other Chinese communities, such as those in Penang and Singapore, where the various bangs attended different schools, worshipped at different temples, and were buried in different cemeteries.

The spirit of bang unity is most evident during the procession that is held every year in Johore Bahru as part of the Chinese New Year celebrations, a three-day affair that is both a carnival and a religious event. The participants include all kinds of cultural bodies and commercial and industrial establishments. I was informed that the procession has been going on annually for more than a hundred years. It must therefore have started in the days of the Ngee Heng. It is managed by the Ancient Temple Committee, a subcommittee of the Chinese Association, and is assisted by the bang associations, each of which is responsible for its respective section of the procession. All participants are required to come under the auspices of one of the bang associations and there is great keenness to participate to win the favor of the gods. For the participants, it has the atmosphere of a family picnic and is definitely a community affair through which the younger generation is socialized into the traditions and beliefs of the community.

The Ngee Heng Kongsi lives on in the public awareness through the streets and public spaces that carry its name or the names of its leaders. It also lives on in local cultural awareness, not only in the school it nurtured, the temple it built, and the successor association its leaders founded, but more importantly, in the traditions it laid down and the goodwill it fostered. The Ngee Heng's organization, from the Major China, the kapitans, and the kangchus down to the cultivators, has become an integral part of history of the Chinese in Johore. The adventurous spirit and rugged determination needed to turn the jungle to productive use is admired. The pioneering planters have become the founding myth of the Johore Chinese. As an informant said to me, "Forget the opium, remember the development."

The history of the Ngee Heng thus provides a strong sense of continuity to the early agriculturists, who are credited as having helped to make Johore what it is today. Running through this narrative also is the theme of connectedness, between past and present, between rural and center, between Chinese and Chinese, and last but not least, between Chinese and Malay. The history of the Ngee Heng under its three leaders corresponds to the history of the Chinese under Johore's first three rulers, showing a continuous process of negotiation and accommodation on both sides. Local history provides a useful means of studying Malay-Chinese relations on the ground, investigating local particularities, and revealing the multiplicity and variation in this complex topic.

Notes

1. This ritual has been described in Carl A. Trocki, *Opium and Empire: Chinese Society in Colonial Singapore, 1800–1910* (Ithaca: Cornell University Press, 1990), 7.

2. I have used the Hanyu Pinyin system of spelling for Chinese characters except for local terms and proper names, for which the commonly used spelling is preferred.

3. For the period under discussion, Johore was a state in Malaya, a British protectorate comprising the Malay Peninsula and Singapore. Since 1963, it has been one of the states of the federation of Malaysia.

4. See "War and Ambivalence: Monuments and Memorials in Johor" in *War and Memory in Malaysia and Singapore*, ed. P. Lim Pui Huen and Diana Wong, 139–59 (Singapore: Institute of Southeast Asian Studies, 2000).

5. "Past and Present Juxtaposed: The Chinese of Nineteenth-Century Johor," *Sojourn* 13 (1998): 114–38.

6. For nineteenth-century works see W. C. Milne, "Some Account of a Secret Association in China, Entitled the Triad Society," *Transactions of the Royal Asiatic Society* 1, 2 (1826): 240–50; Gustave Schlegel, *The Hung League; or, Heaven-Earth-League: A Secret Society with the Chinese in China and India* (Batavia, 1866); W. A. Pickering's two papers in the *Journal of the Straits*

Branch of the Royal Asiatic Society: "Chinese Secret Societies," 3 (1879): 1–18, and "Chinese Secret Societies and Their Origin," 1 (1878): 63–84. Schlegel's book was the authority until the appearance of J. S. M. Ward and W. G. Stirling, *The Hung Society; or, The Society of Heaven and Earth,* 3 vols. (London: Baskerville Press, 1926; New York: AMS Press, 1973 reprint, 1925). Books by former police officers are M. L. Wynne, *Triad and Tabut: A Survey of the Origin and Diffusion of Chinese and Mohamedan Secret Societies in the Malay Peninsula, A.D. 1800–1935* (Singapore: Government Printing Office, 1941); and Leonard Comber, *Chinese Secret Societies in Malaya: A Survey of the Triad Society from 1800 to 1900* (New York: Association for Asian Studies, 1959). For a study by a former secretary for Chinese affairs, Federation of Malaya, see Wilfred Blythe, *The Impact of Chinese Secret Societies in Malaya: A Historical Study* (London: Oxford University Press, 1969). Secret societies were also given prominence in well-known books on the Chinese, such as J. D. Vaughan, *The Manners and Customs of the Chinese of the Straits Settlements* (Singapore, 1879; repr., Kuala Lumpur: Oxford University Press, 1977) and Victor Purcell, *The Chinese in Malaya* (London, 1948; repr., Kuala Lumpur: Oxford University Press, 1967).

7. Mak Lau Fong, *The Sociology of Secret Societies: A Study of Secret Societies in Singapore and Peninsular Malaysia* (Kuala Lumpur: Oxford University Press, 1981).

8. David Ownby, *Brotherhoods and Secret Societies in Early and Mid-Qing China: The Formation of a Tradition* (Stanford: Stanford University Press, 1996).

9. David Ownby and Mary Somers Heidhues, ed., *"Secret Societies" Reconsidered: Perspectives on the Social History of Early Modern South China and Southeast Asia* (Armonk, N.Y.: M. E. Sharpe, 1993).

10. Blythe, *Chinese Secret Societies,* 20. The significance of the adoptive surname can be seen in the fact that this character is printed in the center of many secret society documents.

11. Schlegel, *Hung League,* 12.

12. Ward and Stirling, *Hung Society,* 1:7.

13. Mahani Musa, "Malays and the Red and White Flag Societies in Penang, 1830s–1920s," *Journal of the Malaysian Branch Royal Asiatic Society* 72, 2 (1999): 151–82. See also Ward and Stirling, *Hung Society,* 1:137; and Purcell, *Chinese in Malaya,* 108.

14. Purcell tells us that in 1825, the secret societies' forces comprised three hundred boats, fifteen thousand Siamese, a thousand Chinese and eight thousand Malays—enough that Governor Fullerton felt they posed a potential threat to Penang. Purcell, *Chinese in Malaya,* 156.

15. The revenue farm was an administrative device by which the

government leased out the monopoly of collecting revenue on certain commodities (e.g., opium) and services (e.g., gambling).

16. Some scholars characterize these disturbances as manifestations of a class struggle. See Carl A. Trocki, "The Rise and Fall of the Ngee Heng Kongsi in Singapore," in Ownby and Heidhues, *"Secret Societies" Reconsidered,* 93.

17. Carl A. Trocki, *The Prince of Pirates: The Temenggongs and the Development of Johor and Singapore, 1784–1885* (Singapore: Singapore University Press, 1979), and "Ngee Heng Kongsi," 89.

18. I shall refer to the Johore brotherhood as the Ngee Heng, using the Teochew form of the name by which it is known locally, and to the brotherhoods in other parts of Malaya as the Ghi Hin, using the Hokkien form by which they are usually referred.

19. Wang Tai Peng, *The Origins of the Chinese Kongsi* (Petaling Jaya: Pelanduk, 1994).

20. Sultan Ali was the son of Sultan Hussein, signatory to the treaty establishing Singapore as a British settlement. Under the treaty of 1855, he attained the title of sultan, but the sovereignty of Johore was transferred to Temenggong Daing Ibrahim.

21. Munshi Abdullah bin Abdul Kadir, "The Hikayat Abdullah," trans. A. H. Hill, *Journal of the Malayan Branch Royal Asiatic Society* 28, 2 (1955): 180.

22. In 1846 Tan Tek Hye, "Keeper of the Quinquangular Seal," published a letter in the *Singapore Free Press* stating that the Ngee Heng had commanded four thousand of its members to relocate to Johore. See Trocki, *Prince of Pirates,* 101.

23. Lee Xing, "Roufu Chaoqiao Gaikuang" (The Teochews in Johore), in *Malaiya Chaoqiao tongjian,* ed. Pan Xing Nong (Singapore: Teochew Eight Districts Association, 1950), 42–43.

24. When Sultan Abu Bakar succeeded his father, he was known by the title Temenggong Sri Maharaja, which was not a royal title. In 1868 he adopted the title maharaja, and in 1885 he attained the title of sultan through a treaty negotiated with Britain. To avoid confusion, I have referred to him as Sultan Abu Bakar throughout.

25. Ke Mu Lin, *Sinhua lishi renwu liezhuan* (Biographical dictionary of the Chinese in Singapore) (Singapore: Singapore Federation of Chinese Clan Associations, 1995), 70. The term *yishi* was attached to many Ngee Heng/Ghi Hin personalities, as can be seen in David K. Y. Chng's study of the spirit tablets of its leaders. He identifies the Ghi Hin leaders as "Ming Loyalists," and lists Tan Kee Soon among those holding the rank of Hou Ming, which he translates as "Serving the Ming." See David K. Y. Chng, *Heroic Images of Ming Loyalists: A Study of the Spirit Tablets of the Ghee Hin*

Kongsi Leaders in Singapore (Singapore: Singapore Association of Asian Studies, 1999), 16.

26. Translation from Trocki, *Prince of Pirates*, 104.

27. R. O. Winstedt, *A History of Johore, 1365–1895* (Kuala Lumpur: Malaysian Branch of the Royal Asiatic Society, 1979), 113.

28. Huang Jian Cheng, "Zaonian Kaipi ji Jianshe Xinshan Yougong Huaren Xianxian" (Early Pioneers and Notable Chinese who have contributed to developing Johore) in 40th Anniversary Commemorative Editorial Committee, *Roufuzhou Zhonghua Zonghui sishi zhounian jinian tekan* (Johore Bahru, 1988), 132.

29. There are two aspects to the authority they exercised. On the one hand, the brotherhoods did operate under a certain moral code. Absolute loyalty was of course the cardinal virtue, but respect for each other's women, for example, was another. On the other hand, fear was probably a more significant control factor as brutality was never far from the surface.

30. For a personal account of the war, see Mohamed Salleh bin Perang, *Reputations Live On: An Early Malay Autobiography,* ed. Amin Sweeney (Berkeley: University of California Press, 1980), 89–95.

31. Comber, for example, has pointed out that the role of Yap Ah Loy is not mentioned in accounts of the Selangor War by R. O. Winstedt, "A History of Selangor," *Journal of Malaysian Branch Royal Asiatic Society* 14, 3 (1934): 1–34, 112–14; R. J. Wilkinson, *A History of the Peninsular Malays, with chapters on Perak and Selangor*, 3rd ed. (Singapore: Kelly and Walsh, 1923; and W. Linehan, *A History of Pahang* (Kuala Lumpur: Malaysian Branch Royal Asiatic Society, 1973).

32. Daing Ibrahim to Cavenagh, 4 Oct. 1859, in Letterbook of HH Maharajah of Johore, 1855–65.

33. General Adviser series, GA 275/1913, 276/1913, 278/1913, and 555/1914. Although the edict itself has not been traced, these court records document cases in which the edict was invoked to charge the accused with starting a secret society. Clearly, official recognition of the Ngee Heng did not discourage other brotherhoods from trying to edge in.

34. A. E. Coope, "The Kangchu System in Johore," *Journal of the Malayan Branch of the Royal Asiatic Society* 14, 3 (1936): 253.

35. Song gives his name as Tan Yeok Nee. Song Ong Siang, *One Hundred Years' History of the Chinese in Singapore* (Singapore: University of Malaya Press, 1967), 335.

36. Buku Salinan Surat-surat Maharajah (Transcript of the Letterbook of H.H. The Maharajah of Johore, 1855–65), 248; Johore Archives, National Archives of Malaysia, Johore/Melaka Branch (JA/NAM).

37. The Dutch appointed three ranks of Chinese officers in the colonial

administration—lieutenant, captain, and major—with different levels of responsibilities. See Mona Lohanda, *The Kapitan Cina of Batavia, 1837–1942* (Jakarta: Djambatan, 1996).

38. Yen Ching-hwang, *A Social History of the Chinese in Singapore and Malaya, 1800–1911* (Singapore: Oxford University Press, 1986), 126.

39. The kangchu regulations as described by Coope contain eighty-one clauses. Coope, "Kangchu System," 247–63.

40. In 1863, during the height of the civil war in Pahang in which Sultan Abu Bakar was actively involved, Tan Hiok Nee obtained concessions to four rivers within a one-week period. See Trocki, *Prince of Pirates*, 125.

41. Carl A. Trocki, *Opium and Empire: Chinese Society in Colonial Singapore, 1800–1910* (Ithaca: Cornell University Press, 1990), chs. 5 and 6, describes these syndicates in great detail.

42. Between 1883 and 1914, for example, the annual rent for the Singapore opium farm formed about half the total revenue; in some years it was as high as two-thirds. See Trocki, *Opium and Empire*, 188.

43. I am grateful to Carl A. Trocki for this information. For a discussion on the involvement of Singapore merchants in Johore trade and the dispute between these merchants and Sultan Abu Bakar, see C. M. Turnbull, "The Johore Gambier and Pepper Trade in the Mid-Nineteenth Century," *Journal of the South Seas Society* 15, 1 (1959): 43–55.

44. The building has been designated a national monument, as it is the only surviving building of its kind in Singapore.

45. General Adviser series, GA 82/1911.

46. Trocki, *Opium and Empire*, 151, 192; P. Lim Pui Huen, *Wong Ah Fook, Immigrant and Entrepreneur,* Singapore: Times Media, 2002.

47. Khoo Kay Kim, "Johor's Friendly Secret Societies," *Sunday Star,* 20 April 1997.

48. State Secretariat Letterbook, no. 256, 23 June 1892.

48. State Secretary series, SS 563/1916.

49. Wong Ah Fook was a builder and revenue farmer. He was a Cantonese and, so far as can be ascertained, was not a member of the Ngee Heng. See P. Lim Pui Huen, *Wong Ah Fook.*

50. Lim Jin He was a kangchu. See Wu Hua, *Roufuzhou xinshan huazu huiguan zhi* (History of Chinese associations in Johore) (Singapore: Association of Southeast Asian Studies, 1977), 5.

51. Wong Hei Chor, "Kuanrou Xuexiao Sishiliu Nian Shilue" (Foon Yew School: A forty-six-year sketch) in the 50th anniversary commemoration volume of the Foon Yew School (Johore Bahru, 1963), 9–10. Wong was a Cantonese, a leader of the Guangzhou Huiguan, and one of the founders of the Chinese Association of Johore Bahru. See Wu, *Roufuzhou,* 5.

52. Trocki, *Opium and Empire*, 7.

53. Its name in Chinese was originally Roufu Huaqiao Gongsuo (Johore Overseas Chinese Office). After World War II it was revived in 1946 with the name Xinshanqu Zhonghua Gonghui (Johore Bahru District Chinese Association). About 1948 this was changed to Xinshan Zhonghua Gonghui (Johore Bahru Chinese Association). See Wu, *Roufuzhou*, 5–6.

54. Wong Shee Fun was a Cantonese entrepreneur, banker, politician, and philanthropist. He held leadership positions in many Chinese organizations in both Malaysia and Singapore. In Johore he was a member of the Council of State, chairman of the Board of Governors of Foon Yew School, and president of the Johore Bahru Chinese Association as well as the national Federation of Chinese Associations. He was founder-president of the Malaysian Chinese Association (the Chinese component party in the Malaysian government) in Johore and was its national treasurer for eleven years.

Chapter 14

MIGRANTS IN CONTEMPORARY VIETNAMESE HISTORY

Marginal or Mainstream?

Andrew Hardy

Mr. Tuan was born in Hanoi in the mid-1930s. He was still living there in 1992, when I first met him. But as I got to know him, I discovered that the same was not true for other members of his family. When the Geneva Agreements were signed in 1954, dividing Vietnam into north and south, most of his relatives chose to leave the capital of what had been French Indochina and take their wealth and expertise south to Saigon. Tuan was then studying at university and decided to stay behind. He now receives periodic visits from his relatives, when they fly over from California, where they settled after the war ended, in 1975. He himself expressed no desire to go to America.

This chapter explores an approach to the history of Vietnam whereby choices of historically marginal people like Tuan and his family allow us to chart social, political, and economic changes. Scholars familiar with conventional histories will know many of these changes. The purpose of this approach is to look at the changes from a new perspective, that of people without a defined role in the nation's history but who were nevertheless affected in ways decisive to their everyday lives. In this contemporary history of Vietnam, events in Hanoi, Saigon, Paris, Washington, Moscow, Beijing, Geneva, and other world capitals are relegated to the background. Focus is turned instead on people like Tuan—ordinary people confronted with dramatic life choices by historical events. It is turned also on people living in the margins, in places and contexts like that related by one writer, in an account of his childhood in Phuoc Giang village, in south-central Vietnam. He writes here about the situation in 1954:

> Nobody thought much at all about the division of the country into North and South. In Phuoc Giang, no one ever talked about Hanoi or Saigon, the two great cities. They never even talked about Hue, which was the old capital in the center. As far as I was concerned, Tuy Hoa was the biggest city that had any reality. People talked a lot about Tuy Hoa, but who ever went there? It was fifteen miles away, a long day's walk.[1]

Whether they talked about such far-off places or not, things that happened there affected inhabitants of villages like Phuoc Giang throughout Vietnam. And they happened in ways that, very often, provoked a move.

There are other techniques by which experiences may be analyzed reflectively, as a tool, that is, for casting light from the personal back onto the historical. Duong Van Mai Elliott recently showed, in an account of the experiences of her relatives, how effectively a family history could achieve this.[2] Many of the family events described in Elliott's book involved a move. In Vietnam movements of population, in some cases very substantial ones, accompanied major political and economic changes. In most histories these movements warrant a paragraph or a page. For many people, however, they constituted major events. A focus on these acts of departure, travel, and arrival—at a national level perhaps insignificant events, but nonetheless of tremendous significance for those individuals involved—offers a new approach to history, particularly well adapted to Vietnam. Many ordinary people's decisions were politically motivated; as one commentator noted, "Vietnamese are political animals to a greater degree than Americans: their recent history has forced them to be."[3] And even those springing from more social or economic influences allow us to reflect on matters of broader political import. In Vietnam this perspective is of peculiar, and often painful, appropriateness.

The point I wish to make is that migration highlights people's dilemmas and decisions in response to the historical situations unfolding around them. In 1954, as the Viet Minh moved to fulfill the terms of the Geneva Agreements, occupying the northern half of Vietnam, Tuan's family chose to move south. In 1975, as the South Vietnamese regime collapsed, the family chose to move again, this time to the United States. Tuan opted to stay put. What do the respective decisions of these members of a single family offer in terms of historical insight?

Migration and Choice

A major focus of this approach is on choice. David Chanoff and Doan Van Toai underline the importance of choice in their collection of oral accounts of the Vietnam War. For Americans, they note, the war was a difficult experience, requiring moral choices about whether "to support it or not, to fight or not." But the authors contrast the relatively limited impact of American choices, both in terms of extent and of time, with the experience of Vietnamese.

> For Vietnamese the war was vastly more complex—a maelstrom in which the contending tides of colonialism and liberation, communism and nationalism clashed violently and mixed treacherously. Some Vietnamese found a fixed moral star to guide their actions; others switched allegiance more than once from one phase to another. More were simply pawns of their times. But even the pawns often made decisions.[4]

These decisions could be based on idealism, economic or social interest, the will for survival, or a youthful desire for adventure. They were not made in a vacuum, independent of a socioeconomic environment. Indeed, one of the strengths of this approach is the recognition of the primacy of people's personal interests, of which the most important was often simply making ends meet:

In revolutionary Vietnam, as everywhere, the need to earn a living, to support families and raise children, absorbed most of the attention and energy of most of the people. The propaganda picture of militant village associations devoting themselves to revolutionary "struggle" had some truth to it. But the larger truth is that most Vietnamese paid outward allegiance to whoever held the whip hand and kept their inner allegiance for themselves, their families, and their work.[5]

People make decisions all the time, of course, most of which are related to the minutiae of everyday life. Some of them may also be related to events narrowly understood as historical. But decisions become particularly significant when they come to involve a change in place of residence, for most people a rather important occurrence in their lives. Decisions to move very often become landmark events, turning points people remember and can date years later. In many cases they mark the point at which, in a given situation, strategies aimed at maintaining an "inner allegiance" became untenable. And it is at this conjuncture that we can start speaking about a history from below. For decisions to move commonly reflected changes in political, socioeconomic, or military environments that affected not only those who made the decision to move, but also many other people at the time. Many of these others might have reacted in ways other than a migration. They might have accepted inconveniences, poverty, changes in lifestyles or socioeconomic status, imprisonment, and starvation. They might have resisted change by joining a local political organization, committing suicide, or simply dragging their feet and harboring an inward resentment. But changes often did provoke migration, and the experiences of the migrants inform us as well about the experiences of those who did not move.

The reasons why some people did not move indeed fall within the orbit of this approach, offering structural and psychological perspectives on the society in which they lived. We might ask why, for example, many people chose not to leave their famine-stricken village in the Red River Delta in the spring of 1945. Why did they choose not to beg for food, but preferred instead to select "a spot to lie down and await death, hoping someone there might grant them a decent burial," a question David G. Marr raises in his account of the Vietnamese revolution.[6] We might equally inquire as to the effect of the Hanoi government's use of a household registration policy throughout North Vietnam after 1959 to restrict uncontrolled migration on both the risks people felt they could take and the larger question of social organization at the time. To what extent did membership in a cooperative or employment at a factory—the administrative link between livelihood and residence in a certain place—affect the choices ordinary people made? Decisions not to move, like Tuan's, might be clear-cut responses to specific historical situations. They might, on the other hand, be the result of administrative barriers. Or they could stem from inertia, confusion, procrastination, and lost opportunity. In all these contexts, such decisions tell us much about the political and socioeconomic environments at particular points in time. The more so when they are contrasted with other people's decisions to leave.

Decisions were very often difficult. Their difficulty and above all their fragile basis on uncertain information and one-dimensional perceptions, as well as the need to provide for families, emerges vividly from Elliott's account. She writes of her family's experiences, in early 1947, as refugees from the fighting in Hanoi:

> At this time, my parents still did not have any news of my brothers and sisters in Hanoi. Added to this constant worry, they had to figure out how to keep us fed from day to day. At that moment, our future looked extremely bleak. Considering my parents' fear of the Viet Minh, following them [her sister and brother-in-law] into the safe mountain zone was out of the question. And yet we could not wander around as refugees for much longer, because we were running out of the money my parents had borrowed from relatives. The only alternative was to return to Hanoi. But at that point, my parents did not know whether it was safe to go back, or whether we even had a house to go back to. If, however, we stayed in Ngoc Dong, the war might overtake us again and force us to flee to another village, further and further away from home.[7]

Earlier in their itinerary, the family was offered the chance to move to a relative's farm. This, again, was no easy decision, and gave rise to discussion within the family:

At that time, Uncle Trinh decided to leave Van Dinh to take refuge in Bac Giang Province, where he had bought rice fields and an orange grove. Before leaving Van Dinh, Uncle Trinh told my father, "Why don't you and your family come with us? We don't have money, but we have the rice fields, and we'll have rice to eat. We'll share whatever the land can produce." But when my father mentioned this to my mother, she rejected the offer. She did not want to move further away from Hanoi, where my brothers and sisters might still be alive. It turned out to be a good decision, because Uncle Trinh got stuck in Bac Giang, which later on became a Viet Minh stronghold. He and his family endured a lot of hardships, and eventually paid dearly for opting to return to his land.[8]

The double focus implied in this story, on migration and nonmigration, enables us to take a nuanced perspective on the dynamics of decision making; a perspective that is particularly apt when one begins to speak of refugees and forced migration. In the above story, both those who moved and those who stayed exercised a power of choice and an analysis of risk. Hindsight allows us to assess the risks they chose to take, but those choices were made in situations of extreme uncertainty. With families split, political calculations pressing, and food a constant worry, the experience was one of dilemma.

Vietnam's recent history has hardly been short of such choices. Perhaps the best-known instances are associated with the movement of the boat people after 1975. International attention paid to this problem makes it a particularly fruitful area of inquiry, as its solution occasioned institutional decisions around the world that, in turn, allow us to reflect on those made by individuals and families within Vietnam. Chan Kwok Bun has drawn attention to the changes in attitude of the authorities in Hong Kong toward the exodus from Vietnam. Over a period of ten years, the administration of an asylum policy became gradually less acceptable and growing compassion fatigue culminated in the institution in 1988 of a screening procedure, intended to distinguish "genuine" refugees from economic migrants. Certainly, the people leaving Vietnam in 1987 differed, in regional and political background, from those who left a decade earlier. Nonetheless, an individual considered in the late seventies to be a refugee, one forced to flee, was redefined a decade later as a free migrant, exercising choice.[9]

To make this point clearer, it is better to redefine our terms. Even those people considered by a bureaucratic process to be refugees, with a legitimate cause for fear of ill treatment in their place of departure, should not in the final analysis be regarded as forced migrants. In order to demonstrate the importance of looking at degrees of force, to create conceptual space for the notion of impulsion, Graeme Hugo and Chan Kwok Bun cite Speare's one-dimensional definition of forced migration:

> In the strictest sense migration can be considered to be involuntary only when a person is physically transported from a country and has no opportunity to escape from those transporting him. Movement under threat, even the immediate threat to life, contains a voluntary element, as long as there is an option to escape to another part of the country, go into hiding or to remain and hope to escape persecution.[10]

The scene described by journalist Wilfred Burchett at the Vietnam-China border in 1979 illustrates the usefulness of the conceptual space offered by Speare's approach for the understanding of human decision making. Burchett describes a conversation with a Vietnamese military officer who "spoke of the distressing scenes to which he had been witness during the previous months as Hoa refugees piled up in the area, awaiting their turn to cross into China. 'There were tearful farewell scenes between family members leaving and those who had decided to stay, each trying to persuade the other to change their minds.'"[11] These scenes are reported in the tense circumstances of imminent war between the two countries and unmistakable signals from the Vietnamese government to residents of Chinese origin (Hoa) that it was no longer responsible for their safety. We may legitimately wonder whether the scenes actually took place, given the Vietnamese officer's likely desire to present this migration in terms of free choice and communist sympathizer Burchett's desire to listen. Nevertheless, while many Hoa people decided to leave, by land or by sea, some opted to stay.

Moments and Momentums

How, in terms of time, did personal decisions interact with events of broader significance? The study of choice and migration in Vietnam certainly fits some of the traditional periodicities of its history, as some of the above examples suggest. The major changes in the country's political and economic evolution since 1945 impinged, directly or indirectly, on people's lives in ways that confronted them with choices. In political terms, the importance of the dates 1945, 1954, 1975, and 1979 in Vietnam's recent past is undeniable. These dates correspond to turning points in revolution, war, and civil administration. They were accompanied immediately by events of migration, and their later consequences also affected many people's place of residence. In addition, in those parts of Vietnam governed from Hanoi, two watershed dates emerge corresponding to the announcement of major new policy lines on economic development: 1960 (Third Party Congress) and 1986 (Sixth Party Congress). The latter dates, however, offer less clear cut periodizations, as the economic changes legislated, particularly at the 1986 congress, took root several years before and can be seen in terms of interaction with initiatives from below.

The process of economic transition ratified at the 1986 congress is especially illustrative of the problem of historical time. It is tempting for observers of Vietnam's recent economic history to mark 1986 as the defining date of change, the key moment in the liberalization process known as Doi Moi (renovation). The transitional nature of that change, however, which has been clearly demonstrated in recent studies, belies such rigid periodization.[12] Changes in migration practice that took place during the eighties reinforce these conclusions. Observations of decisions and movements made by many migrants indicate that they operated outside state parameters for years before Doi Moi facilitated such behavior.[13]

Events of military significance were accompanied by migrations, which spilled over into the time not only after, but also immediately before, the event. Duong Van Mai Elliott relates her father's anticipation of the outbreak of hostilities on 19 December 1946:

My family had evacuated to Van Dinh [forty miles south of Hanoi] weeks before, after my father had decided fighting was imminent. We packed up and left for what he believed would be a short stay. He thought that it would take the French just a few days to overcome the fledgling Viet Minh force; then things would be calm again, and we would be able to return home. My brothers Giu and Xuong did not go with us. They knew that there was going to be war and were eager to be part of the action.[14]

These examples emphasize the dangers implicit within chronologically structured history. But as noted above, traditional periodizations of Vietnamese history do bear considerable meaning, and by no means all were transitional or easily anticipated. We should thus bear in mind that each period of time had its own momentum in terms of state policy, as well as individual experience and psychology. Some people anticipated situations of change. Change also had a defining influence on their subsequent situations. Most French, American, and other foreigners—even those closely involved in Vietnam during the different periods of its recent history—spent only a few years in Vietnam. But Vietnamese people lived through these periods, and most of them experienced one change after another without leaving the country. In this analysis, therefore, events and energies discussed in a particular chronological framework are seen in terms of moments, each with its own momentum.

Choices and Their Consequences

Our appreciation of historical momentum is sharpened when the analysis is extended to consider the consequences of choices people made. We now return to the story of Tuan and his family, of which we have so far seen only the basic decisions to migrate or not to migrate. After 1954 Tuan's family members settled in Saigon, where they found themselves members of a powerful elite made up of intellectuals and capitalists from the north. By their very migration they had declared themselves opponents of communism and were adopted as such by Ngo Dinh Diem, becoming closely associated with the

South Vietnamese government. After the communist victory in 1975, these associations impelled them to choose a second migration, this time overseas. Meanwhile, Tuan himself experienced some of the consequences not only of his own, but also of their, decisions. In Hanoi after 1954 he was regarded with the suspicion reserved for one whose relatives had decided to reject rule by the independent communist government, exchanging it instead for life under a regime still regarded as colonial. And after 1975, when the same relatives settled in the United States, he certainly did not throw off that suspicion. But he did become a member of the new economic "elite" within Vietnam, made up of those people with relatives abroad who sent back money and goods, giving them a purchasing power on the black market far beyond that of government officials. The very existence of this purchasing power, conservatively estimated at a total of $100 million annually during the eighties, was a powerful impetus for the transformation of the black market into a free market.[15]

Thus, decisions to migrate, as other decisions, had consequences that went far beyond the particular events and situations to which they responded, affecting the individuals concerned, in what Chanoff and Doan have call the burden of choice, as well as those they left behind and the country as a whole. Decisions not to migrate, especially when made consciously, were no different. One family, many of whose relatives had already left southern Vietnam on boats in the late seventies, hesitated as they made preparations for their own departure. After long consideration, they decided against, saying, "We'll stay and defend to the death." The phrase *tu thu* is used, which evokes the determination of a besieged general refusing to surrender. Having made this difficult decision, as this man recalled later in life, the family found it easier to come to terms with the changes ushered in by the new order.[16]

The Interpretation of Decision Making

In a history relying for source material on interviews, memoirs, and personal accounts in general, the problem of the burden of choice presents a considerable challenge of interpretation. As Ronald Skeldon points out with regard to Chinese migration from Hong Kong in the 1980s and 1990s, migrants interviewed after the event very often come up with post-facto explanations that obscure as much as they reveal of the dilemmas and difficulties of decision making.[17] This is particularly true in the analysis of decision making, where the subjective is necessarily in the foreground. This may be for personal reasons, as people struggle to find justifications, for themselves as much as for anyone else, for the way their lives have turned out. In such cases, clear and linear accounts may be offered, concealing and forgetting elements of dilemma or confusion. But explanations also reflect the social and political context in which the interview was carried out or the account written and, in such cases, require even more careful interpretation. To enter into the dynamics of how a decision was made, it is often necessary to ask how the decision was remembered and related. Two examples suffice in illustration.

Mrs. Lien, whom I met in a village in Vietnam's northern uplands, told me how at the age of twenty she had moved from her home in the Red River Delta: *In those days, we were poor at home, so I came up here to make a living. I came alone, married right away, and by the age of twenty-four had a child.* Her story fitted neatly into the grim saga of a delta with too many people and too little land. She was lucky; she married a local landowner, the owner of a vast tract of paddy land. But her version of events did not fit with that of her son, who spoke to me when she was out of the room: *She came here with an old lady, a trader. She had a marriage problem—her mother wanted to give her to some man she did not like, so she ran away. The old lady was not a member of the family, but agreed to take her along. Here, she met a rich, important man. She was very beautiful, like an actress. . . .* When I met Lien, in her graceful old age, it was not hard to see how she had charmed the valley's biggest landlord. I checked, nevertheless, about her folks back home: were they poor people, did any relatives come and join her? *They have come, but only to visit. My brothers and sisters are all still at home, no one went anywhere.*[18]

Lien's explanation of her move in terms of poverty allowed her to avoid a direct criticism of her family. In conversation with someone from outside her immediate environment, this might have been an uncomfortable experience, and it would have been all the more so to me, a foreigner, for whom such a story might imply a criticism of Vietnamese society as a whole. Poverty was the safe option. It took someone who lived at a certain distance from the migration, or from such considerations of appearance—in this case her son—to provide a less euphemistic account.

The second example relates to people who joined programs of upland settlement organized by the respective governments of South and North Vietnam. In the central highlands province of Dak Lak, migrants gave clear-cut answers when I asked them how they were recruited, in 1959, to participate in Ngo Dinh Diem's strategic hamlet program. One man told me bluntly: *We were forced to go. They brought a vehicle right to your house, and if you didn't want to go, they would use force.*[19] Discussions with two elderly women who had participated in the 1960s land clearance programs in North Vietnam brought a much more nuanced response. One of them put it this way: *If you didn't want to go, they would persuade you further, and if you still didn't want to go, they couldn't force you.* She added that the decision to go was a difficult one: *To go would bring hardship, and to stay would bring hardship.*[20]

In interpreting such data, the context of the interviews may be significant. In the first, I was accompanied by a local policeman, but not in the second. Perhaps the first informant spoke in the terms of a forced migration because he felt he was expected to give a critical opinion of the now defunct government of Ngo Dinh Diem in South Vietnam. The presence of officials in interviews often had an influence on what people said, although this worked in different directions.[21] But the question of officials at interviews is perhaps a red herring, obscuring the fact that, with or without the presence of officials, people were influenced by the political culture in which they lived and told their story. The women in the second interview were genuinely reluctant to speak ill of the government and indeed still expressed heartfelt admiration for the fact that, *thanks to the Party,* they had never again had to live through a famine like that of 1945. Compensating interpretation for the effect of the presence of officials in such cases should not be overemphasized. There is little doubt in my mind, having listened to dozens of informants speak about this issue in different circumstances of interview, that the government of North Vietnam was far more adept in its persuasion than that of Ngo Dinh Diem.[22]

Doubt, however, remains a major feature of the interpretative landscape, particularly when dealing with the very subjective nature of motivation for migration. Even for people with close relationships with the individuals and families involved, the reasons for their decisions may not be apparent. Those making the decisions may do so for reasons that are far from clear cut and may act under confused or conflicting stimuli. This difficulty of understanding is clearly illustrated in a memoir, written in the early 1990s, by a Viet Minh cadre who looked back on the decisions of some of his friends to move to the south in 1954. Nguyen Bac's own political position was clear: he moved about the country and risked his life for the cause of the revolution. But even with hindsight he found it difficult to comprehend the motivation for decisions made by people close to him. In the following selection, he relates his confusion, both at the time and retrospectively, on hearing that his friend Vu Van Hien, a prominent Hanoi lawyer, had decided to leave:

I thought that Mr. Hien would stay. But Dr. Quang told me that Mr. Hien was about to go to the South. I thought that was odd and I hurried to ask him about it. Mr. Hien said calmly: "I supported the resistance then because the resistance was weak! Now the resistance is already very strong!"

I was surprised, and I didn't understand, and I didn't know what to say. I could only look at him as if I wanted him to explain further. Understanding what I meant, he said: "Whether I'm in Saigon or Paris, I will continue to wait and see—you can believe me!"

After going to Saigon, he did not participate in the government of Ngo Dinh Diem and continued to practice in his private law office. A short time later, I heard that he had gone to France and died in France of a brain hemorrhage. Up to this day, whenever I recall Mr.

Hien, I still think about this question: What was the real reason why Mr. Hien did not stay? Was it for complex reasons? Or did he think that the lawyers' profession would have no place for his activities? And what position would he have had when our government returned after the takeover? There were also people who told me that intellectuals were very much listening to their wives and very frightened! Which was the main reason? Perhaps it was all four reasons together![23]

Personal and family reasons, professional reasons, political reasons, and the enigmatic "complex" reasons: whatever was behind it, Vu Van Hien's decision remained a mystery to Nguyen Bac.

The mention of intellectuals and their wives, moreover, raises a further area of difficulty in interpretation: the issue of decisions within the family. In the above story, Mr. Hien migrated. And so, we are led to believe, did Mrs. Hien. The way decisions to move were made within families is one of the most impenetrable areas of research, the more so in Vietnam, where realities were regularly obscured behind jocular stereotypes of henpecked husbands and obedient wives. Mr. Hien was such a husband, if we are to take Nguyen Bac's intimation at face value. And the two elderly women in the example cited above presented themselves as such wives. When I asked them who in the family made the choice to leave, one of them quickly replied, *the whole family decided,* adding that there were cases when the husband wanted to go and the wife did not. She laughed then, saying, *the wife must follow the husband,* but I could not tell whether her laughter indicated a joke, was intended ironically, or whether she actually meant what she had just said.

In many cases, it was possible to get a closer sense of how decisions were reached within the family only when anger was generated. I learned of a cooperative official in the Red River Delta province of Thai Binh who, threatened with loss of position, told his family in 1977 that he was going to clear land in Dak Lak, with or without them. The family had to follow, and his son, who related the story to me, was still furious twenty years later. By contrast, an industrial sector cadre, who accepted a promotion from the Red River Delta town of Hai Duong to a project in an upland part of the province of Ninh Binh, moved back again after his son was attacked on the way back from school, on the deserted mountain paths. The boy's mother understandably refused to bring up a family in such a place. Rather than pursue his career, the cadre chose to follow his wife back to the plains.[24]

In the context of anger, we should note the existence of "forced" decisions within the family. In most instances husbands, particularly during the boat people's exodus, when the need for secrecy was paramount, would present a decision to wives and children as something little short of a fait accompli: *we're leaving tonight*. This was the case of Le Thanh, whose story was related by David Chanoff and Doan Van Toai during an interview in the United States:

> He had planned his escape meticulously, telling no one except the few friends who were essential to getting the boat and supplies. Not even his father knew: he was afraid an emotional reaction might suggest to the block committee or work committee that something was wrong in the family. For the same reason, he didn't tell his wife until everything was set.
>
> In a remote stretch of Haiphong harbor, the thirty-foot sailing junk with twenty-two refugees aboard was becalmed for several hours shortly after its midnight departure. Just before the wind came up again the boat was spotted by a sentry on a little island outpost. Bullets crashed into the boat and broke the main mast. Crouching behind the gunnels shielding their children, some of the women were screaming curses at Thanh for getting them killed.
>
> As we talked in the apartment, friends of his dropped by to visit. They had been on the boat, and the wife had done more than her share of the cursing. Recalling the scene, they all had a good laugh. After their escape from the harbor, it had taken two months to get to Hong Kong.[25]

One partner made a clear ultimatum to the other, which threatened the relationship. This may not give us much insight into the ways in which decisions were made by the whole family, like that of the two elderly women mentioned. In anticipation of further research on the role of gender and the dynamics of family in migration decision making, such extreme positions remain, however, our only indicator.

The decision to leave, however it was reached, constituted an act of positioning. Even in Vu Van Hien's case, a wait-and-see, sit-on-the-fence attitude was still a *prise de position,* to which he and his family gave expression in an act of migration. This may not have been of great encouragement to Nguyen Bac, as he sought to understand the character of his friend. It was, indeed, at the heart of his questioning. For the historian, on the other hand, a separation between the two domains—motivation and migration—creates conceptual space for dealing with interpretative doubt. Migration, seen in these terms, is both decision and action, both thought process and statement. This space—situated after the decision and before the consequences—is created by the very fact of traveling. Its implied commitment to a course of action gives the study of migration great value for the historian. For whatever the distortion of memory or ideology interjected by the informant, whatever the interpretative gloss one might wish to place on the issue of motivation, whatever consequences one might wish to read into subsequent events, the journey provides its own evidence. The move is an act and, for the historian, interpretation of motivation and consequence becomes a matter, simply, of professional practice.

Marginal or Mainstream?

In this perspective, the act of travel—which sheds light on social, economic, or political environments, conjunctures, and changes—is taken as the structuring principle of a "marginal-mainstream" approach to historical writing. We can thus imagine a rewriting of Vietnam's modern history that offers a fresh introduction to the last fifty years of change. A chronological framework is appropriate here, the main aim being to foreground moving people. In the first instance, the purpose is to outline, in a general sense, some of the major events and transformations of the period from a grassroots perspective, to give an "underview" of mainstream change. The skeleton summary that follows is intended to highlight the periods into which this view should be structured. Space does not allow for close-grained insights into people's decision making.

Observers of migration in the Vietnamese colonial era were struck by its low incidence. Population movements were associated with the settlement of the Mekong Delta and the transportation of labor to plantations in the highlands. But, as Pierre Gourou points out in his 1936 study of the Red River Delta, migration in densely settled northern Vietnam was extremely limited. He reckoned that the estimated annual 14,800 rate of out-migration from the delta could make little or no impact on the region's overpopulation (calculated in terms of an "excess of births over deaths") of between 65,000 and 100,000 people. Vietnamese people, he concluded, were hard to uproot.[26]

Their reluctance to migrate was explained by means of a discourse, Confucian in origin but assimilated by colonial commentators, that maintained that Vietnamese villagers were attached to their place of origin, their land, and their ancestors. My own research indicates that this "psychological" attachment had a more down-to-earth explanation, in policies of taxation, identity control, and security implemented by the colonial authorities.[27]

Relative population immobility reflected the reality of rule by a regime concerned, first and foremost, with its own security. Here the word *relative* indicates comparison with precolonial times, when the existence of a floating population was part and parcel of Vietnamese society; vagabonds, or "errants," were described as a separate social class by turn-of-the-century French commentators.[28] They constituted the majority of nineteenth-century settlers in the Mekong Delta.[29] Over the early decades of the twentieth century the colonial state sought to fix Vietnamese in villages, preventing challenges to order represented by roaming bandits and vagabonds. Rural mobility was curtailed. By the 1930s the system of indentured plantation labor, the best-documented instance of population movement, was, most significantly, very highly regulated. The spontaneous movement of population that persisted in the countryside was remarkable only for its numerical insignificance.

1945

Constraints on mobility created the conditions for revolution. This is the argument of Masaya Shiraishi's theory on Vietnamese society, which helps explain the events of 1945 and relies heavily on an analysis of rural population mobility:

> If it is correct to argue that social and economic differentiation in traditional rural society manifested itself as a struggle between those who remained in villages and those who were forced to leave, then differentiation in the colonial period tended to intensify tensions inside village society itself. . . . Now in the colonial period the struggle between the privileged and the unprivileged became a conflict among the inhabitants of the village itself. Hence, at the core of both the Nghe-Tinh Soviet movement in 1930–31 and the August Revolution in 1945 where the revolutionary movement developed, stood an unprivileged peasantry mobilized against the notables, landlords, and officials of their own villages.[30]

The August 1945 revolution owed some of its success to an intensification of internal tensions within villages, resulting from restrictions on mobility during the colonial period. These manifested themselves in an economic form, in the most immediate sense. In 1944–45, desperation was a prime motive for those who moved from the flood- and famine-stricken areas of Vietnam's northern plains, seeking to escape starvation by drifting into the cities and up to the hills. Numerous survivors of that experience expressed a determination never to return to the village they left in that terrible time.[31] In the context of long-standing tensions within rural society, profound economic disruption in the northern countryside provided the Viet Minh with the basis for mobilizing the local population against the French and Japanese, and against collaborating Vietnamese elites.[32]

In addition, desire for an end to foreign rule motivated mobility associated with the revolution. Rumors and representations of the Viet Minh challenge to the existing order circulated widely in mid-1945 and, as Marr relates, had a profound effect on many young people, prompting them to spontaneously leave their homes.

[I]nspired by such rhetoric, hundreds of young men and women in Hanoi, Haiphong, and the Red River Delta started walking into the hills, hoping to join a Viet Minh armed unit. Most were encouraged politely to return home to organize their own self-defense groups; a few were killed as suspected Japanese spies. Those prudent enough to obtain letters of introduction in advance from local Viet Minh leaders might be escorted under armed guard to Tan Trao, where they received revolutionary pseudonyms and eagerly learned how to count off in platoon formation, march in file, maintain route silence, cross open areas with minimum risk, and disperse at sign of danger.[33]

The disruptions of 1945 set a pattern for population mobility that would last for thirty years.

1946–54

The outbreak of war provoked vast movements of population no longer associated with the structures of rural society and colonial rule. People moved now in response to choices, and attempts to avoid them, between colonial and communist versions of rule using varying degrees of force to compete over Vietnamese "hearts and minds." People moved between the French- and Viet Minh–occupied zones of the country. The departure for the maquis of those who supported revolution, to work as soldiers, cadres, and porters, became common. Those associated with the colonial power, by their political or economic activity or their social status, took refuge in the French zones, and particularly urban areas such as Hanoi, Haiphong, Hue, and Saigon. These decisions indicated clear positioning with regard to the conflict, positions that were moreover often determined by the conflict. The establishment, for example, in 1952 of a "surveillance band" along the road between Hanoi and Haiphong, which was to be "an absolute no-man's-land, where nothing circulates, nothing works, nothing lives," occasioned the forced displacement of a hundred thousand people. A French military source reported, "The inhabitants of the prohibited zone will be invited to choose between Vietnam and the Viet Minh."[34]

Many people, however, chose to stay put, and especially in the French zone they had to balance their loyalties, paying lip service to both sides while protecting their interests and families. Migration often indicated the failure of such a balancing act, a reluctant taking of sides. In other cases, mobility was evidence of its success, particularly among clandestine traders who moved back and forth between zones, taking advantage of economic differentials to make money out of war.

This period culminated in 1954, when Vietnam was divided at the Geneva Conference and its people were invited to decide which part they preferred to live in. The partition, and thus the move, was supposed in the first instance to be temporary, for two years until proposed reunification elections, and many people made their decision with this in mind. Others anticipated that the country would be divided for longer. Nearly a million northerners—military and civilian collaborators with the French, Catholics, business people, intellectuals, and victims of the early stages of communist land reform—chose to relocate south of the Seventeenth Parallel. More than a hundred thousand communist supporters and soldiers moved north. This was a moment of difficult decision between competing Vietnamese nationalisms. It lies at the origins of a later migration, after 1975, beyond the borders of Vietnam in rejection of the communist reunification of the country.

1954–75

After independence the population of North Vietnam was organized to contribute to economic reconstruction and an eventual resumption of hostilities, and this is reflected in migration practice. The relocation of people to areas of economic development from the late fifties, in new industrial centers such as Thai Nguyen and Viet Tri, and in state farms and cooperatives in upland areas (new economic zones), was intended to create new resources for national development. Most of these migrations were based on voluntary decisions made by families and individuals, but the decisions were made in a climate of orchestrated patriotism and organized persuasion. Persuasion was backed by a system of household registration linked to economic livelihood by membership of a work unit, usually a cooperative, factory, or state farm, which greatly limited people's freedom to maneuver. From the sixties, the same dynamic enabled the recruitment of large numbers of soldiers for the war in the south.[35]

Much of the population of Hanoi departed, first at the outbreak of hostilities and then during the 1954–55 exodus south. The city was repopulated with cadres and others who had fought with the Viet Minh, including a number of people from the south. The government subsequently discouraged the growth of large cities, and a policy of restricted urbanization was implemented. Evacuation was stepped up after American bombing started in the mid-sixties.[36]

In South Vietnam, meanwhile, during the first few years after independence, the experiences of migrants, in this different political and economic climate, mirrored those in the north. A new elite moved to Saigon, made up of educated people from the countryside and rural towns as well as people who had proven their anticommunism by moving from the north. Economic and military imperatives prompted the organized resettlement of lowland farmers in the strategically important central highlands region. By contrast with North Vietnam, this pattern changed with the escalation of war in the sixties. Populations had to move, both into strategic hamlets and simply away from their village, into the city or to refugee camps.[37] In the countryside, decisions to migrate, when they were possible, increasingly came to resemble those taken in 1946–54 to stay put: people had to balance their loyalties, while migration implied a positioning of some kind. The population of urban centers expanded as security in the countryside deteriorated and people sought refuge from hostilities.[38]

1975–99

Reunification was achieved by the military occupation of the south; soldiers were quickly followed by administrators and settler farmers. Large numbers of southerners who remained in Vietnam were removed from the cities, in an extensive de-urbanization program. Most returned to their villages or were sent to clear land in new economic zones and reeducation camps in the highlands. As the capitalist economy of the south was dismantled and relations with China deteriorated prior to the brief 1979 war, people of Chinese origin started leaving the country. Their departure came on the heels of an exodus, by boat and by land, caused by the collapse of South Vietnam. Those leaving included Vietnamese associated with the defunct regime unable to leave in April 1975, returnees from the new economic zones, and people whose interests were threatened by the new order. There were also many who attempted departure but failed on numerous occasions for different reasons. Many people, of course, decided quite deliberately not to leave.[39] The departures of these members of the population—in response to Hanoi's deteriorating relationship with Beijing and the emergence of an image within Vietnam of the West as a sort of paradise—was mirrored by other departures, in response to Hanoi's improving relationship with Moscow, of workers contracted to the factories and construction sites of the countries of the Soviet bloc.[40]

Economic reforms pursued in the 1980s were formalized as the Doi Moi policy at the Sixth Party Congress in 1986. These included the dissolution of the cooperatives and assignation of land rights to families, which now became the principal unit of agricultural production. The abolition of the subsidy system reduced the efficacy of the household registration system as a means of control over the place of residence of the population. These changes were reflected in growing population mobility, an increasingly important element in people's strategies for social and economic development.[41] A movement of spontaneous migration, notably to the central highlands, reflected lowland people's desire to grow rich on the marketing of coffee and other cash crops. A similar desire for economic gain motivated a movement of rural-urban migration to Hanoi and Ho Chi Minh City.[42] And such desires motivated tens of thousands of people to take to the boats in the late eighties, in search of a better livelihood in the West, until a screening process instituted for refugees in

Hong Kong in 1988, and the development of Vietnam's own economy, stemmed the flow.

Summarized so briefly, this history may at one level be interpreted as simply a political economy of migration in twentieth-century Vietnam. But as I have tried to convey here, the presentation of the voices and stories of individuals and families who lived through the events and processes described leads the analysis. This is a study in dilemma and decision, and its primary aim is to give expression to the difficulty of choice. The choices people made, expressed in migration, enable us to observe the ways in which phenomena occurring in local, national, or international environments—decisions reached in world capitals, laws passed in government buildings, the overturning of those laws in revolution, events of violence, gradual macroeconomic transformations even—impacted on everyday lives. Or put the other way round, the choices reflect our attention onto the phenomena that provoked them. In the process they enable an understanding of people's social, economic, and political positioning. The marginal informs us on the mainstream.

Notes

1. David Chanoff and Doan Van Toai, *Vietnam, A Portrait of Its People at War* (London: I. B. Taurus, 1996), 14–15.
2. Duong Van Mai Elliott, *The Sacred Willow: Four Generations in the Life of a Vietnamese Family* (New York: Oxford University Press, 1999).
3. Chanoff and Doan, *Vietnam*, xviii.
4. Ibid., xxi.
5. Ibid., xviii.
6. David G. Marr, *Vietnam 1945: The Quest for Power* (Berkeley: University of California Press, 1995), 106.
7. Elliott, *Sacred Willow*, 151.
8. Ibid., 146.
9. Chan Kwok Bun, "Hong Kong's Response to the Vietnamese Refugees: A Study in Humanitarianism, Ambivalence, and Hostility," *Southeast Asian Journal of Social Sciences* 18, 1 (1990): 94–95.

10. A. Speare, "The Relevance of Models of Internal Migration for the Study of International Migration," in *International Migration: Proceedings of a Seminar on Demographic Research in Relation to International Migration,* ed. G. Tapinos (Paris: CICRED, 1974), 89; cited in Graeme Hugo and Chan Kwok Bun, "Conceptualizing and Defining Refugee and Forced Migrations in Asia," *Southeast Asian Journal of Social Sciences* 18, 1 (1990): 20.

11. Wilfred Burchett, *At the Barricades* (London: Quartet, 1980), 11.

12. For elaboration of this argument, see Adam Fforde and Stefan de Vylder, *From Plan to Market: The Economic Transition in Vietnam* (Boulder: Westview, 1996). See also Đặng Phong, "Opening the Door: Two Centuries of Markets in Vietnam," manuscript, Hanoi, 1998, ch. 5.

13. For evidence of this, see Andrew Hardy, "A History of Migration to Upland Areas in Twentieth-Century Vietnam" (Ph.D. diss., Australian National University, 1998), 351–52, shortly to be published under the title "Red Hills: Migrants and the State in the Highlands of Vietnam" (Copenhagen: NIAS Press).

14. Elliott, *Sacred Willow,* 138.

15. This aspect of the transition to a market economy in 1980s Vietnam is detailed in Melanie Beresford and Đặng Phong, *Economic Transition in Vietnam: Trade and Aid in the Demise of a Centrally Planned Economy* (Cheltenham, UK: Edward Elgar, 2000), 69–71, 97–101.

16. Pers. comm. from one of this man's relatives, Singapore, June 1999.

17. Ronald Skeldon, introduction to *Reluctant Exiles? Migration from Hong Kong and the New Overseas Chinese,* ed. R. Skeldon (Armonk, N.Y.: M. E. Sharpe, 1994), 3.

18. Interview by author, Thái Nguyên province, January 1997. In the interviews I have given the informants' words in italics to convey the overlap between their voices and my own, which acted by means of language, field notes, and translation.

19. Interview by author, Dak Lak province, May 1996.

20. Interview by author, Thái Nguyên province, October 1996.

21. Sometimes officials corrected or attempted to influence people's version of their experiences, sometimes they went to sleep or slipped outside to smoke a cigarette or buy some local produce, and sometimes they proved very helpful, clarifying points in the discussion in an informative way, and telling me afterward when a particular individual had been spinning a line. At times, after a few days' work in a village, they would get bored of listening to the same questions and leave my Vietnamese colleague and me to continue. In the light of this, I resist the conclusion that carrying out rural fieldwork in Vietnam in the legal manner, which sometimes involves the

presence of such officials, is necessarily detrimental to the quality of the information gathered. It becomes another factor for interpretation.

22. David Chanoff and Doan Van Toai appear to have come to the same conclusion, after the extensive interviewing that went into their collection of oral histories about the war. They make the following observation in an afterword to the book: "Because of their success in communicating their own perception of events and excluding others, the Northern leadership was able to excite emotion and guide logic in a way that Southern strongmen could only dream of and that was wholly alien to Americans." Chanoff and Doan, *Vietnam,* 209.

23. Nguyễn Bắc, *Giữa thành phố bị chiếm* (In the occupied city) (Hanoi: Nhà Xuất bản Hà Nội, c. 1994), 44–45. My thanks to Mark Sidel for permission to use his as yet unpublished translation here.

24. Interviews by author, Dak Lak province, November 1996, and Hanoi, January 1997.

25. Chanoff and Doan, *Vietnam,* 56.

26. Pierre Gourou, *Les paysans du delta tonkinois* (Paris: Editions d'Art et d'Histoire, 1936), 219.

27. For a more detailed analysis, see Hardy, "History of Migration," ch. 4.

28. See, for example, Camille Briffaut, *La cité annamite,* 3 vols. (Paris: E. Larose, 1909), vol. 3, *Les errants.*

29. The fullest account of this may be found in Pierre Brocheux, "L'économie et la société dans l'Ouest de la Cochinchine pendant la période coloniale, 1898–1940" (Ph.D. diss., Université de Paris, Faculté des Lettres, 1969); see also Pierre Brocheux, *The Mekong Delta: Ecology, Economy, and Revolution, 1860–1960* (Madison: University of Wisconsin, Madison, Center for Southeast Asian Studies, 1995).

30. Masaya Shiraishi, "States, Villagers, and Vagabonds," *Senri Ethnological Studies* 13 (1984): 394.

31. Interviews by author, Thái Nguyên province, 1995–96.

32. For concrete expressions of these tensions, see Marr, *Vietnam 1945,* 143–45.

33. Ibid., 230.

34. Report authored by Colonel de Saint Martin, 18.1.1953, Archives of the Service Historique de l'Armée de Terre, Vincennes, carton 10I I 3359, dossier "Blocus Economique (3è Bureau)."

35. Fuller analysis of the decision-making process in these contexts is available in Hardy, "History of Migration," ch. 7.

36. See Nigel Thrift and Dean Forbes, *The Price of War: Urbanization in Vietnam, 1954–1985* (London: Allen and Unwin, 1986), ch. 6.

37. For documentation of this phenomenon, see Jonathan Schell, *The Village of Ben Suc* (New York: Knopf, 1967).

38. These changes are effectively catalogued in Langlet-Quach Thanh Tam, "Notes sur les changements du milieu humain dans la République du Viêt-Nam," *Bulletin de la société des études indochinoises,* new series 49, 1 (1974): 9–31.

39. A good account of this period in Vietnam's history, from the point of view of migrants over international borders, may be found in W. Courtland Robinson, *Terms of Refuge: The Indochinese Exodus and the International Response* (New York: Zed, 1998), chs. 2, 3.

40. For an account of this movement of migration, see Andrew Hardy "Des valeurs de l'amitié: Esquisse éthnographique des travailleurs vietnamiens dans les pays socialistes de l'Europe," *Revue européenne des migrations internationales* 16, 1 (2000): 235–46.

41. These are summarized in a series of articles that appeared in Vietnam's *Journal of Sociology* in 1997 and 1998. See Nguyễn Văn Chính, "Biến đổi kinh tế—xã hôi và vấn đề di chuyển lao động nông thôn-độ thị ở miền Bắc Việt Nam" (Socioeconomic change and the rural-urban migration of labor in the north of Vietnam), *Xã hội học* 2, 58 (1997): 25–38; Đang Nguyên Anh, "Về vai trò của di cư nông thôn-độ thị trong sự nghiệp phát triển nông thôn hiện nay" (The role of rural-urban migration in the cause of rural development), *Xã hội học* 4, 60 (1997): 15–19; Tương Lai, "Về di dân ở Việt Nam trong qúa khứ và hiện nay" (Past and present migration in Vietnam), *Xã hội học* 2, 62 (1998): 3–15; Lê Bach Dương, "Nhà nước, kinh tế thị trường và di dân nội địa ở Việt Nam" (The state, market economy, and internal migration in Vietnam), *Xã hội học* 3, 63 (1998): 38–45.

42. For a review of the impact of Doi Moi on population mobility, see Philip Guest, *The Dynamics of Internal Migration in Vietnam* (Hanoi: United Nations Development Programme, 1998), 5. See also Li Tana, *Peasants on the Move: Rural-Urban Migration in the Hanoi Region* (Singapore: Institute of Southeast Asian Studies, 1996), 4.

Chapter 15

LOCATING CHINESE WOMEN IN MALAYSIAN HISTORY

Tan Liok Ee

Since the 1970s women's history has become a major focus of research for historians of Europe, North America, Australia, and China.[1] But in Malaysian historiography women's history remains largely unexplored territory.[2] Though more work has been done on Chinese than on Malay or Indian women,[3] little is known about the hundreds of thousands of Chinese women who have lived in the territories that today comprise Malaysia.[4] Their family and working lives, economic, social, and political contributions, changing gender relations within and outside the family, the role of women in the transformation of the Chinese population from transient-immigrant to settled communities and in the shaping of Chinese identities are largely "hidden from view."[5] This chapter explores some ways of locating Chinese women in the major historical changes that have taken place since the Chinese began sojourning to, and settling in, different parts of the Malay Peninsula.

The Earliest Chinese Women

When and where we locate the earliest Chinese women in the history of the Malay Peninsula depends on who are identified in historical sources as Chinese women, as well as how we use those sources. Lim Joo Hock's study of Chinese female immigration, the earliest scholarly work in this area, was influential in setting a trend of equating Chinese women with female *sinkeh,* or new arrivals from China.[6] Lim dates the arrival of the first "Chinese woman proper" from reports in the *Singapore Free Press,* in 1853 and 1854, that some merchants in Singapore and Penang had brought their wives and families from their home villages in southern China to escape the socioeconomic devastation after the Taiping Rebellion (1850–64) began. Lim dismissed reports that women had started coming, in small but significant numbers, before 1853 because these reports were disputed or uncorroborated.[7] Undisputed evidence for these earlier arrivals was unlikely as they did not come openly as the wives of respectable merchants, but were probably smuggled out "in men's clothes or in baskets" and brought in to work as prostitutes serving the sexual needs of the large numbers of young male sinkeh who had come to Penang and Singapore since the early nineteenth century.[8] Lim also excluded females living in early Chinese settlements on the peninsula because these women, described in his sources as "natives" or "half-Chinese," were not considered "purebred Chinese" or "Chinese women proper."[9] The first question that arises in trying to locate Chinese women in Malaysian history, therefore, is whether we should begin with officially recorded arrivals of female sinkeh in the mid-nineteenth century or look for other accounts of Chinese women entering, even earlier, into the history of the Malay Peninsula.

The earliest mention of a Chinese woman arriving on the shores of the Malay Peninsula is probably to be found in the *Sejarah Melayu,* or *Malay Annals,* which tells us that some time during the reign of Sultan Mansur Shah (1458–77), the ruler of China sent a princess named Hang Liu to Melaka, together with five hundred youths of noble birth and several hundred beautiful female attendants. Sultan Mansur Shah married Princess Hang Liu after she embraced Islam and the couple had a son, from whom a line of princes can be traced. The descendants of the five hundred youths, who became known as the Chinese yeomen, were ordered to settle in Bukit Cina (Chinese

Hill).[10] Here we have the intriguing figure of a young lady coming from China, not as a sinkeh smuggled in men's clothes or tossed in a basket nor as a prostitute, but in the persona of a princess. The *Sejarah Melayu* story of a princess from China being sent to marry the king of Melaka cannot be corroborated from Chinese records.[11] But, Tome Pires's *Suma oriental* tells us that Iskandar Shah, an earlier ruler of Melaka, married a Chinese woman, purportedly sent by the king of China though she was "not a woman of rank," and from the issue of this marriage were descended the kings of Pahang, Kampar, and Indragiri.[12] It is possible that the two stories are chronologically conflated in the *Sejarah Melayu* or that fake envoys from China brought a woman to Melaka and described her as a princess to gain trading advantages for themselves.[13] In either case, though the woman in question may not have been a Chinese princess, it is not implausible that a Chinese woman, or several women, had arrived in the Malay Peninsula as early as the fifteenth century. Tony Reid suggests that the many variations on the same theme of a ruler or prince of a Southeast Asian kingdom marrying a Chinese princess may be, from the local point of view, "an acceptable way of explaining an infusion of Chinese blood, wealth and technology in the early fifteenth century."[14] The princess from China is a symbolic marker in indigenous historiography of early Chinese influence in the region.

Less debatable and more generally accepted is the fact that male travelers and traders from China had come intermittently to various parts of Southeast Asia from as early as the Tang (618–906) and Sung (960–1279) dynasties, and more regularly during the Ming dynasty (1368–1644). Some of these traders' visits turned into extended stays as they married local women, had families, and maintained homes in the Malay Peninsula or other parts of Southeast Asia, while continuing to return regularly to China. These men were not migrants so much as sojourners, a term suggested by Wang Gungwu to distinguish the fluid and ambivalent nature of their stays from the more defined patterns of immigration and relocation that came much later.[15] Sojourning gave rise to the earliest Chinese settlements in various parts of Southeast Asia in the fourteenth and fifteenth centuries.

These early settlements are believed to have originated from marriages between Chinese traders and local women, whose offspring formed the nucleus of *peranakan,* or local-born, communities.[16]

Chinese families were reported to be living in Melaka and Singapore from the early fifteenth century, though clearer indications of a Chinese settlement in Melaka come from Portuguese reports and Dutch reports in the sixteenth and seventeenth centuries respectively.[17] Governor Balthasar Bort's detailed report of Melaka's population in 1678 describes the Chinese population as comprising 127 men, 140 women, 159 children, 93 male slaves, 234 female slaves, and 105 children of slaves.[18] Victor Purcell, however, contends that the 140 women counted as Chinese by Bort were not "really" Chinese but "mostly Batak and Balinese slaves and some Malays."[19] Should we accept Purcell's, rather than Bort's, categorization of these 140 women, and why? What about the woman who was buried together with her husband in a Chinese-style grave, among the oldest in Bukit Cina, with the surname Ng and "Imperial Ming" inscribed on their tombstone?[20] What other markers of Chinese identity must we find to consider this woman among the earliest Chinese wives to have lived, and in this case also to have died, in Melaka?

By the eighteenth century we have more reports of women using Chinese names and in some cases speaking Chinese, married to Chinese men and mothers of their children. Shortly after Francis Light took over Penang Island from the Sultan of Kedah in 1786, a group of Chinese from Kedah led by Koh Lay Huan, their *kapitan* (leader), paid Light a visit.[21] Koh, later appointed first kapitan of the Chinese in Penang, had two wives, Guan Boey Neoh and Saw It Neoh.[22] Chinese settlement in Kedah had preceded that in Penang; there were 60 Chinese families there in 1787 and 110 Chinese shops, and 425 Chinese families in 1788.[23] In Penang, Light reported in 1794 that Chinese families were rapidly formed as the men would "obtain a wife and go on in a regular domestic mode to the end of their existence" as soon as they acquired a little money. The females were, apparently, kept at home "with the greatest strictness," enjoying more freedom only after marriage.[24]

Early in the eighteenth century Chinese were already reported among the population living in a thousand houses in Kuala Terengganu, on the east coast.[25] A visitor to Terengganu in 1828 described the Chinese population as including women and children who "all speak Chinese, keep very much to themselves, and mix less with the Malays." More intriguing still, we learn that "the Chinese females in Triangano double the number of the males, and the children are more numerous still."[26] To the north, in Kelantan, several hundred people were reported to be arriving every year from China in the late eighteenth century.[27] And to the south, in Pahang, the Chinese were estimated to number twelve thousand out of a total population of forty thousand in the early nineteenth century.[28] All these reports suggest that the history of Chinese settlement, and the formation of Chinese families, had begun long before the arrival of wives of "pure" Chinese descent from China.

The first three censuses, in 1881, 1891 and 1901, showed the local (or "Straits-born") Chinese in the Straits Settlements to have a normal demographic profile, with females slightly outnumbering males and 45 percent comprising children below fifteen years of age (see table 15.1). By then, a distinctive peranakan culture, with its unique blend of Chinese and Malay cuisine and ways of life, had evolved among the Chinese living in Melaka, Penang, and Singapore.[29] J. D. Vaughan's *The Manners and Customs of the Chinese in the Straits Settlements,* first published in 1879 but based on a paper on the Chinese in Penang written in 1854, provides us with a contemporary account of Chinese social life, albeit colored by an Orientalist perspective.[30] By the end of the nineteenth century the peranakan, or Straits Chinese, were an important group, socially, economically, and politically. But numerically they were outnumbered by the sinkeh (see table 15.2), new immigrants who came in large numbers as commerce in the Straits Settlements prospered and tin mining and commercial agriculture in the Malay states became important sectors of the colonial economy. The boundaries between peranakan and sinkeh were porous, not impervious. Important aspects in the history of Chinese women, and Chinese family formation, would be

Table 15.1
Straits Chinese Population in Penang, Melaka, and Singapore, 1881–1911

Year	Place	<15 years		>15 years		Total		Total
		Males	Females	Males	Females	Males	Females	
1881	Penang	2,334	3,150	2,541	2,452	4,875	5,602	10,477
	Singapore	2,461	2,891	2,052	2,123	4,513	5,014	9,527
	Melaka	1,271	1,742	1,159	1,092	2,430	2,834	5,264
	Straits Settlements Total							25,268
1891	Penang	4,173	5,040	3,874	3,894	8,047	8,934	16,981
	Singapore	3,203	3,810	2,881	2,911	6,084	6,721	12,805
	Melaka	1,360	1,791	866	954	2,226	2,745	4,971
	Straits Settlements Total							34,757
1901	Penang	6,359	6,517	5,329	5,364	11,688	11,881	23,569
	Singapore	4,178	4,357	3,541	3,422	7,719	7,779	15,498
	Melaka	1,092	1,540	1,140	1,183	2,232	2,723	4,955
	Straits Settlements Total							44,022
1911	Penang	-	-	-	-	15,966	19,563	35,529
	Singapore	-	-	-	-	20,632	23,251	43,883
	Melaka	-	-	-	-	3,309	4,057	7,366
	Straits Settlements Total							86,778

Source: Ting Shing Chung, "Sejarah wanita Cina pulau Pinang, 1900–1957: Perubahan dan kesinambungan" (History of Chinese women in Penang: Change and continuity) (M.A. thesis, Universiti Sains Malaysia, Penang, 2000), 34.

Table 15.2
Proportion of Straits Chinese to Total Chinese Population in the Straits Settlements, 1881–1901

Year	Straits Chinese	Total Chinese	% Straits Chinese
1881	25,268	174,327	14.5
1891	34,757	227,989	15.2
1901	44,022	281,933	15.6

Source: Report on the Census of the Straits Settlements and the Protected Malay States of the Malay Peninsula, 1891; and *Report on the Census of the Straits Settlements taken on 1ˢᵗ March 1901.*

lost if we were to date this history from the arrival of female sinkeh in the mid-nineteenth century.

Women and Demographic Change

In the 1840s the era of mass migration began as large numbers of *huagong* (Chinese coolies) came to work in tin mines in Perak and Selangor. By 1862 there were twenty to twenty-five thousand Chinese men working in mines in Larut, Perak, and within the next ten years this increased to thirty to forty thousand men.[31] They were soon followed by young women, brought in as prostitutes by mine operators, who controlled their workers through secret societies, which operated opium dens and brothels.[32] Fighting over women featured in the secret society wars that raged in Perak in the 1860s, leading to British intervention in 1874. Women "belonging" to different societies had been kidnapped by their rivals, after which they were either kept or sold off. Some of the women who were kidnapped committed suicide.[33] J. W. W. Birch, who was trying to locate the captured women, discovered that kidnappings of women had been going on for several years and some had been sold off as slaves to Deli, off Java.[34] The women "owned" by the secret societies had little control over their lives but some were courageous enough to make choices, across the lines drawn by the secret society bosses. One woman's story, as told to Frank Swettenham in 1874, provides us with a glimpse of her fate: "a Si Quan woman, the wife of a headman, liked a Gho Quan man better than her husband. The husband discovered this, and inciting his men, they took the Gho Quan man and the woman of their own tribe and put them each into a basket (one of those Chinamen carry pigs in). They carried them to this old mine and threw them into the water, and then held the baskets down till the unfortunate wretches were drowned."[35]

Official records of arrivals of female sinkeh are available after 1877, when the Chinese protectorate began to keep track of all arrivals from China. Indeed one of the reasons for setting up the Chinese protectorate was to "protect" young female sinkeh who had been forced into prostitution after being sold by their families, or abducted or kidnapped by traffickers.[36] By 1877 several thousand female sinkeh had arrived in the Straits Settlements of Melaka, Penang, and Singapore, with smaller numbers going to the Malay states.[37] In 1891 there was barely one female to every twenty males in a total Chinese population of 94,345 in Perak, while in Selangor there were 3,234 females to 47,610 males, roughly one female to every sixteen males.[38]

After the turn of the century, the number of female arrivals from China increased. In Perak there were 1,956 Chinese females to every ten thousand males in 1911, compared to 669 in 1891, while in Selangor the increase was from 679 in 1891 to 2,133 in 1911. Two-thirds of the women in the four Federated Malay states of Perak, Selangor, Pahang, and Negri Sembilan, were concentrated in the mining centers of Kuala Lumpur in Selangor and the Kinta district in Perak.[39] Cantonese and Hakka women together comprised 70 to 80 percent of all female arrivals for 1891 and 1911 in the Malay states, while in the Straits Settlements there were more Cantonese and Hokkien, and fewer Hakka women. Hainanese women were prohibited from leaving China until the 1920s but, after the ban was lifted, there was a fivefold increase in the number of Hainanese females: from 2,510 in 1921 to 12,836 in 1931.[40] Differences between the dialect groups is thus an important dimension to bear in mind in researching the history of Chinese women in Malaya.

W. L. Blythe has suggested that the most intense period of Chinese female immigration was from 1934—when a quota on male immigrants was imposed with the implementation of the Immigration Ordinance of 1930 and the Aliens Ordinance of 1933—to 1938, when a limit was placed on female immigrants. Notwithstanding the significance of the "net migrational gain to Malaya of over 190,000 Chinese female deck passengers" between 1934 and 1938 (highlighted by Blythe),[41] this brief surge in female arrivals was not the main factor in the overall increase in Chinese females (see table 15.3), nor did it mark the most important period of female immigration. Table 15.4 shows that the number of immigrant females born in China in fact

Table 15.3
Number of Chinese Females by State, 1921–1957

Year	Penang	Melaka	Perak	Selangor	N. Sembilan	Johore	Kelantan	Pahang
1921	47,679	12,289	61,895	48,725	11,525	18,187	3,378	6,401
1931	70,533	22,729	109,047	87,027	24,011	56,756	5,583	14,629
1947	119,287	44,514	201,555	166,666	49,446	152,155	9,907	40,454
1957	162,358	57,947	263,282	237,960	70,990	184,276	13,302	49,050

Sources: J. E. Nathan, *The Census of British Malaya, 1921* (London:Waterflow and Sons, 1922); C. A. Vlieland, *British Malaya: A Report on the 1931 Census* (Westminister: Crown Agents for the Colonies, 1932); M. V. del Tufo, *Report on the 1947 Census of Population: Malaya, Comprising the Federation of Malaya and the Colony of Singapore* (Kuala Lumpur: Government Printer, Federation of Malaya, 1948); H. Fell, *1957 Population Census of the Federation of Malaya*, report no. 14 (Kuala Lumpur: Department of Statistics, Federation of Malaya, 1960).

Table 15.4
Number of Chinese Females Born in China, 1921–1957

Year	Penang	Melaka	Perak	Selangor	N. Sembilan	Johore	Kelantan	Pahang
1921	18,975	5,591	39,019	35,257	8,482	12,634	272	4,774
1931	29,170	11,481	60,791	50,492	15,087	37,533	1,181	9,418
1947	29,058	12,654	59,717	51,792	17,875	54,601	1,678	15,773
1957	28,905	11,588	55,863	54,918	17,626	45,300	1,892	12,911

Sources: See table 15.3.

Table 15.5
Percentage of Local-Born Chinese Females by State, 1921–1957

Year	Penang	Melaka	Perak	Selangor	N. Sembilan	Johore	Kelantan	Pahang
1921	58.7	54.2	36.4	27.4	25.9	29.6	90.0	24.8
1931	57.2	49.1	43.8	41.7	36.5	33.4	78.0	35.5
1947	74.5	70.9	69.8	68.3	63.4	63.7	82.2	60.6
1957	81.2	79.5	78.1	76.4	74.7	66.6	85.2	73.3

Sources: See table 15.3.

increased more substantially between 1921 and 1931 than between 1931 and 1947 in most states in the peninsula. In the later intercensus period the increase in numbers of China-born females was far less dramatic, except in Johore. Table 15.5 provides the other side of the picture, showing that by 1921 local-born Chinese females already made up more than half the total number of Chinese females in Penang and Melaka while in Kelantan they accounted for 90 percent. The influx of female sinkeh after 1921 led to marginal drops in the proportion of local-born in Penang, Melaka, and Kelantan in 1931, but the states of Perak, Selangor, Negri Sembilan, and Johore saw significant increases in the proportion of local-born Chinese females. From 1931 onward the trend was clearly a steady increase in the number and proportion of local-born Chinese females until, by 1957, they constituted the majority in all states. This was part of the major demographic transition in the Chinese population.

The first step in this transition was the arrival of the women and the significant fact that after arrival they almost always stayed on.[42] This led to a steady increase in the number of children. In 1891 there was roughly one child to every seven adults in the Straits Settlements while in Perak it was only one to every forty adults.[43] By 1911 the ratio of children to adults in the Federated Malay States had improved to one to three, which, as the writer of the 1911 census of the Federated Malay States noted, pointed to "a considerable increase of Chinese family life in these states."[44] As more children were born the local-born component of the Chinese population increased progressively, from 23 percent in 1911 to 38 percent in 1931 in the Straits Settlements and from 8 to 29 percent for the same years in the Federated Malay States.[45] By the 1930s the Chinese were clearly making the transition from being "mere sojourners" to becoming part of the settled population of the peninsula.[46]

The arrival of wives, often with children in tow, was the beginning of this transition, with entire families relocating themselves from China. As more children were born, raised, and educated locally, families took root and the transition toward permanent settlement was clearly underway. The vast majority of Chinese females were

Table 15.6
Sex Ratio of Chinese Population in the
Malay Peninsula, 1911–1957

Year	Females per 1,000 Males
1911	215
1921	371
1931	486
1947	815
1957	926

Source: Charles Hirschman, *Ethnic and Social Stratification in Peninsular Malaysia* (Washington, D.C.: American Sociological Association, 1974), 12.

Table 15.7
Chinese Population below Fifteen Years of Age,
Malaya, 1921–1957

Year	No. of Chinese < 15
1921	230,211
1931	434,021
1947	747,452
1957	1,129,926

Source: See table 15.3.

wives and mothers. In 1931, 71.5 percent of those 15 to 34 years old and 84 percent of those 35 to 45 were married; and in 1947, 55.6 percent between 20 and 24, 80.6 of those between 25 and 29, 86.8 between 30 and 34, and 88.9 between 40 and 44, were or had been mothers.[47] Women, as wives and mothers, were the nucleus of family life, sustaining and reproducing the labor force. As Victor Purcell points out, the arrival of the women brought with it a "transition from male to *family* labor" as marketing and cooking was carried out by the female for the family, no longer by the contractor for single male coolies.[48]

The Japanese occupation from 1941 to 1945, which put a temporary stop to the prewar migratory movements, had the effect of further consolidating the evolution toward permanent settlement. The

1947 postwar census recorded a further improvement in the female-to-male ratio and noted an "extraordinary" increase of 135.5 percent in children under fifteen, which accounted for two-thirds of the total increase in the Chinese population since the 1931 census.[49] By 1957, the year Malaya became an independent nation, a balanced male-female ratio and a large component of children under fifteen indicated that the Chinese population by then had a normal demographic profile (see tables 15.6, 15.7).

Different Marriage Patterns for Different Women

The *jia* (family, household) is identified in historical and anthropological studies of China, Taiwan, and Hong Kong as the center of social and economic life and the site on which gender relations are constructed and gender identities shaped.[50] The Chinese family was both patrilineal and patriarchal, with female children valued less than males and women subordinated to men. When it came to marriage, however, neither boys nor girls, whether from rich or poor families, were free to choose their partners, as marriage was looked upon as a link between two families, not a relationship between two individuals.[51] What happened to marriage patterns and the power structure of family relationships when Chinese families were reconstituted as its members arrived, usually separately, in Malaya? Was the force of old values and practices so strong that they reinvented and reasserted themselves, or did relocation offer women interstices for seeking new freedoms?

Elite families in China had for centuries built and consolidated their networks of power and influence by carefully selecting marriage partners for their sons and daughters.[52] From Song Ong Siang's encyclopedic *One Hundred Years' History of the Chinese in Singapore,* we can see that this too was the practice of local upper-class families.[53] Women, far less visible than men, appear sporadically as daughters, wives, or mothers, sometimes as sisters or widows, and almost always as the social glue binding families in the upper strata of society. Local

Chinese families, especially in the early nineteenth century, took considerable interest in the arrival of the junks from China, for they brought "welcome batches of eligible sons-in-law for the daughters who could not marry the natives of the country."[54] Peranakan fathers recruited "new blood" for their families and businesses by marrying daughters to talented and hardworking sinkeh while successful sinkeh, who had few local family and kinship ties, enhanced their status by marrying into established peranakan families.

In Song's book we find many examples of bright and hardworking sinkeh who became their employers' sons-in-law and helped run successful family businesses. Lim Kwee Eng, born in 1858, came to Singapore at the age of eighteen and worked for Cheang Hong Lim, an established businessman and community leader. In 1879 his employer gave his eldest daughter's hand in marriage in to him.[55] Seah Eu Chin, who was born in China in 1805 and came to Singapore in 1823, was another highly valued sinkeh son-in-law. In 1837, when he had become a successful businessman, Seah married the eldest daughter of the kapitan of Perak. When this wife died a few months after marriage, Seah married his wife's younger sister.[56] This practice of a widower marrying a sister of his deceased wife to maintain links between the two families is a custom that can be traced to eleventh-century China.[57] It continued in Chinese families in the Malay Peninsula, as can be seen from Seah's case and that of Bebe, the central character in Yeap Joo Kim's *Of Comb, Powder and Rouge,* who was forced by her family to *chiap ow siew,* the Hokkien term for marrying a widower. The widower was Bebe's elder sister's husband and the scion of a wealthy China-born family with whom her Straits Chinese family wanted to maintain links. Set in prewar Penang, Yeap Joo Kim's historical novel conveys the contempt the Straits Chinese had for the China-born, who were considered crude and unlawful. But because of its wealth, marriage with such a family was still sought by a Straits Chinese family facing a downward slide in its fortunes.[58]

In the nineteenth century, during the zenith of Straits Chinese power and influence, Straits Chinese men were sought as sons-in-law by up-and-coming sinkeh families. One such example was Wong

Nai Siong, the famous pioneer of a Foochow settlement in Sarawak.[59] His elder daughter married Lim Boon Keng, a Queen's scholar from a Straits Chinese family in Singapore, and his younger daughter married Wu Lien Teh, a Queen's scholar from a Penang Straits Chinese family.[60] Among the notable sinkeh who married wives from Straits Chinese families was Yap Ah Loy, who came to Malaya from China at the age of eighteen in 1854. In 1865, when Yap was a relatively wealthy man managing Kapitan Liu Ngim Kong's mines (besides owning two mines himself), Liu arranged for him to marry Kok Kang Keow, a Straits Chinese from Malacca.[61] Yap already had a wife in China, who was a *tongyangxi,* a girl raised by her prospective husband's family from young as a daughter-in-law. This was a common practice among poorer families in China and Taiwan.[62] This girl is listed in the family genealogy as Yap's official first wife, but it is not known whether the marriage was formalized or consummated as there were no children from this first wife who died young after an illness.[63]

It was Madam Kok from Melaka who enjoyed the status of being married to one of the most powerful men in Kuala Lumpur. As the bride of the kapitan's right-hand man, she "was an important person" who lived in a house next to his on the edge of the market place.[64] In addition to Kok, Yap had three official concubines.[65] Apart from the women in his own family, Yap controlled the lives of hundreds of other women. As kapitan, he owned and ran public services such as the police, prisons, hospitals, and markets, as well as gambling booths and brothels for workers in his tin mines. Yap had, in 1884, some three hundred Chinese women working for him in the brothel quarter between Pudu Road and Petaling Street. Each earned two dollars per month.[66] The police "turned a blind eye on this particular business venture of the Capitan China" and it was only after Yap's death that investigations revealed the appalling conditions in which these women lived and worked:

> there are over a 100 prostitutes in the Capitan's buildings; the room for each is so small that it is only five feet by five feet and all the women are cramped up without ventilation.

the houses are so soddened with dirt and filth that they are past cleaning. . . . The rooms in which the poor women live are much worse than pig-styes and so dark that lamps are in use all day.[67]

It is hardly surprising that syphilis was a major medical problem in early Kuala Lumpur and that prostitutes from the Chinese brothels "were generally in a very advanced stage of the disease, owing to absolute neglect."[68]

For the thousands of women who were prostitutes, marriage was an unlikely avenue of escape from their harsh lives. The younger and more beautiful among them might become concubines or mistresses of rich clients who could pay the price of releasing them from the brothels. Some tried running away with a sympathetic, but poor, client.[69] It was common practice for a prostitute to "follow" a man, without any of the formalities or ceremonies that marked her as wife or concubine.[70] Dependents with little protection, they could as easily be abandoned or forced back into prostitution. Inspections by protectorate officers sometimes provided the braver women with the chance to seek a life outside the brothel. A report in 1886 mentions that seventy-seven women were married before the registrar and five before magistrates in Penang, most of whom "were released from the brothels against the will of the keeper."[71] Marriage before the registrar was presumably different from following a man or becoming his concubine, but no other details are available on these marriages.

The voices, and lives, of these women are difficult to retrieve except when they surface in newspaper reports or court records. For example, brought before a magistrate in Selangor in 1886, Chui Ah Sip said,

> I came from China with a man whose name I don't know. I was poor in China and he promised to give me wages when I got to Singapore. By mistake we came on to Penang. Here the man sold me to a man in a brothel at Penang. The latter handed me over to this man Chong Lam Yau to turn me into a prostitute. . . . I was three months in the brothel, I didn't know what steps to take in Penang to get free. I want to find someone who is willing to keep me decently.

I don't want to go to Klang to become a prostitute. A towkay here, Goh Boo, has offered to keep me and I wish to stop with him.[72]

After listening to her and Chong Lam Yau, the magistrate allowed Ah Sip to go to the towkay Goh Boo, who had to pay a security for her and vouch that he would not resell her. We do not know Ah Sip's fate after following Goh Boo but Liu Fuk Tak, a twenty-three-year-old who had followed a man for seven years, sought refuge at the Poh Leung Kuk home in Kuala Lumpur in 1911 because her "husband," who was an opium smoker, treated her ill when she refused to prostitute herself to sustain his habit. Fuk Tak ran away when he threatened to sell her son and came to the home to get the committee's help, not to start a new life, but to get her husband to pledge that he would not sell her son if she agreed to return. Fuk Tak's predicament was complex, as her mother had been the mistress of the father while she had followed the son. Mother and daughter had apparently sought refuge from prostitution in the same household.[73]

The Poh Leung Kuk homes, in Penang and Kuala Lumpur, were set up as temporary refuges for prostitutes who ran away from brothels or young girls rescued from them. They also provided a refuge for women who were forced into prostitution by their husbands. Tan Moi, aged twenty and the wife of a miner in Kinta, came to the Kuala Lumpur Poh Leung Kuk home in 1910 because her husband was forcing her to have sex with his friends. More spirited than Fuk Tak, Tan decided to seek a new life and absolutely refused to return to her husband despite the committee's attempts at reconciliation.[74] The limited options available to Poh Leung Kuk inmates were either another marriage or employment as domestic help. From 1909 the Poh Leung Kuk committee in Kuala Lumpur included prominent Chinese community leaders,[75] who were asked to recommend or to vouch for the character of men who applied to marry girls from the home. Marriages arranged through the Poh Leung Kuk perhaps offered a less risky escape from the brothel than following a client or being "bought out" by a rich man.

Husbands for the girls in the Poh Leung Kuk homes came mainly from working-class backgrounds. Among those who applied to the home for wives between 1909 and 1915 were a barber living in Sultan Street, a blacksmith from Sentul, another from Kuala Kubu, a tailor on Petaling Street and another from High Street, a fitter in a Public Works Department factory, a goldsmith in Ulu Langat, and a cook employed by the superintendent of Indian immigration. Though the voices of the women themselves can rarely be heard in the minutes of meetings of the Poh Leung Kuk committee, yet we can get some insight into the choices the women faced and how some of them made decisions. Ng Chen Tho, for example, changed her mind after initially agreeing to marry the tailor on Petaling Street, though they were both from the same dialect group, when she discovered that he was a widower with a daughter.[76] Two men applied to marry Lim A Meng, a sixteen-year-old; Lim, a twenty-six-year-old in Serdang who had eighty coolies working under him and earned about fifty dollars per month; and Chan, a twenty-eight-year-old teacher who earned fifty to sixty dollars per month. A Meng told the committee, "I will have nothing to do with Chan, I wish to marry Lim." She knew Chan, the teacher, as her aunt used to wash clothes for him and she had lived with her aunt, in his house, the previous year.[77] Eighteen-year-old Wong Yam Thai, who had three suitors, was initially prepared to leave the decision to the committee but in the end decided that she did not want to marry any of them.[78]

Girls at the Poh Leung Kuk homes were rarely sought by sinkeh who had achieved some success. Such men usually returned to China to marry a woman chosen by their parents. Chan Wing, who arrived as a poor migrant to work in a tin mine in Sungei Besi in 1887, went back to his home village when he had saved enough money some years later. He married Low Ming Ching, a sixteen-year-old from a neighboring village, chosen by Chan's mother because she met Chan's criteria of being submissive, of good disposition, quiet, and old-fashioned. On their return to Sungei Besi, Chan kept his young wife practically locked up in his new house, forbidding her to look out or make new friends because he did not want anyone to "contaminate" her with ideas contrary to his own and lead her astray.[79] Young, ignorant, and deprived of the support of family and friends, Low's health withered after she lost two babies. The domineering and proud Chan Wing finally allowed the wife of an older relative to visit her when the third child fell ill. The submissive Low did not resist when Chan married another woman even before she had given birth to the first child. Chan's second wife, who was "pleasant, well-dressed, refined, witty and good company," was clearly a more assertive woman who managed not only to cultivate his trust but even to become "his mentor in more ways than one." Despite this, Chan had three more wives after he became more successful and wealthy.[80]

Some sinkeh married fellow sinkeh or local-born women although they already had wives in China. Where the "China wife" and "local wife" stood in the family varied, depending on their relative status and individual characters. The wife from abroad appears in Daniel Kulp's study of life in a rural village in south China as the more assertive, quick-witted, and experienced woman, in comparison to the village wife, whose life was lived entirely within village confines.[81] But sometimes the local wife could be the one threatened by the arrival of the China wife, especially if the latter was clearly recognized as the principal wife.[82] Family photographs showing the China-born wife, identified by her dress, and the local wife, usually dressed in Straits Chinese style, could still be seen in some old family homes in Penang in the 1960s.

Polygamy, arranged marriages, and the traditional family's dominance over the individual came under severe criticism from social and cultural reform movements in China during the first few decades of the twentieth century. Writers and intellectuals argued for the freedom to choose marriage partners and for greater equality for women.[83] Echoes of these movements can be found in the columns of Chinese newspapers in Singapore and Malaya, which gave an increasing amount of space to discussions of issues affecting women. New marriage patterns emerged in the 1930s. Radical young couples announced in newspaper advertisements that they had become man and wife after finding that their emotions and common interests brought them together (*qingtou yihe*), emphasizing that theirs was an individual and personal decision, not a match determined by their families. The reverse advertisement, of a couple announcing that they had agreed to separate, thereby renouncing all claims on one another, sometimes appeared to mark the dissolution of a marriage.[84]

While such revolutionary changes were taking place among the young and educated in big towns, older practices continued among Chinese living in rural areas or smaller towns. In 1947 Wong Yan, a vegetable and pig farmer from Mentakab in Pahang, was detained by immigration officials in Hong Kong because he was traveling with six women, aged seventeen to nineteen. The women were from Wong's home village; one was his newly married wife and the other five were betrothed to friends of his in Mentakab. Each of the women carried a photograph of her prospective husband, to whom she claimed to have been betrothed as a child and who had sent the money for her to travel to Mentakab. Wong and the women were allowed to leave Hong Kong only after their stories were confirmed after investigations in Mentakab. A follow-up check on the situation found the women happily settled, though officials still suspected that Wong had earned a commission for his matchmaking efforts.[85]

More surprising than women coming from China in 1947 to marry men they had never met was the persistence of the custom of tongyangxi, raising a girl-child as a daughter-in-law for a son, as late as the 1960s. In Singapore in 1974 I met a young Chinese woman from a small fishing village in Johore who had been raised as a tongyangxi. Soon after she reached puberty, both her intended husband and his brother had forced her to have sexual relations with them. Subsequently rejected by both of them, she left to seek a life of her own working as a maid in Singapore.

The persistence of marriage patterns from China meant that most women in the Malay Peninsula lived within traditional patrilineal and patriarchal family structures. These structures defined male-female roles in a binary division that circumscribed the lives of females to the "inner" space of family and home, simultaneously limiting women's agency and subordinating them to the authority of men. However, depending on whether they came from rich or poor families, lived in cities or in the countryside, Chinese women faced different options. They could be locked into different worlds though living in the same time frame and the same country.

Women and Work

Work, unwaged as part of household labor or waged as paid labor outside the home, is another important dimension in the lives of Chinese women. Data on women's economic activities is available only after 1911, when the census included information on occupational categories for both sexes in some states. But even after information on the numbers and proportion of "economically active" or "gainfully employed" Chinese women becomes available for all states after 1921 (see table 15.8), these figures should be treated with great caution. First, some of those classified as economically active or gainfully employed, for example the wife who helped her husband on the family smallholding or the daughter who helped in the family shop, were not paid for their work. They received no personal income and had little economic independence. Second, the work of the housewife who "cooks, washes and scrubs for a large family" is not included under the "gainfully employed" category, meaning that, for example, the 37 percent of the total female population categorized as "housewives" in the 1947 census were not considered to be economically

Table 15.8
Percentage of Chinese Females Classified as Economically Active, by State, 1921–1957

Year	Penang	Melaka	Perak	Selangor	N. Sembilan	Johore	Kelantan
1921	9.69	9.49	27.56	30.89	26.55	19.50	34.25
1931	8.47	10.92	21.50	21.13	23.82	13.03	24.05
1947	8.76	10.25	18.46	17.74	26.63	15.18	12.91
1957	8.42	12.29	18.48	17.91	26.33	18.08	17.17

Source: See table 15.3.

active.[86] This helps explain the large proportion of females excluded from the "economically active" workforce (see table 15.8).

Women's domestic work is a notoriously difficult area for historical research and one that has yet to be explored in the history of Chinese women in Malaysia. Ironically, it is easier to locate when the demand for domestic services led to women being employed outside their own homes to do household chores. In the Federated Malay States the number of Chinese females engaged in the domestic and personal services sector increased from 4,061 in 1921 to 11,244 in 1947. By 1957 there were 22,386 Chinese females, outnumbering 18,406 males, working in this sector.[87]

Two groups of Chinese females involved in domestic work have attracted considerable attention. The first are the black and white amahs.[88] The second are the *mui tsai,* an exotic euphemism popular in colonial discourse for young girls who were sold into domestic servitude by their impoverished parents in a centuries-old system of bondage, who were, in effect, domestic slaves doing household chores without pay. The existence of thousands of mui tsai in Chinese households in Malaya in the 1920s and 1930s indicated the need for domestic labor in growing families and expanding households. By convention, suitable marriages were arranged for the girls when they reached marriageable age. When their buyers no longer needed their labor or could not support additional mouths in the household, they were resold, sometimes into prostitution. Most were vulnerable to sexual harassment from male members of the households.[89] In Yeap Joo Kim's *The Patriarch,* the wealthy family of Khoo Sian Ewe owned several such domestic slaves and Khoo was prone to "indiscretions with the slave girls." Khoo's wives tolerated these indiscretions as long as the slave girls did not become pregnant. When such undesired consequences arose, "the popular Malay abortionist of the time was summoned."[90]

Janet Lim was among the three thousand or so mui tsai who were registered with the Chinese protectorate after the 1936 Mui Tsai Ordinance came into effect.[91] Her autobiography, *Sold for Silver,* tells the story of how inspection by Chinese protectorate officers enforcing the new law provided the interstice for her to escape from the cruelty of her owners and her master's persistent attempts to force her into sex with him. From refuge in the Poh Leung Kuk home, Janet Lim was able to move on to schooling and training as a nurse, eventually carving out a life of her own.[92] Less fortunate but more representative of the majority perhaps was Ong Ah Lam, a twelve-year-old Hokkien girl who was found wandering in the streets of Batu Pahat and brought to the Poh Leung Kuk in 1929, after she had been beaten and thrown out by her mistress. An old woman brought Ah Lam from China when she was three and after her parents died. She was first sold to a couple for $380, then resold several times for lower prices before she was brought to the Poh Leung Kuk home.[93]

Prostitutes are another group of workers who have attracted much attention from colonial officials and researchers. There is no doubt that in the late nineteenth century many women were engaged in this occupation. For example, in 1889, when the total adult Chinese female population in the Straits Settlements was estimated to be thirty thousand, registered prostitutes were reported to number 3,673.[94] But as the female population grew, women were engaged in a wider range of occupations. Out of 25,595 Chinese females classified as "economically active" in 1911 in the Federated Malay States, 2,230 worked as registered prostitutes, a figure that did not include the large numbers operating illegally. Even so, it is important to place it against the numbers of women in other occupations; 4,928 tailors and seamstresses, 3,097 ayahs and domestic servants, 5,770 mine workers, 7,264 in the agricultural sector, 5,796 in various light industries, and 42,813 identified as housewives.[95]

By the twentieth century, the number of Chinese women employed in mines had increased from 5,770 in 1911 to 8,712 in 1931 in the Federated Malay States. Dulang washing for tin deposits, carried out entirely by women, bolstered productivity and family incomes as the number of dulang passes issued by the Mines Department increased from 8,278 in 1908 to 15,774 in 1918.[96] By the 1930s there was an "extraordinary increase in the employment of Chinese women on the estates."[97] Women's overall share of the Chinese estate work force increased from 20 percent in 1937 to 33.5 in 1947, while in the Federated Malay States, there were almost thirty thousand females employed in the agricultural sector in 1931 and 58,394 in 1947.[98] Outside mining and agriculture, women were employed in new manufacturing industries such as factories making matches, cigars, shoes, and other rubber goods.[99]

In many fields of work women were confined to jobs regarded as women's work and in positions subordinate to men. In the medical world women were employed mainly as nurses or midwives, rarely as doctors or surgeons. According to the 1931 census there were only three females in the doctor/surgeon category in Penang and another three in Melaka, compared to 279 Chinese male doctor/surgeons in Penang and 142 in Melaka. On the other hand, there were 116 Chinese female nurse/midwives in Penang and 25 in Melaka but only two Chinese male nurse/midwives in Penang and none at all in Melaka. In 1931 there were no Chinese women engineers or accountants at all in Malaya and just one Chinese female barrister/solicitor in Penang.[100] By 1957 the number of Chinese women in these occupations had increased slightly: one in the architect/surveyor/engineer category, three in the chemist/physicist/other scientist category, seven lawyers, and 61 doctor/surgeons. This indicated improved access to education and training for Chinese girls; with a small minority going to English schools while the majority were educated in Chinese schools.[101] The expanding school system in the first five decades of the twentieth century required girls to be trained as teachers or, in the case of the Chinese schools, for teachers to be brought in as immigrants. There were only 13 Chinese women teachers in the Federated Malay States in 1911, but this had increased to 277 in 1931 and 1,086 in 1947. In 1957 the total number of Chinese women teachers in the Federation of Malaya totaled 5,770. By then more women were employed but they remained concentrated in "feminine" occupations; female nurses and midwives at 2,127 outnumbered males at 387, female stenographers and typists at 1,455 also outnumbered males at 579, and female telephone operators at 648 outnumbered males at 105.[102]

Nevertheless, being employed and having their own personal income provided more women with the economic basis for independence and the means to make some decisions for themselves. Some of the women who had trained as teachers or nurses chose to dedicate themselves to their careers, turning their backs on the traditional demand that a Chinese woman's life, and worth, lay in marriage and bearing children. The ability to find work and earn an income had enabled women to support their families since the 1930s, when it became clear that it was not always the males who emigrated and sent money to families in China. Female migrants sometimes came ahead to earn money and support families in their home villages.[103]

From the few dimensions in the lives of Chinese women that are explored in this chapter, we can see that the women who entered into and became part of the making of Malaysian history were not a monolithic or homogenous group. They entered at different points in the history of the peninsula and from different locations in their places of origin. Each wave of arrivals added another layer to the historical process of family and community formation. As immigrants, some Chinese women were at their weakest and most vulnerable while others, paradoxically, found new freedoms and escape routes provided by the unique collision of different structures of social relations in a colonial society. There is no single narrative structure that can capture the range of roles and relations through which the women lived out their lives. Explorations of their agency, and of their subordination, would have to take cognizance of how different women were located in the structures of power relations, within the microcosm of the family as well as in the broader structures of class relations beyond the family.

Notes

This chapter draws on research funded by a short-term research grant from Universiti Sains Malaysia and the opportunity to read and think about different approaches to women's history during a three-month appointment, from October to December 1998, as Sacher Visiting Fellow at

St. Hilda's College, Oxford University. The support of Universiti Sains Malaysia and St. Hilda's College is gratefully acknowledged.

1. The literature is too vast to be surveyed here but a good sampling of research trends can be gleaned from journals such as *History Workshop, Past and Present, Women's History Review, Gender and History; Feminist Studies, Signs: Journal of Women in Culture and Society, Women's Studies International Forum,* and *Journal of Women's History.*

2. Women's studies has attracted greater interest since the 1980s but there are only a handful of historical studies. See Jamilah Ariffin, *Women's Studies in Malaysia: An Overview and a Reference Bibliography* (Kuala Lumpur: National Population and Family Development Board, 1991).

3. Ibid. Important recent additions on Malay women are Wazir Jahan Karim, *Women and Culture: Between Malay Adat and Islam* (Boulder: Westview, 1992); Maznah Mohamad, *The Malay Handloom Weavers: A Study of the Rise and Decline of Traditional Manufacture* (Singapore: Institute of Southeast Asian Studies, 1996); and Cheah Boon Kheng, "Power Behind the Throne: The Role of Queens and Court Ladies in Malay History," *Journal of the Malaysian Branch of the Royal Asiatic Society* 66, 1 (1993): 1–22. The only historical study of Indian women is Nisha Bhatt, "Sejarah sosio-ekonomi pekerja wanita India estet di tanah Melayu, 1900–1957" (Socioeconomic history of Indian women estate workers in Malaya) (M.A. thesis, Universiti Sains Malaysia, 1999).

4. This chapter does not cover Sabah and Sarawak, which became part of Malaysia after 1963 but Singapore, administratively part of the Malay Peninsula until 1946, is included in some parts of the discussion.

5. This is also true of Chinese women in the rest of Southeast Asia; see Leo Suryadinata, ed., *Ethnic Chinese as Southeast Asians* (Singapore: Institute of Southeast Asian Studies, 1997), 296–300, which records the brief discussion provoked by a question from Mely Tan, an Indonesian woman of Chinese descent and a well-known researcher on the Chinese in Indonesia, who asked why the role of women had, as always, been ignored.

6. Lim Joo Hock, "Chinese Female Immigration into the Straits Settlements, 1860–1901," *Journal of the South Seas Society* 22 (1967): 58–110.

7. For example G. W. Earl, who was in Singapore in 1837, claimed that out of every five to eight thousand arrivals from China, forty to fifty were females, and Leonard Wray, a sugar planter in Penang, reported to the Select Committee of the House of Commons in February 1848, "It is beyond all question that they [Chinese women] do emigrate and in great numbers too, for I myself have seen many hundred who have done so." Both are cited in Lim, 61–62.

8. It is likely that this way of smuggling single females out of China, de-

scribed in the Labour Commission Report of 1876 (cited in Lim, 71) had been going on for some time.

9. Terms such as "real Chinese woman" and "Chinese woman proper" are cited frequently in Lim's discussion of his sources.

10. *Sejarah Melayu; or, Malay Annals, an annotated translation by C. C. Brown* (Kuala Lumpur: Oxford University Press, 1970), 82. Bukit Cina, as its name suggests, is the place where the earliest Chinese settlement is located. The oldest Chinese cemetery is to be found there, too.

11. Geoff Wade, "Melaka in Ming Dynasty Texts," *Journal of the Malaysian Branch of the Royal Asiatic Society* 70, 1 (1997): 49.

12. Ibid. See also Tan Chee Beng, *The Baba of Melaka: Culture and Identity of a Chinese Peranakan Community in Malaysia* (Petaling Jaya: Pelanduk Publications, 1988), 30.

13. As suggested by Wade, "Melaka in Ming Dynasty Texts," 49.

14. Anthony Reid, "Flows and Seepages in the Long-Term Chinese Interaction with Southeast Asia," in *Sojourners and Settlers: Histories of Southeast Asia and the Chinese in Honour of Jennifer Cushman,* ed. Anthony Reid, with the assistance of Kristine Alilunas Rodgers (St. Leonards, NSW: Allen and Unwin in association with Asian Studies Association of Australia, 1996), 25.

15. Wang Gungwu, "Sojourning: The Chinese Experience in Southeast Asia" in *Sojourners and Settlers,* 1–14.

16. See G. William Skinner, "Creolized Chinese Societies in Southeast Asia," in *Sojourners and Settlers,* 51–93.

17. According to Tan Chee Beng the first peranakan families or settlements may have existed in Singapore as early as 1349 and in Melaka by 1436. Tan, *Baba of Melaka,* 28,

18. As cited in Victor Purcell, *The Chinese in Malaya* (1948; Kuala Lumpur: Oxford University Press, 1967), 30.

19. Ibid.

20. Ibid., 22; citing an article by Rev. Yeh Hua Fen on the Chinese in Melaka.

21. E. G. Cullin and W. F. Zehnder, *The Early History of Penang, 1592–1827;* cited in Ting Shing Chung, "Sejarah wanita Cina Pulau Pinang, 1900–1957: Perubahan dan kesinambungan" (History of Chinese women in Penang: Change and continuity) (M.A. thesis, Universiti Sains Malaysia, Penang, 2000), 50.

22. Wong Choon San, *A Gallery of Chinese Kapitans* (Singapore: Government Printing Press, 1964), 14.

23. In Ting, "Sejarah wanita Cina," 94.

24. "Notices of Pinang," *Journal of the Indian Archipelago,* 1850; cited in Purcell, *Chinese in Malaya,* 41.

25. Khoo Kay Kim, "Malaysia: Immigration and the Growth of a Plural Society," *Journal of the Malaysian Branch of the Royal Asiatic Society* 71, 1 (1998): 5.

26. M. Medhurst, *Journal of a Tour through the Settlements on the Eastern Side of the Peninsula of Malacca, 1828;* cited in Khoo, "Malaysia."

27. Wang Gungwu, "An Early Chinese Visitor to Kelantan," *Malaysia in History* 6, 1 (1960); cited in Khoo, "Malaysia."

28. Khoo, "Malaysia."

29. See Tan, *Baba of Melaka;* Felix Chia, *The Babas* (Singapore: Times Books International, 1980); and John R. Clammer, *Straits Chinese Society* (Singapore: Singapore University Press, 1980). Arab and Indian traders also gave birth to distinctive peranakan communities; see Khoo, "Malaysia."

30. J. D. Vaughan, *The Manners and Customs of the Chinese of the Straits Settlements* (1879; Kuala Lumpur: Oxford University Press, 1971).

31. Wong Lin Ken, *The Malayan Tin Industry to 1914 with Special Reference to the States of Perak, Selangor, Negri Sembilan, and Pahang* (Tucson: University of Arizona Press for the Association for Asian Studies, 1965), 27.

32. Tan Pek Leng, "Chinese Secret Societies and Labour Control in the Nineteenth-Century Straits Settlements," *Kajian Malaysia* 1, 2 (1983): 14–48.

33. Purcell, *Chinese in Malaya,* 107.

34. J. W. W. Birch, "Diary of Voyage as British Resident to the Malay Peninsula," MSS Indian Ocean S 242/1 and 242/1, Rhodes House Library, Oxford.

35. Sir Frank Swettenham, *Sir Frank Swettenham's Malayan Journals, 1874–1875,* ed. P. L. Burns and C. D. Cowan (Kuala Lumpur: Oxford University Press, 1975), 10. The pages before and after p. 10 describe J. W. W. Birch's attempts to find the Chinese women caught in the secret society battles.

36. On the establishment of the Chinese protectorate and its functioning, see R. N. Jackson, *Pickering: Protector of Chinese* (Kuala Lumpur: Oxford University Press, 1965); Ng Siew Yoong, "The Chinese Protectorate in Singapore, 1877–1900," *Journal of Southeast Asian History* 2, 1 (1961): 76–99; Chu Tee Seng, "The Singapore Chinese Protectorate, 1900–1941," *Journal of the South Seas Society* 20, 1 (1971): 5–45.

37. Collated from annual reports of the Chinese protectorate in *Straits Settlements Government Gazette,* 1880–89.

38. E. M. Merewether, *Report of the Census of the Straits Settlements and the Protected Malay States of the Malay Peninsula, 1891* (Singapore: Government Printing Office, 1892), 28, 29.

39. A. M. Pountney, *The Census of the Federated Malay States, 1911* (London: His Majesty's Stationery Office, 1911), 28–29.

40. C. A. Vlieland, *British Malaya: A Report on the 1931 Census and on Certain Problems of Vital Statistics* (Westminster: Crown Agents for the Colonies, 1932), 82. The 1911 census notes that the Hainanese "stoutly profess that they do not allow their women to emigrate." Pountney, *Census of the Federated Malay States, 1911,* 28.

41. W. L. Blythe, "Historical Sketch of Chinese Labour in Malaya," *Journal of the Malaysian Branch of the Royal Asiatic Society* 20, 1 (1947): 65.

42. Ibid., 52.

43. *Census of the Straits Settlements, 1891;* J. R. Innes, *Report on the Census of the Straits Settlements taken on the 1st March 1901* (Singapore: Government Printing Office, 1901).

44. Pountney, *Census of the Federated Malay States, 1911,* 36.

45. Vlieland, *British Malaya,* 69.

46. T. E. Smith, "Immigration and Permanent Settlement of Chinese and Indians in Malaya: And the Future Growth of the Malay and Chinese Communities," in *The Economic Development of Southeast Asia,* ed. C. D. Cowan (London: Allen and Unwin, 1965), 179.

47. M. V. del Tufo, *A Report on the 1947 Census of Population: Malaya, Comprising the Federation of Malaya and the Colony of Singapore* (Kuala Lumpur: Government Printer, Federation of Malaya, 1948), 67.

48. Purcell, *Chinese in Malaya,* 200; emphasis added.

49. Tufo, *Malaya,* 53.

50. Fei Hsiao-tung, *Peasant Life in China: A Field Study of Country Life in the Yangtze Valley* (London: Kegan Paul, Trench, Trubner, 1947); Daniel Kulp, *Country Life in South China: The Sociology of Familism,* vol. 1, *Phoenix Village, Kwangtung, China* (1925; New York: Paragon Books, 1966); Margery Wolf, *The House of Lim: A Study of a Chinese Farm Family* (New York: Meredith Corporation, 1968); Margery Wolf, *Women and the Family in Rural Taiwan* (Stanford: Stanford University Press, 1972).

51. For an account of pre-Qing upper-class marriage, see Patricia Ebrey, "Women in the Kinship System of the Southern Sung Upper Class," in *Women in China: Current Directions in Historical Scholarship,* ed. Richard W. Guisso and Stanley Johannesen (New York: Philo Press, 1981); see also citations in note 50 for marriages in peasant societies and rural areas in twentieth-century China.

52. For examples from the Southern Sung (1127–1279), see Ebrey. The links by marriage between some of the most well known elite families in late Qing China are visible in Nie Zeng Jifen, *Testimony of a Confucian Woman: The Autobiography of Mrs. Nie Zeng Jifen, 1852–1942,* trans. and annot. Thomas Kennedy, ed. Thomas Kennedy and Micki Kennedy (Athens: University of Georgia Press, 1993).

53. Song Ong Siang, *One Hundred Years' History of the Chinese in Singapore* (Singapore: University Malaya Press, 1967).

54. See Lim Boon Keng's explanation of the importance of daughters in sustaining Straits Chinese families, cited in Song, *One Hundred Years*, 4.

55. Ibid., 204.

56. Ibid., 21.

57. For the example of a Sung scholar-official who was handpicked by his future father-in-law for his elder daughter and upon her demise married his deceased wife's younger sister, see Ebrey, "Women in the Kinship System."

58. Yeap Joo Kim, *Of Comb, Powder, and Rouge* (Singapore: Lee Teng Lay, 1992), ch. 21.

59. Daniel Chew, *Chinese Pioneers on the Sarawak Frontier, 1841–1941* (Singapore: Oxford University Press, 1990), ch. 7.

60. Song, *One Hundred Years*, 236–37.

61. Chen Yacai, "Ye Yalai shenping dashi nianbiao" (Chronology of major events in the life of Yap Ah Loy), in *Jilongpo kaituoje de zhuqi: Jiabidan Ye Yalai de yishen* (In the footsteps of the pioneer of Kuala Lumpur: The life of Kapitan Yap Ah Loy), ed. Li Yeling (Kuala Lumpur: Huazi Resource and Research Centre, 1997), 274, and a photograph of Yap's wife on 280.

62. Fei, *Peasant Life in China,* describes this practice in rural China in the 1940s; Maurice Freedman, *Chinese Family and Marriage in Singapore,* found it still alive in Singapore in 1949–50; and both Arthur and Margery Wolf describe this as a prevalent practice in Taiwan in the 1960s. See Wolf, *Women and the Family.*

63. Chen, "Ye Yalai," 278.

64. S. M. Middlebrook and J. M. Gullick, *Yap Ah Loy* (Kuala Lumpur: Malaysian Branch of the Royal Asiatic Soceity reprint no. 9, 1883), 21.

65. Chen Yacai, "Ye Yalai shenping dashi nianbiao," 278.

66. J. M. Gullick, *Kuala Lumpur, 1880–1895: A City in the Making* (Kuala Lumpur: Malaysian Branch of the Royal Asiatic Society, 1955; repr., Kuala Lumpur: Pelanduk Publications for the Heritage of Malaysia Trust, 1988), 94.

67. Ibid., 95, citing police and medical reports following the investigation.

68. Ibid., 94, citing a medical report on Kuala Lumpur General Hospital in 1893.

69. On some ways Chinese prostitutes tried to leave brothel life, see James Francis Warren, *Ah Ku and Karayuki-san: Prostitution in Singapore, 1870–1940* (Singapore: Oxford University Press, 1993), ch. 13. On "Crossing over" see Wong Sin Kong, "Women for Trade: Chinese Prostitution in Late-Nineteenth-Century Penang," *Journal of the South Seas Society* 53 (1998): 171–84.

70. Mentioned in annual reports of the Chinese Protectorate; for ex-

ample, "49 brothel inmates left to live as wives of Chinese" in 1884; in 1885 the figure was 70, and in 1888, 217 were reported to have left the brothels and "followed" men.

71. Report of the Chinese Protector, *Straits Settlements Gazette,* 1886, Arkib Negara Malaysia, Kuala Lumpur (ANM/KL).

72. Selangor Secretariat File no. 1527/86, ANM/KL.

73. Selangor Secretariat File no. 3701/1911, ANM/KL.

74. Selangor Secretariat File no. 1187/1910, ANM/KL.

75. In 1909 they were Chan Sow Lin, Loke Chow Kit, San Ah Weng, Cheong Yoke Choy, all well-known Chinese leaders from different dialect groups in Kuala Lumpur.

76. Selangor Secretariat File no. 1187/1910, ANM/KL.

77. Selangor Secretariat File no. 3701/1911, ANM/KL.

78. Selangor Secretariat File no. 2950/1911, 3701/1911, ANM/KL.

79. Chan King Nui, *From Poor Migrant to Millionaire: Chan Wing, 1873–1947* (Kuala Lumpur: Malaysian Branch of the Royal Asiatic Society, 1997), 16.

80. Ibid., ch. 4

81. Kulp, *Country Life in South China,* 51.

82. I was told the story of a local wife of a Hainanese man in Negri Sembilan who felt so disgraced and threatened by the arrival of the first and principal wife from Hainan that she ran away.

83. For a succinct account of social and cultural currents in early-twentieth-century China, in particular of the life and literary work of Ding Ling, one of modern China's most well known women activists and writers, see Jonathan Spence, *The Gate of Heavenly Peace: The Chinese and Their Revolution, 1895–1980* (Harmondsworth: Penguin Books, 1981).

84. Examples can be found in issues of the *Lat Pau* and *Nanyang Siang Pao* in the late 1920s and early 1930s.

85. Secretariat for Chinese Affairs File no. 298/1947, ANM/KL. Wong Yan was a widower who returned to China in 1947 to remarry and to bring his son from his first marriage back to Mentakab with him. One of the six women did not make it to Mentakab as it turned out on investigation that her betrothed had died and his father did not wish her to come to Mentakab.

86. Tufo, *1947 Census,* 109.

87. Figures calculated from census for the relevant years.

88. See Lai Ah Eng, *Peasants, Proletarians, and Prostitutes: A Preliminary Investigation into the Work of Chinese Women in Colonial Malaya* (Singapore: Institute of Southeast Asian Studies, 1986), ch. 6; Kenneth Gaw, *Superior Servants: The Legendary Cantonese Amah of the Far East* (Singapore: Oxford University Press, 1988).

89. See Mui Tsai Commission, *Report of the Commission on Mui Tsai in Hong Kong and Malaya* (London: His Majesty's Stationery Office, 1937).

90. Yeap Joo Kim, *The Patriarch* (n.p., 1975), 63–64.

91. From evidence presented to the *Report of the Commission on Mui Tsai in Hong Kong and Malaya,* many doubted that the majority of mui tsai were registered despite the law.

92. Janet Lim, *Sold for Silver: An Autobiography by Janet Lim* (London: Collins, 1958). See also Suzanne Miers, "Mui Tsai through the Eyes of the Victim: Janet Lim's Story of Bondage and Escape" and Koh Choo Chin, "Implementing Government Policy for the Protection of Women and Girls in Singapore: 1948–66," both in *Women and Chinese Patriarchy: Submission, Servitude, and Escape,* ed. Maria Jaschok and Suzanne Miers (London: Zed Books, 1994), 108–21, 122–40, respectively.

93. HCO File no. 819/1929, ANM/KL.

94. *Annual Report of the Chinese Protectorate,* 1889, *Straits Settlements Gazette.*

95. Pountney, *Census of the Federated Malay States, 1911,* 144–48.

96. R. N. Jackson, *Immigrant Labour and the Development of Malaya, 1786–1920* (Kuala Lumpur: Government Press, 1969), 146. Dulang washing is the process of panning for tin; dulang is the Malay word for the tray used in panning.

97. Purcell, *Chinese in Malaya,* 200–201.

98. Figures calculated from census for the respective years. For more detailed accounts, see Lai, *Peasants, Proletarians, and Prostitutes,* chs. 4, 5, 7, and 8.

99. Purcell, *Chinese in Malaya,* 200–201; Lai, *Peasants, Proletarians, and Prostitutes.*

100. Vlieland, *British Malaya,* table 125.

101. See Lenore Manderson, "The Development and Direction of Female Education in Peninsular Malaysia," *Journal of the Malaysian Branch of the Royal Asiatic Society* 51, 2 (1978): 100–122; and Tan Liok Ee, "A Century of Change: Education in the Lives of Four Generations of Chinese Women in Malaysia," in *Asian Migrants and Education: The Tensions of Education in Immigrant Societies and among Migrant Groups,* ed. Michael W. Charney, Brenda S. A. Yeoh, and Tong Chee Kiong, forthcoming.

102. Figures from census for respective years.

103. W. L. Blythe, "Historical Sketch of Chinese Labour in Malaya," *Journal of the Malayan Branch of the Royal Asiatic Society* 20, 1 (1947): 65.

CONTRIBUTORS

Abdul Rahman H.I., currently associate professor, School of Humanities, Universiti Sains Malaysia, teaches East Asian and Malaysian history and has published mainly in Malay on traditional and modern Malay political history.

Abu Talib A. trained at Tsukuba University (Japan) and Monash University (Australia) in twentieth-century Southeast Asian history, especially Myanmar's relations with Japan (1940–1970s). Currently associate professor, School of Humanities, Universiti Sains Malaysia, his research interests are the Japanese occupation of Malaya and the social history of twentieth century Malaya/sia.

Badriyah H.S., formerly associate professor, School of Humanities, Universiti Sains Malaysia, continues to research and write on the socioeconomic history of Malaysia and Malaysian historiography, areas of interest on which she has published in both Malay and English.

M. R. Fernando, Senior Fellow, Humanities and Social Studies Education Academic Group, National Institute of Education, Nanyang Technological University, is author of several publications on the socioeconomic history of Indonesia, economic growth and change in the Malay Archipelago during the early modern period, and the Chinese in Southeast Asia.

Andrew Hardy was educated at Cambridge, in Paris, and at the Australian National University. After completing his Ph.D. on migration in twentieth-century Vietnam, he broadened his research interests to include migrations accompanying Vietnam's late-twentieth-century wars and the formation of diasporas in Western and former Soviet bloc countries.

Hong Lysa, formerly with the Department of History, National University of Singapore, is currently affiliated with the history department of the University of Melbourne. Her primary research work and publications are on nineteenth-century Thai history and historiography but she follows the writing of history in Singapore with interest.

Huang Jianli, associate professor at the history department of the National University of Singapore, has research interests and publications in the history of Republican China from the 1920s to 1940s, especially on topics relating to student political activism and local self-government, and in the history of Chinese intellectual and business elites in postwar Singapore.

Paul H. Kratoska, formerly lecturer at the School of Humanities, Universiti Sains Malaysia, is currently with the history department at the National University of Singapore. His research interests include the Japanese occupation of Malaya, citizenship and nationality, rice cultivation and nutrition, and minorities in Southeast Asia. He is editor of the *Journal of Southeast Asian Studies.*

P. Lim Pui Huen, is currently research fellow at the Institute Sultan Iskandar, Universiti Teknologi Malaysia. Her research interests include Malaysian and Singapore history, Chinese culture and society, and oral and local history.

Ni Ni Myint joined the history department at the University of Yangon after studying history, political science, and philosophy there. She is currently director-general of the Universities Historical Research Centre and concurrently director of the SEAMEO (Southeast Asian Ministers of Education Organization) Regional Centre for History and Tradition (SEAMEO CHAT).

Dhiravat na Pombejra, currently attached to the Department of History, Chulalongkorn University in Bangkok, is one of the few Thai scholars who can and has used Dutch, French, and English (in addition to Thai) materials for his research. He has published in both Thai and English and is known especially for his work on the Ayutthaya period.

Kobkua Suwannathat-Pian, formerly with the National University of Malaysia and currently dean of the Institute of Liberal Studies, Universiti Tenaga Nasional in Malaysia, researches in both Thailand and Malaysia on sociopolitical history and relations between the two countries. She is author of *Thai-Malay Relations: Traditional Intra-Regional Relations from the Seventeenth to Early Twentieth Centuries* and *Thailand's Durable Premier: Phibun through Three Decades, 1932–1957.*

Tan Liok Ee, formerly associate professor at the School of Humanities, Universiti Sains Malaysia, continues to research and write in her areas of interest: Malaysian historiography, history of Chinese women, Chinese education, and Chinese politics.

C. J. W.-L. Wee teaches literature and cultural theory at the Nanyang Technological University, Singapore. He is currently working on the relationship between modernization, memory, art, and culture in Singapore and is author of *Culture, Empire, and the Question of Being Modern* and editor of *Local Cultures and the "New Asia": The State, Culture, and Capitalism in Southeast Asia,* both forthcoming.

Thongchai Winichakul, recipient of the Harry J. Benda prize for his first book, *Siam Mapped: A History of the Geo-Body of a Nation,* and a Guggenheim Fellowship in 1994, is currently professor at the Department of History, University of Wisconsin, Madison. His main research interest is Thai intellectual history, especially changing constructions of knowledge and nationhood.

Brenda S. A. Yeoh, associate professor, Department of Geography, National University of Singapore, specializes in social and historical geography but has a wide range of research and publication interests that include the politics of space in colonial and postcolonial cities, gender, migration, and transnational communities.

Yong Mun Cheong, educated and trained in Singapore and the United States, is currently associate professor in the Department of History, National University of Singapore and associate dean in the Faculty of Arts and Social Sciences. His research experience and interests include broad coverage of Southeast Asian history as well as specific topics such as the maritime history of the region.

INDEX